Programming
the 68000™

Steve Williams

SYBEX®

Berkeley • Paris • Düsseldorf • London

Cover art by Judithe Sager
Book design by Sharon Leong

CP/M is a registered trademark of Digital Research, Inc.
CP/M-68K is a trademark of Digital Research.
Motorola and UNIDOS are trademarks of Motorola, Inc.
PDP-11 is a trademark of Digital Equipment Corporation.
UNIX is a trademark of Bell Labs.
SYBEX is not affiliated with any manufacturer.

Library of Congress Card Number: 85-90327
ISBN 0-89588-133-0
Printed by Haddon Craftsmen
Manufactured in the United States of America
10 9 8 7 6 5 4 3

Acknowledgments

I would like to thank the following people who helped make this book possible: Mike McGrath of SYBEX for suggesting the book in the first place. My mother, Sylvia Williams, for providing that all-important "naive user" viewpoint. Steve Cliff for providing several important ideas for extensions to the book. Fran Borda, for her tireless effort in reviewing vast quantities of material in a very short time. Rod Coleman and Sage Computer Company for providing an affordable yet powerful 68000 machine. Mark of the Unicorn Software for providing the MINCE editor on CP/M-68K. Special thanks to Carole Alden and Scott Loewe, editors, and the SYBEX production staff for all their efforts and expertise: Valerie Robbins, word processing; Dawn Amsberry and Brenda Walker, proofreading; Sharon Leong, book design; Valerie Brewster and Janis Lund, typesetting.

Contents

2 *68000 ARCHITECTURE* 29

3 68000 INSTRUCTION SET

4 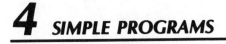 SIMPLE PROGRAMS

251

5 I/O PROGRAMMING 271

6 ADVANCED CONCEPTS 305

APPENDICES

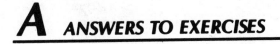

A ANSWERS TO EXERCISES 419

B ASCII CHARACTER SET 441

C PROGRAMMING STYLE 445

D 68010 457

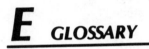

Introduction

This book explains machine-language programming for the 68000 microprocessor family. The material is divided into three parts: an introduction to programming, an explanation of applications programming, and a discussion of systems programming. These three areas can be studied in succession or independently.

Chapter 1 provides an introduction to computer operation and programming for readers with no programming background. It covers basic hardware and software concepts. Experienced readers may wish to skim this material.

Chapters 2 through 6 provide the background necessary to write assembly-language appplication programs or subroutines, including the mechanics of generating programs and debugging them. These chapters also cover high-level languages and interfacing to operating systems. With this information, you will be able to write applications programs in assembly language. It may also be used for calling assembly-language routines from a high-level language program for efficiency or for access to low-level machine resources.

Chapters 7 through 8 are a lower level discussion of programming the 68000. These chapters deal with interrupts and other machine-level primitives. A small multitasking "operating system" is provided as a case study.

An important part of learning machine-language programming is picking up the jargon. Computer scientists have their own language. All terms in this book are explained as they occur. A glossary has also been provided as a study aid.

Computer programming is not difficult to learn. It does not require extreme mathematical proficiency or supernormal intelligence. It does, however, require diligence and, more importantly, practice. There is absolutely no substitute for sitting down at the machine and trying it for yourself. Type in the examples, try them out, make improvements, and above all, make mistakes. You will learn more from your errors than anything else.

Basic Concepts

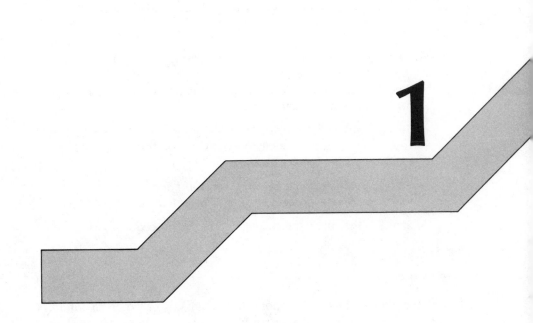

Machine-level computer programming has been called art, engineering, sorcery, and religion. It is all of these and more. Dealing with a computer at its own level can be a very rewarding (and frustrating) experience.

This book will introduce you to the joys and woes of this wondrous craft. We have attempted to minimize the mathematics involved; anyone who can add, subtract, multiply, and divide can make full use of all the material presented here.

This chapter will introduce you to the concepts on which modern computing is founded: algorithms, elementary hardware operations, and the binary and hexadecimal number schemes.

As a start toward learning how to program, consider the process of starting an automobile engine:

1. Insert the key into the lock.

2. Turn the key past the ON position to the START position and hold.

3. If the motor does not crank, stop.

4. If the motor does catch, proceed to step 5. If the motor does not catch within 30 seconds, turn the key OFF and go to step 2.

5. Release the key back to the ON position, and stop.

This simple procedure has all of the same elements of a computer program:

- Step 1 is called an *initialization*. This is an action which is performed once at the start of a program.

- Steps 2 through 4 form a *loop*—a series of actions which is repeated until some condition is satisfied. (In this case, either the car starts or the battery expires.)

- Step 3 is an example of an *error condition*—some condition which causes the procedure to terminate in an abnormal fashion.

- Step 5 is the successful completion of the procedure.

Algorithms

The above procedure, in computer terminology, is called an *algorithm*. Algorithms are stepwise procedures which can be used to define the steps in programs. Any step-by-step description is an algorithm. Some examples from everyday life are kitchen recipes and directions for getting from one place to another.

You can see from these examples that not all algorithms can be made into computer programs. Even if an algorithm is suitable for transforming into a program, it must first be put into a form the computer can recognize. Computers cannot utilize even the simplest English.

Programming Languages

If you want a computer to carry out the steps you define in an algorithm, you must first translate the English description into a language that the computer can execute. Such a language is called a *programming language*. There are many such languages. The task to be performed generally dictates which language is to be used. Some examples of programming languages are:

- BASIC (Beginner's All-purpose Symbolic Instruction Code). BASIC is a very simple language to learn and to use. It is generally used for short, simple programs.

- COBOL (COmmon Business Oriented Language). COBOL is commonly used for business related software, such as payroll and other accounting applications.

- FORTRAN (FORmula TRANslation). FORTRAN is widely used in the scientific community for applications involving large numbers of calculations.

- Pascal (Named for the French mathematician Blaise Pascal). Pascal is often used in universities to teach budding computer scientists how to program.

- Assembly Language. Assembly language is the process of programming a computer at the level of individual machine instructions. This book describes the process of assembly language programming for the 68000 computer.

- Machine Language. Machine language deals with programming a computer at the instruction level, without assistance from development software. Machine language involves using a numeric language: the binary codes directly usable by the computer. This type of programming is incredibly tedious, and is only used for very specialized applications.

Flowcharts

A visual method of representing an algorithm is called *flowcharting*. A flowchart is a series of boxes which are connected by lines to show the possible paths of the algorithm. Flowcharting, like algorithm descriptions, is not done in a computer language.

Flowcharts consist of three basic symbols:

- a square box which indicates an action to be performed

- a diamond shaped box which indicates a decision

- lines which connect the two.

There is an ANSI (American National Standards Institute) standard for flowchart symbols and flowchart layout.

A flowchart for our car-starting algorithm is shown in Figure 1.1.

A flowchart segment should fit on a single page. A flowchart for a computer program will require partitioning into several pages, interconnected by boxes. These boxes typically contain a number, indicating the mating connector on another page. Partitioning a large program flowchart into single-page segments is quite an involved process. It could require so much time that the exercise is not justified.

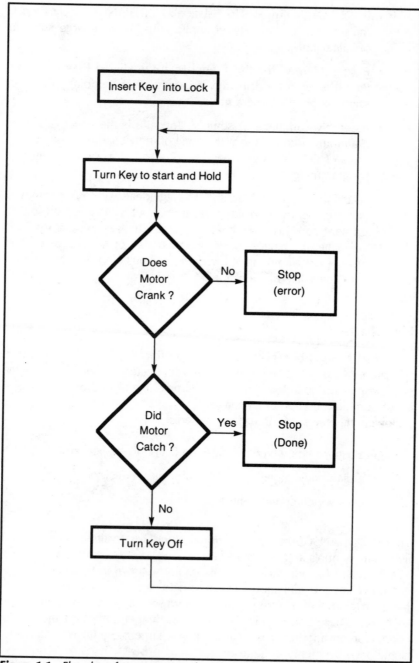

Figure 1.1 – Flowchart for car-starting algorithm

HOW DOES A COMPUTER WORK?

In order to learn programming, one must first understand how computer hardware functions. Figure 1.2 is a block diagram showing the major portions of a typical computer.

The *memory* contains the program which the computer follows, as well as the data on which the computer operates. In this simplified model of a computer, the box labeled *central processing unit* (CPU) is the "brains" behind the computer. The connection between the CPU and the computer's memory is known as the *memory bus*. *Input/output (I/O) devices* are the machines through which the computer interacts with the outside world. Examples of I/O devices are *cathode ray tube* (CRT) terminals (the computer's "TV screen"), floppy disk drives, and printers. The connection between the CPU and the I/O devices is called the *input/ouput bus*. Let us now examine each of these areas in detail.

Memory

Computer memory is a series of numbered slots, called *locations,* each of which contains a number. The number of the location is called its

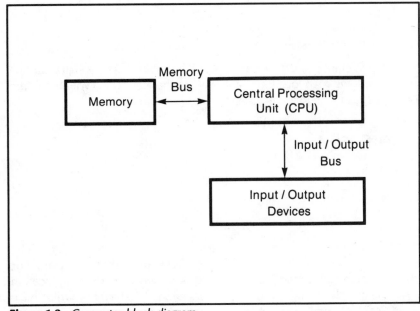

Figure 1.2 – *Computer block diagram*

address (like a street number). The number contained within the slot is called the *memory data* or *memory contents*. There are two operations associated with a computer memory:

- Change the contents of a location to a specific value. This operation is called a memory *write* or a memory *store*. The contents of the location before the write are lost.

- Obtain the present contents of a location. This operation is called a memory *read* or a memory *fetch*. A memory read does not alter the contents of the location—subsequent reads with no intervening writes will return the same value.

For example, suppose we have a four location memory with the following values:

Address	Data
0	21
1	27
2	19
3	100

Note that memory addresses are always numbered sequentially, starting with zero. If we read location 2, we will get the result 19. Writing a 6 into location 1 gives the following values:

Address	Data
0	21
1	6
2	19
3	100

Note that the memory write did not affect any other location. For example, reading location 2 again would again yield 19. Reading location 1 will yield 6. The original contents of location 1 (before the write) have been discarded, and may not be retrieved.

Input/Output Devices

Input/output devices connect the computer to the outside world. These devices typically fall into one of two categories:

1. Low-speed, character-oriented devices used to interact directly with people. Examples of this type of device are: CRT terminals, printers, and plotters.

2. High-speed, block-oriented devices used for bulk storage of programs or data. Devices in this category such as disks, tapes, etc., are usually magnetic.

Character-oriented devices typically interact with human operators. This type of device usually transfers one character at a time. Many computer CRT terminals send and receive characters at 960 characters per second. Although this seems amazingly fast to a human sitting at a terminal, to a computer (which can handle millions of operations per second), it is extremely slow. When interacting with humans, the computer spends a tremendous amount of time just waiting for characters from the terminal.

Block-oriented devices such as disks and tapes, on the other hand, do not normally interact with humans. These devices typically handle multi-character blocks at a time, with a short interval between characters within a block, but a comparatively long interval between blocks.

Central Processing Unit

The CPU is the heart of the computer. It executes the programs and manipulates the input/output devices.

CPU Organization

The organization of a typical CPU is shown in Figure 1.3.

The boxes on the top of the diagram are called *registers*. A register is a single memory location within the CPU which is used to store a temporary result. Different CPUs use different numbers and types of registers. The 68000 register set will be explained in detail in Chapter 2.

The CPU registers, which can be accessed much faster than main memory, are temporary memory locations used to facilitate program execution. There are usually a limited number of these registers.

The memory address and memory data registers are used to access memory. For example, to read memory, the correct address is placed in the memory address register, and then the data can be read from the memory data register. To write to memory, the data is placed in the memory data register, and then the address is placed in the memory address register.

The program counter is a special register that is used to keep track of the next instruction to be executed. This process is detailed in the next section.

The *Arithmetic and Logic Unit* (ALU) performs all of the basic arithmetic operations, such as addition, subtraction, etc. The data on which the ALU operates can come from any of the registers with a path into the top of the ALU: the CPU registers, memory data, or the program counter. The result of the operation can be placed back into any of the registers.

Fortunately, programming the machine does not require attention to the inner operations of the ALU. The control unit supervises the movement of data through the ALU, and defines certain basic machine functions called *instructions*.

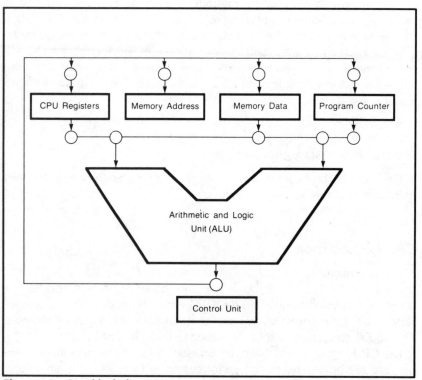

Figure 1.3 – *CPU block diagram*

Stored Program Execution

The process of executing a program works like this:

1. Fetch memory at the address indicated by the program counter, and increment the program counter to the next instruction in memory. The program counter is said to "point to" (i.e., contain the address of) the next instruction.

2. Perform the instruction.

3. Go back to step 1.

To illustrate how all this works together, we will now write a short program to add two numbers together. For simplicity, we will define a computer: Our simple computer has one register, named A. The machine can execute the following instructions:

Instruction	Meaning
1nnn	Copy memory location nnn into A
2nnn	Add memory location nnn to A
3nnn	Copy A into memory location nnn
4000	Stop

Now suppose that the computer memory contains the following:

Location	Contents	Instructions
100	1104	Load location 104 into A
101	2105	Add location 105 to A
102	3106	Store A into location 106
103	4000	Stop
104	0300	(Data)
105	0400	(Data)
106	0000	(Data)

If we then set the program counter to 100 and cause the computer to execute, the program will execute as follows:

1. The contents of memory location 104 (300) will be copied into register A.

2. The contents of location 105 (400) will be added to register A. Register A will then contain 700.

3. Register A will then be copied to memory location 106. This operation is called "Storing register A."

4. The machine will stop.

Upon completion of the above program, Register A and memory location 106 will have been altered to contain the value 700. This example is a program which adds two memory locations together and stores the result in a third memory location.

Programming at its most basic level is the process of putting the right instructions (also called *operations* or *op codes*) into the proper memory locations. The above program is an example of *machine language programming,* where the programmer deals with the actual numeric values of the instructions, and memory locations are assigned by hand. This is a tedious process at best, and programs called "assemblers" have been developed to handle the drudgery involved. Programming using an assembler is commonly called *assembly language programming.* The example program above, might look like this in assembly language:

```
        LOAD      A,X
        ADD       A,Y
        STORE     A,Z
        STOP
   X:   DC        300
   Y:   DC        400
   Z:   DC        0
```

The words LOAD, ADD, STORE and STOP are called *mnemonics.* A mnemonic is a symbolic representation of a machine instruction. X, Y, and Z are called *labels.* A label is a way to tag a memory location without knowing what the final memory address will be. The assembler or another tool called the linker will make the final address assignment.

Finally, the abbreviation "DC" is an *assembler directive.* DC stands for "Define Constant." This directive tells the assembler to place a constant in memory at the location where the DC directive occurs.

Why is assembly language better than machine language? First, it is far more readable. Second, the task of changing an existing program is much simpler. Suppose that we wish to change our example program to add a third number, W, to X and Y. To add this to the assembly language version, we need add only two lines: an

ADD A,W

addition instruction, and a declaration for the new constant:

W: DC 50

To change the machine language version of the program, we must alter all of the instructions that reference memory, since the values to be added are now in a different place, as illustrated below:

Location	Machine Language	Assembly	Language	
100	*1105		LOAD	A,X
101	*2106		ADD	A,Y
102	*2107	*	ADD	A,W
103	*3108		STORE	A,Z
104	4000		STOP	
105	0300	X:	DC	300
106	0400	Y:	DC	400
107	*0050	*W:	DC	50
108	0000	Z:	DC	0

The asterisk character (*) shows lines that have been changed. Note that no machine language location contains the same value as it did in the previous example. In large programs, altering machine code is a tremendous chore.

Data Representation

The vast majority of computers represent numbers in a form involving only two possible values: ON and OFF. This is a property of the hardware used to implement the CPU, memory, and I/O devices. This two-value representation is called *binary*, or base 2.

The Binary System

The binary system represents a number as a string of two-valued quantities. Each such quantity is called a *bit*, which stands for *Binary digIT*. The

ON and OFF values for a bit are 1 and 0, respectively. A bit with a value of 1 is said to be *set;* a bit with a value of 0 is said to be *clear*.

Most computers in use today organize bits in groups of eight to form a quantity known as a *byte*. The bits in a byte are numbered from right to left, starting at zero. Each bit is assigned a value twice the value of its neighbor on the right. Bit 0, the rightmost bit, has the value 1. The values associated with the eight bits in a byte are shown in Table 1.1.

Bit Number	Place Value
7	128
6	64
5	32
4	16
3	8
2	4
1	2
0	1

Table 1.1 – *Binary Bit Values*

Using this table of binary values, the binary number 0010 1111 has the value of 47. This is how the value for our example would be calculated.

The decimal value of a binary number is equal to the bit number value times the place value, as shown in Figure 1.4.

The largest number that can be represented using eight bits is 1111 1111, which is decimal 255. It is the result of adding 128 + 64 + 32 + 16 + 8 + 4 + 2 + 1. For readability, we will write binary numbers as groups of four bits. In computerese, a four bit group, or one half of a byte, is called a *nibble*.

To represent numbers bigger than 255, two or more bytes are used. Common combinations are two bytes (16 bits), and four bytes (32 bits).

These quantities are called a *word* and a *longword,* respectively. Dealing with 16 and 32 digit numbers can be cumbersome, however, so an abbreviated form of binary representation called *hexadecimal* (or base 16) is often used.

Hexadecimal Numbers

In hexadecimal (*hex*) representation, a nibble is encoded as one hexadecimal digit.

These digits have values from 0 to 15. The values for 10 through 15 are represented by the letters A through F. Each digit in a hex number has a place value of sixteen times the value of its neighbor to the right. For instance, the number 22 hex is (2 × 16) + 2, or 34.

Converting Binary to Hex

A hex number can be derived from a binary number by first grouping the binary number into groups of four bits (nibbles), and then computing

Bit Number   7 6 5 4 3 2 1 0
Bit Value   0 0 1 0 1 1 1 1

Bit Number	Binary Value	×	Place Value	=	Decimal Value
7	0	×	128	=	0
6	0	×	64	=	0
5	1	×	32	=	32
4	0	×	16	=	0
3	1	×	8	=	8
2	1	×	4	=	4
1	1	×	2	=	2
0	1	×	1	=	1
Converted decimal value				=	47

Figure 1.4 – *Computing the decimal value of a binary number*

the proper hex digit for each group using the 8–4–2–1 values for the bits in the group. For example, the number 0010 1111 in binary is 2F in hex:

8421

$0010 = (0 \times 8) + (0 \times 4) + (1 \times 2) + (0 \times 1) = 2$

$1111 = (1 \times 8) + (1 \times 4) + (1 \times 2) + (1 \times 1) = F\ (15)$

Converting Hex to Binary

Hex numbers can be converted to binary by first taking each hex digit and then expanding it into four binary bits using the hex, decimal, and binary values shown in Table 1.2.

Hex Value	Decimal Value	Binary Value
0	0	0000
1	1	0001
2	2	0010
3	3	0011
4	4	0100
5	5	0101
6	6	0110
7	7	0111
8	8	1000
9	9	1001
A	10	1010
B	11	1011
C	12	1100
D	13	1101
E	14	1110
F	15	1111

Table 1.2 – *Hex, Decimal, and Binary Values*

When you use this table, the hex number 2F converts to the binary number 0010 1111.

Converting Hex to Decimal

To convert a hex number to a decimal number, first multiply each digit by its appropriate place value, and then add the resulting numbers. The place values for hex numbers are shown in Table 1.3.

Digit	Place Value
0	1
1	16
2	256
3	4,096
4	65,536
5	1,048,576
6	16,777,216
7	268,435,456

Table 1.3 – *Hexadecimal Place Values*

The digit numbered 0 is the rightmost digit in a hex number. Each place value is derived by multiplying the previous place value by 16, starting with a value of 1 for the rightmost digit. The digit number is also known as a "power of 16."

The hex number 54321 converts to its decimal value as shown in Figure 1.5, the hex number A25 converts to its decimal value as shown in Figure 1.6, and the hex number 1234 converts to the decimal value of 4660 as shown in Figure 1.7.

Digit	×	Place Value	=	Decimal Value
5	×	65,536	=	327,680
4	×	4,096	=	16,384
3	×	256	=	768
2	×	16	=	32
1	×	1	=	+ 1
Converted decimal value			=	344,865

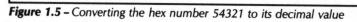
Figure 1.5 – *Converting the hex number 54321 to its decimal value*

Hex Digit	×	Place Value	=	Decimal Value
A(10)	×	256		2,560
2	×	16		32
5	×	1		+ 5
Converted decimal value			=	2,597

Figure 1.6 – *Converting the hex number A25 to its decimal value*

Hex Digit	Place Value	Decimal Value
1	4096	4096
2	256	512
3	16	48
4	1	+ 4
Converted decimal value =		4660

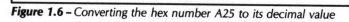
Figure 1.7 – *Converting the hex number 1234 to its decimal value*

Converting Decimal to Hex

Decimal numbers can be converted to hex numbers using the inverse of the above technique. To convert a decimal number to hex, first find the largest place value in Table 1.3 that divides into the number to be converted, then divide the decimal value by this number. The quotient of this division is the hex digit. Divide the remainder by the next smallest place value to obtain the next hex digit (even if it's zero). Divide this remainder by the next smallest place value, to get the next digit and so on.

To convert the decimal number 123,456 to hex, we start with a hex place value of 65,536 and divide this hex value into the decimal value of 123,456. The result of 1 is the first hex digit and the remainder (57,920) is the dividend for the next hex place value.

Decimal Remainder	÷	Hex Place Value	=	Hex Digit
123,456	÷	65,536	=	1
57,920	÷	4,096	=	E (14 decimal)
576	÷	256	=	2
64	÷	16	=	4
0	÷	1	=	0

Read the answer down the Hex Digit column: 1E240. The next remainder can be calculated on a decimal calculator as: Present decimal remainder − (place value × hex digit).

For example, the remainder 576 was calculated above by first dividing 4,096 into 57,920. The answer is 14, or a hex value of E. Then the hex place value was multiplied by 14, which equals 57,344. Finally, the remainder of 576 was arrived at by subtracting 57,344 from the previous remainder, 57,920.

There are several calculators on the market which will do hex and decimal conversions. If you are going to be writing a lot of machine code, a hex calculator will pay for itself in short order.

What's in a K?

The hex number 400 translates to 1,024 in decimal. The term *K* (for "Kilo") is used in computer terminology to represent multiples of 1,024. Memory and disk device capacities are expressed in units of kilobytes. For instance, a 64 kilobyte (64K) memory contains 64 × 1,024, or 65,536 decimal (or 10000 hex) bytes of memory.

Similarly, the number 100000 hex (1,048,576 decimal) is the result of multiplying 1024 × 1024. This number is commonly abbreviated M (for Mega). Megabyte units are used to describe the capacities of larger memory and disk devices. A 5–megabyte (commonly written 5Mb) disk therefore contains 5 × 1,048,576, or 5,242,880 bytes.

Operations on Binary Numbers

Since decimal, binary, and hex are simply alternate ways of representing numbers, the same operations that can be performed on decimal numbers can also be performed on binary or hex numbers. One can apply techniques similar to those used for decimal numbers for the addition, subtraction, multiplication, and division of hex and binary numbers. For programming, however, it is important to understand the operations a computer is capable of performing.

A computer's ALU is capable of performing a number of very simple operations on binary numbers. These include: One's complement, AND, OR, Exclusive OR, addition, two's complement, shifts and rotates. We will now explore these in greater detail.

One's Complement

One of the simpler operations on binary numbers is to take the *one's complement:* Simply invert the values of all the bits. All 0's become 1's and vice versa.

For example, complementing the number 0011 1100 (3C hex) produces 1100 0011 (C3 hex). Complementing 0000 0000 (00 hex) yields 1111 1111 (FF hex). Complementing the complement of a number yields the original number again.

Binary AND

Performing an *AND* operation on two binary numbers produces a third binary number with 1's in each bit position where the original numbers both had a 1. ANDing 0000 1101 (0D hex) with 1001 1001 (99 hex) yields 0000 1001 (09 hex).

The AND operation is commonly used to obtain a remainder for a division by a power of two (2, 4, 8, 16, etc.). To obtain such a remainder,

AND the number with the power of 2 minus 1. For example, to find the remainder when 0011 1101 (3D hex) is divided by 8, AND with 0000 0111 (07 hex). The result is 0000 0101 (05 hex). 3D hex is 3 × 16 + 13, or 61 decimal. Dividing by 8 yields 7, with a remainder of 5.

Binary OR

The *OR* operation takes two binary numbers and produces a third binary number that has a 1 where either of the original numbers had a 1. For example, ORing 1010 1010 (AA hex) with 0101 0101 (55 hex) yields 1111 1111 (FF hex). (ANDing these two numbers gives all zeros.)

Binary XOR

The *XOR* (eXclusive OR) operation takes two binary numbers and produces a third binary number which has 1's in bit positions where one (not both) of the original numbers had a 1. For example, XORing 0101 0101 (55 hex) with 1111 1111 (FF hex) yields 1010 1010 (AA hex). XORing a number with all 1's yields the 1's complement of the number. XORing a number with itself produces zero.

Binary Addition

Adding two binary numbers is similar to adding decimal numbers. You add each pair of digits, starting on the right, and carry any result over 1 to the next column. For example, adding 0011 1101 (3D hex) and 0001 0101 (15 hex) is done as follows:

```
Carry      0011  1010
           0011  1101   (3D hex)
          +0001  0101   (15 hex)
         _____

Sum        0101  0010   (52 hex)
```

This procedure can be used for binary numbers of any length.

2's Complement Arithmetic

Subtraction involves a bit of magic. Negative numbers are stored in a form known as *two's complement*. The two's complement of a number is obtained by taking the one's complement (as explained above), and adding 1 to it. For instance, the two's complement of 0000 0001 is:

Original Number:	0000 0001	(01 hex)
One's Complement:	1111 1110	(FE hex)
Add One:	+0000 0001	(01 hex)
Two's Complement:	1111 1111	(FF hex)

Adding the two's complement of a number is the same as subtracting the number. As an example, consider adding 1111 1111 (FF hex) to 0000 0010 (02 hex). The leftmost bit of a two's complement number will be a 0 if the number is positive (zero or greater), and a 1 if the number is negative (less than 0). For this reason, the leftmost bit is often called the *sign bit.*

Carry 11111	1100	
0000	0010	(02 hex)
+1111	1111	(FF hex)
Sum 0000	0001	(01 hex)

Note that the carry out of the high order bit position is discarded. This is due to the fact that all of the numbers kept in a computer have exactly the same number of bits (eight in this example). Note that the result of adding 02 hex and FF hex is 01. This is the same as subtracting 1 from 2. FF hex is the two's complement of 01 hex, as shown above.

Two's complement changes the range of numbers it is possible to represent using a given number of bits. For instance, without using the two's complement, we could represent from 0 to 255 with eight bits. Using two's complement, however, we can represent from −128 to +127.

The first case is called *unsigned* arithmetic, meaning that only positive numbers can be represented. The second case is called two's complement representation, meaning that both positive and negative numbers can be represented.

Shifts and Rotates

Two other operations commonly performed on binary numbers are shifts and rotates. These operations are similar to the old "bucket brigade" operation used in fighting fires. Bits are moved from one position to the next position. Shifts and rotates can occur in either direction.

There are two types of shifts: logical and arithmetic. In a logical shift operation, the bits are moved left or right as in Figure 1.8.

Zero bits are shifted into the bit vacated by the shift operation. The bit marked C is a special status bit in one of the CPU internal registers. This bit is called the *Carry* bit, and it receives the bit which would otherwise be lost.

An arithmetic left shift is the same as a logical left shift. An arithmetic right shift is similar to a logical right shift, except that the most significant bit is copied into itself. Both of these are shown in Figure 1.9.

Rotates are similar to logical shifts, except that the Carry bit is shifted into the vacated bit, instead of a zero, as illustrated in Figure 1.10.

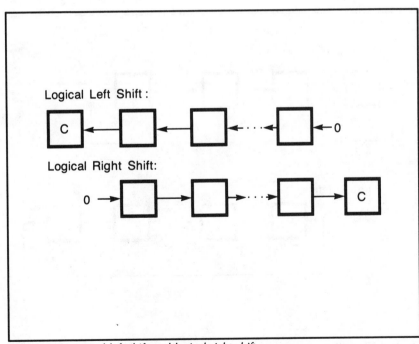

Figure 1.8 – *Logical left shift and logical right shift*

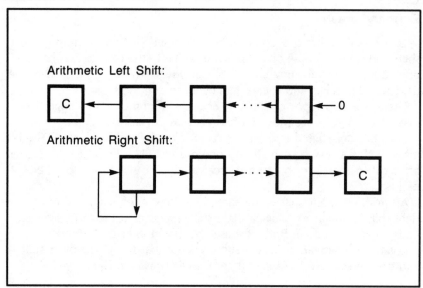

Figure 1.9 – *Arithmetic left shift and arithmetic right shift*

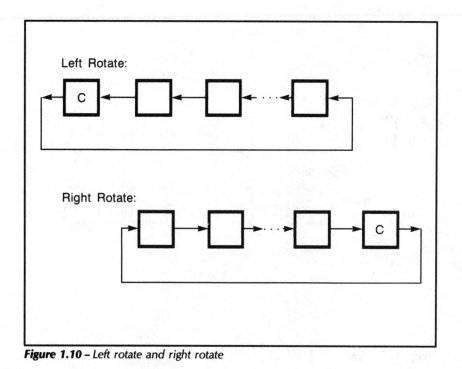

Figure 1.10 – *Left rotate and right rotate*

Examples

The following examples assume that the Carry bit is initially zero. The original number is 1010 1010 (AA hex).

Logical Shifts:

Times	Left			Right		
0	1010	1010	(AA hex)	1010	1010	(AA hex)
1	0101	0100	(54 hex)	0101	0101	(55 hex)
2	1010	1000	(A8 hex)	0010	1010	(2A hex)
3	0101	0000	(50 hex)	0001	0101	(15 hex)
4	1010	0000	(A0 hex)	0000	1010	(0A hex)
5	0100	0000	(40 hex)	0000	0101	(05 hex)
6	1000	0000	(80 hex)	0000	0010	(02 hex)
7	0000	0000	(00 hex)	0000	0001	(01 hex)
8	0000	0000	(00 hex)	0000	0000	(00 hex)

Arithmetic shifts:

Times	Left			Right		
0	1010	1010	(AA hex)	1010	1010	(AA hex)
1	0101	0100	(54 hex)	1101	0101	(D5 hex)
2	1010	1000	(A8 hex)	1110	1010	(EA hex)
3	0101	0000	(50 hex)	1111	0101	(F5 hex)
4	1010	0000	(A0 hex)	1111	1010	(FA hex)
5	0100	0000	(40 hex)	1111	1101	(FD hex)
6	1000	0000	(80 hex)	1111	1110	(FE hex)
7	0000	0000	(00 hex)	1111	1111	(FF hex)
8	0000	0000	(00 hex)	1111	1111	(FF hex)

Rotates:

Times	C	Left			Right			C
0	0	1010	1010	(AA hex)	1010	1010	(AA hex)	0
1	1	0101	0100	(54 hex)	0101	0101	(55 hex)	0
2	0	1010	1001	(A9 hex)	0010	1010	(2A hex)	1
3	1	0101	0010	(52 hex)	1001	0101	(95 hex)	0

Times	C	Left			Right			C
4	0	1010	0101	(A5 hex)	0100	1010	(4A hex)	1
5	1	0100	1010	(4A hex)	1010	0101	(A5 hex)	0
6	0	1001	0101	(95 hex)	0101	0010	(52 hex)	1
7	1	0010	1010	(2A hex)	1010	1001	(A9 hex)	0
8	0	0101	0101	(55 hex)	0101	0100	(54 hex)	1
9	0	1010	1010	(AA hex)	1010	1010	(AA hex)	0

Shifts are very useful for multiplying and dividing. A logical shift left is the same as multiplying a number by 2, and a logical shift right is the same as dividing a number by 2. This is only true for unsigned numbers.

Arithmetic shifts, on the other hand, represent multiplication and division by 2 for two's complement numbers. The one exception is that dividing (shifting right) −1 yields −1 and not zero.

Extensions

When copying an 8-bit quantity into a 16-bit quantity, or when copying a 16-bit quantity into a 32-bit quantity, there is a possibility of losing the two's complement properties of the number.

To illustrate the problem, suppose we copy FF hex (−1 as an 8-bit number) to a 16-bit number. Copying only the lower 8 bits gives us 00FF hex, which is not −1, but 255! The way to fix this situation is to copy the sign bit (most significant bit) into all the "extra" bits in the larger number. This is called *sign extension*. If we sign extend FF hex into 16 bits, we get FFFF hex, which is −1 in two's complement form.

Conclusion

In this chapter we have learned basic concepts that are applicable to most computers on the market today. In the next chapters, we shall see how these concepts are applied to a specific type of computer, the Motorola 68000.

Exercises

Use the following questions to help solidify your understanding of the material presented in Chapter 1. Answers to all exercise questions can be found in Appendix A.

1. Write an algorithm for converting a decimal number to hex.

2. Develop a flowchart for the algorithm in question 1.

3. Suppose the computer on page 9 has an additional instruction 5nnn, which subtracts the contents of memory location nnn from Register A. The assembly form of this instruction is *SUB A,y* where y is a label on the memory location to be subtracted from A. Modify the example of the machine-language program to compute the difference between the contents of location 105 and the contents of location 104. Store the result in location 106. (Hint: You will have to load location 105 into Register A first. Why?)

4. Move the machine-language program you wrote in question 3 to run at address 200.

5. Give the assembly language equivalent of the program for question 3.

6. Write a new assembly language program that computes the sum of the first five integers. Use the labels A through E for the memory locations that contain the numbers to be added. Store the result in a separate memory location, labeled F.

7. Convert the following decimal numbers to their hex and binary equivalents.

    273
    421
    1024
    100

8. Convert the following hex numbers to their binary and decimal equivalents.

    ABE
    100
    64
    1024
    505

9. Give the one's and two's complements for each of the numbers in the previous question.

10. Perform the AND, OR, XOR, and addition operations on the following pairs of hex numbers. Use 16-bit operations. Give the carry out of the high order bit pairs for the addition operation.

   A5A5 5A5A
   FFFF 0001
   1234 4321

11. Prepare shift and rotate tables similar to those in the text for the hex quantities FF and 55. Assume that the carry bit is initially zero.

68000 Architecture

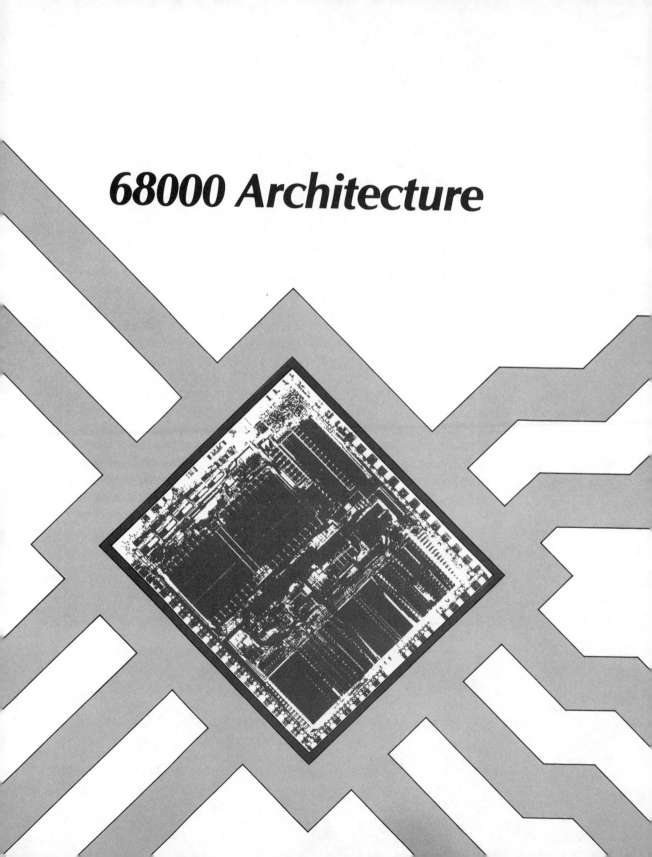

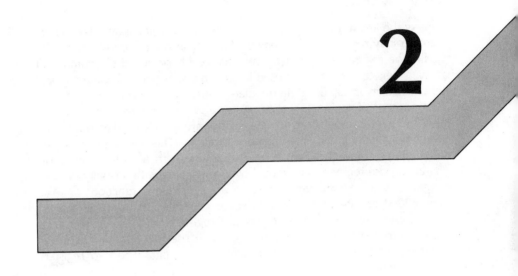

INTRODUCTION

In this chapter, we will expand the general programming concepts presented in Chapter 1 to cover the architecture of the Motorola 68000. The information specific to the 68000 is necessary in order to understand the instruction set contained in Chapter 3.

Most computers can be categorized by the following criteria:

- The number and type of registers that may be used by the programmer in writing software.

- How data is organized in memory, and what data types are supported with hardware instructions.

- How memory is addressed by an instruction.

- Special hardware features, such as hardware support for stacks.

We will now explore each of these areas as it relates to the 68000.

REGISTER SET

One of the first questions you should ask when learning a new computer is "How many registers does it have?" Another important consideration is whether the registers can be used interchangeably or not. If the computer has many registers that *can* be used interchangeably, you will have a great deal of flexibility in handling intermediate values in a computation.

The number of registers in a computer also has an effect on program speed and size. Computations using a register are usually smaller and faster than computations involving a memory location. (This is due primarily to the nature of computer hardware). A machine with a large number of general-purpose registers is preferred over a machine with a small number of registers or a machine whose registers are restricted in function.

The 68000 architecture trades off some generality in order to gain a larger register set. There are two types of registers: *address registers* and *data registers*. Address registers are normally used to contain memory addresses, while data registers normally contain data. The two register classes are not used interchangeably.

Address Registers

There are eight address registers, numbered A0–A7. Each address register is a 32-bit quantity. Address registers can also be used as 16-bit quantities. When a 16-bit quantity is loaded into an address register, it is sign extended to become a 32-bit quantity, as shown in Figure 2.1. The notation A0.W is used to mean the word part of address register A0. (A0.L means the entire 32 bits stored in register A0.) The .B suffix is used to denote an 8-bit quantity. Address registers may not be used as 8-bit quantities, however.

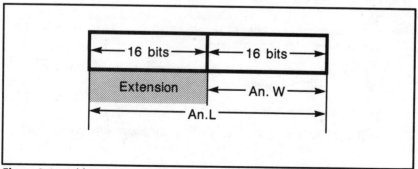

Figure 2.1 – *Address register layout*

Register A7 is a special-purpose register. A7 is the *hardware stack pointer* used by 68000 exceptions and subroutine call instructions. This register is also used by programs for temporary storage of data. The concept of a stack is discussed later in this chapter.

Address registers are used as temporary locations for storing memory addresses. These registers can be used in instructions that reference memory in order to specify the address at which data is located. The upper byte of the register is presently ignored in such usage (by the 68000 and 68010 chips). This limits the amount of memory that you can use to 16 megabytes (16,772,216 bytes). Future processors in the 68000 family will not ignore this byte, so it should always be set to zero for compatibility.

Data Registers

The 68000 also has eight other registers, called *data registers,* numbered D0–D7. A data register can be used as an 8-bit, 16-bit, or 32-bit quantity, as shown in Figure 2.2. Unlike address registers, loading a data register with less than 32 bits does not cause a sign extension to occur into the remaining bits in the register. These remaining bits are left unchanged.

Data registers cannot be used to address memory in an instruction. These registers are used instead as temporary locations where data may be stored. Many instructions require one or more of the operands to reside in a data register.

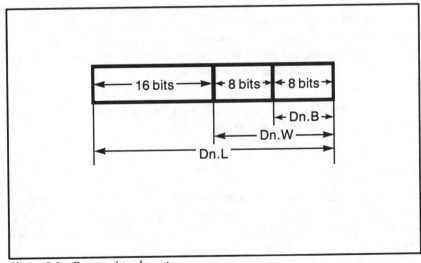

Figure 2.2 – *Data register layout*

Program Counter

A special 32-bit register called the *program counter* is used to control execution of the program in memory. The program counter always contains the memory address of the next instruction to be executed. As an instruction is executed, the program counter is advanced to point to the next instruction.

Certain instructions can be used to affect the contents of the program counter. These are:

- Instructions that alter the contents of the program counter unconditionally. These are called *unconditional branches* or *jumps.* Such an instruction is useful for programming loops, or for merging several alternative sections of the program into one common section.

- Instructions that alter the contents of the program counter based on the result of a previous instruction. These are called *conditional branches,* and enable the computer to make decisions. Using a conditional branch, either a portion of the program can be skipped or a previous portion repeated, based on the result of a previous computation.

- Instructions that cause a given section of code to be repeated a specific number of times, or until a condition is satisfied. Such instructions are called *looping primitives.*

- Instructions that are used to branch to another area of the program and then to return to the location following the original branch. This technique is known as a *subroutine call.* A subroutine call can be used to invoke a common function, such as an I/O routine, at many points in the program, using only a single copy of the instructions that perform the I/O.

As with address registers, the upper eight bits of the program counter are ignored by the 68000 and 68010 processors.

Status Register

The 68000 uses a special register, called the *status register* (SR) to store information about the status of the machine. This register is used by the conditional branch instructions to retrieve information about the last instruction.

The status register is a 16-bit quantity, organized as shown in Figure 2.3.

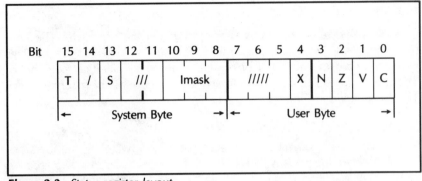

Figure 2.3 – *Status register layout*

System Byte

Bits 15–8 are called the *system byte,* because the information contained here is not normally available to applications programs. The fields in the system byte are:

1. Bit 15 is a hardware aid for debuggers. It is called the *trace bit.* If bit 15 is set, an exception will take place at the end of each instruction. Exceptions are described in Chapter 7, *Exception Processing.* This feature is used by debuggers to regain control as each instruction is executed.

2. Bit 13 is used to regulate access to certain instructions and to the system byte of the status register. It is called the *supervisor bit.* If this bit is set, access is allowed. When the supervisor bit is set, the 68000 is said to be executing in *supervisor mode.* When the bit is reset, the 68000 is said to be executing in *user mode.* User mode software is prevented by the hardware from executing certain privileged instructions that might compromise the integrity of the system software. Access to the status register's system byte is also prohibited when in user mode, ensuring that the user mode program cannot change the supervisor bit.

3. Bits 10–8 are called the *interrupt mask.* This feature is more fully explained in Chapter 7, which deals with 68000 exception conditions.

The system byte of the status register is of concern only to systems software programmers. We will deal more extensively with this topic in later chapters.

User Byte

The lower byte of the status register is called the *user byte*. The user byte contains a set of bits known as *condition codes*, which are bit flags used to record the outcome of the last arithmetic operation performed. The user byte can be accessed at any time regardless of machine state. The bits defined in the user byte are:

- The C (carry) bit carries out the high-order bit position of an arithmetic operation. For example, when two 8-bit numbers are added, the C bit is the ninth bit of the result. This bit also receives bits that are shifted out of a number during shift or rotate operations.

- The V (oVerflow) bit is set whenever an operation yields a result that cannot be properly represented. For example, when adding the bytes 7F hex and 01 hex, the result, 80 hex is not properly represented in eight bits. (Remember, 80 hex is −128 decimal in two's complement notation.) The V bit would be set following such an operation.

- The Z (Zero) bit is set if the result of an operation is zero.

- The N (Negative) bit is set if the high order bit of a result is set. (In two's complement, the high order bit of a number is set if the number is less than zero.)

- The X (eXtended) bit is a copy of the carry bit, but it is not affected by every instruction that affects the carry bit. The purpose of this bit is to facilitate multiprecision instructions. The X bit is affected only by instructions that can be used for multiprecision operations. This allows you to intermix other instructions between multiprecision operations without having to preserve the carry bit.

The descriptions of the instruction set in Chapter 3 describe how the condition codes are used by each operation. Since the lower half of the status register contains nothing but the condition codes, it is sometimes called the *condition code register* (CCR).

DATA ORGANIZATION IN MEMORY

The 68000 instruction set supports several data formats: binary, BCD, and floating point.

Bytes, Words, and Longwords

Binary data items can be 8, 16, or 32 bits long. These data types are known as *bytes, words,* and *longwords,* respectively. Most instructions that operate on binary data support any of these three data lengths. For example, the MOVE instruction, which transfers a binary data item from one place to another, has three forms:

- MOVE.B moves a byte of data

- MOVE.W moves a word of data

- MOVE.L moves a longword of data

Note the use of the suffixes .B, .W, and .L to denote data length.

When a word or a longword is stored in memory, the bytes are stored in order of decreasing magnitude. The most significant bits are stored at the lowest address, and the least significant bits are stored at the highest address. For example, when a 16-bit word is stored at location 1000, the most significant byte is at location 1000, and the least significant byte at 1001. When the long word 01234567 (hex) is stored at address 1000, memory appears as shown in Figure 2.4.

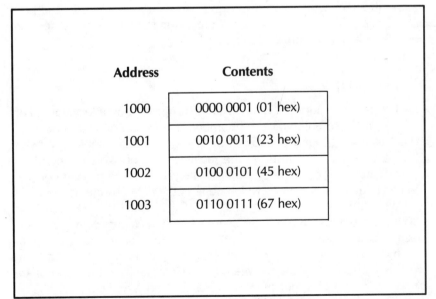

Address	Contents
1000	0000 0001 (01 hex)
1001	0010 0011 (23 hex)
1002	0100 0101 (45 hex)
1003	0110 0111 (67 hex)

Figure 2.4 – *Memory with longword stored at address 1000*

We emphasize this point because all computers do not store multibyte binary quantities in the same way. In particular, the 8080/Z-80, 6502, and 8086/8088 family of microprocessors store words and longwords in ascending order, so that the low byte is stored at the lowest address and the high byte at the highest address. Which order is "correct" is largely a matter of taste, but you should be aware that the difference exists.

BCD

A special form of binary numbers, called *binary coded decimal* (BCD), is often used for digital displays and input devices. The familiar displays on digital clocks and electronic calculators are universally based on BCD. Most computer-based laboratory and factory instruments also use BCD.

BCD is basically hexadecimal without the codes for 10–15 (i.e., A–F). Each nibble represents a digit in a decimal number. Thus, two decimal digits are stored in a byte. The 68000 has instructions for the addition and subtraction of BCD numbers.

BCD is especially useful in commercial applications, such as accounting. Many such applications require only addition and subtraction of numbers in character format. To convert these numbers to binary for calculation and then convert them back to character format for output requires much multiplication and division, which are comparatively slow operations for most computers. Using BCD avoids these expensive operations, and provides quick conversion to and from character format. In many applications, BCD is much more efficient than binary.

Floating Point

Scientific applications require a large range of possible values. For example, to represent Avogadro's number (a common quantity in chemical calculations, roughly 6 followed by 23 zeros) would require ten bytes of storage. To hold the result of the multiplication of two such numbers would require twice this much storage. Then there is the problem of representing fractional numbers, which none of the data representations thus far have addressed.

The clean solution to these problems is found in *floating point numbers*. Floating point numbers are a computerized form of scientific notation, which is taught in grade school mathematics. In scientific notation, a number is written as a quantity between 0 and 10 times 10 to the appropriate power. For example, the quantity 1,935,000,000 is written as 1.935×10^{12}. The quantity 0.000001349 is written as 1.349×10^{-6}.

Scientific notation is extremely useful in a computer. Allocating a fixed number of bits to the exponent and fraction parts of a number yields a very useful approximation to both very large and very small numbers. The 68000, like most microprocessors, does not directly support floating point with instructions. However, there is an additional feature which can be added to provide hardware support for floating point.

The 68000 add-on is called the 68881 Floating Point Processor. It provides hardware instructions to manipulate floating-point numbers. The 68881 uses a floating-point format known as The Institute of Electrical and Electronic Engineers (IEEE) format, named for the organization that proposed the format as a standard. IEEE format provides the following floating point format:

S	Exp	Fraction

The field labeled S is the sign bit for the entire number. If this bit is set, the number is negative. If the bit is not set, the number is positive.

The field labeled EXP is the exponent; it is seven bits long. The exponent field indicates the exponent of 2 by which the fractional part of the number is multiplied. To allow for negative exponents, decimal 64 (40 hex) is subtracted from the exponent field before it is used. The exponent range is 00 hex (interpreted as -64) to 7F hex (interpreted as $+63$). Thus, the range of representation is 2^{63} (approximately 9.2234×10^{18}) to 2^{-64} (approximately 5.421×10^{-20}).

The fraction part is 24 bits, or 6–7 decimal digits. This limits the number of significant digits the floating point number may contain. A limit of 6 digits means that the computer cannot correctly subtract 1 from 10,000,000, for example.

Alternate forms of floating point allow more bits for the fraction and exponent to avoid this and other problems with the range and precision of floating-point representation. The remainder of this book deals strictly with integer arithmetic.

ASCII

The final form of data storage is known as *ASCII* or character format. ASCII stands for American Standard Code for Information Interchange. This code assigns a numeric value for each character. These values are used to represent characters in memory and during I/O. The current

ASCII standard for the United States defines 128 characters, with values from 0–127. The characters are stored one per byte in memory. The eighth bit is used for additional characters in Europe and Japan. For a complete list of United States ASCII values, see Appendix B.

Multicharacter sequences, called *strings* are stored in multiple consecutive bytes in memory. The 68000 provides no instructions explicitly for string manipulation; sequences of byte instructions must be used instead. There are three common types of string storage you may employ:

- Use a fixed length for each string to be stored. This has the advantage of being easy to program, but wastes memory if string length tends to vary. This technique is usually used by the FORTRAN and COBOL languages.

- Prefix each string with a character count. This is more difficult to program, but wastes less memory. If the character count is stored in a byte at the beginning of the string, then strings are limited to 255 characters. Using a word (i.e., two bytes) allows 65,535 characters in a string. This is the technique usually used by the Pascal and BASIC languages.

- Terminate the string with some flag value, usually zero. This technique is used by the C language. Problems arise, however, if strings are processed in a manner other than sequentially from beginning to end.

ADDRESSING MODES

A computer instruction must specify two things:

1. What operation to perform, such as addition or subtraction.

2. On what data to perform the operation. Data for instructions is usually found either in registers or memory.

A portion of the instruction, called the *op code*, indicates the operation to perform. The simple example in Chapter 1 used the first digit of the instruction as the op code. Data was in the machine's single register and a memory location. The memory location was identified by the address contained in the last three digits of the instruction.

Real computers are seldom so simple. In the 68000, instructions specify operands by one of three techniques:

1. Some instructions imply the use of certain operands, usually a register, such as the status register or the Program Counter (PC).

2. Some instructions work only on registers. The register number is contained in the instruction itself.

3. Most 68000 instructions specify operands with a technique called an *effective address*. This is a generalized technique for addressing the registers and memory.

Effective Address

An effective address is specified by six bits in the instruction (usually the lowest six bits). The bit values indicate how to find the data for the instruction. Figure 2.5 shows how these bits are arranged into two groups of three bits.

The mode bits determine the meaning of the entire field. Three bits give eight possible combinations. Values 0–6 mean that a register is to be used, either as the operand, or to determine the address of the operand in memory. If the mode field is 7 (i.e., all 1's), then the entire six bits of the effective address field is used to specify the mode.

In the following examples, we will illustrate the addressing modes using the *MOVE.L* instruction, which moves a longword from one operand to another. Both operands have the effective address format. We will use the D0.L data register as the destination operand, and vary the source operand to illustrate the various addressing modes. Figure 2.6 shows the format of a *MOVE.L* instruction.

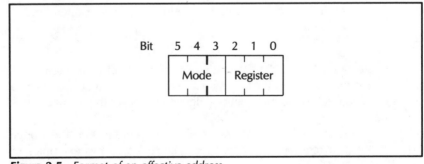

Figure 2.5 – *Format of an effective address*

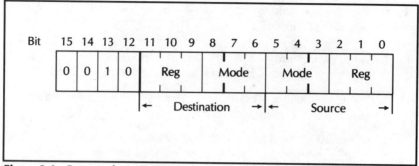

Figure 2.6 – *Format of a MOVE.L instruction*

The *Source* and *Destination* fields are used to select the source and destination operands. Since the register and mode fields are three bits wide, it is difficult to look at the hex representation of an instruction and determine the assembly language equivalent. This process is known as *disassembly*. 68000 instructions in general are difficult to disassemble by hand. Fortunately, most debuggers perform disassembly, so this problem is not as severe as it could be.

Data Register Direct Addressing

Addressing Mode Field: 000
Register Field: 000–111 (Data Register Number)
Assembler Syntax: Dn (n is 0–7)

Description

Data register direct addressing is indicated by an effective address mode field of 000 (binary). The register field contains a number from 000 to 111 (0–7), which indicates a data register. In data register direct addressing, the data register (indicated by the register field) contains the operand.

Example

The instruction *MOVE.L D1,D0* causes the contents of data register D1 to be copied into data register D0. After the instruction executes, the two registers contain the same information. Figure 2.7 shows the format of this instruction.

When only a word or byte is transferred, the contents of the upper bytes of the data register are unchanged. Figure 2.8 shows examples of the *MOVE* instruction with a byte, a word, and a longword.

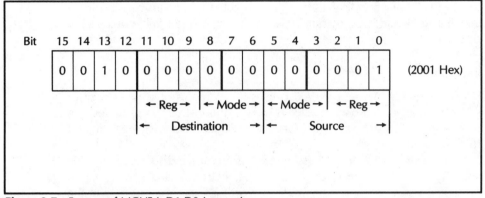

Figure 2.7 – Format of MOVE.L D1,D0 instruction

Instruction	Before	After
MOVE.B D1,D0	D0 = FFFFFFFF D1 = 01234567	D0 = FFFFFF67 D1 = 01234567
MOVE.W D1,D0	D0 = FFFFFFFF D1 = 01234567	D0 = FFFF4567 D1 = 01234567
MOVE.L D1,D0	D0 = FFFFFFFF D1 = 01234567	D0 = 01234567 D1 = 01234567

Figure 2.8 – Moving a byte, word, or longword

Address Register Direct Addressing

Addressing Mode Field: 001
Register Field: 000–111 (Address Register Number)
Assembler Syntax: An (n is 0–7)

Description

Address register direct addressing is indicated by an effective address mode field of 001 (binary). The register field contains a number from 000 to 111 (0–7), which indicates an address register. In address register direct addressing, the address register indicated by the register field contains the operand.

Example

The instruction *MOVE.L A1,D0* causes the contents of address register A1 to be copied into data register D0. After the instruction executes, the two registers contain the same information. Figure 2.9 shows the format of this instruction.

Transfers involving an address register are restricted to word or long size. Byte operations are not allowed. When transferring a word to an address register, bit 15 (the sign bit of a word) is extended throughout the upper word of the address register. Figure 2.10 gives several examples of address register direct addressing.

Bit	15	14	13	12	11	10	9	8	7	6	5	4	3	2	1	0	
	0	0	1	0	0	0	0	0	0	0	0	0	1	0	0	1	(2009 Hex)

← Reg → ← Mode → ← Mode → ← Reg →

← Destination → ← Source →

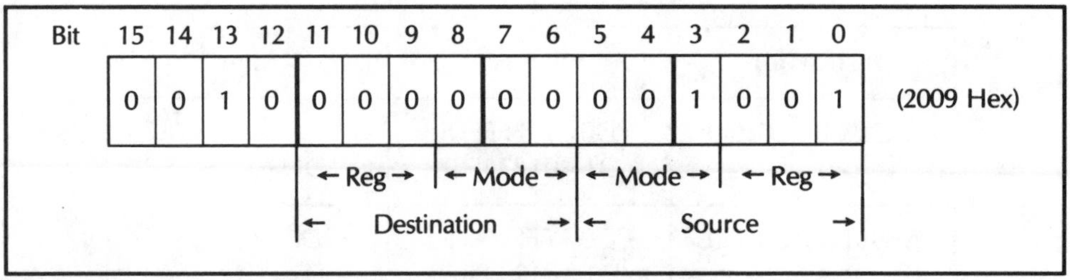

Figure 2.9 – *Format of MOVE.L A1,D0 instruction*

Instruction	Before	After
MOVE.W A1,D0	D0 = FFFFFFFF A1 = 01234567	D0 = FFFF4567 A1 = 01234567
MOVE.W D0,A1	D0 = 01234567 A1 = FFFFFFFF	D0 = 01234567 A1 = 00004567
MOVE.W D0,A1	D0 = 0000FFFF A1 = 00000000	D0 = 0000FFFF A1 = FFFFFFFF
MOVE.L A1,D0	D0 = FFFFFFFF A1 = 01234567	D0 = 01234567 A1 = 01234567

Figure 2.10 – *Examples of address register direct addressing*

Address Register Indirect Addressing

Addressing Mode Field:	010
Register Field:	000–111 (Address Register Number)
Assembler Syntax:	(An) (n is 0–7)

Description

Address register indirect addressing is indicated by an effective address mode field of 010 (binary). The register field contains a number from 000 to 111 (0–7), which indicates an address register.

In address register indirect addressing, the address register indicated by the register field is the address of a memory location that contains the operand. The register is said to point to (contain the address of) the operand. Address register indirection is denoted by enclosing the address register name in parentheses. For example, (A0) denotes indirection on address register A0. Word or longword references require that the address contained in the address register must be even.

Example

The instruction *MOVE.L (A1),D0* causes the contents of the memory location pointed to by address register A1 to be copied into data register D0. After the instruction executes, data register D0 and the memory location contain the same information. Figure 2.11 shows the format of this instruction.

The instruction works as shown in Figure 2.12. $1000 indicates the contents of the longword in memory at address 1000 hex.

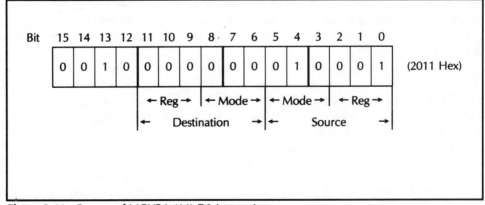

Figure 2.11 – *Format of MOVE.L (A1),D0 instruction*

Instruction	Before	After
MOVE.L (A1),D0	D0 = FFFFFFFF A1 = 00001000 $1000 = 01234567	D0 = 01234567 A1 = 00001000 $1000 = 01234567

Figure 2.12 – *An example of the MOVE.L (A1),D0 instruction*

Address Register Indirect Addressing with Post-Increment

Addressing Mode Field: 011
Register Field: 000–111 (Address Register Number)
Assembler Syntax: (An)+ (n is 0–7)

Description

Address register indirect addressing is indicated by an effective address mode field of 011 (binary). The register field contains a number from 000 to 111 (0–7), which indicates an address register. In address register indirect addressing, the address register indicated by the register field contains the address of a memory location that contains the operand. The register is said to point to (contain the address of) the operand.

The address register is incremented after the data has been obtained from memory. The increment is based on the length of the data item referenced by the instruction. Thus, for a *MOVE.B* instruction, the address register would be incremented by one. For a *MOVE.W* instruction, the address register is incremented by two. For a *MOVE.L* instruction, the address register is incremented by four.

Address register indirection with post-increment is denoted by enclosing the address register name in parentheses followed by a plus (+) symbol. For example, (A0)+ denotes post-increment indirection on address register A0. Word or longword references require that the address contained in the address register must be even.

Example

The instruction *MOVE.L (A1)+,D0* causes the memory location pointed to by address register A1 to be copied into the contents of data register

D0. After the instruction is executed, data register D0 and the memory location contain the same information. Address register A1 is incremented by 4. Figure 2.13 shows the format of this instruction.

The instruction works as shown in Figure 2.14. $1000 indicates the contents of the longword in memory at address 1000 hex.

A special case occurs when the address register specified is A7, which is the hardware stack pointer. Byte operations on address register A7 cause an increment by two rather than one. This ensures that the stack pointer always contains an even address.

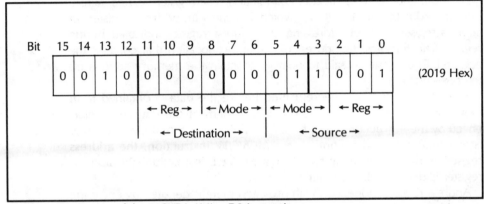

Figure 2.13 – *Format of the MOVE.L (A1)+,D0 instruction*

Instruction	Before	After
MOVE.L (A1)+,D0	D0 = FFFFFFFF A1 = 00001000 $1000 = 01234567	D0 = 01234567 A1 = 00001004 $1000 = 01234567

Figure 2.14 – *An example of the MOVE.L (A1)+,D0 instruction*

Address Register Indirect Addressing with Pre-decrement

Addressing Mode Field: 100
Register Field: 000–111 (Address Register Number)
Assembler Syntax: – (An) (n is 0–7)

Description

Address register indirect addressing with pre-decrement is indicated by an effective address mode field of 100 (binary). The register field contains a number from 000 to 111 (0–7), which indicates an address register. In address register indirect addressing, the address register indicated by the register field contains the address of a memory location that contains the operand. The register is said to point to (contain the memory address of) the operand.

The address register is decremented before the data is obtained from memory. The decrement is based on the length of the data item referenced by the instruction. Thus, for a *MOVE.B* instruction, the address register is decremented by one. For a *MOVE.W* instruction, the address register is decremented by two. For a *MOVE.L* instruction, the address register is decremented by four.

Address register indirection with pre-decrement is denoted by enclosing the address register name in parentheses preceded by a minus (–) symbol. For example, – (A0) denotes pre-decrement indirection on address register A0. Word or longword references require that the address contained in the address register must be even.

Example

The instruction *MOVE.L – (A1),D0* causes address register A1 to be decremented by four. The contents of the memory location pointed to by address register A1 are copied into data register D0. After the instruction executes, data register D0 and the memory location would contain the same information. Figure 2.15 shows the format of this instruction.

The instruction works as shown in Figure 2.16. $1000 indicates the contents of the longword in memory at address 1000 hex.

A special case occurs when the address register specified is A7, which is the hardware stack pointer. Byte operations on address register A7 cause a decrement by two rather than one. This ensures that the stack pointer always contains an even address.

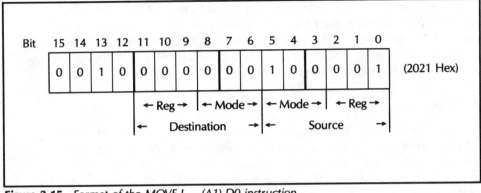

Figure 2.15 – *Format of the MOVE.L – (A1),D0 instruction*

Instruction	Before	After
MOVE.L – (A1),D0	D0 = FFFFFFFF A1 = 00001004 $1000 = 01234567	D0 = 01234567 A1 = 00001000 $1000 = 01234567

Figure 2.16 – *An example of the MOVE.L – (A1),D0 instruction*

Address Register Indirect Addressing with Displacement

Addressing Mode Field: 101
Register Field: 000–111 (Address Register Number)
Assembler Syntax: x(An) (x is 16 bits, n is 0–7)

Description

Address register indirect addressing with displacement is indicated by an effective address mode field of 101 (binary). The register field contains a number from 000 to 111 (0–7), which indicates an address register. In this type of addressing, the address register indicated by the register field is added to the sign-extended 16-bit number following the instruction. The result is the address of a memory location that contains the operand.

Address register indirect addressing with displacement is denoted by enclosing the address register name in parentheses preceded by a 16-bit constant. For example, 8(A0) denotes the memory location whose address is the contents of A0 plus 8. Word or longword references require that the address generated must be even.

Example

The instruction *MOVE.L 4(A1),D0* causes the contents of the memory location pointed to by address register A1 plus 4 to be copied into data register D0. After the instruction executes, data register D0 and the memory location contain the same information. Figure 2.17 shows the format of this instruction.

The instruction works as shown in Figure 2.18. $1004 indicates the contents of the longword in memory at address 1004 hex.

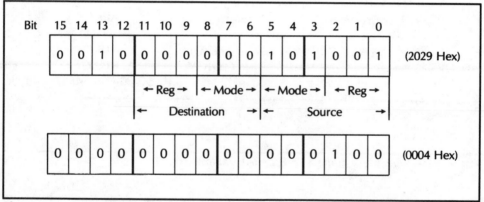

Figure 2.17 – *Format of the MOVE.L 4(A1),D0 instruction*

Instruction	Before	After
MOVE.L 4(A1),D0	D0 = FFFFFFFF A1 = 00001000 $1004 = 01234567	D0 = 01234567 A1 = 00001000 $1004 = 01234567

Figure 2.18 – *An example of the MOVE.L 4(A1),D0 instruction*

Note that displacement values greater than 7FFF (hex) subtract from rather than add to the value in the address register. This is due to the sign extension.

Address Register Indirect Addressing with Index

Addressing Mode Field:	110
Register Field:	000–111 (Address Register Number)
Assembler Syntax:	x(An,Dn.L) (x is 8 bits, n is 0–7)
	x(An,Dn.W)
	x(An,An.W)
	x(An,An.L)

Description

Address register indirect addressing with index is indicated by an effective address mode field of 110 (binary). The register field contains a number from 000 to 111 (0–7), which indicates an address register. In address register indirect addressing with index, the address register indicated by the register field is added to the contents of another register, plus a sign-extended 8-bit displacement. The sum of these three quantities is the address of a memory location that contains the operand.

The second register is called the *index register,* and may be either a data register or an address register. The size of the index register may be either a word or a longword. Word quantities are sign-extended before use.

Indexed address register indirect addressing is denoted by enclosing the index and address register names in parentheses preceded by an 8-bit constant. The desired size of the index register is defined by using the .L or .W suffixes on the register name. For example, *4(A0,D0.L)* denotes the memory location whose address is the contents of data register D0 and the contents of address register A0 plus 4. Word or longword references require that the address so generated must be even.

The information concerning the index register and 8-bit displacement is contained in the 16-bit quantity that follows the instruction. This is called an *extension word,* and is in the format shown in Figure 2.19.

The bit labeled A is 1 if the index register is an address register, and 0 if the index register is a data register. Bits 14–12 contain the register number. The bit labeled L is a 1 if the index register is a long quantity, and 0 if the index is a word.

Example

The instruction *MOVE.L 4(A1,A2.L),D0* causes the contents of the memory location pointed to by the sum of address registers A2 and A1 plus 4 to be copied into data register D0. After the instruction executes, data register D0 and the memory location contain the same information. Figure 2.20 shows the format of this instruction.

Figure 2.21 shows how the instruction works. $2004 indicates the contents of the longword in memory at address 2004 hex.

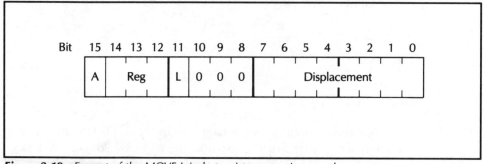

Figure 2.19 – *Format of the MOVE.L index register extension word*

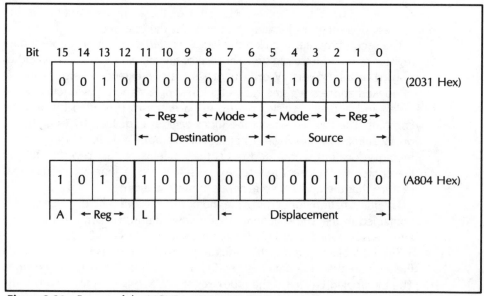

Figure 2.20 – *Format of the MOVE.L 4(A1,A2.L),D0 instruction*

Instruction	Before	After
MOVE.L 4(A1,A2.L),D0	D0 = FFFFFFFF A1 = 00001000 A2 = 00001000 $2004 = 01234567	D0 = 01234567 A1 = 00001000 A2 = 00001000 $2004 = 01234567

Figure 2.21 – *An example of the MOVE.L 4(A1,A2.L),D0 instruction*

Absolute Short Addressing

Addressing Mode Field: 111
Register Field: 000
Assembler Syntax: x (x is a 16-bit constant)

Description

Mode 7 with a register field of zero indicates that the word following the instruction is an absolute 16-bit address. The address is sign-extended before use, so that address specifications 8000 hex and above refer to addresses FFFF8000 and above. Remember, however, that the high byte of the address is presently discarded. The sign extension means that short addressing is useful only for the first 32,768 (32K) bytes of memory.

Example

The instruction *MOVE.L $1000,D0* causes the contents of memory location 1000 (hex) to be copied into data register D0. (Many 68000 assemblers use the $ prefix to indicate hex numbers.)

Figure 2.22 shows the format of this instruction.

Figure 2.23 shows how the instruction works.

$1000 indicates the contents of the longword in memory at the address 1000 hex.

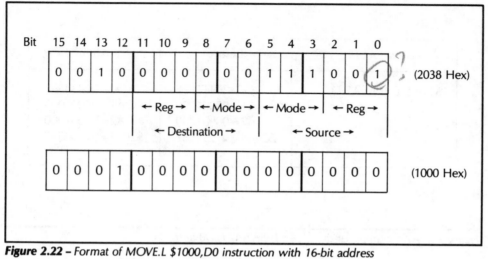

Figure 2.22 – *Format of MOVE.L $1000,D0 instruction with 16-bit address*

Instruction	Before	After
MOVE.L $1000,D0	D0 = FFFFFFFF $1000 = 01234567	D0 = 01234567 $1000 = 01234567

Figure 2.23 – *An example of the MOVE.L $1000,D0 instruction with 16-bit address*

Absolute Long Addressing

Addressing Mode Field: 111
Register Field: 001
Assembler Syntax: x (x is a 32-bit constant)

Description

Mode 7 with a register field of one indicates that the longword following the instruction is an absolute 32-bit address. Remember that the high byte of the address is presently discarded.

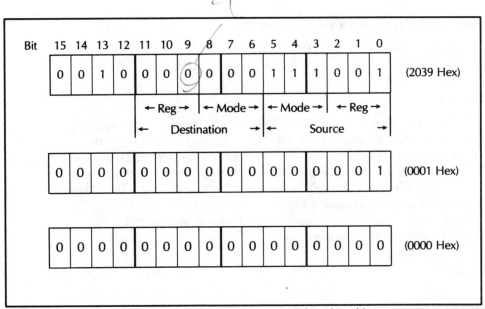

Figure 2.24 – *Format of MOVE.L $10000,D0 instruction with 32-bit address*

Instruction	Before	After
MOVE.L $10000,D0	D0 = FFFFFFFF $10000 = 01234567	D0 = 01234567 $10000 = 01234567

Figure 2.25 – *An example of the MOVE.L $10000,D0 instruction with 32-bit address*

Example

The instruction *MOVE.L $10000,D0* causes the contents of memory location 10000 (hex) to be copied into data register D0. Figure 2.24 shows the format of this instruction. Figure 2.25 shows how the instruction works.

$10000 indicates the contents of the longword in memory at address 10000 hex. Many 68000 assemblers use the prefix $ to indicate hex numbers.

Program Counter with Displacement

Register Field: 010
Assembler Syntax: x(PC) (x is a 16-bit constant)

Description

Mode 7 with a register field of two indicates that the word following the instruction is a displacement to be added to the program counter in order to obtain a memory address. The displacement is sign-extended before the addition takes place. Thus, it is possible to address memory in a range from −32,768 to +32,767 bytes relative to the present instruction. The value used for the program counter is the address of the displacement word.

The program counter with displacement is denoted as *xxxx(PC)*, where *xxxx* is a constant 16-bit number.

Example

The instruction *MOVE.L $100(PC),D0* causes the contents of the memory location specified by the address of the instruction plus 102 hex to be copied into data register D0. Figure 2.26 shows the format of this instruction.

Suppose the first word of the instruction is at location 1000 hex. Figure 2.27 shows how the instruction would work.

$1102 indicates the contents of the longword in memory at address 1102 hex. Many 68000 assemblers use the prefix $ to indicate hex numbers.

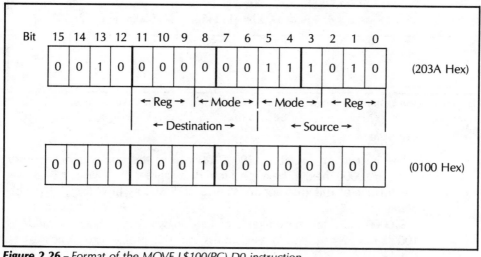

Figure 2.26 – *Format of the MOVE.L$100(PC),D0 instruction*

Instruction	Before	After
MOVE.L $100(PC),D0	D0= FFFFFFFF $1102=01234567	D0=01234567 $1102=01234567

Figure 2.27 – *An example of the MOVE.L $100(PC),D0 instruction*

Program Counter with Index

Addressing Mode Field:	111
Register Field:	011
Assembler Syntax:	x(PC,Dn.L) (x is 8 bits, n is 0–7)
	x(PC,Dn.W)
	x(PC,An.W)
	x(PC,An.L)

Description

Mode 7 with a register field of 3 indicates that the memory address is to be constructed using the value of the program counter, an index register, and a sign-extended 8-bit displacement. This mode is similar to the address register with index mode instruction. The same format extension word is required. Figure 2.28 shows the format of this instruction.

The program counter with index is denoted as xxx(PC,xr.s), where xxx is a constant 8-bit number, and xr.s is a register name with size specification. For example, indexing with the word contained in D0 and a displacement of 10 hex is written $10(PC,D0.W).

Example

The instruction MOVE.L $10(PC,A1.L),D0 causes the contents of the memory location at the address of the instruction plus the contents of A1 plus 12 hex to be copied into data register D0. Figure 2.29 shows the format of this instruction.

Suppose the first word of the instruction is at location 1000 hex. Figure 2.30 shows how the instruction would work.

$2012 indicates the contents of the longword in memory at address 2012 hex.

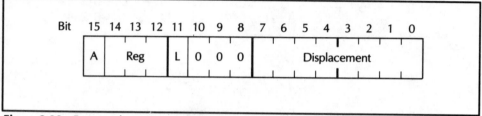

Figure 2.28 – Format of program counter with index extension word

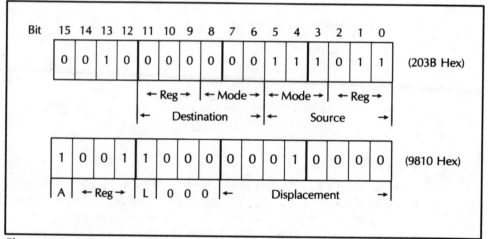

Figure 2.29 – Format of MOVE.L $10(PC,A1.L),D0 instruction

Instruction	Before	After
MOVE.L $10(A1.L,PC),D0	D0 = FFFFFFFF $2102 = 01234567 A1 = 00001000	D0 = 01234567 $2102 = 01234567 A1 = 00001000

Figure 2.30 – An example of the MOVE.L $10(PC,A1.L),D0 instruction

Immediate Mode

Addressing Mode Field:	111 (Source only)
Register Field:	100
Assembler Syntax:	#x (x is 8, 16, or 32 bits)

Description

Mode 7 with a register field of 4 indicates that the source data for an instruction is contained in the word or longword (depending on the size of the instruction) that follows the instruction. Byte data for an immediate mode instruction is contained in the low-order byte of the word following the instruction.

Immediate mode is denoted by #(constant) where (constant) is a hex or decimal number. Many assemblers allow symbols to be defined for use as immediate quantities. (See the section on assemblers in Chapter 3 for additional information.)

Example

The instruction *MOVE.L #$10002000,D0* causes the long constant 10002000 (hex) to be loaded into data register D0. The previous contents of D0 are lost. Figure 2.31 shows the format of this instruction. Figure 2.32 shows how this instruction works.

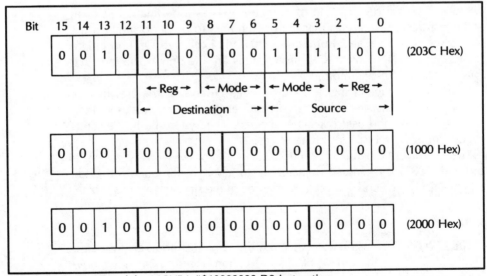

Figure 2.31 – *Format of the MOVE.L #$10002000,D0 instruction*

Instruction	Before	After
MOVE.L #$10002000,D0	D0 = 01234567	D0 = 10002000

Figure 2.32 – An example of the MOVE.L #$10002000,D0 instruction

Status Register Addressing

Addressing Mode Field: 111 (Destination only)
Register Field: 100
Assembler Syntax: SR
                          CCR

Description

Mode 7 with a register field of 4, when used as a destination field on some instructions, indicates that the operation is to be performed on the status register. The And Immediate (ANDI), Exclusive Or Immediate (EORI), and Or Immediate (ORI) instructions are the only operations that can use this addressing mode.

When the instruction specifies a byte length, then only the user byte of the status register is affected. When a word length instruction is used, then both the system and user bytes are affected. The System bit in the status register must be set to 1 in the latter case.

The assembler recognizes the special labels SR (for the whole status register) and CCR (for the user byte). CCR is an acronym for Condition Code Register. Only the condition codes are stored in the status register user byte.

Example

The *ORI #5,CCR* instruction sets both the carry (C) and zero (Z) flags. Figure 2.33 shows the format of this instruction. Figure 2.34 shows how the instruction works.

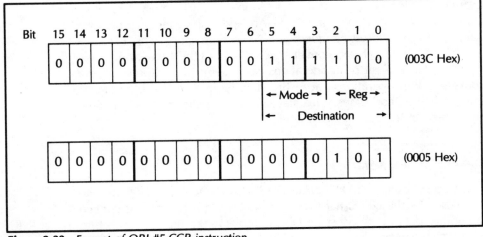

Figure 2.33 – *Format of ORI #5,CCR instruction*

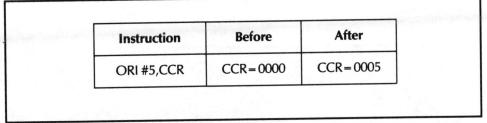

Figure 2.34 – *An example of the ORI #5,CCR instruction*

Stacks and Stack Frames

Many commercial microcomputers today (including the 68000) have a feature called a *stack*. A stack is a storage technique similar to the spring-loaded platforms used for plates in a cafeteria line. The last byte, word, or longword, placed on the stack is the first data item to be removed. This storage scheme is called *Last-In-First-Out* (LIFO). The act of placing a new data item on the stack is known as a *push*. Removing a data item is commonly called a *pop*.

How a Stack Works

Stacks are implemented on the 68000 using the pre-decrement and post-increment addressing modes. An address register (called the *stack pointer*) is used to indicate the top of the stack's position in memory. Data items are pushed onto the stack using the – (An) addressing mode, and popped using the (An)+ addressing mode, as illustrated in Figure 2.35.

The stack pointer always contains the address of the element on top of the stack. Subsequent push operations cause items to be stored at lower addresses. Pop operations cause the stack pointer to be incremented toward higher addresses. The stack is said to "grow toward lower addresses" on the 68000.

68000 Hardware Stack

Register A7 on the 68000 is called the *hardware stack pointer*. This register is used by the 68000 hardware for addressing memory that contains temporary data items. Most 68000 assemblers take the symbol SP (for Stack Pointer) as an alternative to A7 in register specifications.

There are two stack pointers on the 68000: one for when the processor is in user mode (called USP) and one for when the processor is in supervisor mode (called SSP).

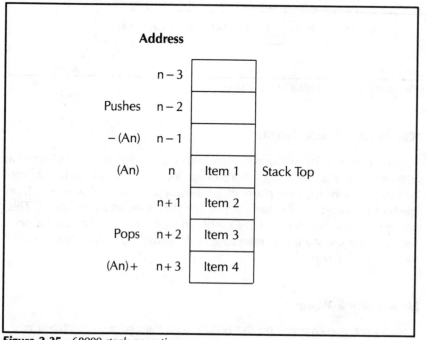

Figure 2.35 – *68000 stack operations*

A special instruction, *MOVE USP,* allows the supervisor program to access the USP. The user mode program is not allowed access to the SSP.

Typically, the stack is used for information that will be required again later. For example, there is a common programming technique called a *subroutine.*

Subroutines

Subroutines are small programs in themselves that can be used as units of other, larger programs. Typical subroutines include I/O routines and common calculations, such as taking the square root of a number.

The 68000 supports instructions known as *subroutine calls.* These instructions place the address of the next instruction on the stack and the address of the subroutine into the program counter (PC). In this way, the next instruction to be executed becomes the first instruction in the subroutine. When the subroutine has completed processing, it executes a *return* instruction, which restores the address currently on top of the stack back into the PC. This causes the program to resume execution at the instruction that immediately follows the subroutine call.

Subroutines are powerful programming tools. A subroutine is essentially an extension to the instruction set of the machine. The programmer can treat subroutine calls as if they were sophisticated machine instructions.

Exceptions

A concept similar to the subroutine call is the 68000 exception mechanism. The 68000 allows the suspension of a program and subsequent resumption of the same program through a technique known as an *exception.* (This same technique is called an *interrupt* on other machines.)

An exception causes the status register and program counter to be pushed onto the stack. A special instruction allows restoration of the program counter/status register combination at a later point. This mechanism is described in detail in Chapter 7, Exception Programming.

Stack Implemented in Software

You can implement a stack using any address register. All that is required is to place the address of the end of the area to be used as a stack into the address register. The pre-decrement and post-increment addressing modes can then be used to push and pop data items from this software stack.

Stack Frames

Stacks are convenient for allocating temporary memory areas. The 68000 supports a hardware mechanism for allocating scratchpads called a *stack frame*.

The 68000 *LINK* and *UNLK* (unlink) instructions allocate and free temporary memory at the top of the stack. An additional address register, called the *frame pointer*, is used to point to the area allocated on the stack. References to the stack frame use the address register with displacement addressing mode. The frame pointer rather than the stack pointer is used to address the frame so that subsequent stack *PUSH* and *POP* operations will not affect the offsets of individual components of the frame.

Summary

The important points that we have covered in this chapter are:

- The 68000 has sixteen registers: eight data registers and eight address registers. Data registers may be used as bytes, words, or longwords. Address registers may be used only as words or longwords. In addition, loading a word into an address register causes the word to be sign-extended to 32 bits.

- There are two special registers: the program counter (PC) and the status register (SR). The program counter contains the address of the next instruction to be executed. The status register contains machine status bits. The upper eight bits of the status register, called the system byte, may not be accessed by ordinary programs. The lower eight bits of the status register, called the condition code register (CCR), contain status bits (condition codes) that indicate the result of the last instruction executed.

- The 68000 supports three principle numeric data types: binary, BCD, and floating-point. Binary data may be used in units of 8 bits (a byte), 16 bits (a word), and 32 bits (a longword). These lengths are indicated on register and instruction names by the suffixes .B, .W, and .L. BCD is a method of storing two decimal digits per byte. Floating-point is a method of representing very large or very small numbers without requiring undue amounts of memory.

- The 68000 supports fourteen distinct methods of specifying data in an instruction. These are called *addressing modes*. They are listed in Table 2.1.

Syntax	Name
Dn	Data register direct
An	Address register direct
(An)	Address register indirect
(An)+	Address register indirect post-increment
−(An)	Address register indirect pre-decrement
w(An)	Address register with displacement
b(An,Rn)	Address register with index
w(.W)	Absolute short
l(.L)	Absolute long
w(PC)	PC with displacement
b(PC,Rn)	PC with index
#x	Immediate
SR	Status register (Privileged)
CCR	Condition code register

b   is a byte constant.

w   is a word constant.

l   is a long constant.

x   can be any of these.

n   is a register number, 0–7.

R   is a register specifier, either A or D.

Table 2.1 *– Addressing Modes of The 68000*

- The post-increment and pre-decrement addressing modes are used to implement data structures called stacks. Stacks are organized in a last-in first-out (or LIFO) scheme in which the last data item to be put on is the first one taken off. Register A7 is used by the 68000 instructions to refer to a special stack called the hardware stack.

• Special 68000 instructions exist that allocate and free temporary scratchpad memory areas on the hardware stack. These scratchpad areas are known as *stack frames*.

Chapter 3 will build on this background to present the 68000 instruction set and the mechanics of writing 68000 assembly language programs.

Exercises

1. Given the following conditions:

   • D0 = 00008000
   • A0 = 00001000
   • A7 = 00010000
   What are the results of the following instructions?

   MOVE.B   D0,A0
   MOVE.W   D0,A0
   MOVE.B   D0,(A0)+
   MOVE.B   D0, – (A7)

   Give the new contents of all registers and memory locations that change. Use the same starting conditions for all the instructions.

2. The ADD binary instruction can add an effective address operand to a data register. The format of this instruction is shown in Figure 2.36.

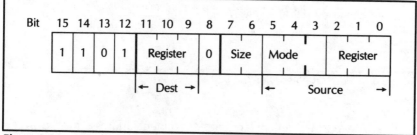

Figure 2.36 – ADD binary instruction format

The Size field is 00 for byte, 01 for word, and 10 for long data. Modify the examples for the addressing modes (except for the status register mode) to use this instruction.

3. The 68000 pre-decrement and post-increment addressing modes are normally used for stacks that grow toward lower addresses. Can these addressing modes be used to implement a stack (in software) that grows toward higher addresses? If so, how would such a stack differ from a normal one? How could the 68000 addressing modes be altered to support such stacks?

68000 Instruction Set

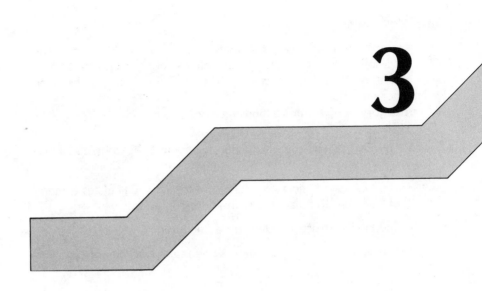

INTRODUCTION

This chapter covers the mechanics of program generation and the details of the 68000 instruction set. It is probably not necessary to study each instruction in detail, but you should pay attention to the section on the mechanics of program generation. This information is vital to understanding the instruction descriptions.

INSTRUCTION CLASSES

The 68000 instructions fall into eight classifications:

- Data movement
- Integer arithmetic
- Logical
- Shift and rotate
- Bit manipulation
- BCD
- Program control
- System control

We will now describe each of these classes in detail.

Data Movement

Data movement instructions transport data from one location in the 68000 to another. Normally, these instructions move from one to four bytes of data between two registers, a register and memory, or between two memory locations.

This category of 68000 instructions includes:

- The EXG (EXchanGe) instruction. Exchanges the contents of two registers.

- The LEA (Load Effective Address) instruction. Calculates a memory address and places it in an address register.

- The LINK instruction. Allocates a stack frame.

- The MOVE instruction. Transfers one register or memory location to another.

- The MOVEM (Move Multiple) instruction. Transfers multiple registers to or from memory.

- The MOVEP (Move Peripheral) instruction. Transfers data to or from an 8-bit peripheral.

- The MOVEQ (Move Quick) instruction. Loads a data register with a constant.

- The PEA (Push Effective Address) instruction. Calculates a memory address, and pushes it onto the hardware stack.

- The SWAP instruction. Swaps the words in a data register.

- The UNLK (UNLinK) instruction. Deallocates a stack frame.

Integer Arithmetic Operations

Integer arithmetic instructions perform basic two's complement operations on binary data. This class of instructions includes:

- The ADD, ADDA, ADDI, ADDQ, and ADDX instructions. Used for two's complement addition.

- The CLR instruction. Moves zero into an operand.

- The CMP, CMPA, CMPI, and CMPM instructions. Compares two quantities.

- The DIVS and DIVU instructions. Perform signed and unsigned integer division.

- The EXT instruction. Sign extends a byte to a word quantity or a word to a long quantity.

- The MULS and MULU instructions. Used for signed and unsigned multiplication operations.

- The NEG and NEGX operations. Form the two's complement of a number.

- The SUB, SUBA, SUBI, SUBQ, and SUBX instructions. Used for two's complement subtraction.

- The TAS (Test and Set) instruction. Used to synchronize multiple processors.

- The TST instruction. Compares an operand to zero.

Logical Operations

The logical operation instruction group performs bit-wise Boolean operations on binary numbers. This class of instructions includes:

- The AND and ANDI instructions. Perform a Boolean AND operation on two binary integers.

- The OR and ORI instructions. Perform a Boolean OR operation.

- The EOR and EORI instructions. Perform a Boolean exclusive OR operation.

- The NOT instruction. Perform a one's complement operation.

Shift and Rotate Operations

The shift and rotate instructions perform arithmetic and logical shifts, as well as rotates with and without an auxiliary Carry bit. This group contains:

- The ASL and ASR instructions. Arithmetic left and right shift operations.

- The LSL and LSR instructions. Logical left and right shift operations.

- The ROL and ROR instructions. Left and right rotates without an auxiliary Carry bit.

- The ROXL and ROXR instructions. Left and right rotates through an auxiliary Carry bit.

Bit Manipulation Operations (4)

The bit-manipulation instructions operate on single bits within a byte. This instruction class contains:

- The BTST instruction. Tests a single bit.

- The BSET instruction. Tests a single bit and then sets the bit.

- The BCLR instruction. Tests a single bit and then clears the bit.

- The BCHG instruction. Tests a single bit and then inverts (complements) the bit.

Binary Coded Decimal Instructions (3)

The binary coded decimal (BCD) instructions manipulate numbers in BCD format. This group contains:

- The ABCD instruction. Performs BCD add operations.

- The SBCD instruction. Performs BCD subtract operations.

- The NBCD instruction. Performs BCD negation.

Program Control Instructions (8)

The program control instructions alter the instruction flow through a program segment. This group contains:

- The Bcc instruction group of fifteen conditional-branch instructions. Conditionally alter the flow of instructions.

- The DBcc instruction group, consisting of sixteen looping-primitive instructions.

- The Scc instruction group of sixteen conditional-set instructions. Set a byte depending on the settings of the condition code.

- The BSR and JSR subroutine call instructions.

- The RTS subroutine return instruction.

- The JMP absolute jump instruction.

- The RTR instruction. Restores the program counter and condition codes from the stack.

System Control Operations ⑦

System control instructions alter the state of the 68000 hardware environment.

Many of these instructions are "privileged," meaning that they require that the 68000 be executing in supervisor mode. This instruction class contains:

- The MOVE USP instruction. Allows a supervisor mode program access to the user mode stack pointer.

- The RESET instruction. Resets external devices.

- The RTE instruction. Returns from an exception condition. (Exceptions are described in Chapter 7.)

- The STOP instruction. Suspends instruction processing until an external event occurs.

- The CHK and TRAPV instructions. These instructions detect catastrophic program errors.

- The TRAP group of sixteen instructions. Provide a method for a user mode program to call a supervisor mode program.

PROGRAM DEVELOPMENT MECHANICS

The process of writing an assembly language program works something like this:

1. Key in the program using a text editor. The disk file resulting from this process is known as the *assembly source file.*

2. Transform the program into machine code using a program called an *assembler.* The machine-code file produced by the assembler is commonly called an *object file.* Most assemblers also

produce a file that contains the instructions from the source file along with the machine code produced (in hexadecimal). Such a file is known as a *listing file.*

3. Some systems require that the object output of the assembler be processed by a program known as a *linker* or *linkage editor* before execution. For other systems, this step is not required. Many large programs are split into separate source files, assembled separately, and then combined with the linkage editor. The final output of this process is a file that may be loaded into memory and executed. This file is commonly called a *load file, executable file,* or a *load module.*

4. The load file produced by the assembler and linker is then loaded into memory and executed.

Usually, each of these steps is repeated many times. The file must be edited many times to get it to assemble without errors. The assembled file may not link properly, necessitating more editing and assembling. Finally, the successfully linked file may not run properly. What to do when this happens?

An error in a program is known as a *bug.* Finding bugs in object programs is more of an art than a science. Fortunately, there are tools that make the task easier. The first of these is the age-old standby of printing out values within the program by inserting a temporary printing code. The second, and most valuable tool is the *interactive debugger.* This wonderful program allows you to stop at certain points in the program and look at the values that are currently in registers and memory. Many debuggers allow references to labels contained in the program source file.

Most systems that support assembly language development are equipped with these tools in one form or another. The instructions on how to use the tools that come with your system are usually contained in the system manuals. For the remainder of this book, we will give examples from two systems—UNIX and CP/M-68K.

Editing

Developing programs requires only a simple editor without word processing capabilities such as word wrap, justification, and so on. Which editor is best is a matter of personal preference. A screen-oriented editor is preferred by most programmers.

Editing a file on the UNIX and CP/M-68K systems starts with a command like:

```
% ed filename.typ
A>ed filename.typ
```

where the % and A> represent the system prompt characters for UNIX and CP/M-68K respectively. Filename.typ is the name of the file to be edited or created. Many editors preserve the original contents of the file in a backup file, often named filename.bak. For UNIX and CP/M-68K, the .typ field is usually .s.

Backups

Maintaining backup copies of source files is essential because of the possibility of a hardware or software failure. While hardware failures are comparatively rare, they still occur from time to time. Software and media failures are all too common. Power failures can also destroy disk files. There is a bit of conventional engineering wisdom known as Murphy's Law:

If anything can go wrong, it will.

You will find that this law applies to programming as well. Most programmers keep *two* backup copies in case the machine crashes while making a backup. (If this occurs, it is possible to destroy *both* the original and the backup.) Recovery from such a disaster is extremely painful. Unfortunately, most people have to learn this lesson the hard way, as Ben Franklin said:

Experience is a dear school, but fools will learn at no other.

Don't be one of them! Back up your files!

Assembling

Assemblers come in a variety of different styles. Most assemblers take a source file and produce an object file and a listing file. The command line for invoking an assembler on UNIX and CP/M-68K is:

```
% as file.s
A>as68 -l -p file.s >file.lis
```

The UNIX assembler "as" creates file.o (the object file) from file.s (the source file). The command given for CP/M-68K does the same, and also produces file.lis (the listing file). Some UNIX assemblers use a command similar to the CP/M-68K command line to produce a listing file.

Source File Format

The source file that you input to the assembler consists of lines of text. Each line in the source file may be classified as one of three things:

- A comment line. Comments in most 68000 assemblers are denoted by placing an asterisk (∗) as the first character on the line.

- A 68000 instruction. Instruction lines consist of an optional label, followed by an instruction mnemonic, followed by one or more operands. Spaces or tabs are required between the label, mnemonic, and operand fields. A comma is used to separate multiple operands. Most assemblers do not allow spaces between operands.

- An assembler directive. Directives are a means of telling the assembler how you want your program treated. For example, the UNIX and CP/M assemblers have the following directives in common:

   a) .text. This directive specifies that the code that follows is to be treated as machine instructions.
   b) .data. This directive specifies that the code that follows is to be treated as data.
   c) .bss. This directive specifies that the code that follows reserves uninitialized memory and has no particular initial value. BSS code is not stored in the executable file. Proper use of this directive can substantially reduce both disk storage and load time for the final program.
   d) .page. This directive causes the assembler to start a new page on the listing file. Proper use of this directive can substantially increase program readability.

Linking

After obtaining an error-free assembly, you may need to link the output file in order to make it executable. Some UNIX systems allow you to execute the object output of the assembler (and some do not). CP/M-68K requires the use of the linker.

The linker command for UNIX has the following syntax:

```
% ld  − o  thisfile file.o
```

The "−o thisfile" construct causes the output file to be named thisfile. The same command on CP/M-68K has the following syntax:

```
A>lo68 −r −o thisfile.68k file.o
```

The −r switch causes the relocation information to be preserved. This flag allows the program to run on any CP/M-68K system. The "−o thisfile.68k" construct causes the output file to be named thisfile.68k.

Debugging

Typing the filename at the system prompt level causes the file to be executed. But what if it doesn't work correctly? How do you figure out what is wrong?

When something goes wrong, use the interactive debugger. Both the UNIX and CP/M-68K systems have debugging programs that allow you to interact with an executing program so that you can identify any problem areas. Debuggers usually have the following features:

- The ability to select a program for debugging.

- The ability to examine and change the contents of a machine register or a memory location.

- The ability to start execution at a desired location, and stop execution at one of several points (commonly called *breakpoints*).

- The ability to execute a single instruction at a time. This is commonly called *tracing*, because the Trace bit in the status register provides this capability.

In explaining the 68000 instruction set, we will make use of the CP/M-68K debugger, DDT-68K. The original version of this debugger is called a *hex debugger* because it lacks the ability to use labels from the source program. A debugger that can use these labels is called a *symbolic debugger*. A later version of DDT-68K provides symbolic capability. We will use the following commands from DDT-68K:

- The Lxxxxx,yyyyy command. This causes memory locations xxxxx through yyyyy to be displayed as 68000 instruction mnemonics.

- The Dxxxxx,yyyyy command. This causes memory locations xxxxx through yyyyy to be displayed in hex.

- The Sxxxxx command. This causes memory location xxxxx to be displayed for possible modification. Pressing Return causes the next location to be displayed. Typing a period causes the debugger to prompt for the next command.

- The G,xxxxx command. This starts program execution at the location contained in the program counter and stops program execution immediately before the instruction at xxxxx.

- The T command. The next instruction is executed, using the Trace bit hardware mechanism.

The UNIX debugger is called *sdb,* and can be used in a similar fashion.

Example

Suppose that we wish to execute the source file shown in Listing 3.1 under CP/M-68K.

```
        .text
*********************************
*       This program adds the first
*       five integers and stores the
*       result in memory.
*********************************
start:  move.w  a,d0    Load first number
        add.w   b,d0
        add.w   c,d0
        add.w   d,d0
        add.w   e,d0
        move.w  d0,f    Store answer
        rts             Return to CP/M
        .data
a:      dc.w    1       Numbers to add
b:      dc.w    2
c:      dc.w    3
d:      dc.w    4
e:      dc.w    5
f:      dc.w    0       Answer goes here
        .end
```

Listing 3.1 – *The source file*

This program adds the first five integers and stores the result in memory. Assume that the program has been entered into file test.s using the text editor. We then assemble the file using the assembler (AS68) as follows:

A>as68 –l –p test.s >test.l

The assembler produces an object file test.o. The file "test.l" is shown in Listing 3.2.

The first number on each line is the number of the line in the source file, starting with one. The assembler reports errors by line number.

The second number is the hex offset at which the present line is assembled. When added to the load address of the text, data, or bss segment (as appropriate) this number yields the absolute memory address of the instruction or data described by the line.

The third number in each line is the actual hex contents of the memory location when the program is loaded into memory. Addresses may not be relocated to their final value until load time. The assembly listing reflects addresses as they are known to the assembler.

The linker relocates all addresses to the values that they will have at execution time. Later, when the program is loaded into memory, it may be

```
 1 00000000                          .text
 2                          ********************************
 3                          *       This program adds the first
 4                          *       five integers and stores the
 5                          *       result in memory
 6                          ********************************
 7 00000000 303900000000    start:   move.w   a,d0    Load first number
 8 00000006 D07900000002             add.w    b,d0
 9 0000000C D07900000004             add.w    c,d0
10 00000012 D07900000006             add.w    d,d0
11 00000018 D07900000008             add.w    e,d0
12 0000001E 33C00000000A             move.w   d0,f    Store answer
13 00000024 4E75                     rts              Return to CP/M
14 00000000                          .data
15 00000000 0001           a:        dc.w     1       Numbers to add
16 00000002 0002           b:        dc.w     2
17 00000004 0003           c:        dc.w     3
18 00000006 0004           d:        dc.w     4
19 00000008 0005           e:        dc.w     5
20 0000000A 0000           f:        dc.w     0       Answer goes here
21 0000000C                          .end
```

Listing 3.2 – *The Listing file*

relocated yet again if the base address of the program does not match the address to which it was linked. By the time the program begins execution, however, all addresses are absolute.

The source line as it appears in the file comes next. Source lines that begin with an asterisk (*) are placed in the listing file as is. Such a line is called a comment line. Comments serve only to help the human reader understand the program.

Other lines consist of an optional label, an opcode or directive, and one or more operands. Additional text on the line following the operands is regarded as comments by the assembler. At least one space is required between the end of the last operand and the beginning of the comment. The leading asterisk is not required for a comment at the end of a line.

A label on a line establishes a symbolic name for a memory location. A label must be the first word on a line, and must be terminated by a colon (or by a space or tab if the label starts in column 1). The label may then be referred to by instructions that reference memory. The memory locations a: through f: in Listing 3.2 illustrate this usage. These labels are tags for the memory locations referenced by the program's MOVE and ADD instructions.

```
A>lo68 −r −o test.68k test.o
```

The linker produces an executable file called test.68k. To run the program under the debugger, we type:

```
A>ddt test.68k
```

```
DDT-68K
Copyright 1982, Digital Research
```

```
text base     = 00000500  data base    = 00000526  bss base    = 00000532
text length   = 00000026  data length  = 0000000C  bss length  = 00000000
base page address = 00000400    initial stack pointer = 0001A2B8
```

This information indicates that the program is loaded into memory starting at 500 hex (text base). The data section of the program begins at address 526 hex (data base). From the assembly listing, we can see that the text portion is 26 bytes long. We can now use the debugger to list out the program in 68000 mnemonics with the l (el) command:

```
−l500,524
00000500 move $526,D0
00000506 add $528,D0
0000050C add $52A,D0
```

```
00000512 add $52C,D0
00000518 add $52E,D0
0000051E move D0,$530
00000524 rts
```

The data area is between addresses 526 and 532. The data base printed out by DDT (526) and data length (0c), when added together, produce the first address beyond the data area (532). We can display the data area with the Display Words (dw) command:

```
-dw526,532
00000526 0001 0002 0003 0004 0005 0000 ............
```

The Trace (t) command is used to execute each instruction. DDT shows the registers *before* the instruction is executed, as shown below:

```
PC = 00000500  USP = 0001A2B0  SSP = 00002000  ST = 0000 = >IM = 0
D 000000D0  000000D1  000000D2  000000D3  000000D4  000000D5  000000D6  000000D7
A 000000A0  000000A1  000000A2  000000A3  000000A4  000000A5  000000A6  0001A2B0
move $526,D0
-t
PC = 00000506  USP = 0001A2B0  SSP = 00002000  ST = 0000 = >IM = 0
D 00000001  000000D1  000000D2  000000D3  000000D4  000000D5  000000D6  000000D7
A 000000A0  000000A1  000000A2  000000A3  000000A4  000000A5  000000A6  0001A2B0
add $528,D0
-t
PC = 0000050C  USP = 0001A2B0  SSP = 00002000  ST = 0000 = >IM = 0
D 00000003  000000D1  000000D2  000000D3  000000D4  000000D5  000000D6  000000D7
A 000000A0  000000A1  000000A2  000000A3  000000A4  000000A5  000000A6  0001A2B0
add $52A,D0
-t
PC = 00000512  USP = 0001A2B0  SSP = 00002000  ST = 0000 = >IM = 0
D 00000006  000000D1  000000D2  000000D3  000000D4  000000D5  000000D6  000000D7
A 000000A0  000000A1  000000A2  000000A3  000000A4  000000A5  000000A6  0001A2B0
add $52C,D0
-t
PC = 00000518  USP = 0001A2B0  SSP = 00002000  ST = 0000 = >IM = 0
D 0000000A  000000D1  000000D2  000000D3  000000D4  000000D5  000000D6  000000D7
A 000000A0  000000A1  000000A2  000000A3  000000A4  000000A5  000000A6  0001A2B0
add $52E,D0
-t
PC = 0000051E  USP = 0001A2B0  SSP = 00002000  ST = 0000 = >IM = 0
D 0000000F  000000D1  000000D2  000000D3  000000D4  000000D5  000000D6  000000D7
A 000000A0  000000A1  000000A2  000000A3  000000A4  000000A5  000000A6  0001A2B0
move D0,$530
```

```
-t
PC=00000524  USP=0001A2B0  SSP=00002000  ST=0000=>IM=0
D 0000000F  000000D1  000000D2  000000D3  000000D4  000000D5  000000D6  000000D7
A 000000A0  000000A1  000000A2  000000A3  000000A4  000000A5  000000A6  0001A2B0
rts
```

Notice how the value of register D0 changes as each number is added. To make the actions of the instructions easier to identify, we will underline registers that change in presenting examples. Just before returning to CP/M, look at the answer in memory. (Location 530 hex corresponds to the label f: in the assembly listing.)

```
-dw530,532
00000530 000F
-g
A>
```

INSTRUCTIONS

The rest of this chapter is devoted to presenting the details of the Motorola 68000 instruction set. For ease of reference, the instructions are listed in alphabetical order. For each instruction, the following items are provided:

- A verbal description of what the instruction does.
- Which addressing modes are allowed. (Very few of the instructions allow all addressing modes.)
- What data sizes (byte, word, long) are allowed.
- Condition codes affected by executing the instruction.
- The layout of the machine code.
- Where possible, an example of how this instruction might be used. We will use the debugger to illustrate the results of executing the instruction.

Effective Address Operands

Most instructions that reference memory do so by means of an effective address operand. Effective address operands consist of a 3-bit mode field and a 3-bit register field. These operands are discussed in detail in Chapter 2. The notation used in the instruction descriptions for an effective address operand is <ea>. For each effective address operand in an instruction, the instruction discussion will present a table of addressing modes that is permitted with the operand.

ABCD Instruction

Binary Coded Decimal Instruction, #1 of 3

The ABCD (Add BCD with extend) instruction adds two bytes in BCD (Binary Coded Decimal) format. The destination operand is replaced with the sum of the source and destination bytes.

Addressing Modes Allowed:

Dn	An	(An)	(An) +	– (An)	x(An)	x(An,xr.s)
Yes	No	No	No	Yes	No	No
x.w	**x.l**	**x(PC)**	**x(PC,xr.s)**	**#x**	**SR**	**CCR**
No	No	No	No	No	No	No

There are only two forms of this instruction:

1. Add data register to data register (Dn addressing modes). The low-order bytes of two data registers are added and the result stored in the destination register.

2. Add memory to memory. This form of the instruction is designed for adding multiple bytes in memory. The only valid addressing mode is – (An). Since the 68000 stores BCD data with the highest byte first, one must start at the highest address and work down to add multibyte quantities. (Hence the use of pre-decrement addressing.) Each instruction sets the X-bit if there was a carry out of the most significant BCD digit in the byte. Then the X-bit is added into the next byte.

Data Sizes: Byte only

Condition Codes Affected:

X   Set by carry out of the most significant BCD digit.
N   Undefined.
Z   Cleared if the result is not zero. Unchanged otherwise.

V   Undefined.

C   Set by carry out of the most significant BCD digit.

The Z-bit is cleared if the result was not zero. Not setting the bit when the result of the present byte is zero allows the Z-bit to be accurate after a series of ABCD instructions is executed. The Z-bit must be set initially in such a case. (Comparing a register to itself is an easy way to set the Z-bit.) The N and V bits are undefined as a result of this instruction.

Assembler Syntax: ABCD   Dx,Dy

                    ABCD   – (Ax), – (Ay)

Machine Code Format:

Bit	15	14	13	12	11	10	9	8	7	6	5	4	3	2	1	0
	1	1	0	0	D. Reg			1	0	0	0	0	F	S. Reg.		

The D. Reg and S. Reg fields specify the destination and source register numbers. If the F (format) bit is 0, then the registers are data registers. If the F bit is a 1, then the registers are address registers and the pre-decrement addressing mode is used.

Example:

This example adds two values in data registers:

```
PC = 0000050C USP = 0001598C SSP = 0007BF08 ST = 0000 = >IM = 0
D 00000099   00000001 00000000 00000000 00000000 00000000 00000000 00000000
A 00000000   00000000 00000000 00000000 00000000 00000000 00000000 0001598C
abcd.b D1,D0
-t
PC = 0000050E USP = 0001598C SSP = 0007BF08 ST = 0011 = >IM = 0 EXT CRY
D 00000000   00000001 00000000 00000000 00000000 00000000 00000000 00000000
A 00000000   00000000 00000000 00000000 00000000 00000000 00000000 0001598C
```

Since we added 1 to 99, the result is zero, with the EXT (extend) bit set in the status register. The next example adds two two-byte BCD numbers in memory. The addresses in registers A0 and A1 point to the ends of the BCD numbers.

```
PC = 0000051E USP = 0001598C SSP = 0007BF08 ST = 0000 = >IM = 0
D 00000000   00000000 00000000 00000000 00000000 00000000 00000000 00000000
A 0000082A   0000082C 00000000 00000000 00000000 00000000 00000000 0001598C
abcd.b – (A0), – (A1)
```

Show the operands before the first add:

```
– dw828,82c
00000828 0099 0001                                              ....
– t
PC = 00000520 USP = 0001598C SSP = 0007BF08 ST = 0011 = >IM = 0 EXT CRY
D 00000000   00000000 00000000 00000000 00000000 00000000 00000000 00000000
A 00000829   0000082B 00000000 00000000 00000000 00000000 00000000 0001598C
abcd.b  – (A0), – (A1)
```

Now look at the operands:

```
– dw828,82c
00000828 0099 0000                                              ....
– t
PC = 00000522 USP = 0001598C SSP = 0007BF08 ST = 0000 = >IM = 0
D 00000000   00000000 00000000 00000000 00000000 00000000 00000000 00000000
A 00000828   0000082A 00000000 00000000 00000000 00000000 00000000 0001598C
```

Now look at the results:

```
– dw828,82c
00000828 0099 0100                                              ....
```

This example adds 99 to 1 to become 100. (The second operand is destroyed.) The memory displays show exactly what happens at each step of the process. Notice how the Extend bit gives the carry between the two add operations.

ADD Instruction

Integer Arith Op Instr   1 of 24

The ADD (Add binary) instruction adds two operands together and stores the result in the destination operand. There are two forms of this instruction:

1. Add an effective address operand to a data register.

2. Add a data register to an effective address operand.

Addressing Modes Allowed:

All addressing modes except SR and CCR are allowed when the effective address specifies a source operand:

Dn	An	(An)	(An) +	– (An)	x(An)	x(An,xr.s)
Yes	Yes	Yes	Yes	Yes	Yes	Yes
x.w	**x.l**	**x(PC)**	**x(PC,xr.s)**	**#x**	**SR**	**CCR**
Yes	Yes	Yes	Yes	Yes	No	No

When the effective address field is the destination, then the following addressing modes are allowed:

Dn	An	(An)	(An) +	– (An)	x(An)	x(An,xr.s)
No	No	Yes	Yes	Yes	Yes	Yes
x.w	**x.l**	**x(PC)**	**x(PC,xr.s)**	**#x**	**SR**	**CCR**
Yes	Yes	No	No	No	No	No

Using a data register as a destination requires the register destination form of the instruction.

Data Sizes: byte, word, long
Using an address register as the source is valid only for word and long data lengths.

Condition Codes Affected:

X   Set by the carry-out of the most significant bit. Cleared otherwise.
N   Set if high-order bit of result was 1. Cleared otherwise.
Z   Set if result was zero. Cleared otherwise.
C   Set by the carry-out of the most significant bit. Cleared otherwise.
V   Set if operation resulted in overflow condition. Cleared otherwise.

Assembler Syntax: ADD   Dn,<ea>
                    ADD   <ea>,Dn

Machine Code Format:

Bit	15	14	13	12	11 10 9	8	7 6	5 4 3	2 1 0
	1	1	0	1	Register	D	Size	Effective	Address
								← Mode →	← Reg. →

The Register field gives the data register that must be one of the operands. The D-bit is 0 if the Register field is the destination operand. The D-bit is 1 if the effective address is the destination.
    The Size field is 00 for byte, 01 for word, and 10 for long operands.

Example:

```
PC = 00000530 USP = 0001598C SSP = 0007BF08 ST = 0000 = >IM = 0
D 0000FFFF  0000FFFF  00000000  00000000  00000000  00000000  00000000  00000000
A 00000000  00000000  00000000  00000000  00000000  00000000  00000000  0001598C
add $82C,D0
```

Examine the Memory Operand:

```
– dw82c,82e
0000082C 0001
– t
PC = 00000536 USP = 0001598C SSP = 0007BF08 ST = 0015 = >IM = 0 EXT ZER CRY
D 00000000  0000FFFF  00000000  00000000  00000000  00000000  00000000  00000000
A 00000000  00000000  00000000  00000000  00000000  00000000  00000000  0001598C
```

Notice that the result of adding −1 and 1 is zero. (This was a word operation.) The Z-bit was set by this operation. We will now add the same two numbers with an ADD.L instruction.

   add.l $82E,D1

Examine the Memory Operand:

```
− dl82e,832
0000082E 00000001   ..
− t
PC = 0000053C USP = 0001598C SSP = 0007BF08 ST = 0000 = >IM = 0
D 00000000   00010000  00000000  00000000  00000000  00000000  00000000  00000000
A 00000000   00000000  00000000  00000000  00000000  00000000  00000000  0001598C
```

ADDA Instruction

Integer Arth Op Instr   2 of 24

The ADDA instruction does a binary ADD operation to an address register. In order to allow address computations to be freely intermixed with data operations, this instruction does not affect the condition codes.

Addressing Modes Allowed:

Dn	An	(An)	(An) +	– (An)	x(An)	x(An,xr.s)
Yes	Yes	Yes	Yes	Yes	Yes	Yes
x.w	**x.l**	**x(PC)**	**x(PC,xr.s)**	**#x**	**SR**	**CCR**
Yes	Yes	Yes	Yes	Yes	No	No

The effective address must be the source operand.

Data Sizes: word, long
The ADDA operation always affects all 32 bits of the destination address register.

Condition Codes Affected: None

Assembler Syntax: ADDA   <ea>,An

Machine Code Format:

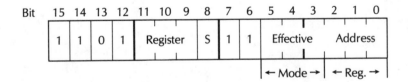

The Register field gives the address register that is to be used as the destination operand. The S-bit is 1 for long operands and 0 for word operands.

Example:

```
PC = 00000548 USP = 0001598C SSP = 0007BF08 ST = 0000 = >IM = 0
D 00000000   00000000 00000000 00000000 00000000 00000000 00000000 00000000
A 0000FFFF   00000000 00000000 00000000 00000000 00000000 00000000 0001598C
adda $830,A0
 - dw830,832
00000830 0001
 - t
PC = 0000054E USP = 0001598C SSP = 0007BF08 ST = 0000 = >IM = 0
D 00000000   00000000 00000000 00000000 00000000 00000000 00000000 00000000
A 00010000   00000000 00000000 00000000 00000000 00000000 00000000 0001598C
```

Notice that the operation size was a word, but the result was a long.

ADDI Instruction

Integer Arith Op Instr 3 of 24

The ADDI instruction adds a constant to an effective address operand. The source operand is always immediate.

Addressing Modes Allowed:

Dn	An	(An)	(An)+	–(An)	x(An)	x(An,xr.s)
Yes	No	Yes	Yes	Yes	Yes	Yes
x.w	**x.l**	**x(PC)**	**x(PC,xr.s)**	**#x**	**SR**	**CCR**
Yes	Yes	No	No	No	No	No

Data Sizes: byte, word, long

Condition Codes Affected:

X   Set on carry out of high-order bit.
N   Set if high bit of result is set.
Z   Set if result is zero.
C   Set on carry out of high-order bit.
V   Set on overflow condition.

Assembler Syntax: ADDI   #x,<ea>

Most assemblers automatically choose the ADDI instruction if the source operand of an ADD instruction is immediate.

Machine Code Format:

Bit   15 14 13 12 11 10 9 8 7 6 5 4 3 2 1 0

0	0	0	0	0	1	1	0	Size	Effective	Address

← Mode → | ← Reg. →

Word data (16 bits)	Byte data (8 bits)

Long data (32 bits, including previous word)

Size is 00 for byte operations, 01 for word operations, and 10 for long operations.

Example:

```
PC = 00000560 USP = 0001598C SSP = 0007BF08 ST = 0000 = >IM = 0
D 00007FFF  0000FFFF  00000000  00000000  00000000  00000000  00000000  00000000
A 00000000  00000000  00000000  00000000  00000000  00000000  00000000  0001598C
addi.l #$10,D0
-t
PC = 00000566 USP = 0001598C SSP = 0007BF08 ST = 0000 = >IM = 0
D 0000800F  0000FFFF  00000000  00000000  00000000  00000000  00000000  00000000
A 00000000  00000000  00000000  00000000  00000000  00000000  00000000  0001598C
```

This instruction adds 10 hex to the contents of register D0.L.

```
-t
PC = 0000056A USP = 0001598C SSP = 0007BF08 ST = 000F = >IM = 0 NEG ZER OFL CRY
D 0000800F  0000FFFF  00000000  00000000  00000000  00000000  00000000  00000000
A 00000000  00000000  00000000  00000000  00000000  00000000  00000000  0001598C
addi #$10,D1
-t
PC = 0000056E USP = 0001598C SSP = 0007BF08 ST = 0011 = >IM = 0 EXT CRY
D 0000800F  0000000F  00000000  00000000  00000000  00000000  00000000  00000000
A 00000000  00000000  00000000  00000000  00000000  00000000  00000000  0001598C
```

This instruction adds 10 hex to register D1.W. (Note that − 1 + 10 = F.)

ADDQ Instruction

Integer Arith Op Instr   4 of 24

The ADDQ instruction adds a three-bit immediate value to an effective address operand. This allows adding a small number to a register or memory address using a small, fast instruction.

Addressing Modes Allowed:

Dn	An	(An)	(An) +	– (An)	x(An)	x(An,xr.s)
Yes	Yes	Yes	Yes	Yes	Yes	Yes
x.w	**x.l**	**x(PC)**	**x(PC,xr.s)**	**#x**	**SR**	**CCR**
Yes	Yes	No	No	No	No	No

Data Sizes: byte, word, long
   When an address register is used as the destination, only word and long sizes are allowed.

Condition Codes Affected:

   X   Set on carry-out of high-order bit position.
   N   Set if high-order bit of result is set.
   V   Set on overflow.
   Z   Set if result is zero.
   C   Set on carry-out of high-order bit position.

   No condition codes are affected if an address register is used as the destination operand.

Assembler Syntax: ADDQ   #<data>,<ea>
#<data> is a constant number between 1 and 8.

Machine Code Format:

Bit	15	14	13	12	11 10 9	8	7 6	5 4 3	2 1 0
	0	1	0	1	Data	0	Size	Effective	Address
								← Mode →	← Reg. →

Data is a three-bit immediate field, with 000 representing 8, 001–111 representing 1–7. Size is 00 for a byte operation, 01 for a word, and 10 for a long operation.

Example:

```
PC = 00000580 USP = 0001598C SSP = 0007BF08 ST = 0000 = >IM = 0
D 00007FFF   00000000  00000000  00000000  00000000  00000000  00000000  00000000
A 00000000   00000000  00000000  00000000  00000000  00000000  00000000  0001598C
addq.l #$1,D0
-t
PC = 00000582 USP = 0001598C SSP = 0007BF08 ST = 0000 = >IM = 0
D 00008000   00000000  00000000  00000000  00000000  00000000  00000000  00000000
A 00000000   00000000  00000000  00000000  00000000  00000000  00000000  0001598C
```

This example adds 1 to register D0.

ADDX Instruction

Integer Arithmetic Operation

The ADDX (ADD eXtended) instruction provides multiple precision ADD operands. Integers of any length can be added using the ADD and ADDX instructions. This makes it possible to represent numbers much larger than the 32-bit longword allows.

There are two forms of this instruction:

1. Add a data register to a data register.

2. Add a memory location to a memory location. The – (An) addressing mode must be used for both the source and destination in this form of the instruction.

Addressing Modes Allowed:

Dn	An	(An)	(An) +	– (An)	x(An)	x(An,xr.s)
Yes	No	No	No	Yes	No	No
x.w	**x.l**	**x(PC)**	**x(PC,xr.s)**	**#x**	**SR**	**CCR**
No	No	No	No	No	No	No

Data Sizes: byte, word, long

Condition Codes Affected:

X Set on carry-out of high-order bit.
N Set if result was negative.
Z Cleared if result is not zero. Unchanged otherwise.
C Set on carry-out of high-order bit.
V Set on overflow condition.

The Z-bit is not set if the result was zero. It is cleared if the result was not zero. This property of the instruction allows the Z bit to correctly indicate the result of a multiprecision addition operation. The Z-bit must be set before the ADD begins, however. (This can be done with a MOVE to CCR, or by comparing a register to itself. The latter instruction is two bytes shorter.)

Assembler Syntax: ADDX   Dy,Dx

                 ADDX   – (Ay), – (Ax)

Machine Code Format:

Bit	15	14	13	12	11	10	9	8	7	6	5	4	3	2	1	0
	1	1	0	1		Reg. Rx		1		Size		0	0	T		Reg. Ry	

The Reg. Rx and Reg. Ry fields contain the destination and source registration numbers, respectively. The size field is 00 for a byte operation, 01 for a word operation, and 10 for a long operation. The T-bit (type) is 0 for the data register to data register form of the instruction. The Reg. Rx and Reg. Ry fields identify data registers in this case. The T-bit is 1 for the memory to memory form of the instruction. The Rx and Ry fields identify the address registers used by this form of the instruction.

Example:

This example adds the 64-bit quantity in (D0,D1) to the 64-bit quantity in (D2,D3). The even numbered registers contain the high order part of the number.

```
PC = 00000596 USP = 0001598C SSP = 0007BF08 ST = 0000 = >IM = 0
D 00000000   FFFFFFFF 00000000 FFFFFFFF 00000000 00000000 00000000 00000000
A 00000000   00000000 00000000 00000000 00000000 00000000 00000000 0001598C
add.l D1,D3
–t
PC = 00000598 USP = 0001598C SSP = 0007BF08 ST = 0019 = >IM = 0 EXT NEG CRY
D 00000000   FFFFFFFF 00000000 FFFFFFFE 00000000 00000000 00000000 00000000
A 00000000   00000000 00000000 00000000 00000000 00000000 00000000 0001598C
addx.l D0,D2
–t
PC = 0000059A USP = 0001598C SSP = 0007BF08 ST = 0000 = >IM = 0
D 00000000   FFFFFFFF 00000001 FFFFFFFE 00000000 00000000 00000000 00000000
A 00000000   00000000 00000000 00000000 00000000 00000000 00000000 0001598C
```

The quantity (0,FFFFFFFF) and (0,FFFFFFFF) when added together become (1,FFFFFFFE). The low-order registers (D1 and D3) were added first. Although the low-order registers both contained negative numbers, the final result was positive.

AND Instruction

Logical Op Instr *1 of 7*

The AND instruction performs a bit-wise AND operation. There are two forms of this instruction:

1. AND the contents of an effective address with a data register, leaving the results in the data register.

2. AND the contents of a data register and an effective address, leaving the results in the effective address.

Addressing Modes Allowed:

Effective address as Source:

Dn	An	(An)	(An) +	– (An)	x(An)	x(An,xr.s)
Yes	No	Yes	Yes	Yes	Yes	Yes
x.w	**x.l**	**x(PC)**	**x(PC,xr.s)**	**#x**	**SR**	**CCR**
Yes	Yes	Yes	Yes	Yes	No	No

Effective address as Destination:

Dn	An	(An)	(An) +	– (An)	x(An)	x(An,xr.s)
No	No	Yes	Yes	Yes	Yes	Yes
x.w	**x.l**	**x(PC)**	**x(PC,xr.s)**	**#x**	**SR**	**CCR**
Yes	Yes	No	No	No	No	No

Data Sizes: byte, word, long

Condition Codes Affected:

X   Not affected.
N   Set if most significant bit of result is set. Cleared otherwise.
Z   Set if result is zero. Cleared otherwise.
C   Always cleared.
V   Always cleared.

Assembler Syntax: AND   <ea>,Dn
                  AND   Dn,<ea>

Machine Code Format:

Bit	15	14	13	12	11	10	9	8	7	6	5	4	3	2	1	0
	1	1	0	0	Register			D	Size		Effective			Address		

← Mode → ← Reg. →

The Register field specifies the Data register used by the instruction, regardless of whether the register is the source or the destination. The D-bit determines the direction of the instruction. If the D-bit is zero, then the Data register is the destination. If the D-bit is one, then the effective address operand is the destination. The Size field specifies the data size: 00 for byte, 01 for word, and 10 for long.

Example:

This example shows the machine operation when two data registers are ANDed together.

```
PC=000005AC USP=0001598C SSP=0007BF08 ST=0000= >IM=0
D AAAAAAAA  01234567  00000000  00000000  00000000  00000000  00000000  00000000
A 00000000  00000000  00000000  00000000  00000000  00000000  00000000  0001598C
and.l D1,D0
-t
PC=000005AE USP=0001598C SSP=0007BF08 ST=0000= >IM=0
D 00220022  01234567  00000000  00000000  00000000  00000000  00000000  00000000
A 00000000  00000000  00000000  00000000  00000000  00000000  00000000  0001598C
```

The long quantities AAAAAAAA and 01234567 are ANDed to become 00220022.

ANDI Instruction

Logical Op Instr   *2 of 7*

The ANDI instruction performs a bit-wise AND between an immediate operand (always the source) and an effective address operand (always the destination).

Addressing Modes Allowed:

Destination only. Source is always immediate.

Dn	An	(An)	(An) +	– (An)	x(An)	x(An,xr.s)
Yes	No	Yes	Yes	Yes	Yes	Yes
x.w	**x.l**	**x(PC)**	**x(PC,xr.s)**	**#x**	**SR**	**CCR**
Yes	Yes	No	No	No	Yes	Yes

Using the status register (SR) as the destination requires that the 68000 executes in Supervisor state. Attempting to execute this form of the instruction in User mode causes a privilege violation exception. (See Chapter 7 on Exception Programming.)

Data Sizes: byte, word, long

Condition Codes Affected:

- X Not affected.
- N Set if the high-order bit of the result is set. Cleared otherwise.
- Z Set if the result is zero. Cleared otherwise.
- C Always cleared.
- V Always cleared.

The condition codes are cleared according to bits 4–0 of the operand if either the status register (SR) or the condition code register (CCR) is used as the destination. The normal condition code settings do not apply for these addressing modes.

Assembler Syntax: ANDI   #<data>,<ea>

Machine Code Format:

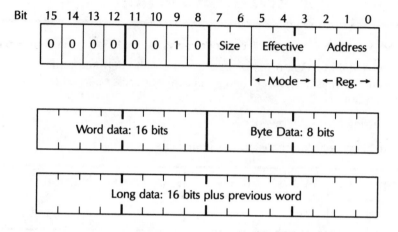

The Size field determines the data size used by the instruction. Size is 00 for byte operation, 01 for word, and 10 for long. Byte and word operations are followed by a word of immediate data. (Byte operations use only the low eight bits of this word.) Long operations are followed by two words (32 bits) of immediate data.

Examples:

The first example ANDs an immediate quantity with a data register.

```
PC = 000005BA USP = 0001598C SSP = 0007BF08 ST = 0000 = >IM = 0
D 55555555   00000000  00000000  00000000  00000000  00000000  00000000  00000000
A 00000000   00000000  00000000  00000000  00000000  00000000  00000000  0001598C
andi #$1234,D0
PC = 000005BE USP = 0001598C SSP = 0007BF08 ST = 0000 = >IM = 0
D 55551014   00000000  00000000  00000000  00000000  00000000  00000000  00000000
A 00000000   00000000  00000000  00000000  00000000  00000000  00000000  0001598C
```

The next example shows the effect of ANDing to the condition code register (CCR). First, we set all the condition codes using the MOVE to CCR instruction:

```
PC = 000005BE USP = 0001598C SSP = 0007BF08 ST = 0000 = >IM = 0
D 55551014   00000000  00000000  00000000  00000000  00000000  00000000  00000000
A 00000000   00000000  00000000  00000000  00000000  00000000  00000000  0001598C
move #$1F,CCR
-t
```

PC = 0005C2 USP = 01598C SSP = 07BF08 ST = <u>001F</u> = >IM = 0 <u>EXT NEG ZER OFL CRY</u>
D 55551014 00000000 00000000 00000000 00000000 00000000 00000000 00000000
A 00000000 00000000 00000000 00000000 00000000 00000000 00000000 0001598C

> Next, we AND the condition code register with 11 hex. This leaves the
> X and C bits set, and clears the other condition codes.

andi.b #$11,ccr
−t
PC = 000005C6 USP = 0001598C SSP = 0007BF08 ST = <u>0011</u> = >IM = 0 <u>EXT CRY</u>
D 55551014 00000000 00000000 00000000 00000000 00000000 00000000 00000000
A 00000000 00000000 00000000 00000000 00000000 00000000 00000000 0001598C

ASL Instruction

Shift & Rotate Instr

The ASL instruction performs an arithmetic left shift on a data register or memory operand. There are three forms of this instruction:

1. Shift a data register to the left by a constant contained in the instruction. Shifts from one to eight bits can be accomplished using this form of the instruction.

2. Shift a data register to the left by the number of bits contained in another data register.

3. Shift a memory word left by one bit only.

Addressing Modes Allowed: Memory form only

Dn	An	(An)	(An) +	– (An)	x(An)	x(An,xr.s)
No	No	Yes	Yes	Yes	Yes	Yes
x.w	**x.l**	**x(PC)**	**x(PC,xr.s)**	**#x**	**SR**	**CCR**
Yes	Yes	No	No	No	No	No

Data Sizes: byte, word, long

Data size is restricted to word for the form of the instruction that is in memory.

Condition Codes Affected:

X   Set according to the last bit shifted out of the operand. Unaffected if the shift count is zero. (This is possible only in the second form of the instruction.)

N   Set if the most significant bit of the result is set. Cleared otherwise.

Z   Set if the result is zero. Cleared otherwise.

C   Set according to the last bit shifted out of the operand. Unaffected if the shift count is zero.

V   Set if the most significant bit is changed at any time during the shift operation. Cleared otherwise.

Assembler Syntax: ASL   #<count>,Dy
                      ASL   Dx,Dy
                      ASL   <ea>

Machine Code Format:

Data Register as destination:

Bit	15	14	13	12	11	10	9	8	7	6	5	4	3	2	1	0
	1	1	1	0	Immed.			1	Size		T	0	0	Register		

Memory location as destination:

Bit	15	14	13	12	11	10	9	8	7	6	5	4	3	2	1	0
	1	1	1	0	0	0	0	1	1	1	Effective			Address		

← Mode → | ← Reg. →

The T-field determines the form of the register-destination form of the instruction. If T is 0, then the Immediate field contains the shift count, with 000 binary representing a count of 8. If T is 1, then the register number that contains the shift count is contained in the Immediate field.

Example:

```
PC = 000005D2 USP = 0001598C SSP = 0007BF08 ST = 0000 = >IM = 0
D 01234567  00000000  00000000  00000000  00000000  00000000  00000000  00000000
A 00000000  00000000  00000000  00000000  00000000  00000000  00000000  0001598C
asl #8,D0
-t
PC = 000005D4 USP = 0001598C SSP = 0007BF08 ST = 0013 = >IM = 0 EXT OFL CRY
D 01236700  00000000  00000000  00000000  00000000  00000000  00000000  00000000
A 00000000  00000000  00000000  00000000  00000000  00000000  00000000  0001598C
```

Notice that the upper half of the register destination is unchanged when a word shift is performed. The sign bit of the word is also changed during the shift, resulting in an overflow condition.

```
PC = 000005E0 USP = 0001598C SSP = 0007BF08 ST = 0000 = >IM = 0
D 01234567   00000010  00000000  00000000  00000000  00000000  00000000  00000000
A 00000000   00000000  00000000  00000000  00000000  00000000  00000000  0001598C
asl.l D1,D0
-t
PC = 000005E2 USP = 0001598C SSP = 0007BF08 ST = 0013 = >IM = 0 EXT OFL CRY
D 45670000   00000010  00000000  00000000  00000000  00000000  00000000  00000000
A 00000000   00000000  00000000  00000000  00000000  00000000  00000000  0001598C
```

This is a long shift with the count specified in a register.

ASR Instruction

Shift & Rotate Inst 2 of 8

The ASR instruction performs an arithmetic right shift on a data register or memory operand. There are three forms of this instruction:

1. Shift a data register to the right by a constant contained in the instruction. Shifts from one to eight bits can be accomplished using this form of the instruction.

2. Shift a data register to the right by the number of bits contained in another data register.

3. Shift a memory word right by one bit only.

Addressing Modes Allowed: Memory form only

Dn	An	(An)	(An) +	– (An)	x(An)	x(An,xr.s)
No	No	Yes	Yes	Yes	Yes	Yes
x.w	**x.l**	**x(PC)**	**x(PC,xr.s)**	**#x**	**SR**	**CCR**
Yes	Yes	No	No	No	No	No

Data Sizes: byte, word, long

Data size is restricted to word for the form of the instruction that is in memory.

Condition Codes Affected:

X Set according to the last bit shifted out of the operand. Unaffected if the shift count is zero. (That is possible only in the second form of the instruction.)

N Set if the most significant bit of the result is set. Cleared otherwise.

Z Set if the result is zero. Cleared otherwise.

C Set according to the last bit shifted out of the operand. Cleared if the shift count is zero.

V Always cleared.

Assembler Syntax: ASR   #<count>,Dy
                  ASR   Dx,Dy
                  ASR   <ea>

Machine Code Format:

Data Register as destination:

Bit	15	14	13	12	11	10	9	8	7	6	5	4	3	2	1	0
	1	1	1	0	Immed.			0	Size		T	0	0	Register		

Memory location as destination:

Bit	15	14	13	12	11	10	9	8	7	6	5	4	3	2	1	0
	1	1	1	0	0	0	0	0	1	1	Effective			Address		

← Mode →   ← Reg. →

The T-field determines the form of the register-destination form of the instruction. If T is 0, then the Immediate field contains the shift count, with 000 binary representing a count of 8. If T is 1, then the register number which contains the shift count is contained in the Immediate field.

Example:

```
PC = 000005EE USP = 0001598C SSP = 0007BF08 ST = 0000 = >IM = 0
D 01234567   00000000  00000000  00000000  00000000  00000000  00000000  00000000
A 00000000   00000000  00000000  00000000  00000000  00000000  00000000  0001598C
asr #8,D0
-t
PC = 000005F0 USP = 0001598C SSP = 0007BF08 ST = 0000 = >IM = 0
D 01230045   00000000  00000000  00000000  00000000  00000000  00000000  00000000
D 00000000   00000000  00000000  00000000  00000000  00000000  00000000  0001598C
```

This instruction shifts register D0 to the right by 8. The upper half of the register is unaffected because the operation is a word operation.

```
PC = 000005FC USP = 0001598C SSP = 0007BF08 ST = 0000 = >IM = 0
D 81234567   00000010  00000000  00000000  00000000  00000000  00000000  00000000
A 00000000   00000000  00000000  00000000  00000000  00000000  00000000  0001598C
asr.l D1,D0
```

```
-t
PC = 000005FE USP = 0001598C SSP = 0007BF08 ST = 0008 = >IM = 0 NEG
D FFFF8123  00000010  00000000  00000000  00000000  00000000  00000000  00000000
A 00000000  00000000  00000000  00000000  00000000  00000000  00000000  0001598C
```

Notice the sign extension due to the upper bit of register D0 being propagated by the right shift.

Bcc (Conditional Branch) Instructions

Program Control   1 of 8

Branch instructions are a vital part of machine-language programs. They provide a way of interrogating the condition codes and executing two or more alternate sets of instructions based on the results of the interrogation. The Bcc group of instructions is the method by which the 68000 performs this function. There are fifteen combinations of the condition codes that may be tested. Each of these has a two-letter mnemonic that takes the place of the cc in Bcc.

The permissible branch instructions are:

BCC   Branch if the C-bit (carry) is clear.

BCS   Branch if the C-bit (carry) is set.

BEQ   Branch on EQual. This instruction branches if the Z (Zero) bit is set.

BGE   Branch on Greater than or Equal. This instruction branches if the N (negative) and V (overflow) bits are either both set or both clear. BGE is used for two's complement binary numbers.

BGT   Branch on Greater Than. This instruction branches if
- The N and V bits are both set AND the Z-bit is clear, or,
- The N, V, and Z bits are *all* clear.

BHI   Branch on HIgher than. This instruction branches if the C and Z bits are both clear. BHI is similar to BGT, except it is used for unsigned numbers.

BLE   Branch on Less than or Equal. This instruction branches if
- The Z-bit is set, or,
- The N-bit is set AND the V-bit is clear, or,
- The N-bit is clear AND the V-bit is set.

       The BLE instruction is used for two's complement binary numbers.

BLS   Branch on Lower or Same. This instruction branches if either the C or Z bits are set. BLS is similar to BLE, except it is used for unsigned numbers.

BLT   Branch on Less Than. This instruction branches if
- The N-bit is set and the V-bit is clear, or,
- The N-bit is clear and the V-bit is set.

BMI   This instruction branches if the N-bit is set.

BRA.s is a preferred instruction

BNE   Branch on Not Equal. This instruction branches if the Z-bit is clear.

BPL   Branch on Plus. This instruction branches if the N-bit is clear.

BVC   Branch on V Clear. This instruction branches if the V-bit is clear, indicating no overflow.

BVS   Branch on V Set. This instruction branches if the V-bit is set, indicating overflow.

BRA   Branch Always. This instruction always branches, regardless of the setting of the condition codes.

The Condition Code Summary is shown in Table 3.1.

Condition Codes				Branch Instructions That Succeed														
N	Z	V	C	BRA	BHI	BLS	BCC	BCS	BNE	BEQ	BVC	BVS	BPL	BMI	BGE	BLT	BGT	BLE
0	0	0	0	x	x		x		x		x		x		x		x	
0	0	0	1	x		x		x	x		x		x		x		x	
0	0	1	0	x	x		x		x			x	x			x		x
0	0	1	1	x		x		x	x			x	x			x		x
0	1	0	0	x		x	x			x	x		x		x			x
0	1	0	1	x		x		x		x	x		x		x			x
0	1	1	0	x		x	x			x		x	x			x		x
0	1	1	1	x		x		x		x		x	x			x		x
1	0	0	0	x	x		x		x		x			x		x		x
1	0	0	1	x		x		x	x		x			x		x		x
1	0	1	0	x	x		x		x			x		x	x		x	
1	0	1	1	x		x		x	x			x		x	x		x	
1	1	0	0	x		x	x			x	x			x		x		x
1	1	0	1	x		x		x		x	x			x		x		x
1	1	1	0	x		x	x			x		x		x	x			x
1	1	1	1	x		x		x		x		x		x	x			x

Table 3.1 – *Condition Code Summary*

Addressing Modes Allowed:

There is a special addressing mode for branch instructions. Branches can either have a byte or word displacement that is sign extended to a long and added to the PC (Program Counter) to perform the branch. (This is done only if the condition is satisfied.)

Data Sizes: byte, word

Condition Codes Affected: None

Assembler Syntax: Bcc.S <label>   Byte displacement
                  Bcc.W <label>   Word displacement

is a label contained in the instruction area of the program (.text area on UNIX and CP/M-68K). The .S and .W suffixes are used to denote the two possible displacement sizes (short and word). Many assemblers perform this selection automatically.

Machine Code Format:

Bit	15	14	13	12	11 10 9 8	7 6 5 4 3 2 1 0
	0	1	1	0	Condition	8-bit displacement

16-bit displacement if 8-bit displacement = 0

The Condition is a four-bit encoding of the branch condition. The conditions are shown in Table 3.2.

The combination 0001 for condition is used to denote the BSR (Branch to Subroutine) instruction, rather than a conditional branch.

The 8-bit displacement field is an 8-bit field that gives a two's complement number to be added to the PC if the branch is successful. *The PC always* contains the address of the word that follows the first word of the branch instruction. If the 8-bit displacement is zero, then the word following the branch instruction contains a 16-bit displacement to be added to the PC.

One-word (8-bit) displacements give a branch range of −128 to +126 bytes away from the branch instruction. With a 16-bit displacement, this range is expanded to −32768 to +32766 bytes. The displacement must always be even. (Instructions must begin on a word boundary.)

Condition	Instruction	Condition	Instruction
0000	BRA	1000	BVC
0001	(NONE)	1001	BVS
0010	BHI	1010	BPL
0011	BLS	1011	BMI
0100	BCC	1100	BGE
0101	BCS	1101	BLT
0110	BNE	1110	BGT
0111	BEQ	1111	BLE

Table 3.2 – *Condition and corresponding instruction*

A one-word (8-bit displacement) branch to the next instruction is impossible. The displacement would have to be zero, and the next word (i.e., the first word of the next instruction) would be taken as a 16-bit branch offset. The Bcc instruction cannot be configured to yield a one word *no operation* (an instruction that does nothing).

Example:

```
PC = 00000606 USP = 0001598C SSP = 0007BF08 ST = 0000 = >IM = 0
D 00000000   00000000 00000000 00000000 00000000 00000000 00000000 00000000
A 00000000   00000000 00000000 00000000 00000000 00000000 00000000 0001598C
beq $60A
 – i606,60e
00000606 beq $60A
00000608 moveq #$FF,D0
0000060A bne $60E
0000060C moveq #$FE,D0
0000060E nop
```

In this segment of sample code, there are two conditional branches, a BNE and a BEQ. The BEQ will not be taken, since the Z-bit is not set at the beginning. Thus, the first MOVEQ instruction will be executed. The Z-bit will remain clear as a result of this instruction. The BNE will be taken, and register D0 will have a value of FFFFFFFF.

```
-t
PC = 00000608 USP = 0001598C SSP = 0007BF08 ST = 0000 = >IM = 0
D 00000000   00000000 00000000 00000000 00000000 00000000 00000000 00000000
A 00000000   00000000 00000000 00000000 00000000 00000000 00000000 0001598C
moveq #$FF,D0
-t
PC = 0000060A USP = 0001598C SSP = 0007BF08 ST = 0008 = >IM = 0 NEG
D FFFFFFFF 00000000 00000000 00000000 00000000 00000000 00000000 00000000
A 00000000   00000000 00000000 00000000 00000000 00000000 00000000 0001598C
bne $60E
-t
PC = 0000060E USP = 0001598C SSP = 0007BF08 ST = 0008 = >IM = 0 NEG
D FFFFFFFF 00000000 00000000 00000000 00000000 00000000 00000000 00000000
A 00000000   00000000 00000000 00000000 00000000 00000000 00000000 0001598C
```

The next example illustrates an anomaly of the 68000 instruction set. The CMP instruction is used to set the condition codes as if the two operands were subtracted. The operands remain unaffected. However, the comparison CMP D0,D1 followed by a BGT instruction will branch if *register D1 is greater than register D0* (i.e., the operands of the compare instruction must be read *backwards*).

```
PC = 00000616 USP = 0001598C SSP = 0007BF08 ST = 0000 = >IM = 0
D FFFFFFFF 00000001 00000000 00000000 00000000 00000000 00000000 00000000
A 00000000   00000000 00000000 00000000 00000000 00000000 00000000 0001598C
cmp.l D0,D1
-l616,620
00000616 cmp.l D0,D1
00000618 bgt $61C
0000061A addq #$2,D2
0000061C bhi $620
0000061E addq #$1,D2
00000620 nop
```

In this code segment, D0 (-1) and D1 (1) are compared. If D1 is greater than D0 (and it is), the first ADDQ instruction will be skipped. The BHI instruction is the unsigned version of a BGT. In this case, -1 (actually $2^{32} - 1$, or about 4 billion) is greater than 1, so the branch will not be taken. (Since we skipped the first ADDQ instruction, the condition codes at the time of executing the BHI are the result of the CMP.L instruction.)

Register D2 will have a value of 1.

```
-t
PC = 00000618 USP = 0001598C SSP = 0007BF08 ST = 0001 = >IM = 0 CRY
D FFFFFFFF  00000001  00000000  00000000  00000000  00000000  00000000  00000000
A 00000000  00000000  00000000  00000000  00000000  00000000  00000000  0001598C
bgt $61C
-t
PC = 0000061C USP = 0001598C SSP = 0007BF08 ST = 0001 = >IM = 0 CRY
D FFFFFFFF  00000001  00000000  00000000  00000000  00000000  00000000  00000000
A 00000000  00000000  00000000  00000000  00000000  00000000  00000000  0001598C
bhi $620
-t
PC = 0000061E USP = 0001598C SSP = 0007BF08 ST = 0001 = >IM = 0 CRY
D FFFFFFFF  00000001  00000000  00000000  00000000  00000000  00000000  00000000
A 00000000  00000000  00000000  00000000  00000000  00000000  00000000  0001598C
addq #$1,D2
-t
PC = 00000620 USP = 0001598C SSP = 0007BF08 ST = 0000 = >IM = 0
D FFFFFFFF  00000001  00000001  00000000  00000000  00000000  00000000  00000000
A 00000000  00000000  00000000  00000000  00000000  00000000  00000000  0001598C
```

BCHG Instruction

Bit Manip Op Inst   *1 of 4*

The BCHG (test a Bit and CHanGe) instruction inverts a single bit in an effective address operand. The Z-bit is set according to the state of the bit *before* the inversion.

The bit number is contained either in a register or in an immediate field inside the instruction itself. The operation is restricted to long data for a data register destination, and to byte data for memory locations. Bits are numbered from 0, with bit 0 being the least significant bit in a byte (or long).

Addressing Modes Allowed:

Dn	An	(An)	(An) +	– (An)	x(An)	x(An,xr.s)
Yes	No	Yes	Yes	Yes	Yes	Yes
x.w	**x.l**	**x(PC)**	**x(PC,xr.s)**	**#x**	**SR**	**CCR**
Yes	Yes	No	No	No	No	No

Data Sizes: byte, long

Condition Codes Affected:

X   Not affected.

N   Not affected.

Z   Set if the bit was zero *before* being inverted. Cleared otherwise.

C   Not affected.

V   Not affected.

Assembler Syntax: BCHG   Dn,<ea>

BGHG   #<data>,<ea>

Machine Code Format:
Bit Number Dynamic:

Bit	15	14	13	12	11	10	9	8	7	6	5	4	3	2	1	0
	0	0	0	0	Register			1	0	1	Effective			Address		

← Mode → | ← Reg. →

Bit Number Static:

Bit	15	14	13	12	11	10	9	8	7	6	5	4	3	2	1	0
	0	0	0	0	1	0	0	0	0	1	Effective			Address		

← Mode → | ← Reg. →

0	0	0	0	0	0	0	0	////////	Bit Number

The Register field indicates the data register in which the bit number resides for the Bit Number Dynamic form of the instruction. In the Bit Number Static case, bits 5–7 of the extension word are ignored for data register destinations. For memory locations, bits 4 and 3 are also ignored. (Bit numbers in a long range from 0–31, and in a byte from 0–7.)

Example:

```
PC = 00000628 USP = 0001598C SSP = 0007BF08 ST = 0000 = >IM = 0
D 00000000   00000000  00000000  00000000  00000000  00000000  00000000  00000000
A 00000000   00000000  00000000  00000000  00000000  00000000  00000000  0001598C
bchg #$0,D0
-t
PC = 0000062C USP = 0001598C SSP = 0007BF08 ST = 0004 = >IM = 0 ZER
D 00000001   00000000  00000000  00000000  00000000  00000000  00000000  00000000
A 00000000   00000000  00000000  00000000  00000000  00000000  00000000  0001598C
```

This example inverts bit 0 of register D0. The Z-bit is set *after* the instruction, indicating that the bit was clear *before* the instruction.

BCLR Instruction

Bit Many Op Inst   *2 of 4*

The BCLR (test a Bit and CLeaR) instruction clears a single bit in an effective address operand. The Z-bit is set according to the state of the bit *before* the instruction.

The bit number is either contained in a register, or in an immediate field inside the instruction itself. The operation is restricted to long data for a data register destination, and to byte data for memory locations. Bits are numbered from 0, with bit 0 being the least significant bit in a byte (or long).

Addressing Modes Allowed:

Dn	An	(An)	(An) +	– (An)	x(An)	x(An,xr.s)
Yes	No	Yes	Yes	Yes	Yes	Yes
x.w	x.l	x(PC)	x(PC,xr.s)	#x	SR	CCR
Yes	Yes	No	No	No	No	No

Data Sizes: byte, long

Condition Codes Affected:

X   Not affected.

N   Not affected.

Z   Set if the bit was zero *before* being cleared. Cleared otherwise.

C   Not affected.

V   Not affected.

Assembler Syntax: BCLR   Dn,<ea>

BCLR   #<data>,<ea>

Machine Code Format:
Bit Number Dynamic:

Bit	15	14	13	12	11	10	9	8	7	6	5	4	3	2	1	0
	0	0	0	0	Register			1	1	0	Effective			Address		

← Mode → | ← Reg. →

Bit Number Static:

Bit	15	14	13	12	11	10	9	8	7	6	5	4	3	2	1	0
	0	0	0	0	1	0	0	0	1	0	Effective			Address		

← Mode → | ← Reg. →

0	0	0	0	0	0	0	0	////////	Bit Number

The Register field indicates the data register in which the bit number resides for the Bit Number Dynamic form of the instruction. In the Bit Number Static case, bits 5–7 of the extension word are ignored for data register destinations. For memory locations, bits 4 and 3 are also ignored. (Bit numbers in a long range from 0–31, and in a byte from 0–7.)

Example:

```
PC = 00000632 USP = 0001598C SSP = 0007BF08 ST = 0000 = >IM = 0
D 00000001   00000000  00000000  00000000  00000000  00000000  00000000  00000000
A 00000000   00000000  00000000  00000000  00000000  00000000  00000000  0001598C
bclr #$0,D0
−t
PC = 00000636 USP = 0001598C SSP = 0007BF08 ST = 0000 = >IM = 0
D 00000000   00000000  00000000  00000000  00000000  00000000  00000000  00000000
A 00000000   00000000  00000000  00000000  00000000  00000000  00000000  0001598C
```

This instruction clears bit 0 of register D0. The Z-bit is not set *after* the instruction, indicating that the bit was set *before* the instruction.

BSET Instruction

Bit Manip Op Instr   3 of 4

The BSET (test a Bit and SET) instruction sets a single bit in an effective address operand. The Z-bit is set according to the state of the bit *before* the instruction.

The bit number is either contained in a register or in an immediate field inside the instruction itself. The operation is restricted to long data for a data register destination, and to byte data for memory locations. Bits are numbered from 0, with bit 0 being the least significant bit in a byte (or long).

Addressing Modes Allowed:

Dn	An	(An)	(An) +	– (An)	x(An)	x(An,xr.s)
Yes	No	Yes	Yes	Yes	Yes	Yes
x.w	x.l	x(PC)	x(PC,xr.s)	#x	SR	CCR
Yes	Yes	No	No	No	No	No

Data Sizes: byte, long

Condition Codes Affected:

X   Not affected.

N   Not affected.

Z   Set if the bit was zero *before* being set. Cleared otherwise.

C   Not affected.

V   Not affected.

Assembler Syntax: BSET   Dn,<ea>
                  BSET   #<data>,<ea>

Machine Code Format:
Bit Number Dynamic:

Bit	15	14	13	12	11	10	9	8	7	6	5	4	3	2	1	0
	0	0	0	0	Register			1	1	1	Effective			Address		

← Mode → ← Reg. →

Bit Number Static:

Bit	15	14	13	12	11	10	9	8	7	6	5	4	3	2	1	0
	0	0	0	0	1	0	0	0	1	1	Effective			Address		

← Mode → ← Reg. →

0	0	0	0	0	0	0	0	////////	Bit Number

The Register field indicates the data register in which the bit number resides for the Bit Number Dynamic form of the instruction. In the Bit Number Static case, bits 5–7 of the extension word are ignored for data register destinations. For memory locations, bits 4 and 3 are also ignored. (Bit numbers in a long range from 0–31, and in a byte from 0–7.)

Example:

```
PC = 00000644 USP = 0001598C SSP = 0007BF08 ST = 0000 = >IM = 0
D 00000000   00000000 00000000 00000000 00000000 00000000 00000000 00000000
A 00000000   00000000 00000000 00000000 00000000 00000000 00000000 0001598C
bset #$0,D0
-t
PC = 00000648 USP = 0001598C SSP = 0007BF08 ST = 0004 = >IM = 0 ZER
D 00000001   00000000 00000000 00000000 00000000 00000000 00000000 00000000
A 00000000   00000000 00000000 00000000 00000000 00000000 00000000 0001598C
```

This instruction sets bit 0 of register D0. The Z-bit is set *after* the instruction, indicating that the bit was clear *before* the instruction.

BSR Instruction

Program Control *2 of 8*

The BSR (Branch to SubRoutine) instruction places the address of the next instruction to be executed on top of the stack. A displacement is then added to the PC register (Program Counter), and execution continues at that address. For the purposes of the addition, the PC points to the word that follows the first word of the BSR instruction.

Addressing Modes Allowed:

There is a special addressing mode for branch instructions. Branch instructions can either have a byte or word displacement that is sign extended to a long and added to the PC (Program Counter) to perform the branch.

Data Sizes: byte, word

Condition Codes Affected: None

Assembler Syntax: BSR.S \<label\>   Byte displacement
                  BSR.W \<label\>   Word displacement

\<label\> is a label contained in the instruction area of the program (.text area on UNIX and CP/M). The .S and .W suffixes are used to denote the two possible displacement sizes (short and word). Many assemblers perform this selection automatically.

Machine Code Format:

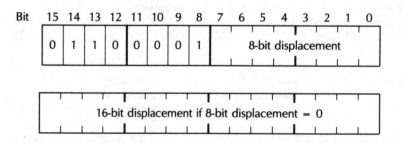

The format of a BSR instruction is the same as that of the Bcc instructions, with a condition field (bits 11–8) of 0001.

As with the Bcc instructions, it is not possible to have a one-word BSR to the next instruction, since the 8-bit displacement in that case would be zero. The next word (which would be the first word of the next instruction) would erroneously be used as the 16-bit displacement in this case. Most assemblers will not allow this error condition to take place.

Example:

```
PC = 0000064E USP = 0001598C SSP = 0007BF08 ST = 0000 = >IM = 0
D 00000000   00000000 00000000 00000000 00000000 00000000 00000000 00000000
A 00000000   00000000 00000000 00000000 00000000 00000000 00000000 0001598C
bsr $652
-t
PC = 00000652 USP = 00015988 SSP = 0007BF08 ST = 0000 = >IM = 0
D 00000000   00000000 00000000 00000000 00000000 00000000 00000000 00000000
A 00000000   00000000 00000000 00000000 00000000 00000000 00000000 00015988
rts
-dl15988,1598c
00015988 00000650                                                  ..
```

The BSR instruction at location 64E branches to location 652, after placing 650 (the address of the next instruction) on the stack (at location 15988).

```
-t
PC = 00000650 USP = 0001598C SSP = 0007BF08 ST = 0000 = >IM = 0
D 00000000   00000000 00000000 00000000 00000000 00000000 00000000 00000000
A 00000000   00000000 00000000 00000000 00000000 00000000 00000000 0001598C
```

Following the RTS instruction, execution picks up at location 650, and the return address has been popped off the stack. (Register A7 now contains 1598C—four bytes have been popped.)

BTST Instruction

Bit Manip Of Instr   *4 of 4*

The BTST (Bit TeST) instruction tests a single bit in an effective address operand. The Z-bit is set according to the state of the bit.

The bit number is either contained in a register or in an immediate field inside the instruction itself. The operation is restricted to long data for a data register destination, and to byte data for memory locations. Bits are numbered from 0, with bit 0 being the least significant bit in a byte (or long).

Addressing Modes Allowed (Bit Number Static):

Dn	An	(An)	(An) +	– (An)	x(An)	x(An,xr.s)
Yes	No	Yes	Yes	Yes	Yes	Yes
x.w	x.l	x(PC)	x(PC,xr.s)	#x	SR	CCR
Yes	Yes	Yes	Yes	No	No	No

Addressing Modes Allowed (Bit Number Dynamic):

Dn	An	(An)	(An) +	– (An)	x(An)	x(An,xr.s)
Yes	No	Yes	Yes	Yes	Yes	Yes
x.w	x.l	x(PC)	x(PC,xr.s)	#x	SR	CCR
Yes	Yes	Yes	Yes	Yes	No	NO

Data Sizes: byte, long

Condition Codes Affected:

X   Not affected.
N   Not affected.

Z   Set if the tested bit is zero. Cleared otherwise.
C   Not affected.
V   Not affected.

Assembler Syntax: BTST   Dn,<ea>
               BTST   #<data>,<ea>

Machine Code Format:

Bit Number Dynamic:

Bit	15	14	13	12	11 10 9	8	7	6	5 4 3	2 1 0
	0	0	0	0	Register	1	0	0	Effective	Address

← Mode → ← Reg. →

Bit Number Static:

Bit	15	14	13	12	11	10	9	8	7	6	5 4 3	2 1 0
	0	0	0	0	1	0	0	0	0	0	Effective	Address

← Mode → ← Reg. →

0	0	0	0	0	0	0	0	/////////	Bit Number

The Register field indicates the data register in which the bit number resides for the Bit Number Dynamic form of the instruction. In the Bit Number Static case, bits 5–7 of the extension word are ignored for data register destinations. For memory locations, bits 4 and 3 are also ignored. (Bit numbers in a long range from 0–31, and in a byte from 0–7.)

Example:

```
PC = 00000658 USP = 0001598C SSP = 000FBF08 ST = 0000 = >IM = 0
D 00000001   00000000   00000000   00000000   00000000   00000000   00000000   00000000
A 00000000   00000000   00000000   00000000   00000000   00000000   00000000   0001598C
btst #$0,D0
```

```
-t
PC = 0000065C USP = 0001598C SSP = 000FBF08 ST = 0000 = >IM = 0
D 00000001   00000000  00000000  00000000  00000000  00000000  00000000  00000000
A 00000000   00000000  00000000  00000000  00000000  00000000  00000000  0001598C
```

This example tests the low-order bit of register D0. The bit is set, so that the Z-bit is not set by the instruction. A BNE instruction will branch in this case.

CHK Instruction

System Control   1 of 7

The CHK (CHecK register against bounds) instruction verifies that a data register contains a number within a certain positive range of values. This instruction is normally used by high-level language systems for range checking subscripts.

The low-order word (16 bits) of the data register is compared to an operand specified by the effective address field of the instruction. If the register is less than zero (i.e., bit 15 of the register is set) or greater than the upper bound, then a CHK exception results. (See Chapter 7 on Exception Processing for details.)

Addressing Modes Allowed:

Dn	An	(An)	(An) +	– (An)	x(An)	x(An,xr.s)
Yes	No	Yes	Yes	Yes	Yes	Yes

x.w	x.l	x(PC)	x(PC,xr.s)	#x	SR	CCR
Yes	Yes	Yes	Yes	Yes	No	No

Data Sizes: word

Condition Codes Affected:

X   Not affected.

N   Set if the data register is less than zero. Cleared if the data register is greater than the effective address operand. Undefined otherwise.

Z   Undefined.

C   Undefined.

V   Undefined.

Assembler Syntax: CHK   <ea>,Dn

Machine Code Format:

Bit	15	14	13	12	11	10	9	8	7	6	5	4	3	2	1	0
	0	1	0	0	Register			1	1	0	Effective			Address		

← Mode → ← Reg. →

Register is the number of the data register to be tested.

Example:

```
PC = 00000660 USP = 0001598C SSP = 000FBF08 ST = 0000 = >IM = 0
D 00000001   00000000  00000000  00000000  00000000  00000000  00000000  00000000
A 00000000   00000000  00000000  00000000  00000000  00000000  00000000  0001598C
chk #$1,D0
-t
PC = 00000664 USP = 0001598C SSP = 000FBF08 ST = 0000 = >IM = 0
D 00000001   00000000  00000000  00000000  00000000  00000000  00000000  00000000
A 00000000   00000000  00000000  00000000  00000000  00000000  00000000  0001598C
chk #$0,D0
-t
Exception $06 at user address 00000668. Aborted.
```

The first CHK instruction in this example does nothing, as the register is equal to the limit (both are 1). In the second example, an exception is generated. The message printed here shows how CP/M-68K treats exceptions in a user program. Other operating systems behave in a similar fashion. Exception 6 is the CHK instruction. (See Chapter 7 on Exception Processing for details.)

CLR Instruction

Integer Arithmetic Op Instr   6 of 24

The CLR (CLeaR) instruction sets an effective address operand to zero. An anomaly of the 68000 hardware causes memory operands to be read and then cleared. This usually makes no difference in program behavior, with two exceptions of initializing some memory units with parity (which may give an erroneous parity error), or accessing memory-mapped hardware.

Addressing Modes Allowed:

Dn	An	(An)	(An) +	– (An)	x(An)	x(An,xr.s)
Yes	No	Yes	Yes	Yes	Yes	Yes
x.w	**x.l**	**x(PC)**	**x(PC,xr.s)**	**#x**	**SR**	**CCR**
Yes	Yes	No	No	No	No	No

Data Sizes: byte, word, long

Condition Codes Affected:

X	Not affected.
N	Always cleared.
Z	Always set.
C	Always cleared.
V	Always cleared.

Assembler Syntax: CLR <ea>

Machine Code Format:

Bit	15	14	13	12	11	10	9	8	7	6	5	4	3	2	1	0
	0	1	0	0	0	0	1	0	Size		Effective			Address		
											← Mode →			← Reg. →		

Size is 00 for byte data, 01 for word, and 10 for long.

Example:

```
PC = 0000066A USP = 0001598C SSP = 000FBF08 ST = 0008 = >IM = 0 NEG
D FFFFFFFF  00000000  00000000  00000000  00000000  00000000  00000000  00000000
A 00000000  00000000  00000000  00000000  00000000  00000000  00000000  0001598C
clr.l D0
-t
PC = 0000066C USP = 0001598C SSP = 000FBF08 ST = 0004 = >IM = 0 ZER
D 00000000  00000000  00000000  00000000  00000000  00000000  00000000  00000000
A 00000000  00000000  00000000  00000000  00000000  00000000  00000000  0001598C
```

This example clears data register D0.

CMP Instruction

Integer Arithmetic Of Instr   7 of 24

The CMP (CoMPare) instruction compares the contents of a data register with an effective address operand. The condition codes are set as if the effective address were subtracted from the data register. Neither operand is altered.

When used with conditional branches, this instruction creates a less than desirable effect. When the combination

```
CMP     D0,D1
BGT     X1
```

is used, the branch takes place if register D1 is greater than register D0.

Addressing Modes Allowed:

Dn	An	(An)	(An) +	– (An)	x(An)	x(An,xr.s)
Yes	Yes	Yes	Yes	Yes	Yes	Yes
x.w	**x.l**	**x(PC)**	**x(PC,xr.s)**	**#x**	**SR**	**CCR**
Yes	Yes	Yes	Yes	Yes	No	No

Data Sizes: byte, word, long

Byte mode is not allowed when address register direct mode is used as the effective address.

Condition Codes Affected:

X   Not affected.
N   Set if the result is negative. Cleared otherwise.
Z   Set if the result is zero. (The operands are equal.) Cleared otherwise.
C   Set if a borrow is generated. Cleared otherwise.
V   Set on overflow in the subtract operation. Cleared otherwise.

Assembler Syntax: CMP   <ea>,Dn

The CMPA instruction is used when the destination is an address register. CMPI compares an immediate source to an effective address operand.
CMPM compares memory to memory. Many assemblers make this distinction automatically.

Machine Code Format:

Bit	15	14	13	12	11 10 9	8	7 6	5 4 3	2 1 0
	1	0	1	1	Register	0	Size	Effective	Address

← Mode → ← Reg. →

The Register field is the number of the data register used as the destination. The size field is 00 for comparing bytes 01 for words, and 10 for longs.

Example:

```
PC = 00000674 USP = 0001598C SSP = 000FBF08 ST = 0000 = >IM = 0
D 00000001   00000002 00000000 00000000 00000000 00000000 00000000 00000000
A 00000000   00000000 00000000 00000000 00000000 00000000 00000000 0001598C
cmp.l $932,D0
– sl932
00000932 00000001 .
– l674,684
   00000674 cmp.l $932,D0
   0000067A beq $67E
   0000067C addq.l #$1,D2
   0000067E cmp.l D0,D1
   00000680 ble $684
   00000682 addq #$2,D2
   00000684 nop
```

This program segment compares register D0 to a memory word containing 1. The BEQ instruction will branch, and the first ADDQ instruction
will not be executed. The BLE instruction will not branch. (Remember that
the compare operands must be read backwards.) Register D2 will have a
value of 2.

```
– t
PC = 0000067A USP = 0001598C SSP = 000FBF08 ST = 0004 = >IM = 0 ZER
D 00000001   00000002 00000000 00000000 00000000 00000000 00000000 00000000
A 00000000   00000000 00000000 00000000 00000000 00000000 00000000 0001598C
beq $67E
```

−t
PC = <u>0000067E</u> USP = 0001598C SSP = 000FBF08 ST = 0004 = >IM = 0 ZER
 D 00000001   00000002   00000000   00000000   00000000   00000000   00000000   00000000
 A 00000000   00000000   00000000   00000000   00000000   00000000   00000000   0001598C
cmp.l D0,D1
−t
PC = 00000680 USP = 0001598C SSP = 000FBF08 ST = <u>0000</u> = >IM = 0
 D 00000001   00000002   00000000   00000000   00000000   00000000   00000000   00000000
 A 00000000   00000000   00000000   00000000   00000000   00000000   00000000   0001598C
ble $684
−t
PC = 00000682 USP = 0001598C SSP = 000FBF08 ST = 0000 = >IM = 0
 D 00000001   00000002   00000000   00000000   00000000   00000000   00000000   00000000
 A 00000000   00000000   00000000   00000000   00000000   00000000   00000000   0001598C
addq #$2,D2
−t
PC = 00000684 USP = 0001598C SSP = 000FBF08 ST = 0000 = >IM = 0
 D 00000001   00000002   <u>00000002</u>   00000000   00000000   00000000   00000000   00000000
 A 00000000   00000000   00000000   00000000   00000000   00000000   00000000   0001598C

CMPA Instruction

Integer Arithmetic Op Instr

The CMPA (CoMPare Address) instruction compares the contents of an address register with an effective address operand. The condition codes are set as if the effective address were subtracted from the address register. Neither operand is altered.

When used with conditional branches, this instruction creates a less than desirable effect. When the combination

```
CMPA      A0,A1
BGT       X1
```

is used, the branch takes place if the value in register A1 is greater than the value in register A0.

Addressing Modes Allowed:

Dn	An	(An)	(An) +	– (An)	x(An)	x(An,xr.s)
Yes	Yes	Yes	Yes	Yes	Yes	Yes
x.w	**x.l**	**x(PC)**	**x(PC,xr.s)**	**#x**	**SR**	**CCR**
Yes	Yes	Yes	Yes	Yes	No	No

Data Sizes: word, long

Condition Codes Affected:

X   Not affected.
N   Set if the result is negative. Cleared otherwise.
Z   Set if the result is zero. (The operands are equal.) Cleared otherwise.
C   Set if a borrow is generated. Cleared otherwise.
V   Set on overflow in the subtract operation. Cleared otherwise.

Assembler Syntax: CMPA <ea>,An

The CMP instruction is used when the destination is a data register. CMPI compares an immediate source to an effective address operand. CMPM compares memory to memory. Many assemblers make this distinction automatically.

Machine Code Format:

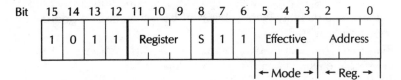

The Register field is the number of the data register used as the destination. The S (Size) bit is 0 for comparing words, and 1 for longs. Comparing a word is performed by sign-extending the source and making a 32-bit compare.

Example:

```
PC = 00000694 USP = 0001598C SSP = 000FBF08 ST = 0008 = >IM = 0 NEG
D FFFFFFFF 00000000 00000000 00000000 00000000 00000000 00000000 00000000
A 00000936  0000094E 00000000 00000000 00000000 00000000 00000000 0001598C
cmpa.l A0,A1
−l694,69a
   00000694 cmpa.l A0,A1
   00000696 bhi $69A
   00000698 clr.l D0
   0000069A nop
```

This code segment compares address registers A0 to A1. The BHI instruction will succeed. (Remember that the compare operands must be read backwards.) Data register D0 will remain unchanged.

```
−t
PC = 00000696 USP = 0001598C SSP = 000FBF08 ST = 0000 = >IM = 0
D FFFFFFFF 00000000 00000000 00000000 00000000 00000000 00000000 00000000
A 00000936  0000094E 00000000 00000000 00000000 00000000 00000000 0001598C
bhi $69A
−t
PC = 0000069A USP = 0001598C SSP = 000FBF08 ST = 0000 = >IM = 0
D FFFFFFFF 00000000 00000000 00000000 00000000 00000000 00000000 00000000
A 00000936  0000094E 00000000 00000000 00000000 00000000 00000000 0001598C
```

CMPI Instruction

Integer Arithmetic Op Instr

The CMPI (CoMPare Immediate) instruction compares an immediate operand with an effective address operand. The condition codes are set as if the immediate quantity were subtracted from the effective address. Neither operand is altered.

When used with conditional branches, this instruction creates a less than desirable effect. When the combination

```
CMPI      #<data>,D0
BGT       X1
```

is used, the branch takes place if the value in data register D0 is greater than the immediate data.

Addressing Modes Allowed:

Dn	An	(An)	(An) +	– (An)	x(An)	x(An,xr.s)
Yes	No	Yes	Yes	Yes	Yes	Yes
x.w	**x.l**	**x(PC)**	**x(PC,xr.s)**	**#x**	**SR**	**CCR**
Yes	Yes	No	No	No	No	No

Data Sizes: byte, word, long

Condition Codes Affected:

X   Not affected.
N   Set if the result is negative. Cleared otherwise.
Z   Set if the result is zero. (The operands are equal.) Cleared otherwise.
C   Set if a borrow is generated. Cleared otherwise.
V   Set on overflow in the subtraction operation. Cleared otherwise.

Assembler Syntax: CMPI #<data>,<ea>

The CMP instruction compares an effective address operand to a data register. The CMPA instruction compares an effective address operand to an address register. The CMPM instruction compares memory to memory. Many assemblers make this distinction automatically.

Machine Code Format:

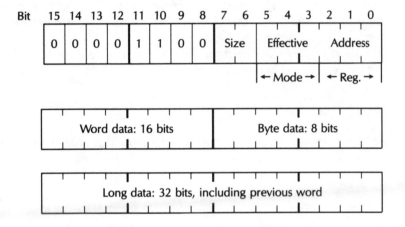

The size field is 00 for byte compares, 01 for words, and 10 for longs.

Example:

```
PC = 000006A2 USP = 0001598C SSP = 000FBF08 ST = 0000 = >IM = 0
D 00000001  00000000  00000000  00000000  00000000  00000000  00000000  00000000
A 00000000  00000000  00000000  00000000  00000000  00000000  00000000  0001598C
cmp.l #$1,D0
-t
PC = 000006A8 USP = 0001598C SSP = 000FBF08 ST = 0004 = >IM = 0 ZER
D 00000001  00000000  00000000  00000000  00000000  00000000  00000000  00000000
A 00000000  00000000  00000000  00000000  00000000  00000000  00000000  0001598C
beq $6AC
-t
PC = 000006AC USP = 0001598C SSP = 000FBF08 ST = 0004 = >IM = 0 ZER
D 00000001  00000000  00000000  00000000  00000000  00000000  00000000  00000000
A 00000000  00000000  00000000  00000000  00000000  00000000  00000000  0001598C
```

This example compares the contents of data register D0 to the constant 1. The BEQ succeeds because D0 also contains a 1.

CMPM Instruction

Integer Arithmetic Op Instr

The CMPM (CoMPare Memory) instruction compares two memory operands using the post-increment addressing mode. The condition codes are set as if the source operand were subtracted from the destination. Neither operand is altered.

When used with conditional branches, this instruction creates a less than desirable effect. When the combination

```
CMPM      (A0)+,(A1)+
BGT       X1
```

is used, the branch takes place if the second operand is greater than the first.

Addressing Modes Allowed: Only post-increment

Data Sizes: byte, word, long

Condition Codes Affected:

X   Not affected.
N   Set if the result is negative. Cleared otherwise.
Z   Set if the result is zero. (The operands are equal.) Cleared otherwise.
C   Set if a borrow is generated. Cleared otherwise.
V   Set on overflow in the subtract operation. Cleared otherwise.

Assembler Syntax: CMPM (Ay)+,(Ax)+

The CMP instruction compares an effective address operand to a data register. The CMPA instruction compares an effective address operand to an address register. The CMPI instruction compares an immediate quantity to an effective address. Many assemblers make this distinction automatically.

Machine Code Format:

Bit	15	14	13	12	11 10 9	8	7 6	5	4	3	2 1 0
	1	0	1	1	Reg Ax	1	Size	0	0	1	Reg Ay

The size field is 00 for comparing bytes, 01 for words, and 10 for longs. The Ay and Ax fields specify the source and destination address registers, respectively.

Example:

```
PC = 0000050C USP = 0001598C SSP = 0007BF08 ST = 0000 = >IM = 0
D 00000000   00000000 00000000 00000000 00000000 00000000 00000000 00000000
A 00000514   00000524 00000000 00000000 00000000 00000000 00000000 0001598C
cmpm (A0) + ,(A1) +
– l50c,510
   0000050C cmpm (A0) + ,(A1) +
   0000050E beq $50C
   00000510 nop
– dw514,534
00000514 0000 0001 0002 0003 0004 0005 0006 0008          ...............
00000524 0000 0001 0002 0003 0004 0005 0006 0007          ...............
– g,510
PC = 00000510 USP = 0001598C SSP = 0007BF08 ST = 0009 = >IM = 0 NEG CRY
D 00000000   00000000 00000000 00000000 00000000 00000000 00000000 00000000
A 00000524   00000534 00000000 00000000 00000000 00000000 00000000 0001598C
```

The example above compares two word strings in memory until it finds a pair that differ. From the *dw* command, we can see that the first pair of words that differ is at locations 522 and 532. The address registers are incremented past these locations by the post-decrement addressing modes.

DBcc Instruction

Program Control   3 of 8

DBcc is an instruction designed for looping. The condition cc is similar
to the conditions for conditional branches (see the Bcc instructions). DBcc
will commonly be placed at the end of a loop. The condition is the termination condition, much like the REPEAT/UNTIL condition of the Pascal
language. The loop may also be terminated on a maximum count.

The termination count is contained in the low word of a data register.
The data register is decremented until it reaches −1. At this point the
loop is terminated. Note that the comparison is for equal to −1. If the
data register initially contains −1, then the loop will be repeated 65,536
times (assuming the termination condition is not satisfied).

The permissible instructions are:

DBCC	Terminate if the C-bit (carry) is Clear.
DBCS	Terminate if the C-bit (carry) is Set.
DBEQ	Terminate on EQual. The loop terminates if the Z (Zero) bit is set.
DBGE	Terminate on Greater than or Equal. The loop terminates if the N (negative) and V (overflow) bits are either both set or both clear. GE is used for two's complement binary numbers.
DBGT	Terminate on Greater Than. The loop terminates if • The N and V bits are both set *and* the Z-bit is clear, or, • The N, V, and Z bits are *all* clear.
DBHI	Terminate on HIgher than. The loop terminates if the C and Z bits are both clear. DBHI is similar to DBGT, except that it works on unsigned numbers.
DBLE	Terminate Less than or Equal. The loop terminates if • The Z-bit is set, or, • The N-bit is set AND the V-bit is clear, or, • The N-bit is clear AND the V-bit is set. The DBLE instruction is used for two's complement binary numbers.
DBLS	Terminate on Lower or Same. The loop terminates if either the C or Z bits are set. DBLS is similar to DBLE, except that it works on unsigned numbers.
DBLT	Terminate on Less Than. The loop terminates if • The N-bit is set and the V-bit is clear, or,

- The N-bit is clear and the V-bit is set.

DBMI   Terminate on MInus. The loop terminates if the N-bit is set.

DBNE   Terminate on Not Equal. The loop terminates if the Z- bit is clear.

DBPL   Terminate on PLus. The loop terminates if the N-bit is clear.

DBVC   Terminate on V Clear. The loop terminates if the V-bit is clear, indicating no overflow.

DBVS   Terminate on V Set. The loop terminates if the V-bit is set, indicating overflow.

DBF   Never terminate. The loop is terminated by count only. Many assemblers accept DBRA as an alternate to DBF.

DBT   Always terminate. This instruction does not loop at all.

The condition is tested before decrementing the data register.

Addressing Modes Allowed:

DBcc instructions use a single addressing mode, where a two's complement displacement is contained in the second word of the instruction. If the loop is executed again, this displacement is sign-extended and added to the PC (Program Counter).

The PC contains the address of the displacement at the time the addition takes place.

Data Sizes: word

Condition Codes Affected: None

Assembler Syntax: DBcc Dn, <label>

is a label on an instruction in the program.

Machine Code Format:

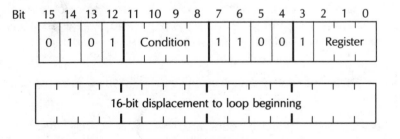

The Register field specifies the data register number to be used as the loop counter. The condition is a four-bit encoding of the branch condition. The conditions are shown in Table 3.3.

Condition	Instruction	Condition	Instruction
0000	DBT	1000	DBVC
0001	DBRA,DBF	1001	DBVS
0010	DBHI	1010	DBPL
0011	DBLS	1011	DBMI
0100	DBCC	1100	DBGE
0101	DBCS	1101	DBLT
0110	DBNE	1110	DBGT
0111	DBEQ	1111	DBLE

***Table* 3.3** – *Conditional corresponding instruction*

Example:

```
PC = 000006CC USP = 0001598C SSP = 000FBF08 ST = 0009 = >IM = 0 NEG CRY
D 00000001   00000000  00000000  00000000  00000000  00000000  00000000  00000000
A 00000952   0000095A  00000000  00000000  00000000  00000000  00000000  0001598C
moveq #$A,D0
-l6ce,6d4
   000006CE move.b (A0) + ,(A1) +
   000006D0 dbeq D0,6CE
   000006D4 nop
```

This sample code segment moves a null-terminated string whose address is contained in register A0 to an area whose address is in register A1. Putting A in D0 (10 decimal) means that if a zero byte is not found, up to eleven bytes will be moved. The areas pointed to by registers A0 and A1 are (conveniently) adjacent. The debugger display command shows:

```
-d952,966
00000952 48 65 6C 6C 6F 20 00 00 00 00 00 00 00 00 00 00    Hello ..........
00000962 00 00 00 00 00                                     .....
```

The string Hello should be duplicated starting at address 95A. Notice the trailing space. Executing the program shows:

```
-g,6d4
PC = 000006D4 USP = 0001598C SSP = 000FBF08 ST = 0004 = >IM = 0 ZER
```

```
D 00000004   00000000  00000000  00000000  00000000  00000000  00000000  00000000
A 00000959   00000961  00000000  00000000  00000000  00000000  00000000  0001598C
```

The count register (D0) is now 4, indicating that six bytes were moved out of a possible eleven. Both address registers have been incremented by seven, and now point to the byte after the first zero byte. (The address registers were incremented once more than the count register was decremented because the *move.b* instruction was executed seven times, while the *dbeq* instruction was executed only six.) Looking at memory again shows:

```
- d952,966
00000952 48 65 6C 6C 6F 20 00 00 48 65 6C 6C 6F 20 00 00    Hello ..Hello ..
00000962 00 00 00 00 00                                      .....
```

The source string has been duplicated in the destination, including the trailing space and the null terminator.

DIVS Instruction

The DIVS (DIVide Signed) instruction divides a 32-bit quantity contained in a data register by a 16-bit quantity contained in an effective address operand. The low-order word of the data register is replaced by the quotient, and the high-order word by the remainder. The remainder and quotient will always have the same sign, except when the remainder is 0.

Two error conditions are possible with a DIVS instruction:

1. An attempt is made to divide by zero. The 68000 processor generates an exception condition when this is attempted (see Chapter 7 on Exception Conditions).

2. A large number is divided by a small number, and the quotient will not fit in 16 bits. This is an Overflow condition. The V-bit in the status register is set, and the contents of the data register remain unmodified.

Addressing Modes Allowed:

Dn	An	(An)	(An) +	– (An)	x(An)	x(An,xr.s)
Yes	No	Yes	Yes	Yes	Yes	Yes
x.w	**x.l**	**x(PC)**	**x(PC,xr.s)**	**#x**	**SR**	**CCR**
Yes	Yes	Yes	Yes	Yes	No	No

Data Sizes: word

Condition Codes Affected:

X   Not affected.
N   Set if the quotient is negative. Cleared otherwise. Undefined on overflow conditions.
Z   Set if the quotient is zero. Cleared otherwise. Undefined on overflow conditions.

C   Always cleared.
V   Set if overflow detected. Cleared otherwise.

Assembler Syntax: DIVS <ea>,Dn

Machine Code Format:

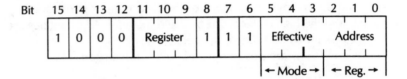

The Register field specifies the data register to be used as the destination (dividend). The Effective Address field specifies the source (divisor).

Example:

```
PC = 000006DC USP = 0001598C SSP = 000FBF08 ST = 0000 = >IM = 0
D 00008887   00000000  00000000  00000000  00000000  00000000  00000000  00000000
A 00000000   00000000  00000000  00000000  00000000  00000000  00000000  0001598C
divs #$2,D0
-t
PC = 000006E0 USP = 0001598C SSP = 000FBF08 ST = 0000 = >IM = 0
D 00014443   00000000  00000000  00000000  00000000  00000000  00000000  00000000
A 00000000   00000000  00000000  00000000  00000000  00000000  00000000  0001598C
```

This example divides 8887 by 2 to yield a quotient of 4443 with a remainder of 1.

DIVU Instruction

Integer Arithmetic Op Instr   12 of 24

The DIVU (DIVide Unsigned) instruction divides a 32-bit quantity contained in a data register by a 16-bit quantity contained in an effective address operand. The low-order word of the data register is replaced by the quotient, and the high-order word by the remainder. All quantities are considered to be unsigned positive integers.

Two error conditions are possible with a DIVU instruction:

1. An attempt is made to divide by zero. The 68000 processor generates an exception condition when this is attempted (see Chapter 7 on Exception Conditions).

2. A large number is divided by a small number and the quotient will not fit in 16 bits. This is an overflow condition. The V-bit in the status register is set and the contents of the data register remain unmodified.

Addressing Modes Allowed:

Dn	An	(An)	(An) +	– (An)	x(An)	x(An,xr.s)
Yes	No	Yes	Yes	Yes	Yes	Yes
x.w	**x.l**	**x(PC)**	**x(PC,xr.s)**	**#x**	**SR**	**CCR**
Yes	Yes	Yes	Yes	Yes	No	No

Data Sizes: word

Condition Codes Affected:

X   Not affected.
N   Set if the quotient is negative. Cleared otherwise. Undefined on overflow conditions.
Z   Set if the quotient is zero. Cleared otherwise. Undefined on overflow conditions.

C   Always cleared.
V   Set if overflow detected. Cleared Otherwise.

Assembler Syntax: DIVU <ea>,Dn

Machine Code Format:

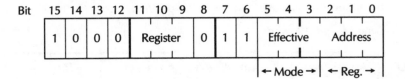

The Register field specifies the data register to be used as the destination (dividend). The Effective Address field specifies the source (divisor).

Example:

```
PC = 000006E8 USP = 0001598C SSP = 000FBF08 ST = 0000 = >IM = 0
D 00008887  00000000  00000000  00000000  00000000  00000000  00000000  00000000
A 00000000  00000000  00000000  00000000  00000000  00000000  00000000  0001598C
divu #$2,D0
-t
PC = 000006EC USP = 0001598C SSP = 000FBF08 ST = 0000 = >IM = 0
D 00014443  00000000  00000000  00000000  00000000  00000000  00000000  00000000
A 00000000  00000000  00000000  00000000  00000000  00000000  00000000  0001598C
nop
```

This example divides 8887 by 2 to yield a quotient of 4443 with a remainder of 1.

EOR Instruction

Logical Op Inst   5 of 79

The EOR (Exclusive OR) instruction performs an exclusive OR function between a data register and memory. The data register is restricted to be the source, and the effective address is the destination.

Addressing Modes Allowed:

Dn	An	(An)	(An) +	– (An)	x(An)	x(An,xr.s)
Yes	No	Yes	Yes	Yes	Yes	Yes
x.w	**x.l**	**x(PC)**	**x(PC,xr.s)**	**#x**	**SR**	**CCR**
Yes	Yes	No	No	No	No	No

Data Sizes: byte, word, long

Condition Codes Affected:

X Not affected.
N Set if the most significant bit of the result is set. Cleared otherwise.
Z Set if the result is zero. Cleared otherwise.
C Always cleared.
V Always cleared.

Assembler Syntax: EOR Dn,<ea>

The EORI instruction is used to exclusive OR immediate data with an effective address. Many assemblers allow using the EOR mnemonic for both, and produce the proper instruction based on the source operand.

Machine Code Format:

Bit	15	14	13	12	11	10	9	8	7	6	5	4	3	2	1	0
	1	0	1	1	Register			1	Size		Effective			Address		

← Mode → ← Reg. →

Register is the data register number to be used as the source operand. Size is 00 for byte, 01 for word, and 10 for long data sizes.

Example:

```
PC = 000006FA USP = 0001598C SSP = 000FBF08 ST = 0000 = >IM = 0
D 11113333  22222222  00000000  00000000  00000000  00000000  00000000  00000000
A 00000000  00000000  00000000  00000000  00000000  00000000  00000000  0001598C
eor.l D1,D0
-t
PC = 000006FC USP = 0001598C SSP = 000FBF08 ST = 0000 = >IM = 0
D 33331111  22222222  00000000  00000000  00000000  00000000  00000000  00000000
A 00000000  00000000  00000000  00000000  00000000  00000000  00000000  0001598C
```

This example executes an exclusive OR on 11113333 with 22222222 to become 33331111. The bits with place value two in all the nibbles in the high-order word of register D0 are initially zero, so the exclusive OR operation sets these bits. The inverse is true for the bits with place value two in the nibbles of the low-order word. (If you're still not sure about how this works, convert the numbers to binary, do the EOR by hand, and then convert them back to hex.)

EORI Instruction

Logical Op Instr   6 of 7

The EORI (Exclusive OR Immediate) instruction performs an exclusive OR function between an immediate operand and an effective address operand. The immediate operand must be the source, and the effective address is the destination.

Addressing Modes Allowed:

Dn	An	(An)	(An) +	– (An)	x(An)	x(An,xr.s)
Yes	No	Yes	Yes	Yes	Yes	Yes
x.w	**x.l**	**x(PC)**	**x(PC,xr.s)**	**#x**	**SR**	**CCR**
Yes	Yes	No	No	No	Yes	Yes

Data Sizes: byte, word, long

Operations specifying the status register (SR) and condition code register (CCR) are restricted to word and byte data lengths, respectively. Operations specifying the status register (SR) are privileged. A 68000 privilege-violation exception will result if this instruction is attempted with the SR addressing mode from User mode. Exceptions are covered in Chapter 7, Exception Processing.

Condition Codes Affected:

X   Not affected.
N   Set if the most significant bit of the result is set. Cleared otherwise.
Z   Set if the result is zero. Cleared otherwise.
C   Always cleared.
V   Always cleared.

When the status register or the condition code register are used as the destination, the condition codes are determined by the operation itself. All bits of the register are affected. Thus, if an EORI instruction to the condition code register leaves all bits in the CCR cleared, the Z-bit is not set as it would be with other operands.

Assembler Syntax: EORI #<data>,<ea>

The EOR instruction executes an exclusive OR on a data register with an effective address. Many assemblers allow using the EOR mnemonic for both EOR and EORI, and produce the proper instruction based on the source operand.

Machine Code Format:

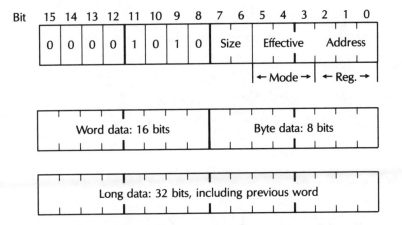

Size is 00 for byte, 01 for word, and 10 for long data sizes.

Example:

```
PC = 00000704 USP = 0001598C SSP = 000FBF08 ST = 0000 = >IM = 0
D 11113333  00000000  00000000  00000000  00000000  00000000  00000000  00000000
A 00000000  00000000  00000000  00000000  00000000  00000000  00000000  0001598C
eori.l #$22222222,D0
-t
PC = 0000070A USP = 0001598C SSP = 000FBF08 ST = 0000 = >IM = 0
D 33331111  00000000  00000000  00000000  00000000  00000000  00000000  00000000
A 00000000  00000000  00000000  00000000  00000000  00000000  00000000  0001598C
```

This example executes an exclusive OR on 11113333 with 22222222 to become 33331111. The bits with place value two in all the nibbles in the high-order word of register D0 are initially zero, so the exclusive OR operation sets these bits. The inverse is true for the bits with place value two in the nibbles of the low-order word. (If you're still not sure about how this works, convert the numbers to binary, do the EOR by hand, and then convert them back to hex.)

EXG Instruction

Data Movement Instruction, # 1 of 10

The EXG instruction exchanges the complete contents of any two address or data registers.

Addressing Modes Allowed:
  Only registers may be specified as operands.

Data Sizes: long

Condition Codes Affected: None

Assembler Syntax: EXG   Rx,Ry

Machine Code Format:

  Exchanging two data registers:

Bit	15	14	13	12	11	10	9	8	7	6	5	4	3	2	1	0
	1	1	0	0	Reg. Dx			1	0	1	0	0	0	Reg. Dy		

Exchanging two address registers:

Bit	15	14	13	12	11	10	9	8	7	6	5	4	3	2	1	0
	1	1	0	0	Reg. Ax			1	0	1	0	0	1	Reg. Ay		

Exchanging an address and a data register:

Bit	15	14	13	12	11	10	9	8	7	6	5	4	3	2	1	0
	1	1	0	0	Reg. Dx			1	1	0	0	0	1	Reg. Ay		

In exchanging an address and a data register, the address register must always be specified in bits 0–3 of the instruction word.

Example:

```
PC = 00000718 USP = 0001598C SSP = 000FBF08 ST = 0000 = >IM = 0
D 11111111   00000000  00000000  00000000  00000000  00000000  00000000  00000000
A 22222222   00000000  00000000  00000000  00000000  00000000  00000000  0001598C
exg D0,A0
–t
PC = 0000071A USP = 0001598C SSP = 000FBF08 ST = 0000 = >IM = 0
D 22222222   00000000  00000000  00000000  00000000  00000000  00000000  00000000
A 11111111   00000000  00000000  00000000  00000000  00000000  00000000  0001598C
```

This instruction exchanges the contents of registers A0 and D0.

EXT Instruction

Integer Arithmetic Op Instr   13 of 29

The EXT (sign EXTend) instruction extends the sign-bit of a byte into a word, or of a word into a long. The EXT instruction takes a single operand, which must be a data register.

When extending a byte to a long, bit 7 of the register is replicated into bits 15–8 of the register. Extension of a word into a long means extending bit 15 of the register into bits 16–31 of the register.

Addressing Modes Allowed: Only data registers

Data Sizes: word, long

Condition Codes Affected:

X   Not affected.
N   Set if the result is negative. Cleared otherwise.
Z   Set if the result is zero. Cleared otherwise.
C   Always cleared.
V   Always cleared.

Assembler Syntax: EXT Dn

Machine Code Format:

Bit	15	14	13	12	11	10	9	8	7	6	5	4	3	2	1	0
	0	1	0	0	1	0	0	0	Size		0	0	0	Register		

The size field is 10 to extend a byte to a word, and 11 to extend a word to a long.

Example:

```
PC = 00000722 USP = 0001598C SSP = 000FBF08 ST = 0000 = >IM = 0
D 00000080   00000000  00000000  00000000  00000000  00000000  00000000  00000000
A 00000000   00000000  00000000  00000000  00000000  00000000  00000000  0001598C
ext D0
```

```
-t
PC = 00000724 USP = 0001598C SSP = 000FBF08 ST = 0008 = >IM = 0 NEG
D 0000FF80  00000000  00000000  00000000  00000000  00000000  00000000  00000000
A 00000000  00000000  00000000  00000000  00000000  00000000  00000000  0001598C
ext.l D0
-t
PC = 00000726 USP = 0001598C SSP = 000FBF08 ST = 0008 = >IM = 0 NEG
D FFFFFF80  00000000  00000000  00000000  00000000  00000000  00000000  00000000
A 00000000  00000000  00000000  00000000  00000000  00000000  00000000  0001598C
```

This example extends the byte 80 hex to a word, and then to a long. Notice that 80 (hex) is a negative number (bit 7 of the byte is set).

ILLEGAL Instruction

The ILLEGAL instruction is not really an instruction at all. It is an operation code guaranteed to cause an illegal-instruction exception on all future 68000 family machines. (Illegal instructions are often used for breakpoints by debugger software.) Exceptions are detailed in Chapter 7, Exception Processing.

Addressing Modes Allowed: None

Data Sizes: None

Condition Codes Affected: None

Assembler Syntax: None

Machine Code Format:

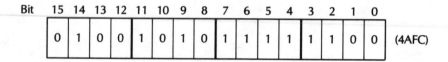

Bit	15	14	13	12	11	10	9	8	7	6	5	4	3	2	1	0	
	0	1	0	0	1	0	1	0	1	1	1	1	1	1	0	0	(4AFC)

JMP Instruction

Program Control   4 of 8

The JMP (JuMP) instruction is used to transfer control to an effective address. The address to which transfer is made is the address generated by the effective address computation. For example, if address register A0 contains 1000 hex, a JMP 4(A0) instruction transfers control to the instruction located at 1004.

Addressing Modes Allowed:

Dn	An	(An)	(An) +	– (An)	x(An)	x(An,xr.s)
No	No	Yes	No	No	Yes	Yes
x.w	**x.l**	**x(PC)**	**x(PC,xr.s)**	**#x**	**SR**	**CCR**
Yes	Yes	Yes	Yes	No	No	No

Data Sizes: Unsized

Condition Codes Affected: None

Assembler Syntax: JMP   <ea>

Machine Code Format:

Bit	15	14	13	12	11	10	9	8	7	6	5	4	3	2	1	0
	0	1	0	0	1	1	1	0	1	1	Effective			Address		

← Mode → ← Reg. →

Example:

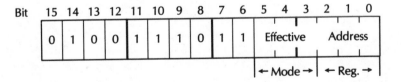

```
PC = 0000072E USP = 0001598C SSP = 000FBF08 ST = 0008 = >IM = 0 NEG
D 00000000  00000000  00000000  00000000  00000000  00000000  00000000  00000000
A 00000736  00000000  00000000  00000000  00000000  00000000  00000000  0001598C
jmp (A0)
```

```
- t
PC = 00000736 USP = 0001598C SSP = 000FBF08 ST = 0008 = >IM = 0 NEG
D 00000000  00000000  00000000  00000000  00000000  00000000  00000000  00000000
A 00000736  00000000  00000000  00000000  00000000  00000000  00000000  0001598C
```

JSR Instruction

Program Control 5 of 8

The JSR (Jump to SubRoutine) instruction calls a subroutine using an effective address operand. The address of the instruction following the JSR is pushed onto the stack (as a long word). The next instruction to be executed is determined by the effective address computation. For example, if address register A0 contains 1000 hex, a JSR 4(A0) instruction would call a subroutine located at address 1004.

Addressing Modes Allowed:

Dn	An	(An)	(An) +	– (An)	x(An)	x(An,xr.s)
No	No	Yes	No	No	Yes	Yes
x.w	**x.l**	**x(PC)**	**x(PC,xr.s)**	**#x**	**SR**	**CCR**
Yes	Yes	Yes	Yes	No	No	No

Data Sizes: Unsized

Condition Codes Affected: None

Assembler Syntax: JSR   <ea>

Machine Code Format:

Bit	15	14	13	12	11	10	9	8	7	6	5	4	3	2	1	0
	0	1	0	0	1	1	1	0	1	0	Effective			Address		
											← Mode →			← Reg. →		

Example:

PC = 0000073A USP = 0001598C SSP = 000FBF08 ST = 0008 = >IM = 0 NEG
D 00000000 00000000 00000000 00000000 00000000 00000000 00000000 00000000
A 00000000 00000000 00000000 00000000 00000000 00000000 00000000 0001598C
jsr $652

```
-t
PC = 00000652 USP = 00015988 SSP = 000FBF08 ST = 0008 = >IM = 0 NEG
D 00000000   00000000 00000000 00000000 00000000 00000000 00000000 00000000
A 00000000   00000000 00000000 00000000 00000000 00000000 00000000 00015988
rts
```

At this point, the subroutine has been called. We can see the return address at the top of the stack (the address in register A7).

```
 - sl15988
00015988 0000073E .
```

Executing the RTS yields:

```
-t
PC = 0000073E USP = 0001598C SSP = 000FBF08 ST = 0008 = >IM = 0 NEG
D 00000000   00000000 00000000 00000000 00000000 00000000 00000000 00000000
A 00000000   00000000 00000000 00000000 00000000 00000000 00000000 0001598C
```

The return address has been popped off the stack.

LEA Instruction

Data Movement Instruction, #2 of 10

The LEA (Load Effective Address) instruction places an effective address in an address register. All 32 bits of the register are affected.

The LEA instruction is normally used to write code that must be position-independent (i.e., can contain no code or data addresses in the program itself). The PC or Address register with displacement addressing modes are normally used for this type of coding.

The LEA instruction also adds a constant to an address register without altering the condition codes. By specifying the address register with displacement or index, either a constant or another register (or both) may be added to an address register in this manner.

Addressing Modes Allowed:

Dn	An	(An)	(An) +	– (An)	x(An)	x(An,xr.s)
No	No	Yes	No	No	Yes	Yes
x.w	**x.l**	**x(PC)**	**x(PC,xr.s)**	**#x**	**SR**	**CCR**
Yes	Yes	Yes	Yes	No	No	No

Data Sizes: long

Condition Codes Affected: None

Assembler Syntax: LEA   <ea>,An

Machine Code Format:

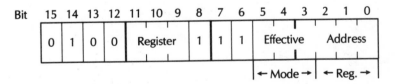

The Register field specifies the address register used as the destination.

The Effective Address field specifies the address to be loaded into the address register.

Example:

```
PC = 00000740 USP = 0001598C SSP = 000FBF08 ST = 0008 = >IM = 0 NEG
D 00000000   00000000  00000000  00000000  00000000  00000000  00000000  00000000
A 00000000   00000000  00000000  00000000  00000000  00000000  00000000  0001598C
lea $736,A0
-t
PC = 00000746 USP = 0001598C SSP = 000FBF08 ST = 0008 = >IM = 0 NEG
D 00000000   00000000  00000000  00000000  00000000  00000000  00000000  00000000
A 00000736   00000000  00000000  00000000  00000000  00000000  00000000  0001598C
lea $2(A0),A0
-t
PC = 0000074A USP = 0001598C SSP = 000FBF08 ST = 0008 = >IM = 0 NEG
D 00000000   00000000  00000000  00000000  00000000  00000000  00000000  00000000
A 00000738   00000000  00000000  00000000  00000000  00000000  00000000  0001598C
```

This example loads a constant address into address register A0 (using absolute long addressing). The second LEA instruction adds 2 to the address register.

LINK Instruction

Data Movement Instruction, #3 of 10

The LINK instruction allocates a temporary area on the stack. Such an area is normally called a *stack frame*. Many block structured high-level languages, such as C, Pascal, and PL/I use this instruction for allocating variables that are local to a procedure. The variables are deallocated when the procedure is deactivated, permitting efficient memory usage.

The LINK instruction takes two operands: an address register and a 16-bit signed displacement. The address register is pushed onto the stack, and the resulting stack pointer is copied into the address register. The displacement (which is usually negative) is added to the stack pointer to allocate memory for the local variables. The stack winds up looking like Figure 3.1.

The local storage area is addressed using negative displacements from the address register, sometimes known as the *frame pointer*. In this way, local variables may be accessed without regard for intervening pushes and pops on the stack.

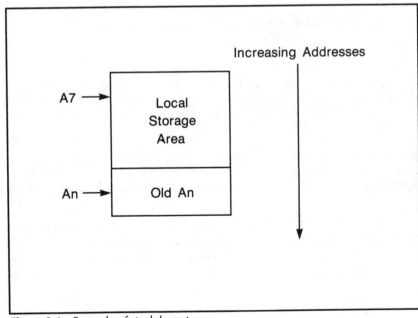

Figure 3.1 – *Example of stack layout*

The UNLK instruction deallocates the stack frame and restores the stack pointer and address register to their original contents.

Addressing Modes Allowed: None

Data Sizes: None

Condition Codes Affected: None

Assembler Syntax: LINK   An, #<displacement>

Machine Code Format:

Bit	15	14	13	12	11	10	9	8	7	6	5	4	3	2	1	0
	0	1	0	0	1	1	1	0	0	1	0	1	0	Register		

16-bit displacement to add to A7

Register is the number of the address register to be used.

Example:

```
PC = 0000074C USP = 0001598C SSP = 000FBF08 ST = 0008 = >IM = 0 NEG
D 00000000   00000000  00000000  00000000  00000000  00000000  00000000  00000000
A 00000000   00000000  00000000  00000000  00000000  00000000  00000000  0001598C
link A6,#$FFF4
-t
PC = 00000750 USP = 0001597C SSP = 000FBF08 ST = 0008 = >IM = 0 NEG
D 00000000   00000000  00000000  00000000  00000000  00000000  00000000  00000000
A 00000000   00000000  00000000  00000000  00000000  00000000  00015988  0001597C
```

This instruction pushes a total of 16 (10 hex) bytes on the stack: four for the address register and twelve due to the displacement field. (FFF4 is −12 decimal.) The long word address contained in register A6 shows the old contents of A6:

```
-sl15988
00015988 00000000
```

```
PC = 00000752 USP = 0001597C SSP = 000FBF08 ST = 0008 = >IM = 0 NEG
D 00000000  00000000  00000000  00000000  00000000  00000000  00000000  00000000
A 00000000  00000000  00000000  00000000  00000000  00000000  00015988  0001597C
unlk A6
-t
PC = 00000754 USP = 0001598C SSP = 000FBF08 ST = 0008 = >IM = 0 NEG
D 00000000  00000000  00000000  00000000  00000000  00000000  00000000  00000000
A 00000000  00000000  00000000  00000000  00000000  00000000  00000000  0001598C
```

The UNLK instruction reverses the action of the LINK instructions.

LSL Instruction

Shift & Rotate Instr   3 of 8

The LSL (Logical Shift Left) instruction performs a logical left shift on a data register or an effective address operand. There are three forms of this instruction:

1. Shift a data register to the left by a constant contained in the instruction. Shifts from one to eight bits can be accomplished using this form of the instruction.

2. Shift a data register to the left by the number of bits contained in another data register.

3. Shift a memory word (16 bits) left by a single bit.

Addressing Modes Allowed: Memory form only

Dn	An	(An)	(An) +	– (An)	x(An)	x(An,xr.s)
No	No	Yes	Yes	Yes	Yes	Yes
x.w	**x.l**	**x(PC)**	**x(PC,xr.s)**	**#x**	**SR**	**CCR**
Yes	Yes	No	No	No	No	No

Data Sizes: byte, word, long

Memory operations are restricted to word length.

Condition Codes Affected:

X   Set according to the last bit shifted out of the high-order bit position of the operand. Unaffected if the shift count is zero.

N   Set if the high order bit of the result is set (indicating a negative result). Cleared otherwise.

Z   Set if the result is zero. Cleared otherwise.

V   Always cleared.

C   Set according to the last bit shifted out of the high-order bit position of the operand. Unaffected if the shift count is zero.

Assembler Syntax: LSL   Dx,Dy
                  LSL   #<data>,Dy
                  LSL   <ea>

Machine Code Format:

Data register as destination

Bit	15	14	13	12	11 10 9	8	7 6	5	4	3	2 1 0
	1	1	1	0	Immed.	1	Size	T	0	1	Register

Memory location as destination

Bit	15	14	13	12	11	10	9	8	7	6	5 4 3	2 1 0
	1	1	1	0	0	0	1	1	1	1	Effective	Address

← Mode → | ← Reg. →

The Immediate field contains either the shift count or the data register number that contains the shift count. A 000 in this field represents a shift count of 8. Values 001 through 111 represent shift counts of 1–7. Size is either 00 for byte data, 01 for words, and 10 for longs. The T-bit (type) is a 0 if the shift count is contained in the instruction, and 1 if the shift count is in a data register. Register is the destination data register number.

Example:

```
PC = 0000075E USP = 0001598C SSP = 000FBF08 ST = 0000 = >IM = 0
D 00001111   00000002 00000000 00000000 00000000 00000000 00000000 00000000
A 00000000   00000000 00000000 00000000 00000000 00000000 00000000 0001598C
lsl D1,D0
−t
PC = 00000760 USP = 0001598C SSP = 000FBF08 ST = 0000 = >IM = 0
D 00004444   00000002 00000000 00000000 00000000 00000000 00000000 00000000
A 00000000   00000000 00000000 00000000 00000000 00000000 00000000 0001598C
```

This example uses the data register form of the instruction. 1111 is shifted left by two places to become 4444.

LSR Instruction

Shift & Rotate Instr   4 of 8

The LSR (Logical Shift Right) instruction performs a logical right shift on a data register or an effective address operand. There are three forms of this instruction:

1. Shift a data register to the right by a constant contained in the instruction. Shifts from one to eight bits can be accomplished using this form of the instruction.

2. Shift a data register to the right by the number of bits contained in another data register.

3. Shift a memory word (16 bits) right by a single bit.

Addressing Modes Allowed: Memory form only

Dn	An	(An)	(An) +	– (An)	x(An)	x(An,xr.s)
No	No	Yes	Yes	Yes	Yes	Yes
x.w	**x.l**	**x(PC)**	**x(PC,xr.s)**	**#x**	**SR**	**CCR**
Yes	Yes	No	No	No	No	No

Data Sizes: byte, word, long

Memory operations are restricted to word length.

Condition Codes Affected:

X   Set according to the last bit shifted out of the low-order bit position of the operand. Unaffected if the shift count is zero.

N   Set if the high order bit of the result is set (indicating a negative result). Cleared otherwise.

Z   Set if the result is zero. Cleared otherwise.

V   Always cleared.

C   Set according to the last bit shifted out of the low-order bit position of the operand. Unaffected if the shift count is zero.

Assembler Syntax: LSR   Dx,Dy
                     LSR   #<data>,Dy
                     LSR   <ea>

Machine Code Format:

Data register as destination

Bit	15	14	13	12	11	10	9	8	7	6	5	4	3	2	1	0
	1	1	1	0	Immed.			0	Size		T	0	1	Register		

Memory location as destination

Bit	15	14	13	12	11	10	9	8	7	6	5	4	3	2	1	0
	1	1	1	0	0	0	1	0	1	1	Effective			Address		

← Mode →   ← Reg. →

The Immediate field contains either the shift count or the data register number that contains the shift count. A 000 in this field represents a shift count of 8. Values 001 through 111 represent shift counts of 1–7. Size is either 00 for byte data, 01 for words, and 10 for longs. The T-bit (type) is a 0 if the shift count is contained in the instruction, and 1 if the shift count is in a data register. Register is the destination data register number.

Example:

```
PC = 0000076A USP = 0001598C SSP = 000FBF08 ST = 0000 = >IM = 0
D 88888888  00000002 00000000 00000000 00000000 00000000 00000000 00000000
A 00000000  00000000 00000000 00000000 00000000 00000000 00000000 0001598C
lsr D1,D0
-t
PC = 0000076C USP = 0001598C SSP = 000FBF08 ST = 0000 = >IM = 0
D 88882222  00000002 00000000 00000000 00000000 00000000 00000000 00000000
A 00000000  00000000 00000000 00000000 00000000 00000000 00000000 0001598C
```

This example shifts data register D0.W (the low word of D0) to the right by two places. The upper half of D0 is unaffected.

MOVE Instruction

Data Movement Instruction, #4 of 10

The MOVE instruction copies a byte, word, or longword from one effective address operand to another. The condition codes are set according to the data that is moved during the operand.

Addressing Modes Allowed: Source operand

Dn	An	(An)	(An) +	– (An)	x(An)	x(An,xr.s)
Yes	Yes	Yes	Yes	Yes	Yes	Yes
x.w	**x.l**	**x(PC)**	**x(PC,xr.s)**	**#x**	**SR**	**CCR**
Yes	Yes	Yes	Yes	Yes	No	No

Addressing Modes Allowed: Destination operand

Dn	An	(An)	(An) +	– (An)	x(An)	x(An,xr.s)
Yes	No	Yes	Yes	Yes	Yes	Yes
x.w	**x.l**	**x(PC)**	**x(PC,xr.s)**	**#x**	**SR**	**CCR**
Yes	Yes	No	No	No	No	No

Use of the An (address register direct) addressing mode is restricted to instructions with word and long data sizes.

Data Sizes: byte, word, long

Condition Codes Affected:

X   Not affected.
N   Set if the high order bit of the result is a one. Cleared otherwise.
Z   Set if the result is zero. Cleared otherwise.

V   Always cleared.
C   Always cleared.

Assembler Syntax: MOVE   <ea>,<ea>

MOVEA moves to an address register. Most assemblers automatically use the right instruction with an address register destination.

Machine Code Format:

Bit	15	14	13 12	11 10 9	8 7 6	5 4 3	2 1 0
	0	0	Size	Destination <ea>		Source <ea>	

← Reg. → |← Mode →|← Mode →| ← Reg. →

Size is the size of the data to be transferred: 01 for bytes, 11 for words, and 10 for longs.

Example:

```
PC = 00000774 USP = 0001598C SSP = 000FBF08 ST = 0000 = >IM = 0
D 11111111   00000000  00000000  00000000  00000000  00000000  00000000  00000000
A 00000000   00000000  00000000  00000000  00000000  00000000  00000000  0001598C
move.b $92D,D0
 -s92d
0000092D 99 .
 -t
PC = 0000077A USP = 0001598C SSP = 000FBF08 ST = 0008 = >IM = 0 NEG
D 11111199   00000000  00000000  00000000  00000000  00000000  00000000  00000000
A 00000000   00000000  00000000  00000000  00000000  00000000  00000000  0001598C
```

This instruction moves a memory location into a data register. Byte moves into a data register leave the upper three bytes of the register unmodified.

MOVE to CCR Instruction

The MOVE to CCR instruction moves the low-order byte of a word operand to the condition code register (CCR), the User byte of the status register. The high-order byte of the source is ignored.

Addressing Modes Allowed:

Dn	An	(An)	(An) +	– (An)	x(An)	x(An,xr.s)
Yes	No	Yes	Yes	Yes	Yes	Yes
x.w	**x.l**	**x(PC)**	**x(PC,xr.s)**	**#x**	**SR**	**CCR**
Yes	Yes	Yes	Yes	Yes	No	No

Data Size: word

Condition Codes Affected:

- X Set from bit 4 of the source operand.
- N Set from bit 3 of the source operand.
- Z Set from bit 2 of the source operand.
- V Set from bit 1 of the source operand.
- C Set from bit 0 of the source operand.

Assembler Syntax: MOVE   <ea>,CCR

Machine Code Format:

Bit	15	14	13	12	11	10	9	8	7	6	5 4 3	2 1 0
	0	1	0	0	0	1	0	0	1	1	Effective	Address

← Mode → ← Reg. →

Example:

PC = 00x0077C USP = 0001598C SSP = 000FBF08 ST = 0000 = >IM = 0
D 00000000   00000000   00000000   00000000   00000000   00000000   00000000   00000000

```
A 00000000   00000000  00000000  00000000  00000000  00000000  00000000  0001598C
move #$1F,CCR
-t
PC = 000780 USP = 01598C SSP = 0FBF08 ST = 001F = >IM = 0 EXT NEG ZER OFL CRY
D 00000000   00000000  00000000  00000000  00000000  00000000  00000000  00000000
A 00000000   00000000  00000000  00000000  00000000  00000000  00000000  0001598C
```

This instruction sets all condition code bits in the status register.

MOVE to SR Instruction

The MOVE to SR (Status Register) instruction transfers a word operand to the CPU status register. All bits of the status register are affected. This instruction requires that the S-bit of the status register (bit 13) be set at the beginning of the instruction (i.e., the CPU must be in Supervisor state).

This instruction may be used to alter the Status register Trace bit, Supervisor bit, interrupt mask, and condition codes. Typical uses include:

- Clearing the Supervisor bit to transfer to User mode.

- Clearing the Interrupt mask to enable CPU interrupts.

- Setting bits in the Interrupt mask to partially or completely disable CPU interrupts.

Changing the condition codes is normally done with the MOVE to CCR instruction, which is not privileged, and can be executed from either supervisor or user mode.

Addressing Modes Allowed:

Dn	An	(An)	(An) +	– (An)	x(An)	x(An,xr.s)
Yes	No	Yes	Yes	Yes	Yes	Yes
x.w	x.l	x(PC)	x(PC,xr.s)	#x	SR	CCR
Yes	Yes	Yes	Yes	Yes	No	No

Data Size: word

Condition Codes Affected:

    X   Set from bit 4 of the source operand.
    N   Set from bit 3 of the source operand.
    Z   Set from bit 2 of the source operand.
    V   Set from bit 1 of the source operand.
    C   Set from bit 0 of the source operand.

Assembler Syntax: MOVE   <ea>,SR

Machine Code Format:

Bit	15	14	13	12	11	10	9	8	7	6	5 4 3	2 1 0
	0	1	0	0	0	1	1	0	1	1	Effective	Address

← Mode → ← Reg. →

Example:

```
- g,786
PC = 00000786  USP = 0001598C  SSP = 0007BF08  ST = 2010 = >SUP  IM = 0
EXT
D 00000000   00000000  00000000  00000000  00000000  00000000  00000000  00000000
A 00000000   00000000  00000000  00000000  00000000  00000000  00000000  0007BF08
move #$200F,SR
- g,78a
PC = 00078A  USP = 01598C  SSP = 07BF08  ST = 200F = >SUP  IM = 0  NEG ZER OFL CRY
D 00000000   00000000  00000000  00000000  00000000  00000000  00000000  00000000
A 00000000   00000000  00000000  00000000  00000000  00000000  00000000  0007BF08
```

This instruction sets the N, Z, O, C, condition codes, as well as the S-bit. The S (Supervisor) bit is set before execution. A Privilege-violation exception results if this instruction is attempted from User mode. Notice that address register A7 reflects the supervisor stack pointer (SSP) rather than the user stack pointer (USP).

MOVE from SR Instruction

The MOVE from SR (Status Register) instruction transfers the entire status register to a word operand. Memory operands are read before writing. This instruction is privileged on the 68010 processor. (A privileged instruction requires that the S-bit [bit 13] in the status register be set prior to execution.)

Addressing Modes Allowed:

Dn	An	(An)	(An) +	– (An)	x(An)	x(An,xr.s)
Yes	No	Yes	Yes	Yes	Yes	Yes
x.w	**x.l**	**x(PC)**	**x(PC,xr.s)**	**#x**	**SR**	**CCR**
Yes	Yes	No	No	No	No	No

Data Size: word

Condition Codes Affected: None

Assembler Syntax: MOVE   SR,<ea>

Machine Code Format:

Bit	15	14	13	12	11	10	9	8	7	6	5	4	3	2	1	0
	0	1	0	0	0	0	0	0	1	1	Effective			Address		
											← Mode →			← Reg. →		

Example:

```
PC = 0000078C  USP = 0001598C  SSP = 0007BF08  ST = 200F = >SUP  IM = 0
NEG ZER OFL CRY
D 00000000   00000000  00000000  00000000  00000000  00000000  00000000  00000000
A 00000000   00000000  00000000  00000000  00000000  00000000  00000000  0007BF08
move SR,D0
```

–t
PC = 0000078E USP = 0001598C SSP = 0007BF08 ST = 200F = >SUP IM = 0
NEG ZER OFL CRY
D <u>0000200F</u> 00000000 00000000 00000000 00000000 00000000 00000000 00000000
A 00000000 00000000 00000000 00000000 00000000 00000000 00000000 0007BF08

This instruction transfers the status register to the low-order word of data register D0. Notice that address register A7 reflects the supervisor stack pointer (SSP) rather than the user stack pointer (USP).

MOVE USP Instruction

System Control   2 of 7

The MOVE USP instruction transfers the user stack pointer to or from an address register. This instruction is a privileged instruction. (The S-bit [bit 13] in the status register must be set.)

A MOVE USP instruction is normally used by a supervisor program to set up a stack area in a user program. The 68000 has separate user and supervisor stack pointer registers, so this special instruction is required to enable the supervisor program to access the user mode stack pointer.

Addressing Modes Allowed: Only An

Data Size: long

Condition Codes Affected: None

Assembler Syntax: MOVE   USP,An
                  MOVE   An,USP

Machine Code Format:

Bit	15	14	13	12	11	10	9	8	7	6	5	4	3	2 1 0
	0	1	0	0	1	1	1	0	0	1	1	0	T	Register

To transfer the address register to the USP, the T field is 0, and 1 to transfer the USP to the address register. The Register field specifies the number of the address register to be used.

Example:

```
PC = 000790 USP = 01558C SSP = 07BF08 ST = 200F = >SUP IM = 0 NEG ZER OFL CRY
D 00000000    00000000    00000000    00000000    00000000    00000000    00000000    00000000
A 00000000    00000000    00000000    00000000    00000000    00000000    00000000    0007BF08
move.l USP,A0
-t
PC = 000792 USP = 01558C SSP = 07BF08 ST = 200F = >SUP IM = 0 NEG ZER OFL CRY
D 00000000    00000000    00000000    00000000    00000000    00000000    00000000    00000000
A 0001558C    00000000    00000000    00000000    00000000    00000000    00000000    0007BF08
```

This example transfers the user stack pointer (USP) to address register A0. The status register S bit must be set for this privileged instruction.

MOVEA Instruction

The MOVEA (Move Address) instruction moves an effective address operand to an address register. Only word and long data sizes are allowed. All 32 bits of the address register are always affected. Word operations are sign extended to 32 bits before loading the address register.

Addressing Modes Allowed:

Dn	An	(An)	(An) +	– (An)	x(An)	x(An,xr.s)
Yes	Yes	Yes	Yes	Yes	Yes	Yes
x.w	**x.l**	**x(PC)**	**x(PC,xr.s)**	**#x**	**SR**	**CCR**
Yes	Yes	Yes	Yes	Yes	No	No

Data Sizes: word, long

Condition Codes Affected: None

Assembler Syntax: MOVEA   <ea>,An

Many assemblers will generate the MOVEA instruction when a MOVE instruction specifies an address register as the destination.

Machine Code Format:

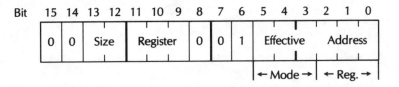

The Size field is 11 for word transfers, and 10 for long transfers. The Register field gives the destination address register. Notice that this instruction is really a MOVE instruction with a destination addressing mode of 001.

Example:

```
PC = 00000796 USP = 0001558C SSP = 0007BF08 ST = 0000 = >IM = 0
D 00000000   00000000  00000000  00000000  00000000  00000000  00000000  00000000
A 00000000   00000000  00000000  00000000  00000000  00000000  00000000  0001558C
move.l #$1234567,A0
-t
PC = 0000079C USP = 0001558C SSP = 0007BF08 ST = 0000 = >IM = 0
D 00000000   00000000  00000000  00000000  00000000  00000000  00000000  00000000
A 01234567   00000000  00000000  00000000  00000000  00000000  00000000  0001558C
```

This example loads address register A0 with the constant 01234567.

MOVEM Instruction

Data Movement Instruction, # 5 of 10

The MOVEM (MOVE Multiple) instruction provides a means for rapidly transferring a group of registers to or from memory. The size of the operation is restricted to word or long data. For word operations that transfer data to the registers, each word is sign-extended to 32 bits before loading the register. All 32 bits of the register are always affected, regardless of whether the register is an address or data register.

The order in which the registers are stored in memory is as follows:

	Address (effective address)	Register
	+0	DO
	+4	D1
	.	
	.	
	.	
	+28	D7
	+32	A0
	+36	A1
	.	
	.	
	.	
	+60	A7
	+64	(Unused)

Any combination of the registers may be loaded or stored using this instruction. The illustration above assumes that all registers are present and long data size.

This instruction is used primarily for pushing a group of registers on the stack so that they may be used temporarily and later reset to their original values, also using a MOVEM instruction. This technique is especially valuable for subroutines and exception-processing routines, where it is often not known which registers can be modified.

An anomaly of 68000 architecture causes an extra memory reference when transferring memory to registers using a MOVEM. In the diagram above, offsets 64 and 65 from the base of the register area in memory would be read (again assuming all registers were present). This is usually not significant, but it can cause problems in certain specialized cases. For example, trying to transfer registers from the very last locations in memory will cause an erroneous BUSERR to occur due to the access of the next word (which is not a valid memory address in this case). The BUSERR exception is explained in Chapter 7, Exception Processing.

Addressing Modes Allowed: Registers to memory

Dn	An	(An)	(An) +	– (An)	x(An)	x(An,xr.s)
No	No	Yes	No	Yes	Yes	Yes
x.w	x.l	x(PC)	x(PC,xr.s)	#x	SR	CCR
Yes	Yes	No	No	No	No	No

Memory to Registers:

Dn	An	(An)	(An) +	– (An)	x(An)	x(An,xr.s)
No	No	Yes	Yes	No	Yes	Yes
x.w	x.l	x(PC)	x(PC,xr.s)	#x	SR	CCR
Yes	Yes	Yes	Yes	No	No	No

Data Sizes: word, long

Condition Codes Affected: None

Assembler Syntax: MOVEM   <register list>,<ea>
              MOVEM   <ea>,<register list>

The register list is composed of a series of register specifications separated by a slash (the / character). For example, D0/D2/A5 specifies registers D0, D2, and A5 as operands. It is also possible to use one or more ranges in the register list. A range consists of two register specifications separated by the – character. For instance, D0–D5/A0–A2 specifies registers D0, D1, D2, D3, D4, D5, A0, A1, and A2.

Machine Code Format:

Registers to Memory:

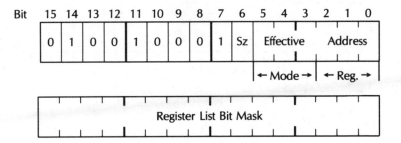

Memory to Registers:

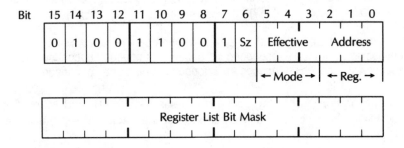

The Sz (size) bit is a 0 for word transfers and a 1 for long transfers. The register list bit mask contains a single bit for each register that can be transferred by a MOVEM instruction (16 registers). If the bit is a 1, then the register is transferred. If the bit is 0, then the register is not transferred.
    The register-list word has two possible orientations, one for predecrement mode addressing and one for all other addressing modes. In all cases, the low-order bit of the mask corresponds to the register that is

to be transferred first. The two sets of correspondence between registers and bits are as follows:

Pre-decrement (– (An)) addressing mode:

Bit	15	14	13	12	11	10	9	8	7	6	5	4	3	2	1	0
	D0	D1	D2	D3	D4	D5	D6	D7	A0	A1	A2	A3	A4	A5	A6	A7

All other addressing modes:

Bit	15	14	13	12	11	10	9	8	7	6	5	4	3	2	1	0
	A7	A6	A5	A4	A3	A2	A1	A0	D7	D6	D5	D4	D3	D2	D1	D0

Example:

```
PC = 0000079E USP = 0001558C SSP = 0007BF08 ST = 0000 = >IM = 0
D 000000D0   000000D1   00000000   00000000   00000000   00000000   00000000   00000000
A 000000A0   000000A1   00000000   00000000   00000000   00000000   00000000   0001558C
movem.l D0 – D1/A0 – A0, – (A7)
–t
PC = 000007A2 USP = 00015580 SSP = 0007BF08 ST = 0000 = >IM = 0
D 000000D0   000000D1   00000000   00000000   00000000   00000000   00000000   00000000
A 000000A0   000000A1   00000000   00000000   00000000   00000000   00000000   00015580
```

This instruction pushes the contents of registers D0, D1, and A0 on the stack. Using the S command, we can look at the stack and see the saved registers.

```
–s15580
00015580 000000D0
00015584 000000D1
00015588 000000A0
–t
PC = 000007A4 USP = 00015580 SSP = 0007BF08 ST = 0000 = >IM = 0
D 00000000   00000000   00000000   00000000   00000000   00000000   00000000   00000000
A 00000000   000000A1   00000000   00000000   00000000   00000000   00000000   00015580
movem.l (A7) + ,D0 – D1/A0 – A0
```

```
-t
PC = 000007A8 USP = 0001558C SSP = 0007BF08 ST = 0000 = >IM = 0
D 000000D0  000000D1  00000000  00000000  00000000  00000000  00000000  00000000
A 000000A0  000000A1  00000000  00000000  00000000  00000000  00000000  0001558C
```

The second half of the example above restores the registers from the
stack. Notice that D0, D1, and A0 are valid hexadecimal numbers as well
as names for registers.

MOVEP Instruction

Data Movement Instruction, #6 of 10

The MOVEP (MOVE Peripheral) instruction provides a convenient method for accessing 8-bit peripheral devices connected to a 68000. The 68000 is a 16-bit microprocessor. This means that there are sixteen data lines connecting the processor to memory, as illustrated in Figure 3.2.

Many I/O devices were designed for 8-bit microprocessors, and thus have only eight data lines. These devices can be connected to the 68000 using either the Upper byte data lines or the Lower byte data lines. Addressing a device connected in such a fashion is done by using alternate memory addresses (for example, 1,3,5 for devices connected to the Lower byte lines, or 0,2,4 for devices connected to the Upper byte lines). The MOVEP instruction is facilitates this process.

The MOVEP instruction transfers a word or a longword contained in a data register to or from these alternate memory addresses. The destination memory address is specified using the address register with displacement addressing mode— x(An).

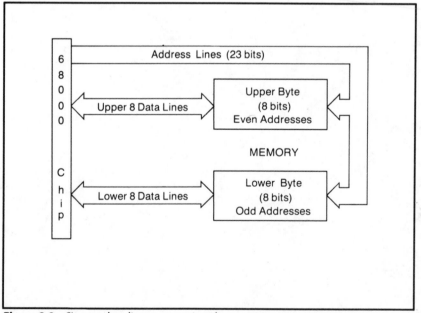

Figure 3.2 – *Sixteen data lines connecting the processor to memory*

The high-order byte of the data register is transferred to or from address x(An), the next byte to or from x+2(An), and so forth. If the original address was odd, then all transfers from the MOVEP will use the Lower byte of the 68000 data bus. Even addresses use the High byte.

Addressing Modes Allowed: x(An) only

Data Sizes: word, long

Condition Codes Affected: None

Assembler Syntax: MOVEP   Dn,x(An)
                  MOVEP   x(An),Dn

Machine Code Format:

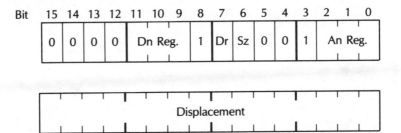

The Dn Register and An Register give the numbers of the data and address registers to be used, respectively. The Dr (direction) bit is 0 for memory to register transfers and 1 for register to memory transfers. The Sz (size) bit is 1 for long data and 0 for words. The displacement field is a 16-bit offset that is added to the address register to form the base memory address at which the transfer begins.

Example:

```
PC = 000007B6 USP = 0001558C SSP = 0007BF08 ST = 0000 = >IM = 0
D 01234567   00000000  00000000  00000000  00000000  00000000  00000000  00000000
A 00000964   00000000  00000000  00000000  00000000  00000000  00000000  0001558C
movep.l D0,0(A0)
-t
PC = 000007BA USP = 0001558C SSP = 0007BF08 ST = 0000 = >IM = 0
D 01234567   00000000  00000000  00000000  00000000  00000000  00000000  00000000
A 00000964   00000000  00000000  00000000  00000000  00000000  00000000  0001558C
-d964,96c
00000964 01 00 23 00 45 00 67 00 00                          ..#.E.g..
```

In this example, register D0 is stored starting at address 964. Since the starting address is even, the bytes in D0 will go into the high-order bytes of successive words, as illustrated by the d command. The high-order byte of D0 is stored first.

a preferred instruction

MOVEQ Instruction

Data Movement Instruction, #7 of 10

The MOVEQ instruction provides a method for loading a small immediate quantity into a data register. The instruction is two bytes in length, and can load any constant in the range − 128 to + 127 (decimal). All 32 bits of the register are affected. (The corresponding MOVE immediate long instruction takes six bytes.)

Data Size: long

Condition Codes Affected:

X   Not affected.
N   Set if the result is negative. Cleared otherwise.
Z   Set if the result is zero. Cleared otherwise.
V   Always cleared.
C   Always cleared.

Assembler Syntax: MOVEQ   #<data>,Dn

Many assemblers automatically convert a move with the appropriate operands into a MOVEQ.
Machine Code Format:

Bit	15	14	13	12	11	10	9	8	7	6	5	4	3	2	1	0
	0	1	1	1	Register			0	Immediate Data							

The Register field identifies the destination data register. The Immediate Data is an 8-bit immediate operand that is sign-extended before loading into the data register.

Example:

```
PC = 000007BC USP = 0001558C SSP = 0007BF08 ST = 0000 = >IM = 0
D 00000000   00000000  00000000  00000000  00000000  00000000  00000000  00000000
A 00000000   00000000  00000000  00000000  00000000  00000000  00000000  0001558C
moveq #$80,D0
```

```
-t
PC = 000007BE USP = 0001558C SSP = 0007BF08 ST = 0008 = >IM = 0 NEG
D FFFFFF80  00000000  00000000  00000000  00000000  00000000  00000000  00000000
A 00000000  00000000  00000000  00000000  00000000  00000000  00000000  0001558C
```

This example loads register D0 with the constant 80 hex (− 128 decimal). The data is sign-extended into a long by the operation.

MULS Instruction

Integer Arithmetic Op Instr   14 of 24

The MULS (MULtiply Signed) instruction multiplies a 16-bit data register operand by a 16-bit effective address operand, leaving the 32-bit result in the data register. The operation assumes two's complement arithmetic.

Addressing Modes Allowed:

Dn	An	(An)	(An) +	– (An)	x(An)	x(An,xr.s)
Yes	No	Yes	Yes	Yes	Yes	Yes
x.w	**x.l**	**x(PC)**	**x(PC,xr.s)**	**#x**	**SR**	**CCR**
Yes	Yes	Yes	Yes	Yes	No	No

Data Size: word

Condition Codes Affected:

X   Not affected.
N   Set if the result is negative. Cleared otherwise.
Z   Set if the result is zero. Cleared otherwise.
V   Always cleared.
C   Always cleared.

Assembler Syntax: MULS   <ea>,Dn

Machine Code Format:

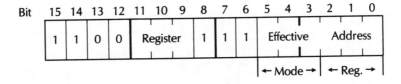

The Register field identifies the data register to be used as the destination.

Example:

```
PC = 000007C6 USP = 0001598C SSP = 0007BF08 ST = 0000 = >IM = 0
D 00001234   00000000  00000000  00000000  00000000  00000000  00000000  00000000
A 00000000   00000000  00000000  00000000  00000000  00000000  00000000  0001598C
muls #$10,D0
–t
PC = 000007CA USP = 0001598C SSP = 0007BF08 ST = 0000 = >IM = 0
D 00012340   00000000  00000000  00000000  00000000  00000000  00000000  00000000
A 00000000   00000000  00000000  00000000  00000000  00000000  00000000  0001598C
```

This example multiplies the contents of register D0 by the constant 10 hex (16 decimal).

MULU Instruction

Integer Arithmetic Op Instr 150/24

The MULU (MULtiply Unsigned) instruction multiplies a 16-bit data register operand by a 16-bit effective address operand, leaving the 32-bit result in the data register. The operation assumes unsigned arithmetic.

Addressing Modes Allowed:

Dn	An	(An)	(An) +	– (An)	x(An)	x(An,xr.s)
Yes	No	Yes	Yes	Yes	Yes	Yes
x.w	x.l	x(PC)	x(PC,xr.s)	#x	SR	CCR
Yes	Yes	Yes	Yes	Yes	No	No

Data Size: word

Condition Codes Affected:

- X   Not affected.
- N   Set if the most significant bit of the result is set. Cleared otherwise.
- Z   Set if the result is zero. Cleared otherwise.
- V   Always cleared.
- C   Always cleared.

Assembler Syntax: MULU   <ea>,Dn

Machine Code Format:

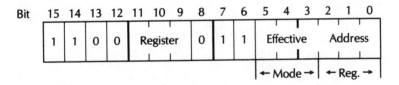

The Register field identifies the data register to be used as the destination.

Example:

```
PC = 000007D2 USP = 0001598C SSP = 0007BF08 ST = 0000 = >IM = 0
D 00008000   00000000  00000000  00000000  00000000  00000000  00000000  00000000
A 00000000   00000000  00000000  00000000  00000000  00000000  00000000  0001598C
mulu #$5,D0
-t
PC = 000007D6 USP = 0001598C SSP = 0007BF08 ST = 0000 = >IM = 0
D 00028000   00000000  00000000  00000000  00000000  00000000  00000000  00000000
A 00000000   00000000  00000000  00000000  00000000  00000000  00000000  0001598C
```

This example multiplies hex 8000 (normally a negative number) by 5. Notice that the result is positive. This is because unsigned arithmetic was used in the MULU instruction.

NBCD Instruction

Binary Coded Decimal Instruction, #2 of 3

The NBCD (Negate BCD) instruction forms the negative of a BCD (binary coded decimal) number. The technique used is ten's complement, analogous to the two's complement used with binary numbers. The ten's complement of a number is formed by subtracting the number from all 9s and then adding one. As with binary numbers, the complementing process works only if you have a fixed number of digits.

For example, assume you have a 4-digit BCD system. The ten's complement of 0001 is (9999 − 0001) + 1, or 9999. Adding this number to a positive decimal number is equivalent to subtracting 1.

As with the other 68000 BCD instructions, NBCD is intended for multiprecision BCD arithmetic. The X (eXtend) bit is added to the ten's complement process. This bit provides the borrow necessary for multiprecision arithmetic. The Z-bit is only cleared by this instruction. This allows the Z-bit to accurately reflect a multiprecision result. Normally, a series of NBCD instructions begins with the X-bit clear and the Z-bit set. The size of the operation is restricted to byte size.

Addressing Modes Allowed:

Dn	An	(An)	(An) +	− (An)	x(An)	x(An,xr.s)
Yes	No	Yes	Yes	Yes	Yes	Yes
x.w	x.l	x(PC)	x(PC,xr.s)	#x	SR	CCR
Yes	Yes	No	No	No	No	No

Data Size: byte

Condition Codes Affected:

X Set if a borrow was generated in the subtraction operation. Cleared otherwise.

N Undefined.

Z Cleared if the result was not a zero. Unchanged otherwise.

V   Undefined.
C   Set if a borrow was generated in the subtraction operation.
Cleared otherwise.

Assembler Syntax: NBCD   <ea>

Machine Code Format:

Bit	15	14	13	12	11	10	9	8	7	6	5	4	3	2	1	0
	0	1	0	0	1	0	0	0	0	0	Effective			Address		

← Mode → | ← Reg. →

Example:

```
PC = 000007DA USP = 0001598C SSP = 0007BF08 ST = 0000 = >IM = 0
D 00000001   00000000  00000000  00000000  00000000  00000000  00000000  00000000
A 00000000   00000000  00000000  00000000  00000000  00000000  00000000  0001598C
nbcd D0
-t
PC = 000007DC USP = 0001598C SSP = 0007BF08 ST = 0019 = >IM = 0 EXT NEG CRY
D 00000099   00000000  00000000  00000000  00000000  00000000  00000000  00000000
A 00000000   00000000  00000000  00000000  00000000  00000000  00000000  0001598C
```

This example takes the ten's complement of 01 to produce 99. (Remember, BCD is the same as hex.)

NEG Instruction

Integer Arithmetic Op Instr   16 of 24

The NEG (NEGate) instruction forms the two's complement of an effective address operand.

Addressing Modes Allowed:

Dn	An	(An)	(An) +	– (An)	x(An)	x(An,xr.s)
Yes	No	Yes	Yes	Yes	Yes	Yes
x.w	**x.l**	**x(PC)**	**x(PC,xr.s)**	**#x**	**SR**	**CCR**
Yes	Yes	No	No	No	No	No

Data Sizes: byte, word, long

Condition Codes Affected:

X   Cleared if the result is zero. Set otherwise.
N   Set if the result is negative. Cleared otherwise.
Z   Set if the result is zero. Cleared otherwise.
V   Set if an overflow is generated. Cleared otherwise.
C   Cleared if the result is zero. Set otherwise.

Assembler Syntax: NEG   <ea>

Machine Code Format:

Bit	15	14	13	12	11	10	9	8	7	6	5	4	3	2	1	0
	0	1	0	0	0	1	0	0	Size		Effective			Address		

← Mode → ← Reg. →

The Size field is 00 for byte data, 01 for words, and 10 for longs.

Example:

```
PC = 000007E2 USP = 0001598C SSP = 0007BF08 ST = 0010 = >IM = 0 EXT
D 00000001   00000000 00000000 00000000 00000000 00000000 00000000 00000000
A 00000000   00000000 00000000 00000000 00000000 00000000 00000000 0001598C
neg D0
-t
PC = 000007E4 USP = 0001598C SSP = 0007BF08 ST = 0019 = >IM = 0 EXT NEG CRY
D 0000FFFF   00000000 00000000 00000000 00000000 00000000 00000000 00000000
A 00000000   00000000 00000000 00000000 00000000 00000000 00000000 0001598C
```

This example takes the two's complement in the low-order word of register D0. (1 is complemented to become − 1.)

NEGX Instruction

Integer Arith Op Instr

The NEGX (Negate with eXtend) instruction provides a method for taking the two's complement of a multiprecision binary number.

Addressing Modes Allowed:

Dn	An	(An)	(An) +	– (An)	x(An)	x(An,xr.s)
Yes	No	Yes	Yes	Yes	Yes	Yes
x.w	**x.l**	**x(PC)**	**x(PC,xr.s)**	**#x**	**SR**	**CCR**
Yes	Yes	No	No	No	No	No

Data Sizes: byte, word, long

Condition Codes Affected:

X   Set if a borrow is generated. Cleared otherwise.

N   Set if the result is negative. Cleared otherwise.

Z   Cleared if the result is not zero. Unchanged otherwise.

V   Set if an overflow is generated. Cleared otherwise.

C   Set if a borrow is generated. Cleared otherwise.

As with other 68000 multiprecision instructions, a group of NEGX instructions should begin with the Z-bit set and the X-bit clear. At the completion of the multiprecision operation, the Z-bit will then correctly indicate whether the entire operand is zero. The usual storage order for multiprecision integers on the 68000 is to place the high-order portion at the lowest address, and the low-order portion at the highest address. ADDs, SUBtracts, and NEGates begin with the low-order word and normally use the pre-decrement addressing mode.

Assembler Syntax: NEGX <ea>

Machine Code Format:

Bit	15	14	13	12	11	10	9	8	7	6	5	4	3	2	1	0
	0	1	0	0	0	0	0	0	Size		Effective			Address		

← Mode → ← Reg. →

The Size field is 00 for byte operands, 01 for words, and 10 for longs.

Example:

```
PC = 000007EA USP = 0001598C SSP = 0007BF08 ST = 0014 = >IM = 0 EXT ZER
D 00000001  00000000  00000000  00000000  00000000  00000000  00000000  00000000
A 00000000  00000000  00000000  00000000  00000000  00000000  00000000  0001598C
neg.l D0
-t
PC = 000007EC USP = 0001598C SSP = 0007BF08 ST = 0019 = >IM = 0 EXT NEG CRY
D FFFFFFFF  00000000  00000000  00000000  00000000  00000000  00000000  00000000
A 00000000  00000000  00000000  00000000  00000000  00000000  00000000  0001598C
negx.l D1
-t
PC = 000007EE USP = 0001598C SSP = 0007BF08 ST = 0019 = >IM = 0 EXT NEG CRY
D FFFFFFFF  FFFFFFFF  00000000  00000000  00000000  00000000  00000000  00000000
A 00000000  00000000  00000000  00000000  00000000  00000000  00000000  0001598C
```

This example uses data registers D0 and D1 as an 8-byte (64 bit) binary integer. Register D1 is the high-order part of the integer. The example complements 1 to become −1 across 64 bits.

NOP Instruction

The NOP (No OPeration) instruction provides a way for idling the 68000 for one instruction. Nothing is changed, except that the Program Counter is advanced to the next instruction. NOP instructions are often used for inserting small delays, or for providing space in a program for patching purposes.

Addressing Modes Allowed: None

Data Sizes: None

Condition Codes Affected: None

Assembler Syntax: NOP

Machine Code Format:

Bit	15	14	13	12	11	10	9	8	7	6	5	4	3	2	1	0	
	0	1	0	0	1	1	1	0	0	1	1	1	0	0	0	1	(4E71 hex)

Example:

```
PC = 000007F2 USP = 0001598C SSP = 0007BF08 ST = 0019 = >IM = 0 EXT NEG CRY
D 00000000  00000000  00000000  00000000  00000000  00000000  00000000  00000000
A 00000000  00000000  00000000  00000000  00000000  00000000  00000000  0001598C
nop
-t
PC = 000007F4 USP = 0001598C SSP = 0007BF08 ST = 0019 = >IM = 0 EXT NEG CRY
D 00000000  00000000  00000000  00000000  00000000  00000000  00000000  00000000
A 00000000  00000000  00000000  00000000  00000000  00000000  00000000  0001598C
```

NOT Instruction

Logical Op Instr   7 of 7

The NOT instruction forms the one's complement of an effective address operand.

Addressing Modes Allowed:

Dn	An	(An)	(An) +	– (An)	x(An)	x(An,xr.s)
Yes	No	Yes	Yes	Yes	Yes	Yes
x.w	**x.l**	**x(PC)**	**x(PC,xr.s)**	**#x**	**SR**	**CCR**
Yes	Yes	No	No	No	No	No

Data Sizes: byte, word, long

Condition Codes Affected:

X   Not affected.
N   Set if the result is negative. Cleared otherwise.
Z   Set if the result is zero. Cleared otherwise.
V   Always cleared.
C   Always cleared.

Assembler Syntax: NOT   <ea>

Machine Code Format:

Bit	15	14	13	12	11	10	9	8	7	6	5	4	3	2	1	0
	0	1	0	0	0	1	1	0	Size		Effective			Address		

← Mode →   ← Reg. →

The Size field is 00 for byte operations, 01 for words, and 10 for longs.

Example:

```
PC = 000007F6 USP = 0001598C SSP = 0007BF08 ST = 0010 = >IM = 0 EXT
D 00000001   00000000  00000000  00000000  00000000  00000000  00000000  00000000
A 00000000   00000000  00000000  00000000  00000000  00000000  00000000  0001598C
not D0
-t
PC = 000007F8 USP = 0001598C SSP = 0007BF08 ST = 0018 = >IM = 0 EXT NEG
D 0000FFFE   00000000  00000000  00000000  00000000  00000000  00000000  00000000
A 00000000   00000000  00000000  00000000  00000000  00000000  00000000  0001598C
```

This example takes the one's complement of the 16-bit quantity 0001 hex to form FFFE hex.

OR Instruction

Logical Op Instr

The OR instruction performs a bit-wise inclusive binary OR operation between a data register and an effective address operand. There are two forms of this instruction:

1. OR the contents of the effective address operand with a data register, leaving the result in the data register.

2. OR the contents of the effective address operand with a data register, leaving the result in the effective address operand.

Addressing Modes Allowed:

Effective address as source:

Dn	An	(An)	(An) +	– (An)	x(An)	x(An,xr.s)
Yes	No	Yes	Yes	Yes	Yes	Yes
x.w	**x.l**	**x(PC)**	**x(PC,xr.s)**	**#x**	**SR**	**CCR**
Yes	Yes	Yes	Yes	Yes	No	No

Effective address as destination:

Dn	An	(An)	(An) +	– (An)	x(An)	x(An,xr.s)
No	No	Yes	Yes	Yes	Yes	Yes
x.w	**x.l**	**x(PC)**	**x(PC,xr.s)**	**#x**	**SR**	**CCR**
Yes	Yes	No	No	No	No	No

Data Sizes: byte, word, long

Condition Codes Affected:

X   Not affected.
N   Set if the most significant bit of the result is set. Cleared otherwise.
Z   Set if the result is zero. Cleared otherwise.
V   Always cleared.
C   Always cleared.

Assembler Syntax: OR   <ea>,Dn
                  OR   Dn,<ea>

The ORI instruction is used when the source is immediate data and the destination is not a data register. Many assemblers use the ORI instruction when OR is specified with this combination of operands.

Machine Code Format:

Bit	15	14	13	12	11 10 9	8	7 6	5 4 3	2 1 0
	1	0	0	0	Register	Dr	Size	Effective	Address
								← Mode →	← Reg. →

The Register field indicates which data register is to be used. The Dr bit is 0 if the data register is the destination, and 1 if the effective address is the destination. Size is 00 for byte operations, 01 for words, and 10 for longs.

Example:

```
PC = 00000806 USP = 0001598C SSP = 0007BF08 ST = 0010 = >IM = 0 EXT
D 11111111  22222222  00000000  00000000  00000000  00000000  00000000  00000000
A 00000000  00000000  00000000  00000000  00000000  00000000  00000000  0001598C
or.l D0,D1
−t
PC = 00000808 USP = 0001598C SSP = 0007BF08 ST = 0010 = >IM = 0 EXT
D 11111111  33333333  00000000  00000000  00000000  00000000  00000000  00000000
A 00000000  00000000  00000000  00000000  00000000  00000000  00000000  0001598C
```

This example ORs the contents of registers D0 and D1, leaving the result in D1. Notice that this is the data register destination form of the instruction.

ORI Instruction

Logical Op Instr   4 of 7

The ORI (OR Immediate) performs a bit-wise OR between an immediate operand (always the source) and an effective address operand (always the destination).

Addressing Modes Allowed:

Dn	An	(An)	(An) +	− (An)	x(An)	x(An,xr.s)
Yes	No	Yes	Yes	Yes	Yes	Yes
x.w	**x.l**	**x(PC)**	**x(PC,xr.s)**	**#x**	**SR**	**CCR**
Yes	Yes	No	No	No	Yes	Yes

When the status register is specified as the destination, the S-bit in the status register must be set (i.e., the 68000 must be executing in Supervisor state).

Data Sizes: byte, word, long

Condition Codes Affected:

X   Not affected.
N   Set if the high-order bit of the result is set. Cleared otherwise.
Z   Set if the result is zero. Cleared otherwise.
V   Always cleared.
C   Always cleared.

If the status register (SR) or condition code register (CCR) is specified as the destination, the condition code bits are set according to bits 5–0 of the immediate source.

Assembler Syntax: ORI   #<data>,<ea>

Machine Code Format:

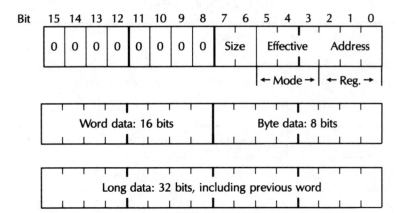

The Size field is 00 for byte data, 01 for word data, and 10 for long data.

Example:

```
PC = 00000810 USP = 0001598C SSP = 0007BF08 ST = 0010 = >IM = 0 EXT
D 11111111  00000000  00000000  00000000  00000000  00000000  00000000  00000000
A 00000000  00000000  00000000  00000000  00000000  00000000  00000000  0001598C
ori.l #$22222222,D0
 −t
PC = 00000816 USP = 0001598C SSP = 0007BF08 ST = 0010 = >IM = 0 EXT
D 33333333  00000000  00000000  00000000  00000000  00000000  00000000  00000000
A 00000000  00000000  00000000  00000000  00000000  00000000  00000000  0001598C
```

This example performs an OR operation on the contents of register D0 with a long constant.

PEA Instruction

Data Movement Instruction, #8 of 10

The PEA (Push Effective Address) instruction places a computed address on top of the stack. The size of the instruction is restricted to long data.

Addressing Modes Allowed:

Dn	An	(An)	(An) +	– (An)	x(An)	x(An,xr.s)
No	No	Yes	No	No	Yes	Yes
x.w	**x.l**	**x(PC)**	**x(PC,xr.s)**	**#x**	**SR**	**CCR**
Yes	Yes	Yes	Yes	No	No	No

Data Size: long

Condition Codes Affected: None

Assembler Syntax: PEA <ea>

Machine Code Format:

Bit	15	14	13	12	11	10	9	8	7	6	5	4	3	2	1	0
	0	1	0	0	1	0	0	0	0	1	Effective			Address		

← Mode → ← Reg. →

Example:

```
PC = 00000816 USP = 0001598C SSP = 0007BF08 ST = 0010 = >IM = 0 EXT
D 00000000  00000000  00000000  00000000  00000000  00000000  00000000  00000000
A 00000000  00000000  00000000  00000000  00000000  00000000  00000000  0001598C
pea $81E
-t
PC = 0000081C USP = 00015988 SSP = 0007BF08 ST = 0010 = >IM = 0 EXT
D 00000000  00000000  00000000  00000000  00000000  00000000  00000000  00000000
A 00000000  00000000  00000000  00000000  00000000  00000000  00000000  00015988
-sl15988
00015988 0000081E .
```

This example pushes the absolute long address 81E. The PUSH is verified by examining memory at the address contained in address register A7 after the instruction executes.

RESET Instruction

System Control.   3 of 7

The RESET instruction is a privileged operation that causes all external devices to be reset.

Addressing Modes Allowed: None

Data Sizes: unsized

Condition Codes Affected: None

Assembler Syntax: RESET

Machine Code Format:

Bit	15	14	13	12	11	10	9	8	7	6	5	4	3	2	1	0	
	0	1	0	0	1	1	1	0	0	1	1	1	0	0	0	0	(4E70 hex)

ROL Instruction

Shuft & Rotate Instr   5 of 8

The ROL (ROtate Left) instruction performs a left rotate on a data register or memory operand. There are three forms of this instruction:

1. Rotate a data register to the left by a constant contained in the instruction. Shifts from one to eight bits can be accomplished using this form of the instruction.

2. Rotate a data register to the left by the number of bits contained in another data register.

3. Rotate a memory word left by one bit only.

The Rotate operation is performed without an auxiliary bit. Bits shifted out of the high-order bit position go to both the carry bit and the low-order bit position.

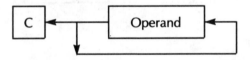

Addressing Modes Allowed: Memory form only

Dn	An	(An)	(An) +	− (An)	x(An)	x(An,xr.s)
No	No	Yes	Yes	Yes	Yes	Yes
x.w	**x.l**	**x(PC)**	**x(PC,xr.s)**	**#x**	**SR**	**CCR**
Yes	Yes	No	No	No	No	No

Data Sizes: byte, word, long

Data size is restricted to word for the in-memory form of the instruction.

Condition Codes Affected:

X Not affected.
N Set if the most significant bit of the result is set. Cleared otherwise.
Z Set if the result is zero. Cleared otherwise.
C Set according to the last bit shifted out of the operand. Cleared if the shift count is zero.
V Always cleared.

Assembler Syntax: ROL   #<count>,Dy
                  ROL   Dx,Dy
                  ROL   <ea>

Machine Code Format:

Data Register as destination:

Bit	15	14	13	12	11	10	9	8	7	6	5	4	3	2	1	0
	1	1	1	0	Immed.			1	Size		T	1	1	Register		

Memory location as destination:

Bit	15	14	13	12	11	10	9	8	7	6	5	4	3	2	1	0
	1	1	1	0	0	1	1	1	1	1	Effective			Address		
											← Mode →			← Reg. →		

The T-field determines the type of the register-destination form of the instruction. If T is 0, then the Immediate field contains the shift count, with 000 binary representing a count of 8. If T is 1, then the register number that contains the shift count is contained in the Immediate field.

Example:

```
PC = 00000830 USP = 0001598C SSP = 0007BF08 ST = 0000 = >IM = 0
D 11111111   00000000 00000000 00000000 00000000 00000000 00000000 00000000
A 00000000   00000000 00000000 00000000 00000000 00000000 00000000 0001598C
rol #3,D0
```

−t
PC = 00000832 USP = 0001598C SSP = 0007BF08 ST = <u>0008</u> = >IM = 0 <u>NEG</u>

D 11118888 00000000 00000000 00000000 00000000 00000000 00000000 00000000
A 00000000 00000000 00000000 00000000 00000000 00000000 00000000 0001598C

This instruction rotates the lower word of register D0 left by three bits. Notice that the high word of D0 is unaffected.

ROR Instruction

Shift & Rotate Inst   6 of 8

The ROR (ROtate Right) instruction performs a right rotate on a data register or memory operand. There are three forms of this instruction:

1. Rotate a data register to the right by a constant contained in the instruction. Shifts from one to eight bits can be accomplished using this form of the instruction.

2. Rotate a data register to the right by the number of bits contained in another data register.

3. Rotate a memory word right by one bit only.

The Rotate operation is performed without an auxiliary bit. Bits shifted out of the low-order bit position go to both the carry bit and the high-order bit position.

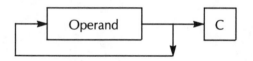

Addressing Modes Allowed: Memory form only

Dn	An	(An)	(An) +	– (An)	x(An)	x(An,xr.s)
No	No	Yes	Yes	Yes	Yes	Yes
x.w	**x.l**	**x(PC)**	**x(PC,xr.s)**	**#x**	**SR**	**CCR**
Yes	Yes	No	No	No	No	No

Data Sizes: byte, word, long

Data size is restricted to word for the in-memory form of the instruction.

Condition Codes Affected:

X Not affected.
N Set if the most significant bit of the result is set. Cleared otherwise.
Z Set if the result is zero. Cleared otherwise.
C Set according to the last bit shifted out of the operand. Cleared if the shift count is zero.
V Always cleared.

Assembler Syntax: ROR #<count>,Dy

ROR Dx,Dy

ROR <ea>

Machine Code Format:

Data Register as destination:

Bit	15	14	13	12	11 10 9	8	7 6	5	4	3	2 1 0
	1	1	1	0	Immed.	0	Size	T	1	1	Register

Memory location as destination:

Bit	15	14	13	12	11	10	9	8	7	6	5 4 3	2 1 0
	1	1	1	0	0	1	1	0	1	1	Effective	Address

← Mode → ← Reg. →

The T-field determines the type of the register-destination form of the instruction. If T is 0, then the Immediate field contains the shift count, with 000 binary representing a count of 8. If T is 1, the register number that contains the shift count is contained in the Immediate field.

Example:

```
PC = 0000083E USP = 0001598C SSP = 0007BF08 ST = 0000 = >IM = 0
D 11111111  00000000  00000000  00000000  00000000  00000000  00000000  00000000
A 00000000  00000000  00000000  00000000  00000000  00000000  00000000  0001598C
ror #3,D0
```

```
-t
PC = 00000840 USP = 0001598C SSP = 0007BF08 ST = 0000 = >IM = 0
D 11112222  00000000  00000000  00000000  00000000  00000000  00000000  00000000
A 00000000  00000000  00000000  00000000  00000000  00000000  00000000  0001598C
```

This instruction rotates the low-order word of register D0 right by three bits. The upper word of register D0 is unaffected.

ROXL Instruction

Shift & Rotate Instr   7 of 8

The ROXL (ROtate Left with eXtend) instruction performs a left rotate on a data register or memory operand. There are three forms of this instruction:

1. Rotate a data register to the left by a constant contained in the instruction. Shifts from one to eight bits can be accomplished using this form of the instruction.

2. Rotate a data register to the left by the number of bits contained in another data register.

3. Rotate a memory word left by one bit only.

The Rotate operation is performed using the X-bit as an auxiliary bit. Bits shifted out of the high-order bit position go to both the carry bit and the X-bit. The X-bit is rotated into the low-order bit position.

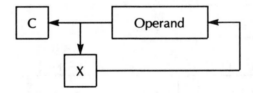

Addressing Modes Allowed: Memory form only

Dn	An	(An)	(An) +	– (An)	x(An)	x(An,xr.s)
No	No	Yes	Yes	Yes	Yes	Yes
x.w	**x.l**	**x(PC)**	**x(PC,xr.s)**	**#x**	**SR**	**CCR**
Yes	Yes	No	No	No	No	No

Data Sizes: byte, word, long

Data size is restricted to word for the in-memory form of the instruction.

Condition Codes Affected:

X Set according to the last bit shifted out of the operand. Unaffected if the shift count is zero.
N Set if the most significant bit of the result is set. Cleared otherwise.
Z Set if the result is zero. Cleared otherwise.
C Set according to the last bit shifted out of the operand. Set to the value of the X-bit if the shift count is zero.
V Always cleared.

Assembler Syntax: ROXL   #<count>,Dy
                  ROXL   Dx,Dy
                  ROXL   <ea>

Machine Code Format:

Data Register as destination:

Bit	15	14	13	12	11	10	9	8	7	6	5	4	3	2	1	0
	1	1	1	0	Immed.			1	Size		T	1	0	Register		

Memory location as destination:

Bit	15	14	13	12	11	10	9	8	7	6	5	4	3	2	1	0
	1	1	1	0	0	1	0	1	1	1	Effective			Address		
											← Mode →		← Reg. →			

The T-field determines the type of the register-destination form of the instruction. If T is 0, then the Immediate field contains the shift count, with 000 binary representing a count of 8. If T is 1, then the register number that contains the shift count is contained in the Immediate field.

Example:

```
PC = 0000084C USP = 0001598C SSP = 0007BF08 ST = 0000 = >IM = 0
D 11111111   00000000  00000000  00000000  00000000  00000000  00000000  00000000
A 00000000   00000000  00000000  00000000  00000000  00000000  00000000  0001598C
roxl #4,D0
```

```
-t
PC = 0000084E USP = 0001598C SSP = 0007BF08 ST = 0011 = >IM = 0 EXT CRY
D 11111110   00000000  00000000  00000000  00000000  00000000  00000000  00000000
A 00000000   00000000  00000000  00000000  00000000  00000000  00000000  0001598C
```

This example rotates the low-order word of register D0 to the left by four bits. The high-order word of register D0 is unaffected. The X-bit is set following the instruction.

ROXR Instruction

Shift & Rotate instr   8 of 8

The ROXR (ROtate Right with eXtend) instruction performs a right rotate on a data register or memory operand. There are three forms of this instruction:

1. Rotate a data register to the right by a constant contained in the instruction. Shifts from one to eight bits can be accomplished using this form of the instruction.

2. Rotate a data register to the right by the number of bits contained in another data register.

3 Rotate a memory word right by one bit only.

The Rotate operation is performed using the X bit as an auxiliary bit. Bits shifted out of the low-order bit position go to both the carry-bit and the X bit. The X bit is rotated into the high-order bit position.

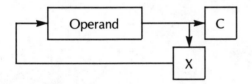

Addressing Modes Allowed: Memory form only

Dn	An	(An)	(An) +	– (An)	x(An)	x(An,xr.s)
No	No	Yes	Yes	Yes	Yes	Yes
x.w	**x.1**	**x(PC)**	**x(PC,xr.s)**	**#x**	**SR**	**CCR**
Yes	Yes	No	No	No	No	No

Data Sizes: byte, word long
Data size is restricted to word for the in-memory form of the instruction.

Condition Codes Affected:

X   Set according to the last bit shifted out of the operand. Unaffected if the shift count is zero.
N   Set if the most significant bit of the result is set. Cleared otherwise.
Z   Set if the result is zero. Cleared otherwise.
C   Set according to the last bit shifted out of the operand. Set to the value of the X-bit if the shift count is zero.
V   Always cleared.

Assembler Syntax: ROXR   #<count>,Dy
                  ROXR   Dx,Dy
                  ROXR   <ea>

Machine Code Format:

Data Register as destination:

Bit	15	14	13	12	11 10 9	8	7 6	5	4	3	2 1 0
	1	1	1	0	Immed.	0	Size	T	1	0	Register

Memory location as destination:

Bit	15	14	13	12	11	10	9	8	7	6	5 4 3	2 1 0
	1	1	1	0	0	1	0	0	1	1	Effective	Address

← Mode → ← Reg. →

The T-field determines the type of the register-destination form of the instruction. If T is 0, then the Immediate field contains the shift count, with 000 binary representing a count of 8. If T is 1, then the register number that contains the shift count is contained in the Immediate field.

Example:

```
PC = 0000085A USP = 0001598C SSP = 0007BF08 ST = 0000 = >IM = 0
D 11111111   00000000  00000000  00000000  00000000  00000000  00000000  00000000
A 00000000   00000000  00000000  00000000  00000000  00000000  00000000  0001598C
roxr #4,D0
```

```
-t
PC = 0000085C USP = 0001598C SSP = 0007BF08 ST = 0000 = >IM = 0
D 11112111  00000000 00000000 00000000 00000000 00000000 00000000 00000000
A 00000000  00000000 00000000 00000000 00000000 00000000 00000000 0001598C
```

This example rotates the low-order word of register D0 to the right by four places. The upper word of register D0 is not affected.

RTE Instruction

System Control   4 of 7

The RTE (ReTurn from Exception) is used to load the status register and the program counter (PC) with a single instruction. This type of operation is required when an operating system in supervisor mode passes control to a user program in user mode. The new contents of the status register and PC are popped off the stack. The status register is taken from the first 16-bit word on the stack, and the PC from the next 32-bit long word. The stack pointer is incremented by six bytes.

This is a privileged instruction. The processor must be in supervisor state (i.e., bit 13 of the status register must be set) at the beginning of the RTE instruction. The RTE instruction changes all the bits of the status register, so the processor might be in user mode at the *completion* of the instruction.

Condition Codes Affected:

The condition codes are all loaded from the word at the top of the stack.

Assembler Syntax: RTE

Machine Code Format:

Bit	15	14	13	12	11	10	9	8	7	6	5	4	3	2	1	0	
	0	1	0	0	1	1	1	0	0	1	1	1	0	0	1	1	(4E73 hex)

Example:

```
PC = 00000868 USP = 0001598C SSP = 0007BF08 ST = 2004 = >SUP IM = 0 ZER
D 00000000   00000000  00000000  00000000  00000000  00000000  00000000  00000000
A 00000000   00000000  00000000  00000000  00000000  00000000  00000000  0007BF08
pea $876
```

The following code pushes a new status register contents (with all the condition code bits set), and a new PC. Since the PC is lower on the stack than the status register, it must be pushed first.

Here is a disassembly of the program:

```
- I868,876
  00000868 pea $876
```

```
0000086E move #$1F, - (A7)
00000872 rte
00000874 moveq #$FF,D0
00000876 nop
```

Executing this program yields the following results

```
-g,876
PC = 00000876 USP = 0001598C SSP = 0007BF08 ST = 001F = >IM = 0 EXT NEG ZER OFL CRY
D 00000000    00000000   00000000   00000000   00000000   00000000   00000000   00000000
A 00000000    00000000   00000000   00000000   00000000   00000000   00000000   0001598C
```

Notice that the breakpoint was set on the address that the RTE instruction loads into the PC. (The debugger will not trace RTE instructions.)

This example shows how a supervisor mode program can transfer control to a user mode program. Note how register A7 reflects the supervisor stack pointer (SSP) before the RTE and the user stack pointer (USP) afterward.

RTR Instruction

Program Control 7 of 8

The RTR (ReTurn and Restore) instruction loads the condition codes and the program counter (PC) from the stack. The condition codes are loaded from the low byte from the word at the top of the stack. The high byte of this word is discarded. The PC is loaded from the long word immediately after the word containing the condition codes. The stack pointer is incremented by six by an RTR instruction.

Condition Codes Affected:

The condition codes are loaded from the first word popped from the stack.

Assembler Syntax: RTR

Machine Code Format:

Bit	15	14	13	12	11	10	9	8	7	6	5	4	3	2	1	0	
	0	1	0	0	1	1	1	0	0	1	1	1	0	1	1	1	(4E77 hex)

Example:

```
PC = 00000888 USP = 00015986 SSP = 0007BF08 ST = 0000 = >IM = 0
D 00000000   00000000 00000000 00000000 00000000 00000000 00000000 00000000
A 00000000   00000000 00000000 00000000 00000000 00000000 00000000 00015986
rtr
```

At this point, we are about to execute an RTR instruction. Using the *s* command, we will examine the information on the stack.

```
- sw15986          (Contents of A7)
00015986 001F      (New condition codes)
00015988 0000      (High word of PC)
0001598A 088C .    (Low word of PC)
- t
PC = 0000088C USP = 0001598C SSP = 0007BF08 ST = 001F = >IM = 0 EXT NEG ZER OFL CRY
D 00000000   00000000 00000000 00000000 00000000 00000000 00000000 00000000
A 00000000   00000000 00000000 00000000 00000000 00000000 00000000 0001598C
```

The stack pointer was incremented by six bytes and the PC and status register now have different contents.

RTS Instruction

Program Control 6 of 8

The RTS (ReTurn from Subroutine) instruction reverses the action of a BSR (Branch to SubRoutine) or JSR (Jump to SubRoutine) instruction. The PC is loaded from the long word at the top of the stack. This causes execution to resume at the instruction that follows the JSR or BSR instruction.

Condition Codes Affected: None

Assembler Syntax: RTS

Machine Code Format:

Bit	15	14	13	12	11	10	9	8	7	6	5	4	3	2	1	0	
	0	1	0	0	1	1	1	0	0	1	1	1	0	1	0	1	(4E75 hex)

Example:

```
PC = 0000089A USP = 00015988 SSP = 0007BF08 ST = 0000 = >IM = 0
D 00000000   00000000 00000000 00000000 00000000 00000000 00000000 00000000
A 00000000   00000000 00000000 00000000 00000000 00000000 00000000 00015988
rts
 - sl15988
00015988 0000089E .
 - t
PC = 0000089E USP = 0001598C SSP = 0007BF08 ST = 0000 = >IM = 0
D 00000000   00000000 00000000 00000000 00000000 00000000 00000000 00000000
A 00000000   00000000 00000000 00000000 00000000 00000000 00000000 0001598C
```

This RTS instruction causes a transfer to address 89E. The stack pointer is incremented by four bytes (which is the size of the address that was popped off the stack).

SBCD Instruction

Binary Coded Decimal Instruction, #3 of 3

The SBCD (Subtract BCD with extend) instruction subtracts two bytes in BCD format. The destination operand is replaced with the difference (Destination − Source − Extend bit).

Addressing Modes Allowed:

Dn	An	(An)	(An) +	− (An)	x(An)	x(An,xr.s)
Yes	No	No	No	Yes	No	No
x.w	**x.l**	**x(PC)**	**x(PC,xr.s)**	**#x**	**SR**	**CCR**
No	No	No	No	No	No	No

There are two forms of this instruction:

1. Subtract data register from a data register (Dn addressing modes). The low-order bytes of two data registers are subtracted and the result stored in the destination register.

2. Subtract memory to memory. This form of the instruction allows multiple bytes to be subtracted. The only valid addressing mode is − (An). Since the 68000 stores BCD data with the highest byte first, to subtract multibyte quantities, one must start at the highest address and work down. (Hence the use of pre-decrement addressing.) if there is a carry out of the most significant BCD digit in the byte, each instruction sets the X bit. The X bit is then subtracted from the next pair of bytes.

Data Sizes: byte only

Condition Codes Affected:

X   Set by a borrow-out of the most significant BCD digit.
N   Undefined.
Z   Cleared if result is not zero. Unchanged otherwise.

V   Undefined.

C   Set by a borrow-out of the most significant BCD digit.

The Z bit is cleared if the result is not zero. Not setting the bit when the result of the present byte is zero allows the Z bit to be accurate after a series of SBCD instructions is executed. The Z bit must be set before beginning such a series. (Comparing a register to itself is an easy way to set the Z bit.) The N and V bits are undefined as a result of this instruction.

Assembler Syntax: SBCD   Dx,Dy
                   SBCD   – (Ax), – (Ay)

Machine Code Format:

Bit	15	14	13	12	11 10 9	8	7	6	5	4	3	2 1 0
	1	0	0	0	D. Reg	1	0	0	0	0	F	S. Reg.

The D. Reg and S. Reg fields specify the destination and source register numbers, respectively. If the F (format) bit is 0, then the registers are data registers. If the F bit is a 1, then the registers are address registers, and the pre-decrement addressing mode is used.

Example:

```
PC = 00000510 USP = 0001598C SSP = 0007BF08 ST = 0000 = >IM = 0
D 00000000  00000000  00000000  00000000  00000000  00000000  00000000  00000000
A 00000518  0000051A  00000000  00000000  00000000  00000000  00000000  0001598C
sbcd – (A0), – (A1)
– d516,519
00000516 00 01 01 00                                                        ....
– t
PC = 00000512 USP = 0001598C SSP = 0007BF08 ST = 0019 = >IM = 0 EXT NEG CRY
D 00000000  00000000  00000000  00000000  00000000  00000000  00000000  00000000
A 00000517  00000519  00000000  00000000  00000000  00000000  00000000  0001598C
sbcd – (A0), – (A1)
– d516,519
00000516 00 01 01 99                                                        ....
– t
PC = 00000514 USP = 0001598C SSP = 0007BF08 ST = 0000 = >IM = 0
D 00000000  00000000  00000000  00000000  00000000  00000000  00000000  00000000
A 00000516  00000518  00000000  00000000  00000000  00000000  00000000  0001598C
– d516,519
00000516 00 01 00 99                                                        ....
```

This example illustrates how to do a multiprecision BCD subtraction operation. A two-byte subtraction operation is executed, subtracting 1 from 100 to obtain 99. The operands are displayed using the *d* command after each step of the process. Notice the action of the borrow.

Scc Instruction

Program Control   *8 of 8*

The Scc instruction sets a byte specified by an effective address operand to all ones if a specified condition is true. The byte is cleared if the condition is false. The permissible instructions are:

SCC   Set <ea> if the C-bit (carry) is clear.

SCS   Set <ea> if the C-bit is set.

SEQ   Set<ea> on EQual. The byte is set if the Z- bit is set.

SGE   Set <ea> on Greater than or Equal. The byte is set if the N (negative) and V (overflow) bits are either both set or both clear. SGE is used for two's complement binary numbers.

SGT   Set <ea> on Greater Than. The byte is set if:

- The N and V bits are both set *and* the Z-bit is clear, or,
- The N, V, and Z-bits are *all* clear.

SHI   Set <ea> on HIgher than. The byte is set if the C and Z bits are both clear. SHI is similar to SGT, except it works on unsigned numbers.

SLE   Set <ea> on Less than or Equal. The byte is set if:

- The Z-bit is set, or,

- The N-bit is set *and* the V-bit is clear, or,

- The N-bit is clear *and* the V-bit is set.

The SLE instruction is used for two's complement binary numbers.

SLS   Set <ea> on Lower or Same.
The byte is set if either the C or Z bits are set. SLS is similar to the SLE instruction, except it works on unsigned numbers.

SLT   Set <ea> on Less Than. The byte is set if:
- The N-bit is set and the V-bit is clear, or,
- The N-bit is clear and the V-bit is set.

SMI   Set <ea> on MInus. The byte is set if the N-bit is set.

SNE   Set <ea> on Not Equal. The byte is set if the Z-bit is clear.

SPL   Set <ea> on Plus. The byte is set if the N-bit is clear.

SVC   Set <ea> on V Clear. The byte is set if the V-bit is clear, indicating no overflow.

SVS   Set <ea> on V Set. The byte is set if the V-bit is set, indicating overflow.

SF   Never set <ea>.

ST   Always set <ea>.

Addressing Modes Allowed:

Dn	An	(An)	(An) +	– (An)	x(An)	x(An,xr.s)
Yes	No	Yes	Yes	Yes	Yes	Yes
x.w	**x.l**	**x(PC)**	**x(PC,xr.s)**	**#x**	**SR**	**CCR**
Yes	Yes	No	No	No	No	No

Data Size: byte

Condition Codes Affected: None

Assembler Syntax: Scc   <ea>

Machine Code Format:

15	14	13	12	11	10	9	8	7	6	5	4	3	2	1	0
	0	1	0	1	Condition			1	1	Effective			Address		

← Mode → ← Reg. →

The Condition is a four-bit encoding of the condition code combination. The conditions are as follows:

Condition	Instruction	Condition	Instruction
0000	ST	1000	SVC
0001	SF	1001	SVS
0010	SHI	1010	SPL
0011	SLS	1011	SMI
0100	SCC	1100	SGE
0101	SCS	1101	SLT
0110	SNE	1110	SGT
0111	SEQ	1111	SLE

Example:

```
PC = 000008BC USP = 0001598C SSP = 0007BF08 ST = 0000 = >IM = 0
D 00000001   00000002  00000000  00000000  00000000  00000000  00000000  00000000
A 00000000   00000000  00000000  00000000  00000000  00000000  00000000  0001598C
cmp.l D0,D1
-t
PC = 000008BE USP = 0001598C SSP = 0007BF08 ST = 0000 = >IM = 0
D 00000001   00000002  00000000  00000000  00000000  00000000  00000000  00000000
A 00000000   00000000  00000000  00000000  00000000  00000000  00000000  0001598C
slt D2
-t
PC = 000008C0 USP = 0001598C SSP = 0007BF08 ST = 0000 = >IM = 0
D 00000001   00000002  00000000  00000000  00000000  00000000  00000000  00000000
A 00000000   00000000  00000000  00000000  00000000  00000000  00000000  0001598C
sgt D2
-t
PC = 000008C2 USP = 0001598C SSP = 0007BF08 ST = 0000 = >IM = 0
D 00000001   00000002  000000FF  00000000  00000000  00000000  00000000  00000000
A 00000000   00000000  00000000  00000000  00000000  00000000  00000000  0001598C
```

This example illustrates the use of the Scc instruction with a compare instruction. Since the value in register D1 is greater than the value in register D0, the SLT instruction *did not* set D2, and the SGT instruction *did* set D2. With the Scc instruction, as with the Bcc and DBcc instructions, the operands of a compare instruction must be read in reverse order.

STOP Instruction

System Control   5 of 7

The STOP instruction provides a way to simultaneously enable interrupts and to wait for an interrupt to occur. Other processors, notably the PDP-11, had separate instructions for enabling interrupts and for waiting for interrupts. An interrupt between the enabling instruction and the waiting instruction could result in waiting for an interrupt that has already occurred.

The STOP instruction is a privileged instruction and is used only by code that must service interrupts. The Supervisor bit in the status register must be set at the beginning of the instruction. The contents of a 16-bit immediate data field are loaded into the Status Register. Bit 13 (which corresponds to the S-bit in the status register) of the immediate data must be set or a privilege violation exception will occur. See Chapter 7 on Exception Processing for additional information.

Addressing Modes Allowed: None

Data Size: unsized

Condition Codes Affected:
   The condition codes are set from bits 5–0 of the immediate operand.

Assembler Syntax: STOP   #<data>

Machine Code Format:

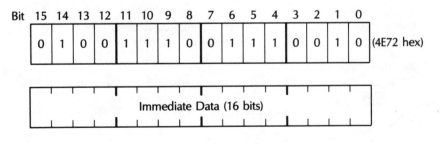

Bit	15	14	13	12	11	10	9	8	7	6	5	4	3	2	1	0	
	0	1	0	0	1	1	1	0	0	1	1	1	0	0	1	0	(4E72 hex)

Immediate Data (16 bits)

SUB Instruction

Integer Arith Op Instr   18 of 24

The SUB (SUBtract binary) instruction subtracts a source operand from a destination operand and stores the result in the destination operand. There are two forms of this instruction:

1. Subtract an effective address operand from a data register.

2. Subtract a data register from an effective address operand.

Addressing Modes Allowed:

All Addressing modes (except SR and CCR) are allowed when the effective address specifies a source operand. When the effective address field is the destination, then the following addressing modes are allowed:

Dn	An	(An)	(An) +	– (An)	x(An)	x(An,xr.s)
No	No	Yes	Yes	Yes	Yes	Yes
x.w	**x.l**	**x(PC)**	**x(PC,xr.s)**	**#x**	**SR**	**CCR**
Yes	Yes	No	No	No	No	No

Using a data register as a destination must be accomplished using the register destination form of the instruction.

Data Sizes: byte, word, long

Using an address register as the source is valid only for word and long data lengths.

Condition Codes Affected:

X   Set by borrow out of most significant bit. Cleared otherwise.
N   Set if high-order bit of result was 1. Cleared otherwise.
Z   Set if result is zero. Cleared otherwise.
C   Set by borrow-out of most significant bit. Cleared otherwise.
V   Set if operation resulted in overflow condition. Cleared otherwise.

Assembler Syntax: SUB   Dn,<ea>
                      SUB   <ea>,Dn

The SUBA instruction is used when the destination is an address register. The SUBI and SUBQ instructions are used when the source is immediate data. Many assemblers will accept the SUB mnemonic for these instructions, and choose the correct instruction based on the operands.

Machine Code Format:

Bit	15	14	13	12	11 10 9	8	7 6	5 4 3	2 1 0
	1	0	0	1	Register	D	Size	Effective	Address
								← Mode →	← Reg. →

The Register field gives the data register that must be one of the operands. The D bit is 0 if the Register field is the destination operand, and 1 if the effective address is the destination.

The Size field is 00 for byte, 01 for word, and 10 for long operands.

Example:

```
PC = 000008CE USP = 0001598C SSP = 0007BF08 ST = 0000 = >IM = 0
D 00000002   00000001  00000000  00000000  00000000  00000000  00000000  00000000
A 00000000   00000000  00000000  00000000  00000000  00000000  00000000  0001598C
sub.l D1,D0
-t
PC = 000008D0 USP = 0001598C SSP = 0007BF08 ST = 0000 = >IM = 0
D 00000001   00000001  00000000  00000000  00000000  00000000  00000000  00000000
A 00000000   00000000  00000000  00000000  00000000  00000000  00000000  0001598C
```

This instruction subtracts 1 from 2 to form 1. When both operands are data registers, the data register destination form of the instruction is used.

SUBA Instruction

Integer Arith Op Instr.   19 of 24

The SUBA instruction does a binary subtraction operation with an address register destination. In order to allow address computations to be freely intermixed with data operations, this instruction does not affect the condition codes.

The source operand is subtracted from the address register. The result is placed in the address register.

Addressing Modes Allowed:

Dn	An	(An)	(An) +	– (An)	x(An)	x(An,xr.s)
Yes	Yes	Yes	Yes	Yes	Yes	Yes
x.w	**x.l**	**x(PC)**	**x(PC,xr.s)**	**#x**	**SR**	**CCR**
Yes	Yes	Yes	Yes	Yes	No	No

All addressing modes are allowed, except SR and CCR. The effective address must be the source operand.

Data Sizes: word, long

The SUBA operation always affects all 32 bits of the destination address register.

Condition Codes Affected: None

Assembler Syntax: SUBA   <ea>,An

Many assemblers will generate a SUBA instruction if a SUB instruction is specified with an address register as the destination operand.

Machine Code Format:

Bit	15	14	13	12	11	10	9	8	7	6	5	4	3	2	1	0
	1	0	0	1	Register			S	1	1	Effective			Address		

| ← Mode → | ← Reg. → |

The Register field gives the address register to be used as the destination operand. The S-bit is 1 for long operands and 0 for word operands.

Example:

```
PC = 000008D8 USP = 0001598C SSP = 0007BF08 ST = 0000 = >IM = 0
D 00000000   00000000  00000000  00000000  00000000  00000000  00000000  00000000
A 000008DC   00000000  00000000  00000000  00000000  00000000  00000000  0001598C
suba #$22,A0
-t
PC = 000008DC USP = 0001598C SSP = 0007BF08 ST = 0000 = >IM = 0
D 00000000   00000000  00000000  00000000  00000000  00000000  00000000  00000000
A 000008BA   00000000  00000000  00000000  00000000  00000000  00000000  0001598C
```

This example subtracts a constant 22 hex from the address contained in address register A0.

SUBI Instruction

Integer Arith Op Instr, #20 of 24

The SUBI instruction subtracts an immediate quantity from an effective address operand. The result is left in the effective address operand.

Addressing Modes Allowed:

Dn	An	(An)	(An) +	– (An)	x(An)	x(An,xr.s)
Yes	No	Yes	Yes	Yes	Yes	Yes
x.w	**x.l**	**x(PC)**	**x(PC,xr.s)**	**#x**	**SR**	**CCR**
Yes	Yes	No	No	No	No	No

Data Sizes: byte, word, long

Condition Codes Affected:

X   Set on borrow out of high-order bit. Cleared otherwise.

N   Set if high-order bit of result is set. Cleared otherwise.

Z   Set if result is zero. Cleared otherwise.

C   Set on borrow out of high-order bit. Cleared otherwise.

V   Set on overflow condition. Cleared otherwise.

Assembler Syntax: SUBI   #x, <ea>

Most assemblers automatically choose the SUBI instruction if the source operand of a SUB instruction is immediate.

Machine Code Format:

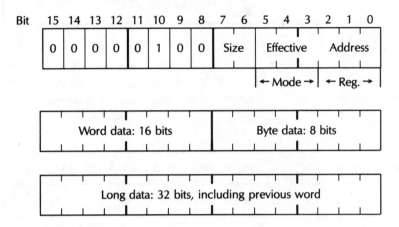

The Size field is 00 for byte operands, 01 for words, and 10 for longs.

Example:

```
PC = 000008E4 USP = 0001598C SSP = 0007BF08 ST = 0000 = >IM = 0
D 00000100  00000000  00000000  00000000  00000000  00000000  00000000  00000000
A 00000000  00000000  00000000  00000000  00000000  00000000  00000000  0001598C
subi.l #$10,D0
 −t
PC = 000008EA USP = 0001598C SSP = 0007BF08 ST = 0000 = >IM = 0
D 000000F0  00000000  00000000  00000000  00000000  00000000  00000000  00000000
 A 00000000  00000000  00000000  00000000  00000000  00000000  00000000  0001598C
```

This instruction subtracts the constant 10 hex (16 decimal) from data register D0.

SUBQ Instruction

Integer Arith Op Instruc   21 of 24

The SUBQ instruction subtracts a three-bit immediate value from an effective address operand. This allows you to subtract a small number from a register or memory address using a small, fast instruction.

Addressing Modes Allowed:

Dn	An	(An)	(An)+	–(An)	x(An)	x(An,xr.s)
Yes	Yes	Yes	Yes	Yes	Yes	Yes
x.w	**x.l**	**x(PC)**	**x(PC,xr.s)**	**#x**	**SR**	**CCR**
Yes	Yes	No	No	No	No	No

Data Sizes: byte, word, long
When an address register is used as the destination, only word and long sizes are allowed.

Condition Codes Affected:

X   Set on borrow out of high-order bit position. Cleared otherwise.

N   Set if high-order bit of result is set. Cleared otherwise.

V   Set on overflow. Cleared otherwise.

Z   Set if result is zero. Cleared otherwise.

C   Set on borrow out of high-order bit position. Cleared otherwise.

No condition codes are affected if an address register is used as the destination operand.

Assembler Syntax: SUBQ   #<data>,<ea>
                  #<data> is a constant number in the range
                  1 to 8.

Machine Code Format:

Bit	15	14	13	12	11 10 9	8	7 6	5 4 3	2 1 0
	0	1	0	1	Data	1	Size	Effective	Address
								← Mode →	← Reg. →

Data is a three-bit immediate field, with 000 representing 8, 001–111 representing 1–7. Size is 00 for byte operations, 01 for word, and 10 for long operations.

Example:

```
PC = 000008EE USP = 0001598C SSP = 0007BF08 ST = 0000 = >IM = 0
D 00000001   00000000  00000000  00000000  00000000  00000000  00000000  00000000
A 00000000   00000000  00000000  00000000  00000000  00000000  00000000  0001598C
subq.l #$2,D0
−t
PC = 000008F0 USP = 0001598C SSP = 0007BF08 ST = 0019 = >IM = 0 EXT NEG CRY
D FFFFFFFF   00000000  00000000  00000000  00000000  00000000  00000000  00000000
A 00000000   00000000  00000000  00000000  00000000  00000000  00000000  0001598C
```

This example subtracts 2 from 1 (in data register D0) to form −1.

SUBX Instruction

Integer Arithmetic Op Instr , 22 of 24

The SUBX (SUBtract eXtended) instruction executes multiple precision subtraction operations. Integers of any length can be subtracted using the SUB and SUBX instructions. This makes it possible to represent numbers much larger than the 32-bit longword allows.

There are two forms of this instruction:

1. Subtract a data register from a data register.

2. Subtract a memory location from a memory location. The – (An) addressing mode is used for both the source and destination in this form.

In both cases, the difference (Destination – Source – X-bit) is placed in the destination operand.

Addressing Modes Allowed:

Dn	An	(An)	(An) +	– (An)	x(An)	x(An,xr.s)
Yes	No	No	No	Yes	No	No
x.w	**x.l**	**x(PC)**	**x(PC,xr.s)**	**#x**	**SR**	**CCR**
No	No	No	No	No	No	No

Data Sizes: byte, word, long

Condition Codes Affected:

- X   Set on borrow out of high-order bit. Cleared otherwise.
- N   Set if result is negative. Cleared otherwise.
- Z   Cleared if result is not zero. Unchanged otherwise.
- C   Set on carry out of high-order bit. Cleared otherwise.
- V   Set on overflow condition. Cleared otherwise.

The Z bit is not set if the result is zero, but it is cleared if the result is not zero. This property of the instruction allows the Z bit to correctly indicate the result of a multiprecision subtraction operation. The Z bit must be set before subtraction begins, however. (This can be done with a MOVE to CCR, or by comparing a register to itself. The latter instruction is two bytes shorter.)

Assembler Syntax: SUBX   Dy,Dx
                    SUBX   − (Ay), − (Ax)

Machine Code Format:

Bit	15	14	13	12	11 10 9	8	7 6 5	4	3	2 1 0
	1	0	0	1	Reg. Rx	1	Size	0	0 T	Reg. Ry

The Reg. Rx and Reg. Ry fields contain the destination and source register numbers, respectively. The size field is 00 for byte operations, 01 for word, and 10 for long operations. The T (type) bit is 0 for the data register to data register form of the instruction. The Reg. Rx and Reg. Ry fields identify data registers in this case. The T-bit is 1 for the memory to memory form of the instruction. The Rx and Ry fields identify the address registers used by the pre-decrement addressing mode for this form.

Example:

```
PC = 000008FE USP = 0001558C SSP = 0007BF08 ST = 0004 = >IM = 0 ZER
D 00000001   00000000  00000000  00000001  00000000  00000000  00000000  00000000
A 00000000   00000000  00000000  00000000  00000000  00000000  00000000  0001558C
subx.l D3,D1
-t
PC = 00000900 USP = 0001558C SSP = 0007BF08 ST = 0019 = >IM = 0 EXT NEG CRY
D 00000001   FFFFFFFF  00000000  00000001  00000000  00000000  00000000  00000000
A 00000000   00000000  00000000  00000000  00000000  00000000  00000000  0001558C
subx.l D2,D0
-t
PC = 00000902 USP = 0001558C SSP = 0007BF08 ST = 0000 = >IM = 0
D 00000000   FFFFFFFF  00000000  00000001  00000000  00000000  00000000  00000000
A 00000000   00000000  00000000  00000000  00000000  00000000  00000000  0001558C
```

This operation subtracts the register pair (D2,D3) from the register pair (D0,D1). The high-order longword of each pair is contained in the even numbered register. The example shows that (1,0) − (0,1) is (0,FFFFFFFF).

SWAP Instruction

Data Movement Instruction, # 9 of 10

The SWAP instruction exchanges the 16-bit words in a data register. Bits 31–16 are exchanged with bits 15–0.

Addressing Modes Allowed: Dn only

Data Size: word

Condition Codes Affected:

X   Not affected.
N   Set if bit 31 of the result is set. Cleared otherwise.
Z   Set if all 32 bits of the register are zero. Cleared otherwise.
V   Always cleared.
C   Always cleared.

Assembler Syntax: SWAP   Dn

Machine Code Format:

Bit	15	14	13	12	11	10	9	8	7	6	5	4	3	2	1	0
	0	1	0	0	1	0	0	0	0	1	0	0	0	Register		

The Register field specifies which data register is to be swapped.

Example:

```
-x
PC = 0000090A USP = 0001558C SSP = 0007BF08 ST = 0000 = >IM = 0
D 11112222  00000000  00000000  00000000  00000000  00000000  00000000  00000000
A 00000000  00000000  00000000  00000000  00000000  00000000  00000000  0001558C
swap D0
-t
PC = 0000090C USP = 0001558C SSP = 0007BF08 ST = 0000 = >IM = 0
D 22221111  00000000  00000000  00000000  00000000  00000000  00000000  00000000
A 00000000  00000000  00000000  00000000  00000000  00000000  00000000  0001558C
```

This example swaps the words in data register D0.

TAS Instruction

Integer Arithmetic Op Instruc, #23 of 24

The TAS (Test And Set) instruction tests a byte specified by an effective address operand. The high-order bit of the byte is set to 1. The N- and Z-bits are set according to the value of the byte *before* the operation. The operation is indivisible, using a read-modify-write memory operation.

The TAS operation provides synchronization when two or more CPU chips have access to the same area of memory. Since TAS is indivisible, a processor can claim a resource and mark it as claimed before another processor can test the memory location. If the operation were not indivisible, two processors could test the flag and set it in such a way that they both assess the resource as free and claim it erroneously. The TAS instruction guarantees that one processor will win and all others lose.

Addressing Modes Allowed:

Dn	An	(An)	(An) +	– (An)	x(An)	x(An,xr.s)
Yes	No	Yes	Yes	Yes	Yes	Yes

x.w	x.l	x(PC)	x(PC,xr.s)	#x	SR	CCR
Yes	Yes	No	No	No	No	No

A TAS operation on a data register (which is allowed) is of no value for synchronization purposes.

Data Size: byte

Condition Codes Affected:

- X Not affected.
- N Set if the high-order bit of the operand is set prior to the operation. Cleared otherwise.
- Z Set if all bits of the operand are zero prior to the operation. Cleared otherwise.
- V Always cleared.
- C Always cleared.

Assembler Syntax: TAS   <ea>

Machine Code Format:

Bit	15	14	13	12	11	10	9	8	7	6	5	4	3	2	1	0
	0	1	0	0	1	0	1	0	1	1	Effective			Address		

← Mode →   ← Reg. →

Example:

```
PC = 0000090C USP = 0001558C SSP = 0007BF08 ST = 0000 = >IM = 0
D 00000000   00000000   00000000   00000000   00000000   00000000   00000000   00000000
A 00000000   00000000   00000000   00000000   00000000   00000000   00000000   0001558C
tas $97C
 -s97c
0000097C 00 .
 -t
PC = 00000912 USP = 0001558C SSP = 0007BF08 ST = 0004 = >IM = 0 ZER
D 00000000   00000000   00000000   00000000   00000000   00000000   00000000   00000000
A 00000000   00000000   00000000   00000000   00000000   00000000   00000000   0001558C
 -s97c
0000097C 80 .
```

This example executes a TAS operation on memory location 97C. The memory location contained zero before the operation and 80 hex afterward. The Z-bit is set, indicating that the operand *was* zero initially.

TRAP Instruction

System Control   6 of 7

The TRAP instruction stacks the PC and the status register on the supervisor mode stack. The Processor is switched to supervisor state, and the PC is taken from one of sixteen trap vectors specified by a four-bit quantity in the TRAP instruction.

This instruction is normally used by user mode programs to call supervisor mode programs (such as operating systems). The TRAP instruction provides a method for the user mode program to request an operating system function, such as I/O, without having to know where the operating system is located in memory.

Condition Codes Affected: None

Assembler Syntax: TRAP   #<vector>

Machine Code Format:

Bit	15	14	13	12	11	10	9	8	7	6	5	4	3	2	1	0	
	0	1	0	0	1	1	1	0	0	1	0	0		Vector			(4E4x hex)

Vectors used by the trap instruction are located at the following absolute memory locations:

Vector	Address	Vector	Address
0	80	8	A0
1	84	9	A4
2	88	10	A8
3	8C	11	AC
4	90	12	B0
5	94	13	B4
6	98	14	B8
7	9C	15	BC

TRAPV Instruction

System Control   7 of 7

The TRAPV instruction tests for overflow. The TRAPV instruction does nothing if the V-bit is clear. If the V-bit is set, the PC and the status register are pushed onto the stack, and a new PC is loaded from absolute location 1C hex. The CPU is switched into Supervisor state. This action is called a TRAPV exception.

The TRAPV instruction is used after computations in which an overflow condition would result in meaningless data. Many high-level languages use this instruction to detect overflow.

Data Size: unsized

Condition Codes Affected: None

Assembler Syntax: TRAPV

Machine Code Format:

Bit	15	14	13	12	11	10	9	8	7	6	5	4	3	2	1	0	
	0	1	0	0	1	1	1	0	0	1	1	1	0	1	1	0	(4E76)

TST Instruction

Integer Arith Op Instruc, #24 of 24

The TST instruction tests an effective address operand for negative or zero. The results are not saved, except that the condition codes are set appropriately.

Addressing Modes Allowed:

Dn	An	(An)	(An) +	– (An)	x(An)	x(An,xr.s)
Yes	No	Yes	Yes	Yes	Yes	Yes
x.w	**x.l**	**x(PC)**	**x(PC,xr.s)**	**#x**	**SR**	**CCR**
Yes	Yes	No	No	No	No	No

Data Sizes: byte, word, long

Condition Codes Affected:

- X   Not affected.
- N   Set if the high-order bit of the operand is set. Cleared otherwise.
- Z   Set if the operand is zero. Cleared otherwise.
- V   Always cleared.
- C   Always cleared.

Assembler Syntax: TST   <ea>

Machine Code Format:

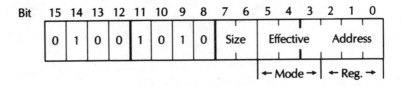

Bit	15	14	13	12	11	10	9	8	7	6	5 4 3	2 1 0
	0	1	0	0	1	0	1	0	Size		Effective	Address
											← Mode →	← Reg. →

Size is 00 to test a byte, 01 for a word, and 10 for a long.

Example:

```
PC = 00000918 USP = 0001558C SSP = 0007BF08 ST = 0004 = >IM = 0 ZER
D 00000001   00000000   00000000   00000000   00000000   00000000   00000000   00000000
A 00000000   00000000   00000000   00000000   00000000   00000000   00000000   0001558C
tst.l D0
 −t
PC = 0000091A USP = 0001558C SSP = 0007BF08 ST = 0000 = >IM = 0
D 00000001   00000000   00000000   00000000   00000000   00000000   00000000   00000000
A 00000000   00000000   00000000   00000000   00000000   00000000   00000000   0001558C
tst.l D1
 −t
PC = 0000091C USP = 0001558C SSP = 0007BF08 ST = 0004 = >IM = 0 ZER
D 00000001   00000000   00000000   00000000   00000000   00000000   00000000   00000000
A 00000000   00000000   00000000   00000000   00000000   00000000   00000000   0001558C
```

This example shows two TST instructions: one on a register that is non-zero and one on a register that is zero.

UNLK Instruction

Data Movement Instruction, #10 of 10

The UNLK (UNLinK) instruction frees a stack frame that was allocated previously by a LINK instruction. (See the description of the LINK instruction.) The instruction works like this:

The specified address register (normally the frame pointer) is placed in the stack pointer. A long word is then popped off the stack into the address register. This is exactly the opposite of the action of the LINK operation. The UNLK instruction functions properly regardless of stack PUSHes and POPs between the LINK and UNLK instructions.

Data Size: unsized

Condition Codes Affected: None

Assembler Syntax: UNLK   An

Machine Code Format:

Bit	15	14	13	12	11	10	9	8	7	6	5	4	3	2	1	0
	0	1	0	0	1	1	1	0	0	1	0	1	1	Register		

The Register field is the address register specified as the frame pointer.

Example:

```
PC = 0000091E USP = 0001558C SSP = 0007BF08 ST = 0004 = >IM = 0 ZER
D 00000000   00000000  00000000  00000000  00000000  00000000  00000000  00000000
A 00000000   00000000  00000000  00000000  00000000  00000000  00000000  0001558C
link A0,#$FFF4
-t
PC = 00000922 USP = 0001557C SSP = 0007BF08 ST = 0004 = >IM = 0 ZER
D 00000000   00000000  00000000  00000000  00000000  00000000  00000000  00000000
A 00015588   00000000  00000000  00000000  00000000  00000000  00000000  0001557C
-sl15588
00015588 00000000 . (Old A0 contents)
PC = 00000924 USP = 0001557C SSP = 0007BF08 ST = 0004 = >IM = 0 ZER
D 00000000   00000000  00000000  00000000  00000000  00000000  00000000  00000000
A 00015588   00000000  00000000  00000000  00000000  00000000  00000000  0001557C
unlk A0
```

```
-t
PC = 00000926 USP = 0001558C SSP = 0007BF08 ST = 0004 = >IM = 0 ZER
D 00000000   00000000   00000000   00000000   00000000   00000000   00000000   00000000
A 00000000   00000000   00000000   00000000   00000000   00000000   00000000   0001558C
```

This example shows a typical pair of LINK and UNLK instructions. The LINK instruction pushes sixteen bytes (four for the address register and twelve specified by the link instruction), which are in turned popped by the UNLK instruction.

SUMMARY

In this chapter we have covered:

1. The 68000 instruction classes

2. Program development mechanics

3. The 68000 instruction set

This material is primarily for reference in later chapters. It is important that you at least know how to generate a program on your system before continuing, however.

EXERCISES

1. Use your own computer to run the program shown in Listing 3.1.

2. Learn how to make backup copies of your files on your system.

3. Why do the ADDX and SUBX instructions use the pre-decrement (−(An)) addressing mode while CMPM uses the post-increment ((An)+) addressing mode?

4. Why won't the debugger trace RTE instructions? What other instructions will the debugger fail to trace?

Simple Programs

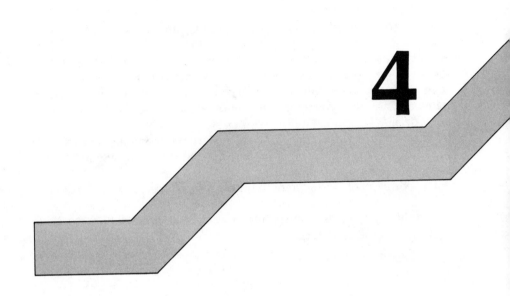

INTRODUCTION

Now that we've been over the necessary background material, we can start to write programs for the 68000 in earnest. Computer programming is the art of combining a small number of simple concepts to produce something both innovative and functional, much as an artist combines oils and canvas to produce a painting. The materials of computer programming are relatively commonplace and simple. What you can create with them is limited only by your own ability and imagination.

DISPLAYING A LINE ON THE TERMINAL

Let's begin by writing a routine that displays a line of text on the CRT terminal (or screen). There are two basic techniques we can use to perform this task. We could read the computer's hardware manual, see how the terminal interface is programmed, and then write a program that deals with the terminal at a hardware level. This is not a terribly difficult task, but it has the disadvantage of working on only one brand of computer (or worse, a particular model of one brand of computer).

An alternate technique is to write a program that uses the computer's operating system to display a line of text for us. This method has the advantage that it will work on any machine that runs the operating system for which we write our program. This is, in fact, the reason operating systems exist: programs can be written that can run on widely disparate hardware, and the programmer need not be concerned with most hardware details.

We will return to the topic of hardware-level programming in Chapters 7 and 8. system. But for now, we will use the operating system for the service it is intended to provide.

The operation of our program to print a string works something like this:

1. If any characters remain in the string to be printed, print the next one. Otherwise, quit.

2. Go back to step 1.

One implementation of this program is shown in Listing 4.1.

```
 1                          ******************************************
 2                          *
 3                          * This program prints "Hello World" on
 4                          * a CP/M-68K system.
 5                          *
 6                          ******************************************
 7                          start:
 8 00000000 41F900000000            lea      string,a0 * a0 -> string
 9 00000006 1218       loop:        move.b   (a0)+,d1  * d1 = next character
10 00000008 6708                    beq      done      * If eq, then quit
11 0000000A 303C0002                move.w   #2,d0     * Print char code
12 0000000E 4E42                    trap     #2        * Call CP/M
13 00000010 60F4                    bra      loop      * Repeat until done
14 00000012 4E75       done:        rts                * Exit to CP/M
15 00000000                         .data
16 00000000 48656C6C6F20 string: .dc.b  'Hello World',13,10,0
```

Listing 4.1 – CP/M-68K string-print routine

The program generally works like this:

- line 8. Address register A0 is initialized to the address of the string to be printed.
- lines 9–10. Data register D1 is loaded with the next character to be printed. If this character has the binary value zero, then the program returns to CP/M-68K (line 14).
- lines 11–12. The character in D1 is printed on the terminal.
- line 13. The program branches back to line 9 to print the next character.

To print a character on the terminal under CP/M-68K, you first load the character to be printed into register D1 and the constant 2 into register D0, and then execute a *trap #2* instruction.

This program uses a zero byte to indicate the end of a string. The loop that prints one character at a time terminates when the *move.b* instruction into D1 loads the register with a zero byte, causing the Z flag to be set. The subsequent beq instruction causes a branch to the label done, thereby terminating the program.

Bytes 13 and 10 at the end of the Hello World text string (line 16) are used to move the terminal cursor to the beginning of the next line. A character with the decimal value of 13 is defined as a *carriage return,* and causes the terminal cursor to move to the leftmost character position on the current line. A character with decimal value of 10 is defined as a *line feed* and causes the cursor to move to the next line. Most terminals require both a carriage return and a line feed to position the cursor at the beginning of the next line.

The same program under UNIX is shown in Listing 4.2.

Lines 6–12 instruct the UNIX system to print the string to standard output (file descriptor 1), which in UNIX is the terminal. Lines 13–15 cause the program to exit to the operating system.

The sequence for calling the system shown here is for a system by Motorola called UNIDOS. This is a UNIX-like operating system that has UNIX-compatible system calls. Each 68000 UNIX or UNIX-like system uses slightly different conventions for calling the operating system. These conventions can usually be found in their system manuals.

For each line that is to be printed, UNIX requires a single line-feed character at the end of the line. This accounts for the value 10 in line 17. Sending a line feed (called a *newline* in UNIX documentation) to the terminal under UNIX causes both a carriage return and a line feed to be sent to the output device.

PROGRAM PORTABILITY

One of the major concerns facing an applications programmer today is the number of machines on which his program will run, particularly for programs to be made available to the public. A program that runs on a large number of machines and operating systems is said to be a *portable* program.

Achieving Program Portability Across Operating Systems

It is possible to write a program that runs on any machine that supports the chosen operating system when you use a machine language program in conjunction with that operating system. Listings 4.1 and 4.2 fall into this category. In most instances, you may take the *load file* from one machine and directly execute that file on another machine that uses the same operating system. This is called *object-code portability.*

```
 1                              ***************************************
 2                              * This Program prints "Hello, World"
 3                              * on a UNIDOS System.
 4                              ***************************************
 5  00000000                            .text
 6  00000000 3F3C000E          start:   move.w   #length,-(a7)  * Push length
 7  00000004 487900000000               pea      string         * Push address
 8  0000000A 3F3C0001                   move.w   #1, -(a7)       * Push file description
 9  0000000E 204F                       move.l   a7,a0          * Copy stack
10  00000010 7004                       move.l   #4,d0          * Write
11  00000012 4E40                       trap     #0             * Do the call
12  00000014 508F                       add.l    #8,a7          * Pop arguments
13  00000016 41F90000000E               lea      status,a0      * Now
14  0000001C 7001                       move.l   #1,d0          * Exit
15  0000001E 4E40                       trap     #0             *
16  00000000                            .data                  *
17  00000000 48656C6C6F2C      string:  .dc.b    'Hello, World',10,0
17  00000008 6F726C640A00
18                             length:  .equ                    *-string
19  0000000E 00000000          status:  .dc.l    0              * Exit status
```

Listing 4.2 – *UNIX string-print routine*

To achieve portability between machines that use the same CPU but different operating systems, you first define a set of subroutines that handles the operating-system interface, and then write the bulk of the program using calls to these subroutines.

To make a program that is designed for one operating system run on a different operating system, you need only rewrite the operating-system interface subroutines. This concept is called *modularity*. A modular program isolates a given function, such as printing a string on the terminal, into a single subroutine. Then the required subroutine is used whenever the program performs a particular function.

Making a modular program run under a different operating system usually involves reassembling the source code for the main body of the program as well as rewriting the operating-system interface subroutines. The reassembly process may call for making changes to the source program in order to accommodate any differences in assembler syntax between the two operating systems. The ability to move programs between different operating systems in this fashion is called *source-code portability.*

A PORTABLE STRING-PRINT PROGRAM

To illustrate this concept, we are going to rewrite the previous string-print program (see Listing 4.2) to run under both CP/M-68K and UNIX. The program, common to both CP/M-68K and UNIX, is shown in Listing 4.3.

```
 1                          ******************************************
 2                          *
 3                          * This program prints "Hello World" on
 4                          * a CP/M-68K or UNIX system.
 5                          *
 6                          ******************************************
 7 00000000                     .text
 8                              .globl  prtstr      * String print
 9 00000000 207C00000000  start: movea.l #string,a0 * a0 -> string
10 00000006 4EB900000000         jsr     prtstr      * Call print routine
11 0000000C 4E75                 rts                 * Exit
12 00000000                      .data
13 00000000 48656C6C6F20  string: .dc.b   'Hello World',10,0
```

Listing 4.3 – A portable "Hello World" program

We have defined a routine called prtstr that takes a string address in address register A0 and prints it on the terminal. The .globl directive (line 8) specifies that prtstr is a label defined in a separate source file. The linker program combines the two assembler-output files into one executable file and corrects the instructions that reference external labels.

Note that we have adopted the UNIX convention—a single line-feed character—to indicate the end of a line. On CP/M-68K, the prtstr routine (or a subsequent routine called by prtstr) must output issue both a carriage return and a line feed whenever a line feed is encountered in the string to be printed.

When designing subroutines, put as much of the work in the subroutine as possible. Following this rule means that work is done once (i.e., in the subroutine), rather than many times in each program that calls the subroutine.

The prtstr routine can also be written in a way that makes it independent of the operating system. By calling a routine to output individual characters (a function that is is dependent on the operating system), we can write a single version of prtstr as well, shown in Listing 4.4.

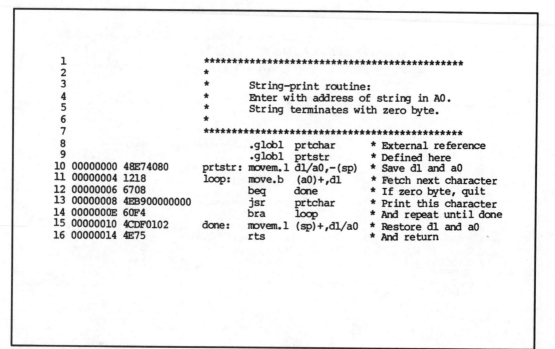

```
 1                      **********************************************
 2                      *
 3                      *       String-print routine:
 4                      *       Enter with address of string in A0.
 5                      *       String terminates with zero byte.
 6                      *
 7                      **********************************************
 8                              .globl  prtchar      * External reference
 9                              .globl  prtstr       * Defined here
10 00000000 48E74080     prtstr: movem.l d1/a0,-(sp)  * Save d1 and a0
11 00000004 1218         loop:   move.b  (a0)+,d1     * Fetch next character
12 00000006 6708                 beq     done         * If zero byte, quit
13 00000008 4EB900000000         jsr     prtchar      * Print this character
14 0000000E 60F4                 bra     loop         * And repeat until done
15 00000010 4CDF0102     done:   movem.l (sp)+,d1/a0  * Restore d1 and a0
16 00000014 4E75                 rts                  * And return
```

Listing 4.4 – Prtstr routine

There are two things to note about prtstr. First, the .globl statement is used two ways:

1. To define labels that are referenced but not defined in the present assembly. Such labels are called *external symbols.*

2. To define labels defined in the present source file and which are referenced as external symbols by other assembly source files.

The second item of note about the prtstr routine concerns registers used by subroutines. Registers A0 and D1 are modified by this routine and are saved and restored so that the contents (as seen by the calling program) do not change.

This is another example of good subroutine design. Register contents altered by a subroutine should be saved and restored.

The prtchar routine for CP/M-68K is coded as shown in Listing 4.5.

This subroutine prints a single character that is passed in the low byte of register D1. Lines 12 through 17 issue a carriage return/ line feed for each

```
 1                    ************************************************
 2                    *
 3                    *   Print a single character on the
 4                    *   terminal. Enter with character in D1.
 5                    *
 6                    *   CP/M-68K Version
 7                    *
 8                    ************************************************
 9                            .globl  prtchar    * Defined here
10                    prtchar:
11 00000000 2F00              move.l  d0,-(sp)   * Save D0
12 00000002 0C01000A          cmpi.b  #10,d1     * Line feed?
13 00000006 660C              bne     notlf      * No, just print
14 00000008 123C000D          move.b  #13,d1     * Print C/R first
15 0000000C 7002              move.l  #2,d0      * CP/M print code
16 0000000E 4E42              trap    #2         * Call CP/M
17 00000010 123C000A          move.b  #10,d1     * Now print LF
18 00000014 7002      notlf:  move.l  #2,d0      * CP/M Print code
19 00000016 4E42              trap    #2         * Call CP/M
20 00000018 201F              move.l  (sp)+,d0   * Restore D0
21 0000001A 4E75              rts                * And return
```

Listing 4.5 – *CP/M-68K prtchar routine*

line feed character passed by the caller. Lines 18–19 output the character passed by the caller in register D1. Note that register D0 is preserved in the same fashion as was register D1 by the putstr subroutine.

The UNIX version of this routine is shown in Listing 4.6.

This routine writes a single character using the same sequence we used to write several characters in Listing 4.2.

CONVERSION ROUTINES

Our print-string program is useful in that we can now print strings on the terminal. To perform useful computational functions as well, we need to be able to print numeric quantities. This process involves *conversion routines*, which transform raw binary numbers into printable strings.

Binary to Hexadecimal Conversion

The easiest conversion is to write a program that converts binary to hexadecimal as shown in Listing 4.7.

```
1                         ***********************************************
2                         * Prtchar Routine for UNIX
3                         * Enter with character in D1.
4                         ***********************************************
5                                   .globl   prtchar
6  00000000 48E78080      prtchar:  movem.l  d0/a0,-(a7)   * Save registers
7  00000004 13C100000000            move.b   d1,char       * Set character
8  0000000A 3F3C0001                move.w   #1,-(a7)      * Push count
9  0000000E 487900000000            pea      char          * Push address
10 00000014 3F3C0001                move.w   #1,-(a7)      * Push file description
11 00000018 204F                    move.l   a7,a0         * Transfer to A0
12 0000001A 7004                    move.l   #4,d0         * Function Code
13 0000001C 4E40                    trap     #0            * Do the call
14 0000001E DFFC00000008            adda.l   #8,a7         * Pop arguments
15 00000024 4CDF0101                movem.l  (a7)+,d0/a0   * Restore registers
16 00000028 4E75                    rts                    * Return
17 00000000                         .data
18 00000000 00            char:     .dc.b    0             * Buffer
```

Listing 4.6 – UNIX prtchar routine

The basic technique employed by this subroutine is to take a nibble and index into the hex character table hextab. Characters are processed from right to left since we need the nibble in the low four bits of the index register to select the appropriate character. In line 11, we initialize a temporary pointer (A1) to the address of the character table. Data register D1 is initialized to the character count minus 1 (as required by the *dbra* instruction). Address register A0 is incremented by 8 to point one byte beyond the rightmost digit (as required by the pre-decrement addressing mode).

Lines 14–18 implement the actual conversion process. The current rightmost digit is isolated in data register D2 using the *andi* instruction. (This instruction guarantees that D2 will be in the range 0–15.) The indexed-addressing mode selects the proper hex character and places it in the next byte in the output area. We then shift data register D0 right one nibble to prepare for converting the next character.

Following the completion of the process, the contents of register A0 will have been decremented eight times, so that it then contains its original value, i.e., the address of the output area. It is therefore unnecessary to preserve this register explicitly.

```
 1                            ***********************************************
 2                            * This routine converts binary to ASCII hex
 3                            *
 4                            * Enter with:
 5                            *    D0  = binary value (long)
 6                            *    A0 -> Output area (8 bytes)
 7                            ***********************************************
 8  00000000                          .text
 9                                     .globl  binhex
10  00000000 48E7E040         binhex:  movem.l d0-d2/a1,-(sp)  *Save input registers
11  00000004 43F90000002A              lea     hextab,a1       *a1 -> character table
12  0000000A D1FC00000008              adda.l  #8,a0           *a0 -> end of area
13  00000010 7207                      move.l  #7,d1           *Loop counter
14  00000012 2400             loop:    move.l  d0,d2           *Copy present number
15  00000014 02820000000F              andi.l  #15,d2          *Get low 4 bits
16  0000001A 11312000                  move.b  0(a1,d2),-(a0)  *Store character
17  0000001E E888                      lsr.l   #4,d0           *Shift 1 hex place
18  00000020 51C9FFF0                  dbra    d1,loop         *Loop until done
19  00000024 4CDF0207                  movem.l (sp)+,d0-d2/a1  *Restore registers
20  00000028 4E75                      rts                     *Return to caller
21  0000002A 303132333437    hextab:  .dc.b   "0123456789ABCDEF"
```

Listing 4.7 – Routine to convert binary to hexadecimal

Binary to Decimal Conversion

A more generally useful function is a routine that converts numbers from binary to decimal ASCII. This function is harder to implement, because you must use division to determine each new digit. This process is further complicated by the lack of a 32-bit division instruction in the 68000. Our program to convert binary to decimal only works on 16-bit numbers. Fortunately, this is usually adequate.

Listing 4.8 shows the decimal conversion routine.

Lines 11–15 put either a space or a minus sign in front of the converted number. The main body of the routine (lines 18–24) work as follows:

1. Divide whatever is left of the number by 10.

2. Place the remainder (which is the high word in the data register following the *divs* instruction) in the buffer. Add the ASCII code for 0 (hex 30) to this byte, making it a character between 0 and 9.

```
 1                         **************************************************
 2                         * Binary to decimal ascii conversion routine.
 3                         *
 4                         * Enter with:
 5                         *    D0.W = number to convert
 6                         *    A0  -> Output area (6 bytes)
 7                         **************************************************
 8                                 .globl  bindec
 9 00000000 48E7C080       bindec: movem.l d0-d1/a0,-(sp)  * Save registers
10 00000004 123C0020               move.b  #' ',d1         * Assume positive
11 00000008 4A40                   tst.w   d0              * Negative?
12 0000000A 6A06                   bpl     notneg          * No, use ' '
13 0000000C 123C002D               move.b  #'-',d1         * Negative, use '-'
14 00000010 4440                   neg.w   d0              * Convert to positive
15 00000012 10C1           notneg: move.b  d1,(a0)+        * Move in sign
16 00000014 D1FC00000005           adda.l  #5,a0           * A0 -> end of area
17 0000001A 323C0004               move.w  #4,d1           * Count register
18 0000001E 48C0           loop:   ext.l   d0              * Extend to long
19 00000020 81FC000A               divs    #10,d0          * Divide by 10
20 00000024 4840                   swap    d0              * Remainder -> low word
21 00000026 1100                   move.b  d0,-(a0)        * Move to area
22 00000028 06100030               add.b   #'0',(a0)       * Adjust to ascii
23 0000002C 4840                   swap    d0              * Quotient -> low word
24 0000002E 51C9FFEE               dbra    d1,loop         * Loop until done
25 00000032 4CDF0103               movem.  (sp)+,d0-d1/a0  * Restore registers
26 00000036 4E75                   rts
```

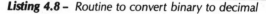

Listing 4.8 – Routine to convert binary to decimal

3. Use the quotient from Step 1 as the new number and repeat Steps 1 through 3 until five digits have been processed.

The output of this routine is a little crude. Possible improvements include a floating minus sign and suppression of leading zeros. Although this routine is not sophisticated, it is adequate for the programs in the remaining part of this chapter.

SUMMING THE FIRST FIVE INTEGERS

Now that we have built a set of tools with which we can write programs, let's begin by looking at the program that sums the first five integers. We can now write a version of this program that prints its output on the terminal, so that we no longer have to use the debugger to look at the output. We can also use the *dbra* instruction to make the program considerably shorter, as shown in Listing 4.9.

Lines 10–16 form the sum of the first five numbers in data register D0. Lines 20–23 convert this sum to hex and decimal at the data areas labeled "hex" and "dec" respectively. Finally, lines 24–25 print the message on the screen as follows:

Sum is: 0000000F (hex) or 00015 (decimal)

It is important to notice how much easier it is to write this program given the output and conversion tools we developed earlier. This is the essence of modular programming—build the right routines to help you do the job in an expedient manner. We are able to treat the conversion or output process as if it were three instructions instead of the twenty to thirty instructions these routines actually require. Indeed, we don't even have to know how the routines work, only how to call them.

READING TERMINAL INPUT

Many programs require user interaction or input to function properly. Examples of this type of software include editor programs, calculator programs, game programs, spreadsheets, and data-base management software.

Let's look at the design of a subroutine that performs terminal input in a manner independent of the operating system. Our subroutine will perform the following actions:

1. Read a line of input from the terminal up to 80 characters in length.

2. Place the characters in a buffer supplied by the user. The address of this buffer will be passed in register A0.

3. Place a terminating null character at the end of the line. No line-termination character will be placed in the user's buffer.

```
 1                        ********************************************
 2                        * This program sums the first five  numbers and
 3                        * prints the result on the terminal.
 4                        ********************************************
 5                                .globl  prtstr  * String-print routine
 6                                .globl  binhex  * Hex-conversion routine
 7                                .globl  bindec  * Decimal-conversion routine
 8                        *
 9                        * Compute the sum first.
10                        *
11 00000000 4280                  clr.l   d0      * Initialize sum
12 00000002 7201                  move.l  #1,d1   * Initialize counter
13 00000004 7404                  move.l  #4,d2   * Loop counter
14 00000006 D081          loop:   add.l   d1,d0   * Add to sum
15 00000008 5281                  add.l   #1,d1   * Increment integer
16 0000000A 51CAFFFA              dbra    d2,loop * Loop until done
17                        *
18                        *       Now print, both in hex and decimal
19                        *
20 0000000E 41F900000009          lea     hex,a0  * A0 -> output area
21 00000014 4EB900000000          jsr     binhex  * Convert to hex
22 0000001A 41F90000001B          lea     dec,a0  * A0 -> decimal area
23 00000020 4EB900000000          jsr     bindec  * Convert to decimal
24 00000026 41F900000000          lea     mess,a0 * A0 -> string to print
25 0000002C 4EB900000000          jsr     prtstr  * Print entire string
26 00000032 4E75                  rts             * Return to CP/M
27 00000000                       .data           *
28                        *
29                        *       Output message area
30                        *
31 00000000 2053756D2069  mess:   .dc.b ´ Sum is: ´
32 00000009 787878787878  hex:    .dc.b ´xxxxxxxx (hex) or ´
33 0000001B 787878787878  dec:    .dc.b ´xxxxxx (decimal)´,10,0
```

Listing 4.9 – *Sum of the first five integers*

The routine should be constructed so that the user can use the normal line editing keys (e.g., Backspace and Delete) during keyboard input. This is typically a function of the operating system.

Listing 4.10 shows the keyboard-input function for CP/M-68K.

CP/M-68K function code 10 reads a line from the console into a buffer consisting of two prefix bytes and an area for input. The first prefix byte (at label "buffer") contains the number of bytes in the input area. The second byte is set by CP/M-68K, and contains the number of characters actually read. CP/M-68K does not place a line-termination character in the buffer.

```
 1                              *************************************************
 2                              * This routine reads a line from the terminal
 3                              * using CP/M-68K I/O.
 4                              *
 5                              * Enter with:
 6                              *
 7                              *   A0 -> area to store the line
 8                              *
 9                              *************************************************
10                                      .globl  getlin
11                                      .globl  prtchar
12 00000000 48E7C0C0         getlin: movem.l d0-d1/a0-a1,-(sp)
13 00000004 43F900000000             lea     buffer,a1       * A1 -> Buffer
14 0000000A 2209                     move.l  a1,d1           * Copy to D1
15 0000000C 700A                     move.l  #10,d0          * D0 =  Function Code
16 0000000E 4E42                     trap    #2              * Call CP/M
17 00000010 12290001                 move.b  1(a1),d1        * Load character count
18 00000014 4881                     ext.w   d1              * Extend to word
19 00000016 5341                     sub.w   #1,d1           * Decrement for dbra
20 00000018 6D0C                     blt     blank           * Blank line entered
21 0000001A D3FC00000002             adda.l  #2,a1           * A1 -> First character
22 00000020 10D9             loop:   move.b  (a1)+,(a0)+     * Move a character
23 00000022 51C9FFFC                 dbra    d1,loop         * Repeat until done
24 00000026 4218             blank:  clr.b   (a0)+           * Null at end
25 00000028 720A                     move.l  #10,d1          * D1 = Line feed char
26 0000002A 4EB900000000             jsr     prtchar         * Go to next line
27 00000030 4CDF0303                 movem.l (sp)+,d0-d1/a0-a1
28 00000034 4E75                     rts                     * Return
29 00000000                          .data
30 00000000 50              buffer: .dc.b   80              * 80 bytes in buffer
31 00000001 00                      .dc.b   0               * Characters actually read
32 00000002                         .ds.b   80              * Reserve space
```

Listing 4.10 – CP/M-68K keyboard line input routine

Lines 13–16 perform a CP/M-68K function 10, reading characters into the local buffer defined by lines 30–32. Lines 17–21 are code to set up the loop that moves the characters read into the user-supplied buffer.

The byte value returned by CP/M-68K must be extended to word size for proper operation of the *dbra* loop. The characters are moved by the code in lines 22 and 23. The *clr.b* instruction at line 24 provides a null terminator at the end of the input in the user buffer.

CP/M-68K does not echo a line feed at the end of a read-buffer function. (It can be argued that this is not a feature.) Lines 25–26 output a line-feed character so that subsequent *prtstr* calls will not overwrite the keyboard input. The equivalent UNIX routine is shown in Listing 4.11.

Lines 7–12 perform a UNIX read system call, which reads data from the keyboard into the local buffer. Lines 13–18 move this data into the user's buffer in a manner compatible with the CP/M-68K routine. A null character is added at the end.

```
 1                            **********************************************
 2                            * This program reads a line from the
 3                            * console using the UNIX read call.
 4                            **********************************************
 5                                    .globl  getlin
 6  00000000 48E780C0         getlin: movem.l d0/a0-a1,-(a7)   * Save registers
 7  00000004 3F3C0050                 move.w  #length,-(a7)    * Max length
 8  00000008 487900000000             pea     buffer           * Buffer address
 9  0000000E 4267                     clr.w   -(a7)            * File 0
10  00000010 7003                     move.l  #3,d0            * Read code
11  00000012 4E40                     trap    #0               * Do the trap
12  00000014 DFFC00000008             adda.l  #8,a7            * Pop arguments
13  0000001A 206F0004                 move.l  4(sp),a0         * Reload A0
14  0000001E 5540                     sub.w   #2,d0            * Take two less
15  00000020 6F0C                     ble     nobytes          * LE => No data bytes
16  00000022 43F900000000             lea     buffer,a1        * A1 -> Temporary buffer
17  00000028 10D9             loop:   move.b  (a1)+,(a0)+      * Move buffer
18  0000002A 51C8FFFC                 dbra    d0,loop          * Util done
19  0000002E 4218             nobytes:clr.b   (a0)+            * Drop in null
20  00000030 4CDF0301                 movem.l (a7)+,d0/a0-a1   * Restore registers
21  00000034 4E75                     rts                      * Return
22  00000000                          .bss                     * Data area
23  00000000             buffer: .ds.b   80               * 80 bytes
24                       length: .equ    *-buffer         * Length
```

Listing 4.11 – UNIX getlin routine

INPUT CONVERSION

In order to use numeric keyboard input, one must first convert it from ASCII characters to binary. This is the reverse of output conversion and is perhaps the most difficult input routine to write.

The routine called *decbin,* shown in Listing 4.12, converts decimal input. Register A0 contains the address of the ASCII input and the binary equivalent is returned in D0.

The routine works using a technique called an *accumulator variable* (which is register D0 in this case). The input is processed from left to right, starting with the most significant digit. For each digit processed, the accumulator is multiplied by 10 and the digit added. (This obviates the need to assign a place value to the first digit encountered.) Processing stops when a

```
 1                              ************************************************
 2                              *
 3                              * This subroutine converts decimal ASCII to
 4                              * longword binary.
 5                              *
 6                              * Enter with:
 7                              *      A0 -> Decimal string
 8                              * Exit with:
 9                              *      D0 =  Converted number
10                              *
11                              * Conversion terminates on first non-decimal
12                              * character. No overflow detection.
13                              *
14                              ************************************************
15                                      .globl  decbin
16 00000000 48E74080           decbin: movem.l d1/a0,-(sp)  * Save starting registers
17 00000004 4280                       clr.l   d0           * Zero out accumulator
18 00000006 0C100039           loop:   cmpi.b  #'9',(a0)    * Upper bound
19 0000000A 621A                       bhi     notdec       * Not a decimal digit
20 0000000C 0C100030                   cmpi.b  #'0',(a0)    * Lower bound
21 00000010 6514                       blo     notdec       * Not a decimal digit
22 00000012 E388                       lsl.l   #1,d0        * Multiply by 2
23 00000014 2200                       move.l  d0,d1        * Save this
24 00000016 E588                       lsl.l   #2,d0        * Now multiplied by 8
25 00000018 D081                       add.l   d1,d0        * Now by 10
26 0000001A 1218                       move.b  (a0)+,d1     * Fetch digit
27 0000001C 02810000000F               andi.l  #$0f,d1      * Isolate binary digit
28 00000022 D081                       add.l   d1,d0        * Add into accumulator
29 00000024 60E0                       bra     loop         * Try another digit
30 00000026 4CDF0102           notdec: movem.l (sp)+,a0/d1  * Unsave registers
31 0000002A 4E75                       rts                  * Return to caller
```

Listing 4.12 – Routine to convert decimal ASCII to binary

non-decimal digit is encountered. There is no provision for overflow detection or for the calling program to learn how many digits were processed.

Lines 18–21 perform a range check to ensure that the next byte in the buffer does, in fact, contain a decimal digit. Lines 22–25 multiply register D0 by 10. This technique is a holdover from machines that had no hardware multiplication feature. You use shift operations to calculate 2n and 8n. Adding these two quantities yields 10n. We used this trick because the 68000 hardware multiply instruction does not work on 32-bit quantities. Lines 26–28 convert the digit to binary and add it to the accumulator.

DECIMAL TO HEX CONVERSION

Now that we have both input and output routines, let's use them to write a program that receives a decimal number as input and gives its hexadecimal equivalent. The program should prompt for input, read the number from the keyboard, and produce both the original number and its hex equivalent.

Listing 4.13 shows the finished conversion program.

Lines 13–19 print a prompt on the screen and read a line from the terminal. If the line is null (i.e., the user only presses Return), the program goes back to the operating system. Lines 20–24 convert the number to binary and then to ASCII hex and finally to ASCII decimal. Line 25 prints the answer on the screen.

Consider how long this program would have been if all the subroutines that we developed earlier had destroyed register contents or had taken their inputs in different registers. The program to convert decimal to hex is very short because the subroutines all expect parameters in the same registers. This allows you to code many *move* instructions, which set up parameters, only once.

Running the program with a few sample inputs shows:

```
A>dechex
Enter decimal number: 100 <Return>
00100 decimal is 00000064 hex
Enter decimal number: 16 <Return>
00016 decimal is 00000010 hex
Enter decimal number: 9999 <Return>
09999 decimal is 0000270F hex
Enter decimal number: 99999 <Return>
 -31073 decimal is 0001869F hex
Enter decimal number:
A>
```

```
 1                                   ****************************************************
 2                                   *
 3                                   * This program converts decimal numbers to hex.
 4                                   * Numbers are input from the keyboard and output to
 5                                   * the screen.
 6                                   *
 7                                   ****************************************************
 8                                          .globl   prtstr          * Line print routine
 9                                          .globl   binhex          * Output converter
10                                          .globl   bindec          * Output converter
11                                          .globl   decbin          * Input converter
12                                          .globl   getlin          * Keyboard input
13 00000000 41F900000000   loop:          lea      prompt,a0       * A0 -> output area
14 00000006 4EB900000000                  jsr      prtstr          * Print prompt
15 0000000C 41F900000000                  lea      inbuf,a0        * A0 -> input  area
16 00000012 4EB900000000                  jsr      getlin          * Get keyboard input
17 00000018 4A10                          tst.b    (a0)            * Null line?
18 0000001A 6602                          bne      gotnum          * No, continue
19 0000001C 4E75                          rts                      * Yes, exit to CP/M
20 0000001E 4EB900000000   gotnum:        jsr      decbin          * Convert to binary
21 00000024 41F900000029                  lea      hexbuf,a0       * A0 -> conversion area
22 0000002A 4EB900000000                  jsr      binhex          * Convert to hex
23 00000030 41F900000017                  lea      decbuf,a0       * Reconvert to decimal
24 00000036 4EB900000000                  jsr      bindec          *
25 0000003C 4EB900000000                  jsr      prtstr          * Print answer
26 00000042 60BC                          bra      loop            * Repeat until done
27 00000000                               .data
28 00000000 456E74657220   prompt:  .dc.b    'Enter decimal number: ',0
29 00000017 585858585858   decbuf:  .dc.b    'XXXXXX decimal is '
30 00000029 585858585858   hexbuf:  .dc.b    'XXXXXXXX hex',10,0
31 00000038                               .bss
32 00000000                 inbuf:  .ds.b    80              * Input buffer
```

Listing 4.13 – *Routine to convert decimal to hex*

Notice that the value 99999 caused an incorrect decimal value. Recall that, due to the limitation of the 68000 *divs* instruction, the binary to decimal routine (see Listing 4.8) works only for 16-bit quantities. (See the exercises at the end of the chapter for the solution to this bug.)

SUMMARY

In this chapter, we have developed the background material for writing sophisticated programs: terminal input, terminal output, and numeric conversion. This basic tool kit provides us with the building blocks necessary to construct larger programs.

EXERCISES

1. A division instruction may be simulated as a loop that subtracts until the dividend is reduced to a number less than the divisor. Write a subroutine called "ldiv" that divides a 32-bit number. Use the following calling convention:

    Enter with:

    D0 = dividend

    D1 = divisor

    Exit with:

    D0 = quotient

    D1 = remainder

    What is the major disadvantage of this scheme?

2. Use the "ldiv" subroutine developed in question 1 to create a new routine that successfully converts 32-bit decimal numbers to decimal ASCII. Use a 10-byte output area.

3. Modify the decimal to hex conversion program (Listing 4.13) to use the "ldiv" conversion routine developed for question 2.

4. Write a routine that converts hexadecimal ASCII to binary in a manner similar to Listing 4.12. Allow both upper and lower case letters for the hex digits A through F.

5. Write a program that converts hex numbers to decimal.

I/O Programming

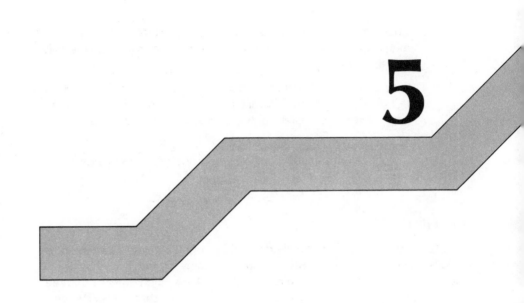

5

INTRODUCTION

In this chapter, we will explore the various methods of I/O available to assembly language programmers. As with the previous chapters, we will confine ourselves to using an operating system to perform the I/O. In Chapter 7, we will explore performing I/O directly to the hardware interface.

Another topic we will explore in this chapter is mixing assembly language with a high-level language. Writing assembly language subroutines for high-level language programs is a common practice and a powerful tool. Programming in this fashion allows you to retain the speed of assembly-language routines, while taking advantage of the large library of subroutines available with most high-level languages. Our discussion will center around accessing the language I/O routines from assembly language.

TYPES OF I/O

Most I/O performed by applications programs falls into one of four categories:

1. Terminal I/O. This is used for interaction with the operator.

2. File I/O. This type of I/O generally involves the retrieval or storage of large amounts of data.

3. Character I/O. Output to printers and plotters, I/O over communications links, and other I/O performed a byte at a time falls into this class.

4. Special I/O. Devices that do not meet the standard model of an I/O device belong to this category. This includes things like real-time devices, computer control devices, and instrumentation.

The remainder of this chapter will deal with the first three types of I/O listed above.

Terminal I/O

I/O to the terminal is normally done either one character at a time or a block of characters at a time. In addition, many operating systems perform line editing on the incoming characters. Line editing means that the operating system attaches special meaning to certain characters. The person using the computer can use these keys to correct simple typing mistakes. Here is a sample of line editing characters and their functions.

- The BACKSPACE key causes the last character typed to be deleted. On video terminals, the character is erased and the cursor moves left one position.

- The Control-R key advances the terminal to the next line and echoes any characters typed on the current line. This is particularly useful on terminals that do not support the erasing of characters on the screen (such as hardcopy terminals, which produce output on paper rather than on the screen).

- The Control-U key cancels all input on a partially typed line (i.e., before the operator presses Return).

- The Control-C key interrupts the program that is currently executing and returns control to the operating system. This provides the user with a way to stop a program that is out of control.

- The Control-Z key is used to indicate the end of terminal input, or to a program reading the terminal, Control Z indicates an end-of-file condition.

- The carriage return (Control-M) and line feed (Control-J) keys indicate the end of a line.

Each operating system interprets terminal input in its own peculiar fashion. The control keys listed above are common to CP/M-68K and most 68000 implementations of UNIX.

You can also perform terminal input without line editing. In this case, your program receives each character, including control characters, exactly as typed. This is called *raw mode* in many operating systems. (Line editing is also occasionally referred to as *cooked mode*.)

Raw mode is extremely useful for programs that are highly interactive or visual in nature. Such programs often perform some action on every keystroke. This type of program includes word processors, spreadsheets, and many data-base management systems.

A significant side effect of raw mode is that you lose the ability to terminate the program via Control-C. For this reason, some operating systems, including UNIX, define yet a third way of reading the terminal, called *rare mode,* in which all characters *except* Control-C are given to the program as they are typed.

For the remainder of this chapter, we will use cooked mode, or line editing, for console input.

File I/O

Devices such as floppy or hard disks are generally accessed through a part of the operating system known as the "file system." A file is simply a way of associating a name with a group of bytes. Files may contain executable programs, text, data, and operating system commands.

The operating system provides the programmer with ways of creating, deleting, modifying, and retrieving the information contained in a file. Providing a user with access to files is the single most important function that the computer system provides. Typical file access operations provided by an operating system are:

- *Open* an existing file or *Create* a new file. This causes the operating system to logically connect program I/O to a file on the disk.

- *Read* data from the file. A Read operation transfers data from the file into the program's memory. The CP/M-68K *type* command or the UNIX *cat* command Reads a file and displays the contents on the screen.

- *Write* data to the file. A Write operation transfers part of the program's memory to a file. When you instruct a text editor to save a file on disk, the editor performs Write operations to accomplish your request.

- *Close* a file. The Close operation tells the operating system that you are through with a file. Many systems impose a limit on the number of files you can have open at any one time. Thus, it is good programming practice to use Opens and Closes in pairs.

File access techniques vary widely from system to system. UNIX files are simply considered as streams of bytes. You can read or write any number of bytes starting at any arbitrary location in the file.

CP/M-68K, on the other hand, does file I/O in 128 byte units. You can transfer only 128 bytes at a time and data transfers must start on 128-byte boundaries within the file.

Other operating systems use different schemes. To write portable programs that access files, you must define a set of subroutines that hide the differences in the way operating systems perform file operations.

For CP/M-68K and UNIX, this work has already been done. A high-level language called C contains a set of file access routines that can be used to write programs that are portable between CP/M-68K and UNIX.

Character I/O

Other devices commonly found on microcomputers include printers, modems (a device that connects a computer to a telephone line), and plotters. I/O to these devices is typically done one character at a time. Operating-system support for such devices usually consists of single-character or block (multicharacter) I/O.

Special I/O

Instrumentation and control devices are typically not accessed in a manner similar to the other, more standard devices. Many operating systems have separate facilities for accessing these devices. The facilities for special I/O often perform special functions on devices normally accessed by other means. Examples of such functions include formatting disks, forwarding and rewinding magnetic tape drives, and controlling modem signals such as "answer the phone" and "dial this number."

DEVICE INDEPENDENCE

Many operating systems have a feature known as *device independence*. This means that most of the devices on the system can be accessed as if they were files. UNIX is an example of such a system. On UNIX, you use the same I/O functions to access the terminal, disk files, and the printer. CP/M-68K is an example of a system that is *not* device independent. CP/M-68K uses different function calls for each of these device types.

The advantage of device-independent I/O is that you do not have to be concerned with what type of device your program uses for I/O. For most programs, this is a tremendous advantage. Device independence makes it possible to enter input to a program that normally receives input from a disk file or to output information to a printer that normally goes to a disk file. It is device independence that makes the highly-touted UNIX pipes, filters, and I/O redirection possible.

Fortunately for users of CP/M-68K and other operating systems that do not provide device independence, it is possible to use calls to a high-level language to obtain this feature. Most high-level languages incorporate the necessary code for device independence in the language *run-time library*. A run-time library is a set of routines that are called by the machine code (which is generated by the language compiler). These routines are normally added to the program by the linker program.

INTERFACING TO HIGH-LEVEL LANGUAGES

One of the most common uses for assembly language is to add functionality or speed to a program written in a high-level language. Since this is a such a common technique, there are very few high-level language compilers that do not allow it. You can take advantage of this capability in your assembly-language programs by using features from the language run-time library.

The technique for interfacing assembly language to a high-level language is different for each compiler. Some compilers insist on having a main program written in a high-level language. Others allow a main program to be in assembly language, but require certain initialization procedures in the main program. Still others have no such restrictions. The proper techniques are usually documented (although not always well) in one of the manuals associated with the high-level language you are using.

In interfacing to a high-level language, you need to answer the following questions:

1. Does the language require a high-level main program? Certain compilers, such as the UCSD P-system require this.

2. If the language allows the main program to be in assembly language, does the main program have to do anything to make the run-time library work?

3. How does one call a high-level procedure from assembly language? Is the sequence any different for calling the run-time modules directly?

4. What registers are preserved by the run-time modules and the routines written in the high-level language? What registers are destroyed?

5. Do you have to do anything special to exit to the operating system? Many languages automatically close all open files upon exiting. If you are coding a main program in assembly language, you may have to code a call to the language exit or stop routine.

6. What techniques are available for accessing global data areas from assembly language? Do you have to pass all data as parameters to the assembly language procedure?

For the rest of the chapter, we will explore techniques for interfacing to the CP/M-68K run-time library for the C language. The same techniques can also be used to access C routines under most UNIX systems.

INTERFACING TO C

The C language used by CP/M-68K allows a main program to be written in assembly language. The program begins execution at the label "_main," which must be declared in a ".globl" statement. No run-time initialization is required. Any run-time library routine that may be called from C may be called from assembly language. There are no special considerations for calling run-time routines.

Calling Sequences

Names of functions and global data areas are the same as the C identifier with an underscore character as the first character of the name. Thus, the C function "main" becomes "_main," and so on. The C language does distinguish between upper- and lower-case, so the label "_main" is different from "_MAIN."

You call a C-language library routine by pushing its arguments in reverse order onto the stack and then executing a JSR instruction (Jump to SubRoutine) to the desired routine. Following the return from the C routine, you normally pop the arguments off the stack. (The routine called by the JSR instructions does not do this for you.) This prevents running out of stack space, and allows you to easily find the return address of the run-time initializer routine. Table 5.1 shows the data sizes of arguments on the stack.

Notice that although the character data type (char) is 8 bits, it is passed on the stack as a 16-bit word. All addresses in C are 32 bits. A character in single quotes is treated as an argument of type "char." A string in double quotes is treated as a "char ∗", i.e., the address of the string is passed to the subroutine.

This C call

```
int   x,a,c;
char ∗b;
x = xyz(a,b,c);
```

generates assembly code that appears as shown in Listing 5.1.

This code which is generated by the compiler, puts the local variables a, b, c, and x on the stack. The variables are accessed as negative offsets from address register A6, which is used as the frame pointer. You can look at the assembly language generated by many compilers to see what instructions are used for subroutine calls.

C Argument Type	Size in Bytes (Bits)	
char	2	(16)
char ∗	4	(32)
int	2	(16)
int ∗	4	(32)
long	4	(32)
long ∗	4	(32)
double quoted string	4	(32)
single quoted character	2	(16)

Table 5.1 – *Sizes of argument types in C*

Many other C compilers use four bytes on the stack for each argument, regardless of argument type. On the 68000, many compilers also use 32 bits for the "int" data type instead of the 16 bits used by the CP/M-68K compiler.

C functions that return values place the return value in register D0 just before the *rts* (Return from Subroutine) instruction. (Some compilers use data register D7 for this purpose.) Byte (char) values are placed in the low-order 8 bits of D0. Word (int or short) values are returned in the low-order 16 bits of D0. Longs and addresses occupy the entire 32 bits of register D0.

The CP/M-68K C compiler treats registers D0, D1, D2, A0, A1, and A2 as "scratch" registers; they are not preserved across C function calls. When you call routines from the C library, the contents of these registers may be altered upon return.

Two Arguments: Argc and Argv

The C function "main" is called with two arguments: argc and argv. The argument called argc is a 16-bit quantity that gives the number of arguments typed on the command line. The argument called argv is the address of an array of pointers to each of the argument strings. Each argument string is terminated with a null character. Figure 5.1 shows the arrangement of the stack and argc and argv arguments for a sample command.

Some systems do not correctly fill in the argv[0] pointer with the program name. It is recommended, therefore, that you not use this argument for anything critical to the program's results.

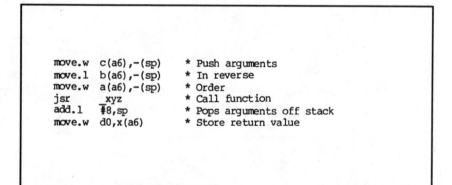

```
        move.w   c(a6),-(sp)      * Push arguments
        move.l   b(a6),-(sp)      * In reverse
        move.w   a(a6),-(sp)      * Order
        jsr      xyz              * Call function
        add.l    #8,sp            * Pops arguments off stack
        move.w   d0,x(a6)         * Store return value
```

Listing 5.1 – *Code generated by the C compiler*

Using Printf from Assembly Language

By far, the most commonly used C-language routine is printf—a formatted print routine. A famous C program is the "Hello, world" program, which uses printf to print the string "Hello, world" on the screen. Listing 5.2 shows how assembly language can be used to code the same program.

The "\n" character in C is a line feed (decimal 10) byte. Double-quoted strings in C also end with a null character (hence the zero byte in line 16).

C PROGRAM I/O

C programs can perform I/O in two ways:

- I/O can use the operating system primitives open, creat, read, write, lseek, and close. These routines are known collectively as *unbuffered I/O routines.*

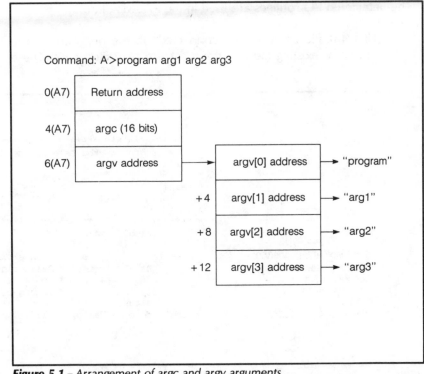

Figure 5.1 – Arrangement of argc and argv arguments

- I/O can use routines from the C-language run-time library that perform local buffering in the application. These routines are fopen, fclose, fread, fwrite, gets, fgets, fgetc, getw, fputc, putw, puts, fputs, feof, and fseek. This type of I/O is called *buffered I/O*, or *stream I/O*.

Which of these two sets of routines to use depends on the amount of I/O performed at any one time. Unbuffered I/O yields very high *throughput* when large amounts of data are transferred in a single read or write call. Transferring small amounts of data at a time is very slow using unbuffered I/O, however.

Stream I/O, on the other hand, performs well when only a few bytes are transferred at a time and poorly when large numbers of bytes are transferred at once.

Unbuffered I/O

The unbuffered I/O routines are used in the following fashion:

1. First, the file or device is "connected" to the program via the open (for existing files) or the creat (for new files) calls. These

```
 1                     *********************************************
 2                     * This program is the same as the C "hello
 3                     * world" program:
 4                     *
 5                     * main() {
 6                     *     printf("Hello, world\n");
 7                     * }
 8                     *********************************************
 9                             .globl   _main
10                             .globl   _printf
11 00000000 487900000000   _main:  pea    hello    * Push string address
12 00000006 4EB900000000           jsr    _printf  * Call printf routine
13 0000000C 588F                   addq.l #4,sp    * Pop argument
14 0000000E 4E75                   rts             * Return to library
15 00000000                        .data           *
16 00000000 48656C6C6F2C2077  hello: .dc.b  "Hello, world",10,0
```

Listing 5.2 – The "Hello world" program

routines return a 16-bit quantity called a *file descriptor* which identifies the file on subsequent read or write calls. A value of − 1 (FFFF hex) is returned if the file cannot be accessed.

2. The read and write routines are called to transfer data to and from the file. Use the lseek call to select the position within the file for starting the transfer.

3. Terminate file access with the close call.

Unbuffered Calling Sequences

Unbuffered I/O routines are relatively simple to call and use. Here is a brief summary of the routines and how they are called.

Open Routine

The open routine is called with two parameters:

1. The name of the file to be opened as a string terminated with a null character, and

2. A 16 bit integer that determines how the file is to be accessed. The integers are 0 for read only, 1 for write only, and 2 for read and write.

The file descriptor is returned in data register D0.W. The filename string can contain a disk drive specification. Listing 5.3 shows the code for reading the file foo.bar on drive A:.

The file descriptor of the open file is contained in register D0. If the file cannot be opened, register D0.W will have the value FFFF (− 1).

Creat Routine

The creat function is called in the following manner. Push the file's *protection mask* (16 bits) followed by a pointer to the null-terminated filename.

The protection mask is the access permission mechanism under UNIX. This word contains three 3-bit fields for read, write, and execute permission by the owner, group, and world. The value 511 (decimal) allows all access by all users. CP/M-68K ignores this field. Listing 5.4 shows the sequence of code that creates a new foo.bar file:

The file descriptor of the open file is contained in register D0. If the file cannot be created, D0.W will have the value FFFF (− 1).

Read and Write Routines

Data transfer is accomplished by the read and write routines, which transfer data from and to the file. Call these routines as follows:

1. Push the number of bytes you wish transferred (16 bits).

2. Push the address of the memory area where the file data is to be transferred. This address is a buffer which receives data on a read call and is a data source on a write call.

3. Push the file descriptor (16 bits).

4. Call _read or _write.

5. Register D0.W contains the number of bytes actually transferred. For a read request, this may be less than the number of bytes requested. For a write request, if D0.W is different from the number of bytes requested, an error occurred.

```
          move.w   #0,-(sp)      * Push "open type" word
          pea      foo           * Push filename address
          jsr      _open         * Call open routine
          add.l    #6,sp         * Pop arguments
          tst.w    d0            * Is file open?
          blt      badopen       * If LE, no, branch
                   .
                   .
                   .
foo:      .dc.b    'a:foo.bar',0 * File name
```

Listing 5.3 – *Calling the open routine*

```
          move.w   #511,-(sp)    * Push protection word
          pea      foo           * Push filename address
          jsr      _creat        * Call creat routine
          add.l    #6,sp         * Pop arguments
          tst.w    d0            * Is file open?
          blt      badcreat      * If LE, no, branch
                   .
                   .
                   .
foo:      .dc.b    'foo.bar',0   * File name
```

Listing 5.4 – *Calling the creat routine*

Listing 5.5 shows code that reads 42 bytes from the file whose file descriptor is in D3.W:

The write routine is called in the same fashion, except the error check should compare D0.W to the number of bytes requested, and branch if not equal to an error-handling routine.

Close Routine

The close routine is called by pushing the file descriptor and calling _close via a *jsr* instruction. Listing 5.6 shows the code that closes the file whose file descriptor is contained in D3.W.

Lseek Routine

The lseek routine alters the position within the file at which the next read or write begins. Normally, each read or write begins where the last one left off. Thus, the file is normally processed sequentially, from beginning to end.

```
        move.w   #42,-(sp)      * Push byte count
        pea      buffer         * Push buffer address
        move.w   d3,-(sp)       * Push file descriptor
        jsr      _read          * Call read routine
        add.l    #8,sp          * Pop arguments
        tst.w    d0             * Any bytes read?
        beq      eof            * If no bytes, end of file
        blt      readerr        * If LE, error on read
                    .
                    .
                    .
buffer: .ds.b    42             * Receives file data
```

Listing 5.5 – *Calling the read routine*

```
        move.w   d3,-(sp)       * Push file descriptor
        jsr      _close         * Call close routine
        add.l    #2,sp          * Pop argument
```

Listing 5.6 – *Calling the close routine*

Lseek allows the file to be accessed in a random fashion. You call·lseek by pushing a word which determines the interpretation of the file offset. A value of 0 means an offset from the beginning of the file, a value of 1 indicates an offset from the current file position, and a value of 2 indicates an offset from the end of the file. You then push the file offset (32 bits). This can be a negative quantity (making it possible to back up from your current position, or from the end of the file). Next, push the file descriptor and call lseek. D0.L returns with the resulting absolute offset from the beginning of the file. Listing 5.7 shows the code that sets the file pointer to 1000H from the beginning of the file.

If the seek could not be performed, D0.L is set to a value of −1.

A File-Copy program

Now that we've learned how to call I/O routines from the C library, let's write a program that copies one file to another. The program should be invoked as follows:

```
A>copy file1 file2
```

The program should duplicate the contents of file1 in file2. (File1 should be left unchanged.) Our program should be a professional quality program. It should report errors on open, creat, read, and write, identifying the file by name.

Stop for a moment and consider the value of device-independent I/O in a program like this. In addition to copying files, we can use the CP/M-68K con: (terminal) and lst: (printer) devices to perform other functions as well.

- *copy file1 con:* transfers a disk file to the console. This is the equivalent of the CP/M-68K TYPE command.

- *copy file1 lst:* transfers a disk file to the printer. This is a function which normally must be performed with the CP/M-68K PIP program.

```
move.w    #0,-(sp)        * Push sense word
move.l    #$1000,-(sp)    * Push file offset
move.w    d3,-(sp)        * Push file descriptor
jsr       _lseek          * Call lseek routine
add.l     #8,sp           * Pop arguments
```

Listing 5.7 – *Calling the lseek routine*

- *copy con: file1* allows you to create a disk file by typing it at the terminal. This is useful for short files.

The completed program is shown in Listing 5.8. Lines 18 to 21 load values for argc and argv into registers D0 and A5. Lines 28 to 33 open the input file, and lines 35 to 40 create the output file.

Lines 46 to 62 execute the file copy operations. Notice the use of the equated label "buffsiz," which controls the number of bytes copied by each iteration of the loop. You can control how many bytes are read and the size of the buffer by changing the .equ (equates) directive on line 16. *Equates* are used extensively in large programs to facilitate program changes. Imagine having to change the constant 1024 to 2048 everywhere in a 300 page program. Clearly, equates can save enormous amounts of time.

The _read routine returns the number of bytes actually read in D0.W. This number does not always equal the number of bytes requested. When reading from the terminal, input is processed one line at a time. When copying files, it is very important to ensure that the number of bytes written is the same as the number of bytes read.

A value of zero bytes read indicates the end of the input file. Upon sensing this condition, the program branches to the label done:. In lines 64 to 70, the program closes the input and output files and returns to the operating system.

Lines 76 to 110 are error routines that print out error messages whenever anything goes wrong. In this program, the error routines print out a message and cause the program to exit to the operating system.

Buffered I/O

Buffered I/O run-time routines in the C language are designed to process I/O a few characters at a time. These functions are used in the following fashion:

1. The file or device is connected to the program via the fopen call. fopen returns the address of a memory structure. This address is known as the *stream pointer.* If the open fails, fopen returns a value of zero.

2. I/O operations use a variety of routines. These routines are listed in Table 5.2. Each of these routines operate on the stream pointer returned by fopen. In addition, a modified version of printf, called fprintf, produces formatted output to a stream file.

```
***********************************************************
*
* This program copies one file to another using unbuffered I/O.
*
* Command:
* a>copy source destination
*
***********************************************************
             .globl  _main       * Global definitions
             .globl  _open       * C library open routine
             .globl  _creat      * C library file creation routine
             .globl  _read       * C library file read routine
             .globl  _write      * C library file write routine
             .globl  _close      * C library file close routine
             .globl  _printf     * C library printf routine
buffsiz:     .equ    1024        * Number of bytes copied at one time

_main:       move.w  4(sp),d0    * "argc"
             move.l  6(sp),a5    * "argv"
             cmp.w   #3,d0       * Proper arg count?
             bne     argcerr     * if EQ, yes, continue

***********************************************************
*
* Open the input and output files. Print an error message and exit
* if either "open" or "creat" fails.
*
***********************************************************
             move.w  #0,-(sp)    * 0 => open for read
             move.l  4(a5),-(sp) * -> Input file name
             jsr     _open       * Try to open the file
             add.l   #6,sp       * Pop arguments
             move.w  d0,d3       * Save returned file descriptor
             bmi     notopen     * If >= 0, then file is open
             move.w  #511,-(sp)  * Creation mode
             move.l  8(a5),-(sp) * -> Output file name from argv
```

Object code:

```
18  00000000  302F0004
19  00000004  2A6F0006
20  00000008  B07C0003
21  0000000C  6670

28  0000000E  3F3C0000
29  00000012  2F2D0004
30  00000016  4EB900000000
31  0000001C  5C8F
32  0000001E  3600
33  00000020  6B6C

35  00000022  3F3C01FF
36  00000026  2F2D0008
```

Listing 5.8 – Unbuffered file copy routine

```
37 0000002A 4EB900000000        jsr    creat            * Try to create the output file
38 00000030 5C8F                add.l  #6,sp            * Pop arguments
39 00000032 3800                move.w d0,d4            * Save output file descriptor
40 00000034 6B6C                bmi    nocreat          * If >= 0, then file created OK
41 00000036                     .page
42
43                     *****************************************************
44                     *  This is the main file copy loop.
45                     *****************************************************
46 00000036 3F3C0400  loop:     move.w #buffsiz,-(sp)   * Push buffer size
47 0000003A 4EB900000000        pea    buffer           * Push buffer address
48 00000040 3F03                move.w d3,-(sp)          * Push input file descriptor
49 00000042 4EB900000000        jsr    read             * Call read routine
50 00000048 508F                add.l  #8,sp            * Pop arguments
51 0000004A 3C00                move.w d0,d6            * Save return from read
52 0000004C 671A                beq    done             * If eq, then end of file
53 0000004E 6B66                bmi    readerr          * if < 0, a read error occurred
54
55 00000050 3F00                move.w d0,-(sp)          * Push byte count from read
56 00000052 4EB900000000        pea    buffer           * Push buffer address
57 00000058 3F04                move.w d4,-(sp)          * Push output file descriptor
58 0000005A 4EB900000000        jsr    write            * Output the buffer
59 00000060 508F                add.l  #8,sp            * Pop arguments
60 00000062 BC40                cmp.w  d0,d6            * Did we write all that we asked for?
61 00000064 665C                bne    writerr          * If NE, no, print error message and exit
62 00000066 60CE                bra    loop             * Repeat until end of file
63
64 00000068 3F03      done:     move.w d3,-(sp)          * Close the input file
65 0000006A 4EB900000000        jsr    close            * Call close routine
66 00000070 548F                add.l  #2,sp            * Pop arguments
67 00000072 3F04                move.w d4,-(sp)          * Close the output file
68 00000074 4EB900000000        jsr    close            * Call close routine
69 0000007A 548F                add.l  #2,sp            * Pop arguments
70 0000007C 4E75                rts                      * Return to runtime library routine
71 0000007E                     .page
```

Listing 5.8 – Unbuffered file copy routine (continued)

```
72
73
74            ***********************************************************
75            * These sections of code are used to print error messages
76  0000007E 48790000000   argcerr pea    usage        * -> command line reminder message
77  00000084 4EB900000000          jsr    printf       * Print error message
78  0000008A 588F                  add.l  #4,sp        * Pop arguments
79  0000008C 4E75                  rts                 * and exit
80
81  0000008E 2F2D0004      notopen move.l 4(a5),-(sp)  * Push input file name address
82  00000092 48790000023           pea    openerr      * Push message address
83  00000098 4EB900000000          jsr    printf       * print open error message
84  0000009E 508F                  add.l  #8,sp        * Pop printf arguments
85  000000A0 4E75                  rts                 * Exit to operating system
86
87  000000A2 2F2D0008      nocreat move.l 8(a5),-(sp)  * Push output file name address
88  000000A6 48790000033           pea    createrr     * Push pointer to error message
89  000000AC 4EB900000000          jsr    printf       * Print error message
90  000000B2 508F                  add.l  #8,sp        * Pop printf arguments
91  000000B4 4E75                  rts                 * Exit
92
93  000000B6 2F2D0004      readerr move.l 4(a5),-(sp)  * Push input filename address
94  000000BA 48790000045           pea    inerr        * Push message address
95  000000C0 600A                  bra    rwerr        * Branch to common error code
96  000000C2 2F2D0008      writerr move.l 8(a5),-(sp)  * Push output filename address
97  000000C6 48790000057           pea    outerr       * Push message address
98  000000CC 4EB900000000  rwerr:  jsr    printf       * Call output routine
99  000000D2 508F                  add.l  #8,sp        * Pop printf args
100 000000D4 6092                  bra    done         * Close input and output files; exit
101
```

Listing 5.8 – *Unbuffered file copy routine (continued)*

```
102                          ***********************************************
103                          * Error message definitions
104                          ***********************************************
105  00000000                         .data
106  00000000  5573616765203A2020      usage:   .dc.b   "Usage:  copy inputfile outputfile",10,0
106  00000008  636F707920696E70
106  00000010  7574666696C65206F
106  00000018  7574707574666696C
106  00000020  650A00
107  00000023  43616E6E6F74206F      openerr:.dc.b   "Cannot open %s",10,0
107  0000002B  70656E2025730A00
108  00000033  43616E6E6F742063      createerr:.dc.b   "Cannot create %s",10,0
108  0000003B  726561746520257320
108  00000043  0A00
109  00000045  5265616420657272      inerr:   .dc.b   "Read error on %s",10,0
109  0000004D  6F72206F6E202573
109  00000055  0A00
110  00000057  5772697465206572      outerr:  .dc.b   "Write error on %s",10,0
110  0000005F  726F72206F6E2025
110  00000067  730A00
111                                   .even
112                                   .bss
113  00000000               buffer:  .ds.b   buffsiz
114  00000000
```

Listing 5.8 – Unbuffered file copy routine (continued)

3. Random access to the file can be performed using the fseek routine, which is analogous to the unbuffered lseek routine.

4. The stream buffer may be emptied using the fflush routine. This procedure guarantees that all data output to the stream is actually transferred to the output device.

5. The fclose routine closes the file.

Buffered Calling Sequences

The buffered I/O routines have calling sequences that are relatively easy to use. We will examine each of them.

Fopen Routine

You must supply two arguments to the fopen routine: the address of the filename string, and the address of a string that describes how the file is to be accessed:

First Character	Access Type
r or R	Read only
w or W	Write only
a or A	Append

Opening a file for write access causes any existing data in the file to be destroyed. Requesting access to Read or append requires that the file already exist. Write access will create a new file if necessary.

Data Size	Input	Output
byte	fgetc	fputc
word	getw	putw
long	getl	putl
string	fgets	fputs

Table 5.2 – *List of I/O routines*

Listing 5.9 shows how fopen is called to create a new file, foo.bar.

A non-zero value in data register D0 (the stream pointer) indicates a successful open operation. Notice that it is necessary to save the entire 32-bit quantity returned in D0.L for subsequent I/O calls.

Input Routines

The routines fgetc, getw, getl, and fgets produce input from the stream. The fgetc, getw, and getl routines share a common calling sequence, as shown in Listing 5.10.

Register D0 contains the data read from the input stream. Fgetc, getw, and getl return, respectively, a byte in D0.B, a word in D0.W and a longword in D0.L. If an attempt is made to read past the end of the file, the return value is −1. Since this value is also a legitimate data value within the file, a function called feof is available to determine if the stream is at end-of-file. feof is a routine implemented via *macros*. You can call this routine by building a brief C program, as shown in Listing 5.11.

```
          .globl    _fopen
          pea       wstring        * Push access string
          pea       fname          * Push filename string
          jsr       _fopen         * Call open routine
          add.l     #8,sp          * Pop argument
          tst.l     d0             * Open succeed?
          beq       badopen        * If EQ, error
          move.l    d0,d3          * Save stream pointer
          .data
wstring:.dc.b       "w",0          * String for write
fname:  .dc.b       "foo.bar",0    * Filename
```

Listing 5.9 – *Calling the fopen routine*

```
     .globl    _fgetc
     move.l    d3,-(sp)      * Push stream pointer
     jsr       _fgetc        * Call routine
     add.l     #4,sp         * Pop argument
```

Listing 5.10 – *A common calling sequence for input routines*

Then use Listing 5.12 to call the C routine from assembly language.

Feof is not necessary when using fgetc, as the value of −1 returned as an error is placed in register D0.W, and thus cannot be a value obtained from the file.

The fgets routine obtains a line terminated by a line-feed character (decimal 10) from the stream. Fgets adds a null (zero) byte to the end of the line (following the line-feed character). The calling sequence for fgets is shown in Listing 5.13.

The value returned from fgets is 0 for the end of file; otherwise, the value returned is the address of the string buffer.

Output Routines

The input routines described above have corresponding counterparts for output. Fputc, putw, putl, and fputs, output a byte, word, long, and string, respectively. Fputc and putw share a common calling sequence, as shown is Listing 5.14.

Putl has a slightly different calling sequence, as shown in Listing 5.15.

```
#include <stdio.h>
int xeof(p)
FILE *p;
  {
        return(feof(p));
  }
```

Listing 5.11 – Calling the feof routine

```
        .globl  _xeof
        move.l  d3,-(sp)        * Push stream pointer
        jsr     _xeof           * Call routine
        add.l   #4,sp           * Pop argument
        tst.w   d0              * At end of file?
        beq     ateof           * EQ => Yes
```

Listing 5.12 – Calling the C feof routine

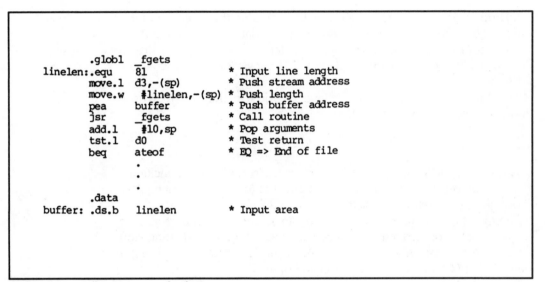

```
            .globl  _fgets
linelen:.equ        81              * Input line length
        move.l  d3,-(sp)            * Push stream address
        move.w  #linelen,-(sp)      * Push length
        pea     buffer              * Push buffer address
        jsr     _fgets              * Call routine
        add.l   #10,sp              * Pop arguments
        tst.l   d0                  * Test return
        beq     ateof               * EQ => End of file
                .
                .
                .
        .data
buffer: .ds.b   linelen             * Input area
```

Listing 5.13 – *Calling sequence for fgets*

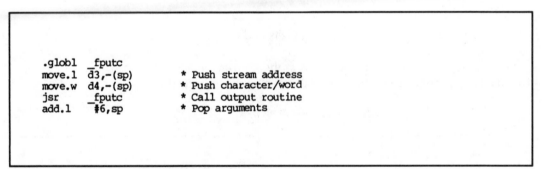

```
.globl  _fputc
move.l  d3,-(sp)            * Push stream address
move.w  d4,-(sp)            * Push character/word
jsr     _fputc              * Call output routine
add.l   #6,sp               * Pop arguments
```

Listing 5.14 – *Calling sequence for fputc and putw*

```
.globl  _putl
move.l  d3,-(sp)            * Push stream address
move.l  d4,-(sp)            * Push long word
jsr     _fputc              * Call output routine
add.l   #8,sp               * Pop arguments
```

Listing 5.15 – *Calling sequence for putl*

In both of these examples, register D3 contains the stream pointer returned by fopen, and register D4 contains the data to be output.

The fputs routine is used to output a null-terminated string to a stream file. The trailing null is not output. Listing 5.16 shows the calling sequence for fputs.

This listing outputs the string "Hello, World" to the stream whose address is contained in register D3.

Fprintf Routine

Fprintf, a formatted-print routine, produces formatted output, including numeric conversion. The output can be directed to a stream. Listing 5.17 shows the calling sequence for this routine.

The fprintf routine takes a format string and a series of arguments. The arguments are converted and output as defined by the format string. You specify the conversion of the arguments in the format string by using a percent sign (%) followed by a conversion operator.

Conversion operators take the form:

   – *ddd.dddlc*

where *ddd* represents a string of decimal digits and *c* represents the conversion specifier.

All of the fields are optional, except for *c*, the conversion specification. The minus sign indicates that the field is to be left-justified instead of right-justified.

```
        .globl  _fputs
        move.l  d3,-(sp)        * Push stream address
        pea     string          * Push string address
        jsr     _fputs          * Call routine
        add.l   #8,sp           * Pop arguments
                .
                .
                .
        .data
string: .dc.b   "Hello, World",10,0
```

Listing 5.16 – *Calling sequence for fputs*

The first decimal field (i.e., before the period) specifies the width of the field for the converted output. The next set of digits (i.e., after the period) specifies the number of decimal places to the right of the decimal point. This specification is only valid for floating-point numbers.

The l specifies that the argument is a 32-bit quantity instead of a 16-bit quantity. This is meaningful only for numeric conversion. Capitalizing the conversion character also causes the argument to be taken as a 32-bit rather than a 16-bit quantity.

Table 5.3 shows the conversion characters accepted by fprintf.

```
        .globl   _fprintf
        move.w   d4,-(sp)        * Arg 1
        pea      format          * format string
        move.l   d3,-(sp)        * Stream address
        jsr      _fprintf        * Call routine
        add.l    #10,sp          * Pop arguments
                 .
                 .
                 .
format: .dc.b    "D4 = %d",10,0  * Format string
```

Listing 5.17 – Calling sequence for fprintf

Character	Argument is
c	A single character
d	A 16-bit number output as decimal
x	A 16-bit number output as hex
o	A 16-bit number output as octal
s	Address of a string terminated by a null character

Table 5.3 – Conversion characters accepted by fprintf

Fseek Routine

The fseek routine in the C library positions a stream file just as the lseek positions an unbuffered file. The calling sequence for the fseek routine is described below.

1. Push a word that describes how you want the offset to be interpreted. This quantity is known as the "sense word." You have three options, as shown below.

   Word   Offset

   0   From the beginning of the file
   1   From the current position
   2   From the end of the file

2. Push the offset (32 bits).

3. Push the stream pointer (32 bits) and call the routine.

You should pop the arguments following the call (10 bytes). Fseek returns the absolute offset from the beginning of the file, or −1 if the seek could not be performed, fseek returns a value of −1. Thus, you can determine the current position by specifying an offset of 0 and a sense word of 1.

Listing 5.18 positions the stream whose stream pointer is contained in register D3 to offset 1000 (decimal).

Fclose Routine

The fclose routine is used to deactivate a stream that has been opened with an fopen call. Listing 5.19 shows the calling sequence for this routine. This code assumes the stream pointer is in register D3.L.

```
        .globl  _fseek
        move.w  #0,-(sp)        * Seek "sense" word
        move.l  #1000,-(sp)     * Offset
        move.l  d3,-(sp)        * Stream pointer
        jsr     _fseek          * Call routine
        add.l   #10,sp          * Pop arguments
```

Listing 5.18 – The fseek routine

BUFFERED FILE COPY PROGRAM

Listing 5.20 is a revised version of Listing 5.8, the unbuffered file copy utility. The routine has been rewritten to use stream I/O instead of unbuffered I/O.

The principal advantages of using buffered I/O are:

1. The copy loop (see lines 44 to 54) is shorter.

2. There is no need for the 1024 byte buffer.

These advantages are offset by the difficulty in checking for I/O errors and increased execution time.

STANDARD I/O

Most implementations of the C language define a set of three files that are open when the program starts. Table 5.4 shows how these files are accessed.

In most implementations, the standard input and standard output may be redirected from the command line. The default is to attach these files to the terminal. The standard error file provides a mechanism for printing error messages on a file (usually the terminal) that is different from the standard output. These standard files are used in UNIX to implement the UNIX concept of *pipes* and *filters*.

Accessing the standard I/O files from assembly language is difficult because the symbols stdin, stdout, and stderr are defined by the C preprocessor. To circumvent this problem, use a C program to define external variables that contain the stream addresses, as shown in Listing 5.21.

```
        .globl  _fclose
        move.l  d3,-(sp)        * Push stream pointer
        jsr     _fclose         * call routine
        add.l   #4,sp           * Pop arguments
```

Listing 5.19 – *The fclose routine*

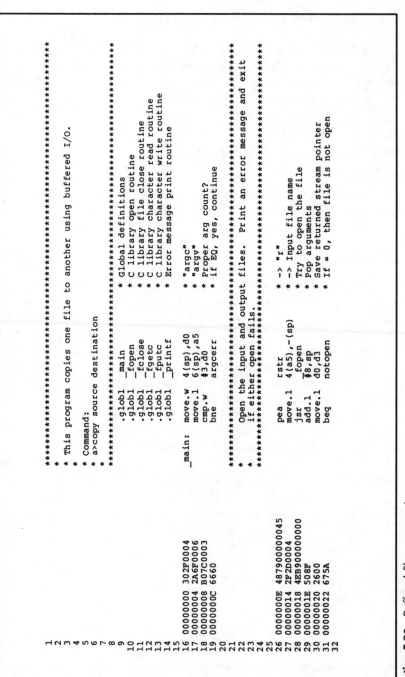

```
 1                      *********************************************
 2                      *
 3                      * This program copies one file to another using buffered I/O.
 4                      *
 5                      * Command:
 6                      * a>copy source destination
 7                      *
 8                      *********************************************
 9                              .globl  _main       * Global definitions
10                              .globl  _fopen      * C library open routine
11                              .globl  _fclose     * C library file close routine
12                              .globl  _fgetc      * C library character read routine
13                              .globl  _fputc      * C library character write routine
14                              .globl  _printf     * Error message print routine
15
16  00000000 302F0004   _main:  move.w  4(sp),d0    * "argc"
17  00000004 2A6F0006           move.l  6(sp),a5    * "argv"
18  00000008 B07C0003           cmp.w   #3,d0       * Proper arg count?
19  0000000C 6660               bne     argcerr     * if EQ, yes, continue
20
21                      *********************************************
22                      * Open the input and output files. Print an error message and exit
23                      * if either open fails.
24                      *********************************************
25
26  0000000E 487900000045       pea     rstr        * -> "r"
27  00000014 2F2D0004           move.l  4(a5),-(sp) * -> Input file name
28  00000018 4EB900000000       jsr     _fopen      * Try to open the file
29  0000001E 508F               add.l   #8,sp       * Pop arguments
30  00000020 2600               move.l  d0,d3       * Save returned stream pointer
31  00000022 675A               beq     notopen     * If = 0, then file is not open
32
```

Listing 5.20 – Buffered file copy routine

```
33  00000024  4879000000047       pea     wstr             * -> "w"
34  0000002A  2F2D0008            move.l  8(a5),-(sp)      * -> Output file name from argv
35  0000002E  4EB900000000        jsr     fopen            * Try to create the output file
36  00000034  508F                add.l   #8,sp            * Pop arguments
37  00000036  2800                move.l  d0,d4            * Save output stream pointer
38  00000038  6758                beq     nocreat          * If = 0, then file created OK
39  0000003A
40                                .page
41                          *******************************************************
42                          * This is the file copy loop.
                            *******************************************************
43  0000003A  2F03         loop:  move.l  d3,-(sp)         * Push input stream pointer
44  0000003C  4EB900000000        jsr     fgetc            * Read a character
45  00000042  588F                add.l   #4,sp            * pop argument
46  00000044  B07CFFFF            cmp.w   #-1,d0           * End of file?
47  00000048  670E                beq     done             * yes, close files and exit
48
49  0000004A  2F04                move.l  d4,-(sp)         * Push output stream pointer
50  0000004C  3F00                move.w  d0,-(sp)         * Push output character
51  0000004E  4EB900000000        jsr     fputc            * Output the byte
52  00000054  5C8F                add.l   #6,sp            * Pop argument
53  00000056  60E2                bra     loop             * Loop till done
54
55  00000058  2F03         done:  move.l  d3,-(sp)         * Close the input file
56  0000005A  4EB900000000        jsr     fclose           * Call close routine
57  00000060  588F                add.l   #4,sp            * Pop arguments
58
59  00000062  2F04                move.l  d4,-(sp)         * Close the output file
60  00000064  4EB900000000        jsr     fclose           * Call close routine
61  0000006A  588F                add.l   #4,sp            * Pop arguments
62  0000006C  4E75                rts                      * Return to runtime library routine
63
```

Listing 5.20 – Buffered file copy routine (continued)

```
64                                   ***********************************************************
65                                   * These sections of code are used to print error messages
66                                   ***********************************************************
67  0000006E  487900000000  argcerr  pea     usage         * -> command line reminder message
68  00000074  4EB900000000           jsr     printf        * Print error message
69  0000007A  588F                   add.l   #4,sp         * Pop arguments
70  0000007C  4E75                   rts                   * and exit
71
72  0000007E  2F2D0004      notopen  move.l  4(a5),-(sp)   * Push input file name address
73  00000082  487900000023           pea     openerr       * Push message address
74  00000088  4EB900000000           jsr     printf        * print open error message
75  0000008E  508F                   add.l   #8,sp         * Pop printf arguments
76  00000090  4E75                   rts                   * Exit to operating system
77
78  00000092  2F2D0008      nocreat  move.l  8(a5),-(sp)   * Push output file name address
79  00000096  487900000033           pea     createrr      * Push pointer to error message
80  0000009C  4EB900000000           jsr     printf        * Print error message
81  000000A2  508F                   add.l   #8,sp         * Pop printf arguments
82  000000A4  4E75                   rts                   * Exit
83                                   ***********************************************************
84                                   * Error message definitions
85                                   ***********************************************************
86  00000000                         .data
87  00000000  5573616753A2020 usage:    .dc.b  "Usage:  copy inputfile outputfile",10,0
88  00000023  43616E6E6F74206F openerr:  .dc.b  "Cannot open %s",10,0
89  00000033  43616E6E6F742063 createrr: .dc.b  "Cannot create %s",10,0
90  00000045  7200            rstr:     .dc.b  "r",0
91  00000047  7700            wstr:     .dc.b  "w",0
92  00000049                            .end
```

Listing 5.20 – Buffered file copy routine (continued)

You can then reference the symbols _xstdin, _xstdout, and _xstderr as external in your assembly-language program.

CALLING AN ASSEMBLY LANGUAGE ROUTINE FROM C

To call an assembly-language routine from C, you need only follow these three conventions:

- register usage
- argument passing
- global routine naming

Listing 5.22 shows a function that initializes an area of memory when called from C.

This function may be used in C to initialize large *arrays* or *structures* more efficiently than the compiler-generated code would.

File Function	Stream Pointer	File Descriptor
Standard input	stdin	STDIN (0)
Standard output	stdout	STDOUT (1)
Standard error	stderr	STDERR (2)

Table 5.4 – *Standard input, output, and error*

```
#include <stdio.h>
FILE *xstdin  = stdin;
FILE *xstdout = stdout;
FILE *xstderr = stderr;
```

Listing 5.21 – *Defining external variables*

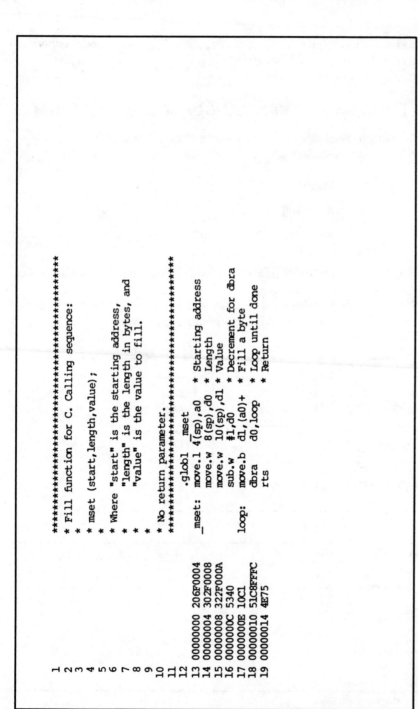

```
 1   *************************************
 2   * Fill function for C. Calling sequence:
 3   *
 4   * mset (start,length,value) ;
 5   *
 6   * Where "start" is the starting address,
 7   *       "length" is the length in bytes, and
 8   *       "value" is the value to fill.
 9   *
10   * No return parameter.
11   *************************************
12           .globl  _mset
13 00000000 206F0004   _mset:  move.l  4(sp),a0    * Starting address
14 00000004 302F0008           move.w  8(sp),d0    * Length
15 00000008 322F000A           move.w  10(sp),d1   * Value
16 0000000C 5340               sub.w   #1,d0       * Decrement for dbra
17 0000000E 10C1       loop:   move.b  d1,(a0)+    * Fill a byte
18 00000010 51C8FFFC           dbra    d0,loop     * Loop until done
19 00000014 4E75               rts                 * Return
```

Listing 5.22 – Memory-fill routine in the C language

SUMMARY

In this chapter, we have covered the following material:

- The various types of I/O performed by applications programs, including Terminal I/O, File I/O, Character I/O, and Special I/O.

- The concept of device-independent I/O and why this concept is important.

- The requirements for interfacing to a high-level language in general, and to CP/M-68K C in particular.

- C run-time library routines for unbuffered and stream I/O, including the calling sequences and samples of how to use these routines.

- How to write assembly-language subroutines to be called from C.

Now that we have a good understanding of I/O techniques, we will apply these techniques in Chapter 6 to write more complicated applications programs.

EXERCISES

1. Write Listing 4.9 (Sum of the first five integers) using the "%d" feature of printf. (see Listing 5.17).

2. Write a program that produces a table of the powers of two from 1 hex to 100000 hex. Print the answers in both decimal and hex. Use the fprintf function, and print the answers to the filename contained in argv[1]. Hint: You can derive the powers of two starting with 1 and shifting left one bit at a time.

3. Write a function to be called from C that copies one area of memory to another. Use the calling sequence:

```
char    *src;
char    *dst;
int     count;
mcpy(src,dst,count);
```
where
- src is the source address
- dst is the destination address
- count is the number of bytes to copy.

Advanced Concepts

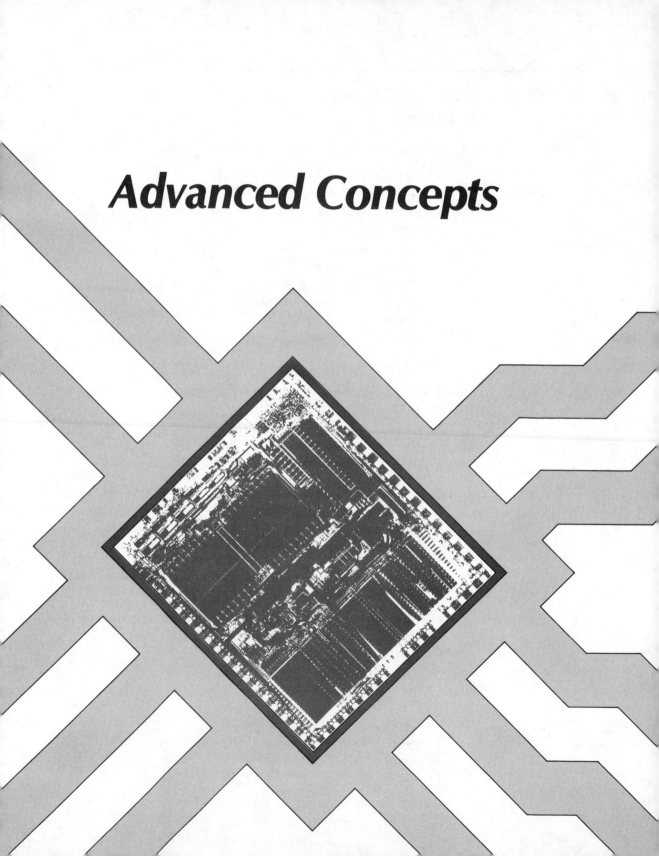

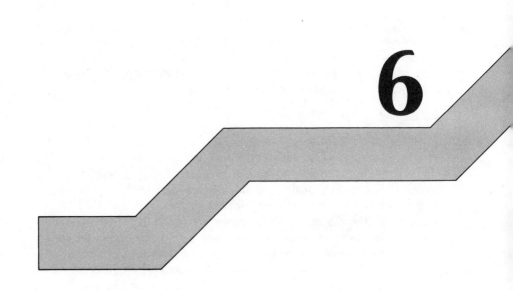

INTRODUCTION

In this chapter we will introduce topics essential to writing advanced applications. These include data storage techniques, sorting, and searching.

We will develop a computerized telephone directory as a sample application. This sample application will use many of the advanced concepts presented here and will have many of the characteristics of a large commercial application system.

DATA ORGANIZATION

One of the most important considerations in writing a large program is how to organize the data both inside and outside the program. You can organize data in the form of records, arrays, linked lists, trees, queues, and dequeues. We will now look at each of these types in detail.

Records

One of the simplest forms of data structure is called a *record*. A record is a set of contiguous memory locations that contains related data. Records are also called *structures,* especially in the C language. For instance, a program that organizes data into a telephone directory would probably have a record with fields for name, address, and telephone number.

Records may exist both in primary memory or on disk. There is an almost infinite variety of record formats. Two of the most popular ones are fixed length records and variable length records.

Fixed Length Records

Fixed-length records (abbreviated FLR) have the same number of bytes in each record. This has distinct advantages when accessing records randomly.

When the records in a file contain differing amounts of information, however, the FLR technique wastes storage space.

Fixed-length records are a natural outgrowth of the days when punched cards were used to run programs and enter data into a computer. Cards had a fixed number of columns, usually 80 or 96. Each column held one byte of information. A common practice in programming machines that used punched-cards was to place each field of the record in a particular card column. When the card was read into memory, the fields would always be offset the same distance from the beginning of the card image in memory.

The FORTRAN language is an example of a holdover from this technique. FORTRAN statements begin in column 7 of the card, which is very difficult on a terminal! If a FORTRAN statement overflows from one line to the next, you have to put a nonblank character in column 6. Fortunately, most systems no longer use cards.

Many present-day storage techniques rely on fixed-length techniques. This is especially true for records contained in primary memory. The simplicity and speed of the FLR technique often outweigh considerations of storage inefficiency.

Variable Length Records

Variable-length records (abbreviated VLR) allow for having a different number of bytes in each record. This technique avoids the problem of wasted space inherent in fixed-length records, but it makes random access slower and more difficult. ASCII text files often use one of the VLR techniques. Here are some of the more popular methods.

1. Records are prefixed with a count field that gives the number of bytes in the record. Minor variations on this technique are the number of bytes dedicated to the count field, whether the count

field includes the number of bytes in the count field, and counting units other than bytes. Most implementations of BASIC on microcomputers use the count technique for string variables. This technique is also used to store text files on many operating systems for mainframes and minicomputers.

2. Records are terminated with some special character or character sequence that cannot occur within the record itself. For example, UNIX text files terminate lines of text with a newline character (decimal 10). CP/M text files terminate each line with a carriage return (decimal 13) / newline sequence. The C language uses a null byte (decimal 0) to terminate strings.

3. The beginning of a record is marked with a unique sequence. This technique is often used in work involving communications, where faulty transmission may distort, add, or delete bytes within a record. A unique sequence of bytes helps resynchronize the receiver and transmitter.

Hybrid Techniques

A number of techniques have been devised that combine the desirable features of fixed and variable length techniques. These "hybrid" techniques usually allow reasonable random access with reasonable storage efficiency.

For records that are processed sequentially, a common technique is to use a fixed portion of the record in combination with a variable portion of the record. The fixed portion of the record contains an indication of how big the variable portion is. This technique is useful for applications that must represent variable-length tables.

Another common technique is to split the fixed and variable portions of the records and store the fixed portions together and the variable portions separately. The fixed portion contains the address of the variable portion. In this way, the capability of fixed-length records to enhance random access is combined with the storage efficiency of variable-length records.

Describing Records in Assembly Language

There are some common techniques for manipulating records in assembly language that are advantageous on the 68000 chip. If a record is less than 32K (as most are), then the "address register indirect with displacement" addressing mode can be used to access the individual fields. This is particularly advantageous when more than one record must be handled at one time.

In coding references to records, it is good practice to use equated names for the different fields in the record. This allows you to go back later and change the size and order of the fields in the record without changing all the references to those fields.

Listing 6.1 gives the definition of the records used in our sample applications program—a computerized telephone directory. For simplicity, we store only the person's name and telephone number, not the address or any other information. The record stores the last name, first name, and middle name, each as ASCII strings terminated with a null character. Each name field can have up to twenty characters. The telephone number (14 characters) and its extension (6 characters) are also stored as null-terminated ASCII strings.

Note how the fields in the record are defined with symbolic expressions (lines 48 to 53). Using the previous field name in defining the next field allows you to change the size of a single field without changing the rest of the description. It is usually helpful to have an equate that gives the total size of the record, such as found in line 53.

STORAGE ALLOCATION

The way in which records are arranged in memory is often critical to a program's performance. There are two techniques commonly used to allocate memory:

1. Allocating the records contiguously, i.e., one following the other. A collection of records arranged this way is called an *array*.

2. Allocating the records non-contiguously, with each record containing the address of the next record in logical order. This is called a *linked list*.

Arrays

An array is composed of records arranged contiguously in memory. When used with fixed-length records, the array technique makes random access extremely easy. To access the record n, you calculate the address as:

address = (n − 1) × (record size) + the starting address of the array

This technique is used in many programs for matrix calculations, tables, and other data that must be accessed randomly. The same technique can

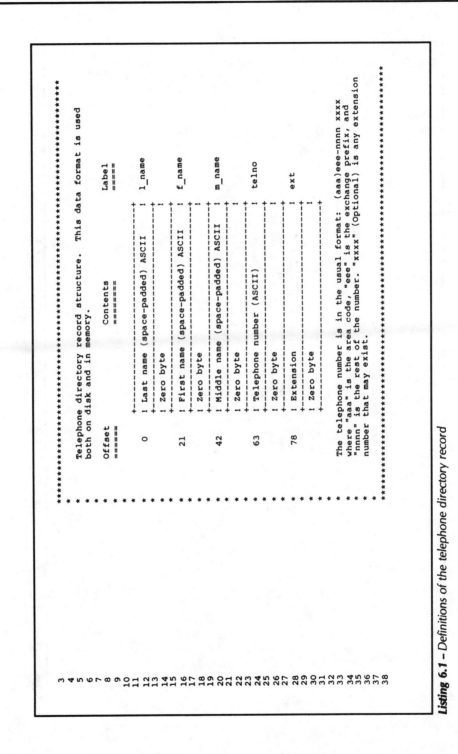

```
 3    ****************************************************************
 4    *
 5    *    Telephone directory record structure.  This data format is used
 6    *    both on disk and in memory.
 7    *
 8    *      Offset        Contents                        Label
 9    *      ======        ========                        =====
10    *                    +--------------------------------+
11    *        0           ! Last name (space-padded) ASCII !    l_name
12    *                    !                                !
13    *                    ! Zero byte                      !
14    *                    +--------------------------------+
15    *                    !                                !
16    *       21           ! First name (space-padded) ASCII !   f_name
17    *                    !                                !
18    *                    ! Zero byte                      !
19    *                    +--------------------------------+
20    *       42           ! Middle name (space-padded) ASCII !  m_name
21    *                    !                                !
22    *                    ! Zero byte                      !
23    *                    +--------------------------------+
24    *       63           ! Telephone number (ASCII)       !    telno
25    *                    !                                !
26    *                    ! Zero byte                      !
27    *                    +--------------------------------+
28    *       78           ! Extension                      !    ext
29    *                    !                                !
30    *                    ! Zero byte                      !
31    *                    +--------------------------------+
32    *
33    *    The telephone number is in the usual format:  (aaa)eee-nnnn xxxx
34    *    where "aaa" is the area code, "eee" is the exchange prefix, and
35    *    "nnnn" is the rest of the number. "xxxx" (Optional) is any extension
36    *    number that may exist.
37    *
38    ****************************************************************
```

Listing 6.1 – *Definitions of the telephone directory record*

```
39
40           *
41           *         Field length definitions
42           *
43           namelen: .equ    20          * Length of name fields
44           numlen:  .equ    14          * Length of phone number field
45           extlen:  .equ    6           * Length of extension field
46           *
47           *         Record definition:
48           *
49           l_name:  .equ    0               * Last name
50           f_name:  .equ    l_name+namelen+1 * First name
51           m_name:  .equ    f_name+namelen+1 * Middle name
52           telno:   .equ    m_name+namelen+1 * Telephone number
53           ext:     .equ    telno+numlen+1   * Extension
54 00000000 length:  .equ    ext+extlen+1     * Record length
                      .page
```

Listing 6.1 – *Definitions of the telephone directory record (continued)*

be used for accessing fixed length records in a disk file. This is sometimes called *direct access*.

The disadvantage of arrays comes in adding or deleting items. The rapid retrieval of information often depends on the information occurring in some particular order. Adding items to or deleting items to an ordered array requires moving all items below the insertion or deletion point. For example, consider the array of numbers displayed in Figure 6.1.

Let's say that we need to insert the number 101 into this array. In order to make room for a new entry between 100 and 103, we must move the lower three elements down. When manipulating large tables, this process can require a lot of time.

Another example of array storage is the argv array of pointers passed to the main routine of a C program (as illustrated in Chapter 5).

Linked Lists

Another technique for allocating storage to a group of records is a linked list. With a linked list, each element of the list contains a way of finding the next entry. This is usually accomplished by inserting the address of the next element in each item of the list. There are several variations of the linked list technique.

Linked lists may be either *linear* or *circular*. Examples of both types are shown in Figure 6.2. Both types of linked lists start at some known point called the *list head*. This is usually a memory location that contains the address of the first element in the list. The linear list terminates with some

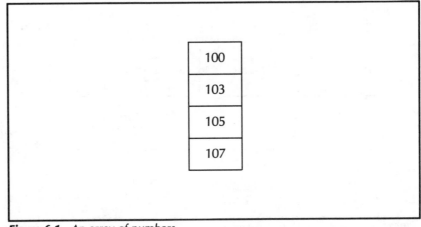

Figure 6.1 – *An array of numbers*

special value in the link portion of the record (usually zero). This value indicates that there are no more records in the list. The circular list is linked in a circle, with the last element pointing either to the first element in the list or the list head.

Linked lists are extremely flexible for inserting and deleting items. To insert an item, you modify two links: the link in the item before the item to be inserted and the link in the item to be inserted. To delete an item, you only need to modify the link that points to the item to be deleted. The cost of this flexibility is the additional processing time it requires to access a random element of a linked list. To access element number k in a linked list, it is necessary to access the previous k − 1 elements.

One advantage of a circular list is that you can tell whether one of the links in the list is corrupt. If you cannot reach the list head within a reasonable number of tries, something is amiss. This reliability is purchased at the cost of extra processing time.

A second variation of a linked-list is to use two pointers in each record in the list; one to the next record and one to the previous record. This

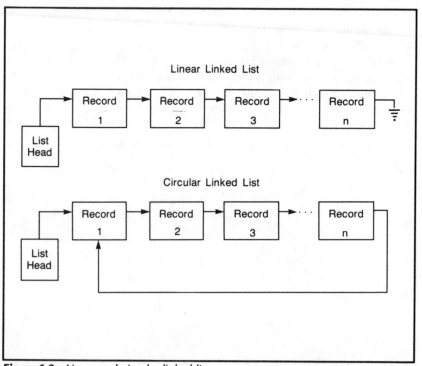

Figure 6.2 – *Linear and circular linked lists*

technique is called a *doubly-linked list*. To insert or delete items from a linked list, you need to know the address of the previous element in the list. The advantage of a having a pointer to the previous element is that it speeds insertion and deletion of random elements in the list.

Yet another variation of the linked list technique is to maintain a pointer to the last element in the list. Such a pointer is known as a *tail pointer*. This is useful when elements are added to the end of a list. To facilitate removal from the end of a list, you would need to use a doubly-linked list with a tail pointer or alternatively, a circular doubly-linked list.

It is poor programming practice to use a linked list on a disk or other form of external memory. The reason for this is that in order to add or delete items from a list, you need to modify *two* items in the list. If the machine crashes between these updates (and this does happen), the linked-list structure is no longer consistent. This can lead to situations where a disk block appears in two files or cannot be used at all. This was a problem in many early versions of UNIX.

DATA STRUCTURES

There are several logical data structures that can be superimposed on top of arrays or linked lists such as stacks, queues, and trees. We will now explore these structures in more detail.

Stacks

You are already familiar with the concept of a stack (the 68000 has a stack implemented in hardware). A stack is a data structure in which the last item added is the first item removed. This is also called a *Last In First Out* (LIFO) arrangement.

Stacks may be implemented either as arrays or linked lists. Implementation of a stack as an array requires a separate variable that defines the top of the stack. The 68000 hardware stack pointer (register A7) is an example of such a variable. Implementation of a stack as a linked list requires adding and removing elements of the list only at the beginning of the list.

Two types of error conditions that you will probably encounter when using stacks are:

1. Running out of room for new stack entries. This condition is known as a *stack overflow*. This can happen, for example, when a program gets caught in an infinite loop that pushes items on the stack.

2. Popping more entries off the stack than were pushed on the stack. This condition is known as a *stack underflow*.

Queues

A *queue* is a list of items in which the first item added is the first item removed. This is also known as a *First In First Out* (FIFO) or a *First Come First Served* (FCFS) arrangement. FIFO arrangements can be observed in any environment where people wait in lines for service. The first person to arrive is the first person served.

You can implement a queue either as an array or as a linked list. Efficient implementation as an array often uses a *circular* (or *ring*) *buffer,* as shown in Figure 6.3. This data structure consists of two pointers: an insertion pointer and a removal pointer.

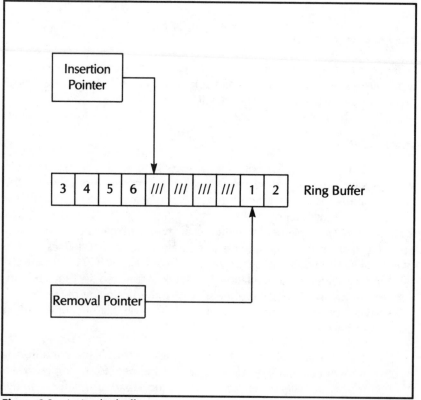

Figure 6.3 – *A circular buffer*

Items are added using an insertion pointer and removed using a removal pointer. When the pointers are equal, the buffer is empty. If adding an element causes the pointers to become equal, the buffer is full. Notice that this means you can't use one of the locations in the buffer (i.e., if the pointers are equal, you can't tell if the buffer is empty or full). You can eliminate this problem by keeping a counter of the number of items in the buffer.

Figure 6.3 shows an example of a circular buffer. Items are added and removed from left to right. Whenever a pointer runs off the right end of the buffer, it is moved back to the left end. Thus, the pointers move in a circular fashion. The shaded areas represent unused elements in the buffer.

Implementing a queue with a linked list is best done using a tail pointer. This makes both insertion and deletion operations quite simple.

Several modifications to the basic queue technique are also useful in many applications. For example, a queue may be based on some order other than chronological. The most common example of this technique is the notion of a *priority order* list of jobs in a larger computer system. A linked list organized according to priorities is often used in an operating system to determine who gets what resources. For additional information, see the discussion of priority-driven scheduling in Chapter 8.

A special form of queue, called a *double-ended queue,* or *dequeue* (pronounced "deck"), allows insertion and removal of elements at both ends. Altered forms of this technique provide for insertion at both ends but removal at only one, or removal at both ends and insertion at only one. These are called *output-restricted* and *input-restricted* dequeues respectively.

Trees

A *tree* is a data structure in which each item can point to more than one item. A tree begins with a single element, called the *root*. The root points to other *nodes,* which in turn point to still other nodes, and so on. (An element in a tree is often called a node.) Figure 6.4 shows an example of a tree structure. The elements of the tree are shown as numbered boxes.

Borrowing terminology from genealogy, element two is termed a *child* of the root, as are elements three and four. The root is said to be the *parent* of these elements. Elements that are children of the same node are termed *siblings*. Nodes five and six in Figure 6.4 are siblings. A node which has no children is called a *leaf* of the tree. Any given node and all its descendants is called a *subtree*. For example, nodes two, five, and six form a subtree of the root.

A tree is useful for describing something that may be defined in terms of itself. This is called *recursion*. For example, on the UNIX operating system, disk devices have a directory of files on the disk. It is also possible for one of these files to be another directory. This directory can contain other directories, which can contain other directories, and so on.

A tree is an ideal representation for this concept. There is a single directory, called the *root directory*, which corresponds to the root of the tree. Nodes in the tree are either directories or ordinary files. Ordinary files are always leaves of the tree, as are empty directories.

Modifying the definition of a tree so that each node has at most two children gives us a special kind of tree called a *binary tree*. The children of

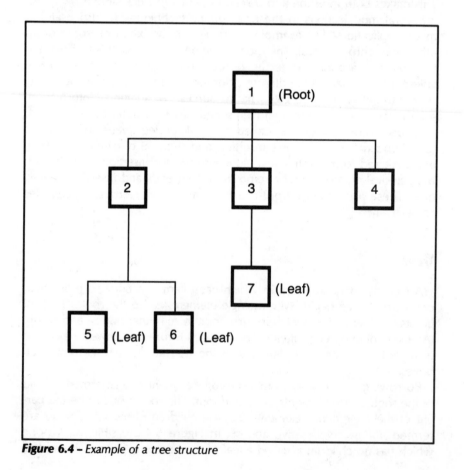

Figure 6.4 – *Example of a tree structure*

a binary tree are called the *left and right descendants,* and the distinction between the two is meaningful. A node with a single right descendant is different from the same node with a single left descendant. Binary trees are used extensively in many areas of computer science. One of the best examples is an *expression tree,* which is found in many high-level language compilers and interpreters.

An excellent example of an expression tree is the handling of arithmetic expressions in assignment statements. For example, the statement

$$x = (a+b)/2$$

would cause the compiler to generate instructions to first add a and b, divide this sum by 2, and then place the result in x. A compiler would represent this expression in a tree as shown in Figure 6.5.

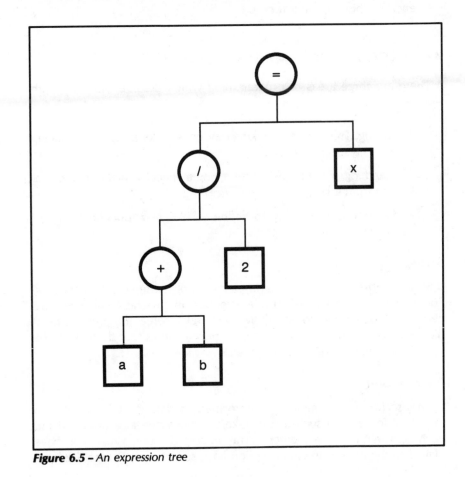

Figure 6.5 – *An expression tree*

Note how the assignment for the equal sign operator (=) is treated as if it were an arithmetic operation. Since most arithmetic operations involve an operator and two operands, the binary tree is a convenient way of representing expressions.

In evaluating this expression, you evaluate the subtree on the left first, and then the subtree on the right. In order to evaluate the equal sign operator, you must first evaluate the division operator (/). To evaluate the division operator you must evaluate the plus sign operator (+). This is called *traversing* the tree. Notice that traversing the binary tree produces the same evaluation order that you would use in evaluating the expression by hand.

There is a great deal more to the area of data structures than we have presented in the brief overview. See the Recommended Reading List for reference on this and other topics.

ADVANCED PROGRAMMING CONCEPTS

There are three areas of programming which deserve more in-depth study:

1. *Sorting.* The process of taking randomly ordered data and placing it into a specified order.

2. *Searching.* The process of retrieving a specified piece of information from a large set of data.

3. *Recursion.* The ability to define a particular function or set of functions in terms of itself.

Sorting

Sorting is the process of ordering a randomly ordered set of records. Sorting has received considerable attention in programming literature because it is so easy to do poorly. We will discuss some of the simple techniques used to sort records. Our discussion assumes that the data to be sorted is in memory rather than on disk.

Insertion Sort

An *insertion sort* is generally performed as data is being input to a program. To perform such a sort, take the items one at a time and put each item that is in the memory array in sorted order. When you have placed all the records in the array, you have sorted data. Due to the large number of insertions required, this technique is particularly suited to a linked-list structure in memory.

Interchange Sort

An *interchange sort* is usually performed on data that is arranged continguously in memory. The simplest form of interchange sort involves taking the top element and comparing it to each element in turn, exchanging where items are out of order. When all the elements have been compared, the top element is certain to be correct. Each element is then compared to all the elements below it. This type of sort requires n – 1 passes through the data, where "n" is the number of records.

Bubble Sort

A more efficient type of sort is the *bubble sort,* which compares successive pairs of elements throughout an array and then swaps elements that are out of order. When a pass is made through the data without exchanging any items, the sort is complete. This method takes advantage of data that may already be in a partially correct order.

Listing 6.2 shows a simple bubble sort program that sorts an array of memory words at the label "list." Lines 5 through 17 constitute a single

```
 1                                    *********************************
 2                                    * Sample bubble sort. Sorts
 3                                    * words at "list."
 4                                    *********************************
 5   000000  41F900000000  bubble:  lea      list,a0      * A0 -> Data
 6   000006  4240                    clr.w    d0           * D0 is flag
 7   000008  3210          bloop:   move.w   (a0),d1      * Load for cmp
 8   00000A  B2680002               cmp.w    2(a0),d1     * Compare 2 elts
 9   00000E  6F0C                   ble      noswap       * LE => Don't swap
10   000010  30A80002               move.w   2(a0),(a0)   * Swap pair of words
11   000014  31410002               move.w   d1,2(a0)     *
12   000018  303C0001               move.w   #1,d0        * Set flag
13   00001C  5488          noswap:  add.l    #2,a0        * A0 -> Next word
14   00001E  B1FC0000000C           cmp.l    #endbuf,a0   * Past end?
15   000024  65E2                   bio      bloop        * No, continue
16   000026  4A40                   tst.w    d0           * Flag set?
17   000028  66D6                   bne      bubble       * Yes, another pass
18   00002A  4E75                   rts                   * Return
19   000000                         .data
20   000000  0006000500030004 list:  .dc.w   6,5,3,4,1,2,0
21                          endbuf:  .equ     *-2
```

Listing 6.2 – Bubble sort routine

pass through the data. Register D0.W is used as a flag to indicate whether any exchanges have taken place on the current pass. Lines 7 through 15 perform one pass on the data, with the comparison taking place at lines 7 through 9 and the exchange at lines 10 through 12.

Searching

Searching is the process of finding an arbitrary record in a large collection. For large amounts of data or frequent searches, the search algorithm can be extremely important.

Sequential Searches

The simplest technique for finding an entry in the table is to start at the beginning of the table and look at each entry in the table until you find the desired one. If you run off the end of the table, then the item you want is not in the table. The average number of comparisons using this technique is one-half the number of entries in the table (assuming that all the entries in the table are accessed an equal number of times). Significant improvements in search times can be made if the data is not accessed in an evenly distributed manner. Simply placing the most commonly accessed data at the beginning of the table can make an amazing difference in performance.

The advantage of the sequential technique is that it does not require the data to be in any particular order. Most of the faster search techniques impose some ordering criteria on the data. A linear search may well be the best method to use, especially if the effort to sort the data outweighs the effort expended in the search. The decision is based on the relative frequency of sorts to searches. For rapidly changing data that is searched infrequently, a linear search is probably the best technique.

Binary Search

For data that is in sorted order, a *binary search* technique can be used to substantially reduce search time. A binary search works like this:

1. Given a table of n elements in sorted order, establish two pointers to the first and last entries in the table.

2. Compute the element that is halfway between the two pointers. (We'll call this element *H*.) Compare this element to the desired element. If the elements are equal, then you have found the

desired data. If the element is less than the desired value, move the bottom pointer to element H. If element H is greater than the desired element, move the top pointer. Reverse these conditions if the table is in descending order instead of ascending order.

3. If the two pointers are equal or adjacent, then the item is not in the table. Otherwise, repeat step 2.

Figure 6.6 shows a sample search sequence. *T* is the Top pointer, *B* is the Bottom pointer, and *H* is the Halfway pointer. In this example, the desired entry is found in three tries, as opposed to five for a sequential search. The desired entry is 135.

The size of the table being considered is reduced by a factor of two for each iteration of the search. For large tables, this is a substantial savings over sequential-search techniques. This is true only if the effort to maintain a sorted table is less than the effort saved by the binary search technique. Effort is measured in terms of program execution time and programming time. The number of times a program is used determines the wisdom of spending a lot of time putting in features which save execution time.

Hashing

Another technique for reducing search times is called *hashing*. Hashing imposes a different kind of structure on the table to be searched. A

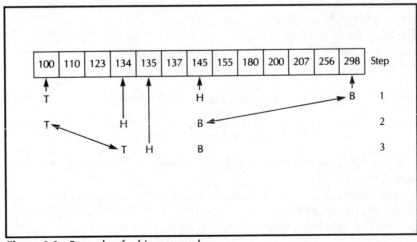

Figure 6.6 – *Example of a binary search*

transformation is performed on the data to be looked up in the table. This transformation is called a *hash function*. The hash function yields a number indicating a position in the table. This number is called a *hash code*. Entries are placed in the table at the locations dictated by their hash codes. A simple way to generate a hash code for alphanumeric (i.e., string) data is to add each of the characters in the string and take the resulting sum as the hash code.

When two or more different table entries have the same hash code, a situation known as a *hash collision* results. The number of hash collisions is an indication of the quality of the hash function. A good hash function will produce few collisions. A hash collision is normally detected when you need to add an entry to the table and you find that an old entry has the same hash code as the new entry. One solution to this problem is to place the new entry in the next free slot in the table. Then do a sequential search starting at the position indicated by the hash code.

Another technique for dealing with hash collisions is to use a large number of linked-list heads. The hash code determines the list in which a given element belongs. Then the lists are searched sequentially. If the hash function yields a reasonably even distribution of elements across the lists, the savings over a sequential search is the number of list heads divided by two. Thus if you used fifty list heads, you would expect to see an improvement of 25 to 1 over a sequential search.

Recursion

Recursion is the ability to define a function in terms of itself. For example, the factorial function can be defined recursively. A factorial multiplies a number by all the integers less than the desired number. Thus, five factorial (written 5!) is $5 \times 4 \times 3 \times 2 \times 1$, or 120. Zero factorial is defined to be 1. The factorial function for a number *n* may be defined recursively as:

1. If *n* is 0 or 1, then n factorial is 1.

2. Otherwise, n factorial is *n* times n − 1 factorial.

Listing 6.3 shows a factorial routine that uses this definition to compute factorials.

Lines 8 through 11 handle the case where n is 0 or 1. Lines 12 through 16 handle the case where n is greater than 1. The fact function is called with n − 1 as the argument. Note that when n reaches 1, the recursion will stop.

In general, recursive routines may not modify registers or static variables without saving and restoring them on the stack. Languages such as C and Pascal, which support recursion, put all variables local to a procedure on the stack. You can do the same in assembly language using the LINK and UNLK instructions to allocate the stack space and the Address register indirect with displacement addressing mode to access the data.

SAMPLE APPLICATION SYSTEM

Our sample telephone directory system performs three functions:

- Adding a new telephone number to the file.
- Recalling a number for a given person.
- Listing the entire file.

In designing this system, we are faced with a fundamental choice: one program or three? We could write three separate programs, each of which would perform one of these three functions. Or we could write a single program that performs all three. To make this decision, consider

```
 1                              ******************************************
 2                              *         Recursive factorial routine
 3                              *
 4                              *         Enter with number in D0.W
 5                              *         Exit  with answer in D0.W
 6                              ******************************************
 7                                      .globl  fact
 8 00000000 B07C0001           fact:   cmp.w   #1,d0       * Easy?
 9 00000004 6E06                       bgt     dofact      * No, do recursion
10 00000006 303C0001                   move.w  #1,d0       * 1! or 0! is 1
11 0000000A 4E75                       rts                 * Done
12 0000000C 3F00               dofact: move.w  d0,-(a7)    * Save present value
13 0000000E 5340                       sub.w   #1,d0       * Decrement
14 00000010 61EE                       jsr     fact        * Take (n-1)!
15 00000012 C1DF                       muls    (a7)+,d0    * n! = n * (n-1)!
16 00000014 4E75                       rts                 * Quit
```

Listing 6.3 – *Recursive factorial routine*

how the program will be used. Recall operations are very frequent, addition operations are relatively infrequent, and listing the file even more infrequent. Addition volume is also quite low. A typical user will add only one or two numbers at a time.

These facts argue for three separate programs. Two of the programs will be used infrequently. Thus, the user can find and add phone numbers from the operating system command level with a minimum of interference with his other activities. The command set we will use is:

PADD first middle last (aaa)eee – nnnn xxxxxx

PFIND name

PLIST

PADD is the command to add a phone number to the existing phone number file. (If no file exists, the PADD program should create it, thereby sparing the user additional inconvenience.) The "first," "middle," and "last" arguments comprise the name of the person. The next two arguments are the phone number. "Aaa" is the area code, "eee" is the exchange, and "nnnn" is the rest of the number. "Xxxxxx" is an optional extension.

PFIND is used to locate a phone number. PFIND prints a list of phone numbers whose first or last names match the given name. This helps locate a person whose full name you can't remember.

PLIST prints the entire phone list on the terminal, sorted by name. By typing *PLIST >filename,* you can also put the listing in a file. The command *PLIST >lst:* sends the listing to the printer.

The record layout for the telephone number file was shown in Listing 6.1. The file on disk consists of an array of these records, sorted by name. All three programs use the length of the file to determine the number of records present.

The PADD Program

Listing 6.4 shows the main entry point for the PADD program. This program is designed in a "top-down" fashion. This means that the program is partitioned into modules, each of which perform a single function. The PADD program has the following modules:

1. The setfield routine, which moves the arguments from the command line into a local storage area called irec. The command line data is also checked for errors at this point.

2. The readfile routine, which reads the entire file into memory at a location called buffer. If the file does not exist, readfile creates it. If the file will not fit in memory, an error message is generated and the program exits to the operating system.

3. The insert routine, which takes the data in the command line record irec and inserts it into the buffer read from disk. This is a type of insertion sort.

4. The wrtfile routine, which writes the modified buffer back out to disk.

Writing programs in this fashion allows you to partition a large task into several smaller and more manageable ones. The main routine in such programs often consists of only subroutine calls.

The Setfield Function

Listing 6.5 shows the code for the setfield function, which moves the fields from the command line (argv) into a temporary area called irec. Setfield mainly checks for the proper number of arguments on the command line and moves the arguments into the proper fields. Two subsidiary functions are used:

- A function called movestr, which moves a variable length string into a fixed-length area. Nulls are added to fill out unused space in the destination area.

- A function called valid, which checks a telephone number for the proper syntax.

The Readfile Function

The function called readfile is shown in Listing 6.6. This function uses read calls in the C run-time library file to open the file, read it, and close it. Lines 223 through 235 open the file PHONE.DAT. If the file does not exist (see lines 228 through 235), it is created. Failure to create the file terminates the program with an error message.

Lines 239 through 253 read the file. Each call to the C _read routine attempts to read 4K into the buffer. (4K is a purely arbitrary size.) When the read operation returns zero bytes read, the program has reached the end of the file.

```
*********************************************************************
*
*                        P A D D   P r o g r a m
*                        =======================
*
*       This program adds a new phone number to the existing phone number file.
*
*       Command:
*
*       A>padd first middle last (aaa)eee-nnnn Xxxxx
*
*       Where "first", "middle", and "last" are the names to be associated with
*       the phone number. "aaa" is the area code, "eee" is the exchange, and
*       "nnnn" is the rest of the number. "xxxx" is an optional extension.
*
*       The number is added to the PHONE.DAT file as follows:
*
*       1).    Move the command line data into a record in memory
*       2).    Read the entire file into a temporary buffer
*       3).    Insert the new record into the proper position
*       4).    Write the file back out.
*
*       Note that this technique requires that the entire file fit into memory
*       at once. Using a 64K buffer gives about 750 phone number entries.
*
*       Main entry point. This program is designed for use with the CP/M-68K
*       C runtime library, and hence can use argc/argv.
*
*********************************************************************
bufsize:.equ     $10000                             *  64K buffer
        .globl   _exit                              *  Exit routine
*
        .globl   main
_main:  move.w   4(a7),d7                            *  Entry point.
        move.l   6(a7),a5                            *  Fetch "argc"
        jsr      setfield                            *  Fetch "argv"
        jsr      readfile                            *  Pick up fields from argc/argv
        jsr      insert                              *  Read file into memory
        jsr      wrtfile                             *  Insert record into file copy
        jsr      _exit                               *  Write file back to disk
        .page                                        *  Call exit routine
```

```
89  00000000  3E2F0004
90  00000004  2A6F0006
91  00000008  6112
92  0000000A  610000E6
93  0000000E  61000166
94  00000012  610001D2
95  00000016  4EB900000000
96  0000001C
```

Listing 6.4 – The main routine for the PADD program

```
 97                              ************************************************
 98                              *
 99                              *    Setfield routine.  This subroutine moves the fields from argv into
100                              *    a local record structure for later insertion into the buffer.
101                              *
102                              ************************************************
103                              setfield:
104  0000001C  48E7FFFE                   movem.l  d0-d7/a0-a6,-(a7)   * Save registers
105  00000020  49F900000000               lea      irec,a4            * a4 -> Record to insert
106  00000026  BE7C0005                   cmp.w    #5,d7              * Must have at least 5 args
107  0000002A  6D00021E                   blt      usage              * Don't have enough args
108  0000002E  BE7C0006                   cmp.w    #6,d7              * Can't have more than 6
109  00000032  6E000216                   bgt      usage              * Got too many
110  00000036  660C                       bne      noext              * If 5, no extension
111  00000038  206D0014                   move.l   20(a5),a0          * a0 -> source
112  0000003C  43EC004E                   lea      ext(a4),a1         * a1 -> dest.
113  00000040  7006                       move.l   #extlen,d0         * *      6 chars max
114  00000042  613E                       jsr      movestr            * Move string into record
115                              *
116                              *    Move the name fields from the command line into the record
117                              *
118  00000044  206D0004          noext:   move.l   4(a5),a0           * a0 -> First name
119  00000048  43EC0015                   lea      f_name(a4),a1      * a1 -> dest
120  0000004C  7014                       move.l   #namelen,d0        * 20 chars max
121  0000004E  6132                       jsr      movestr            * Do the move
122
123  00000050  206D0008                   move.l   8(a5),a0           * a0 -> Middle Name
124  00000054  43EC002A                   lea      m_name(a4),a1      * a1 -> dest
125  00000058  7014                       move.l   #namelen,d0        * 20 chars max
126  0000005A  6126                       jsr      movestr            * Do the move
127
128  0000005C  206D000C                   move.l   12(a5),a0          * a0 -> Last name
129  00000060  43EC0000                   lea      l_name(a4),a1      * a1 -> destinaion
130  00000064  7014                       move.l   #namelen,d0        * 20 chars max
131  00000066  611A                       jsr      movestr            * Do the move
132                              *
133                              *    Validate and move the telephone number
134                              *
```

***Listing 6.5** – The Setfield function*

```
135  00000068  206D0010          move.l  16(a5),a0            * a0 -> Telephone #
136  0000006C  612E              jsr     valid               * Do the validation
137  0000006E  4A80              tst.l   d0                  * If d0 <> 0,
138  00000070  660001E0          bne     badno               *             Bad tel #
139  00000074  700E              move.l  #numlen,d0          * d0 = length
140  00000076  43EC003F          lea     telno(a4),a1        * a1 -> destination
141  0000007A  6106              jsr     movestr             * Move it
142  0000007C  4CDF7FFF          movem.l (a7)+,d0-d7/a0-a6   * Restore registers
143  00000080  4E75              rts                         * Return to caller
144  00000082                    .page
145
146          *************************************************************
147          *
148          *  Movestr routine.  This routine moves a null-terminated string whose
149          *  address is in a0 to an area pointed to by a1.  D0 has the number of
150          *  bytes in the output area.  Destination area is null (zero) padded.
151          *
152          *  A trailing null character is placed at the end of each field, which
153          *  guarantees the strings are null-terminated.
154          *
155  00000082  48E7FFFE  movestr:movem.l d0-d7/a0-a6,-(a7)   * Save registers
156  00000086  5340              subq.w  #1,d0               * d0 = dbra adjusted count
157  00000088  1218      mloop:  move.b  (a0)+,d1            * Fetch next byte
158  0000008A  6602              bne     notnull             * If NE, then not end of string
159  0000008C  5388              subq.l  #1,a0               * Decrement a0
160  0000008E  12C1      notnull:move.b  d1,(a1)+            * Put in destination
161  00000090  51C8FFF6          dbra    d0,mloop            * Loop till done
162  00000094  4219              clr.b   (a1)+               * Install guaranteed null byte
163  00000096  4CDF7FFF          movem.l (a7)+,d0-d7/a0-a6   * Pop registers
164  0000009A  4E75              rts                         * And return
165  0000009C                    .page
166
167          *************************************************************
168          *
169          *  Valid routine.  This routine checks a phone number whose address is in
170          *  a0 for valid syntax.  D0 is zero if all ok, non-zero if not.
171          *
            *************************************************************
```

Listing 6.5 - The Setfield function (continued)

```
172  0000009C  48E77FFE  valid:   movem.l  d1-d7/a0-a6,-(a7)      * Save registers
173  000000A0  0C180028           cmp.b    #'(',(a0)+             * Must start with area code
174  000000A4  6630               bne      vbad                  * Didn't
175  000000A6  303C0003           move.w   #3,d0                 * D0 = count
176  000000AA  6130               bsr      digstr                * Look for 3 digits
177  000000AC  6628               bne      vbad                  * Didn't find them
178  000000AE  0C180029           cmp.b    #')',(a0)+            * Look for end of area code
179  000000B2  6622               bne      vbad                  * Didn't find it
180  000000B4  303C0003           move.w   #3,d0                 * Look for 3 digits
181  000000B8  6122               bsr      digstr                *
182  000000BA  661A               bne      vbad                  * Didn't find them
183  000000BC  0C18002D           cmp.b    #'-',(a0)+            * look for "-"
184  000000C0  6614               bne      vbad                  * Didn't find
185  000000C2  303C0004           move.w   #4,d0                 * Look for   4 more digits
186  000000C6  6114               bsr      digstr                *
187  000000C8  660C               bne      vbad                  * Didn't find
188  000000CA  4A10               tst.b    (a0)                  * End of string?
189  000000CC  6608               bne      vbad                  * No
190  000000CE  4280               clr.l    d0                    * Indicate good return
191  000000D0  4CDF7FFE  vret:    movem.l  (a7)+,d1-d7/a0-a6     * restore registers
192  000000D4  4E75               rts                            *
193  000000D6  303CFFFF  vbad:    move.w   #-1,d0                * Set d0 non-zero
194  000000DA  60F4               bra      vret                  * return
195
196                           *  Look for a string of contiguous digits
197                           *
198  000000DC  5340      digstr:  sub.w    #1,d0                 * Adjust for dbra
199  000000DE  0C100030  dloop:   cmp.b    #'0',(a0)             * check   digit
200  000000E2  6D0C               blt      baddig                *
201  000000E4  0C180039           cmp.b    #'9',(a0)+           *         range
202  000000E8  6E06               bgt      baddig                *
203  000000EA  51C8FFF2           dbra     d0,dloop              * Until done
204  000000EE  4240      baddig:  clr.w    d0                    * Set condition codes
205  000000F0  4E75               rts                            * Return
206  000000F2                     .page
```

Listing 6.5 – *The Setfield function (continued)*

```
207   *********************************************************************
208   *
209   *      Readfile routine.  This subroutine opens the telephone data file and
210   *      reads it into memory at location "buffer".
211   *
212   *********************************************************************
213             .globl  _open              * C runtime open routine
214             .globl  _creat             * C runtime file create routine
215             .globl  _read              * C runtime file read routine
216             .globl  _close             * C runtime file close routine
217   READ:     .equ    0                  * Read parameter to open
218   readfile:
219   000000F2 48E7FFFE        movem.l d0-d7/a0-a6,-(a7)    * Save registers
220         *
221         *      Open the telephone # file
222         *
223   000000F6 3F3C0000        move.w  #READ,-(a7)    * Push Read code
224   000000FA 4879000000CC    pea     telfil         * And filename
225   00000100 4EB900000000    jsr     open           * Call File Open routine
226   00000106 5C8F            add.l   #6,a7           * Pop parameters
227   00000108 4A40            tst.w   d0             * File found?
228   0000010A 6E18            bgt     openok         * Yes, don't create it
229   0000010C 3F3C01FF        move.w  #511,-(a7)     * Push protection word
230   00000110 4879000000CC    pea     telfil         * and filename address
231   00000116 4EB900000000    jsr     creat          * Try to create file
232   0000011C 5C8F            add.l   #6,a7           * Pop parameters
233   0000011E 4A40            tst.w   d0             * Did we get the file created?
234   00000120 6B000138        bmi     badopen        * No, bomb out
235   00000124 3E00    openok: move.w  d0,d7          * Remember file descriptor
236         *
237         *      Now read the file into memory
238         *
```

Listing 6.6 – The Readfile function

```
239  00000126  47F900000055              lea     buffer,a3           * a3 -> Buffer
240                          readloop:
241  0000012C  3F3C1000                  move.w  #4096,-(a7)         * Push byte count (4K)
242  00000130  48790000055               pea     buffer              * Push buffer address
243  00000136  3F07                      move.w  d7,-(a7)            * Push file number
244  00000138  4EB900000000              jsr     read                * Read as much as possible
245  0000013E  DFFC00000008              adda.l  #8,a7               * Pop arguments
246  00000144  4A40                      tst.w   d0                  * D0 > 0?
247  00000146  6714                      beq     eof                 * No, must be end of file
248  00000148  6B000128                  bmi     readerr             * If negative, read error
249  0000014C  48C0                      ext.l   d0                  * Extend to long
250  0000014E  D7C0                      adda.l  d0,a3               * Bump to next byte to read
251  00000150  B7FC000100AA              cmpa.l  #endbuff,a3         * Overflowing buffer?
252  00000156  6400010A                  bhis    boverfl             * Yes, quit
253  0000015A  60D0                      bra     readloop            * And re-try read
254  0000015C  3F07              eof:    move.w  d7,-(a7)            * Push file number
255  0000015E  4EB900000000              jsr     close               * Call close routine
256  00000164  DFFC00000002              adda.l  #2,a7               * Pop parameter
257  0000016A  23CB000100AA              move.l  a3,lastb            * Save the end of the buffer
258  00000170  4CDF7FFF                  movem.l (a7)+,d0-d7/a0-a6   * Restore registers
259  00000174  4E75                      rts                         * Return
260  00000176                            .page
```

Listing 6.6 – *The Readfile function (continued)*

Lines 254 through 256 perform the file close operation. The first free byte in the buffer is recorded at line 257. This address is used by later portions of the program to determine the number of records to process.

The Insert Routine

Listing 6.7 shows the insertion routine called insert and its subsidiary function ncmp. Inserting a new record in the buffer requires three actions:

1. Finding the place to insert the new record (lines 271–278). The function ncmp (lines 297–328) compares the name fields in two records. This function is called repeatedly until either the end of the buffer is encountered or the record in the buffer is greater than the record in irec. When either case becomes true, control is transferred to line 282.

2. Moving the entire buffer down to make a space in the middle of the buffer in order to insert the new record (lines 282–286).

3. Moving the new record into the newly vacated space in the buffer (lines 290–294). Notice that the buffer size was adjusted at line 283 to reflect the insertion of the new record.

The ncmp function takes advantage of the fact that the fields in the record are arranged in the proper order for comparison. Ncmp compares the three name fields as if they were one very large string. The null-padding of these fields ensures that this technique will work.

The Wrtfile Routine

Listing 6.8 contains the code for the wrtfile routine, which copies the modified file from memory back out to disk. Lines 341 through 346 create a new copy of the file. (The old file is deleted by _creat.) Lines 350 through 367 write the file out in segments 4K bytes long. (Again, 4K was chosen quite arbitrarily.)

The only tricky code comes when less than 4K remains to be written to disk. Register A5 is set to point to the first byte not to be written at lines 352 through 356. This byte is either at the top of the buffer or 4K beyond the first byte to be written.

```
261
262           **********************************************************
263           *        Insert routine. This routine inserts the record at "irec" into the
264           *        buffer at the appropriate place. The buffer is moved down to
265           *        accommodate the new entry.
266           *
267           **********************************************************
268  00000176 48E7FFFE     insert: movem.l d0-d7/a0-a6,-(a7)   * Save registers
269  0000017A 43F900000055         lea     buffer,a1            * a1 -> Buffer
270  00000180 267900100AA          move.l  lastb,a3             * a3 -> End of buffer
271  00000186 41F900000000 find:   lea     irec,a0              * a0 -> Comparison string
272  0000018C B3CB                 cmpa.l  a3,a1                * Past the end
273  0000018E 640E                 bhis    found                * Yes, insert at end
274  00000190 6132                 jsr     ncmp                 * Compare the two
275  00000192 4A40                 tst.w   d0                   * record : buffer
276  00000194 6B08                 bmi     found                * Found place to insert
277  00000196 D3FC00000055         adda.l  #length,a1           * a1 -> Next record in buffer
278  0000019C 60E8                 bra     find                 * Loop till done
279           *
280           *        Now move the buffer down to make room for the new entry
281           *
282  0000019E 49EB0055     found:  lea     length(a3),a4        * a4 -> New end of buffer
283  000001A2 23CC000100AA         move.l  a4,lastb             * Record this
284  000001A8 1923         moveit: move.b  -(a3),-(a4)          * transfer a byte
285  000001AA B3CB                 cmpa.l  a3,a1                * Just moved last?
286  000001AC 65FA                 blo     moveit               * No, continue to move
287           *
288           *        Insert the record into the buffer
289           *
290  000001AE 41F900000000 rinsrt: lea     irec,a0              * a0 -> record
291  000001B4 303C0054             move.w  #length-1,d0         * d0 = dbra count
292  000001B8 12D8                 move.b  (a0)+,(a1)+          * Move a byte
293  000001BA 51C8FFFC             dbra    d0,rinsrt            * Continue till done
294  000001BE 4CDF7FFF             movem.l (a7)+,d0-d7/a0-a6    * Pop registers
295  000001C2 4E75                 rts                          * And return
```

Listing 6.7 – The insert routine

```
296 000001C4                .page
297              ******************************************************************
298              *
299              *   Ncmp routine. This routine compares two name fields, whose addresses
300              *   are in a0 and a1.
301              *
302              *   Returns: (in d0)
303              *
304              *        +1    if    (a0) > (a1)
305              *         0    if    (a0) = (a1)
306              *        -1    if    (a0) < (a1)
307              *
308              ******************************************************************
309 000001C4 48E77FFE ncmp:   movem.l  d1-d7/a0-a6,-(a7)    *    Save registers
310              ******************************************************************
311              *
312              *   Note that the fields in the record are cleverly arranged so that we
313              *   can just compare the entire name field as a single string.
314              *
315              ******************************************************************
316
317 000001C8 303C003E nloop:  move.w  #(namelen*3)+2,d0     *    DBRA adjusted count
318 000001CC B308             cmp.b   (a0)+,(a1)+           *    compare next byte
319 000001CE 6E0A             bgt     retneg                *    if GT, (a1) > (a0)
320 000001D0 6D0C             blt     retpos                *    if LT, (a0) > (a1)
321 000001D2 51C8FFF8         dbra    d0,nloop
322 000001D6 4280             clr.l   d0                    *    if neither, must be equal
323 000001D8 6006             bra     nret                  *    Return 0
324 000001DA 70FF     retneg: move.l  #-1,d0                *    Return -1
325 000001DC 6002             bra     nret
326 000001DE 7001     retpos: move.l  #1,d0                 *    Return +1
327 000001E0 4CDF7FFE nret:   movem.l (a7)+,d1-d7/a0-a6     *    Restore registers
328 000001E4 4E75             rts                           *    Return
329 000001E6                  .page
```

Listing 6.7 – The insert routine (continued)

```
330        ***************************************************
331        *
332        *   Wrtfile routine. This routine writes the file back to disk from the
333        *   buffer. The buffer is written 4K at a time.
334        *
335        ***************************************************
336                      .globl  write                        * C Runtime library write routine
337 000001E6 48E7FFFE   wrtfile:movem.l  d0-d7/a0-a6,-(a7)    * Save registers
338        *
339        *   First, Create the file
340        *
341 000001EA 3F3C01FF        move.w  #511,-(a7)               * Push protection word
342 000001EE 4879000000CC    pea     telfil                   * And file name
343 000001F4 4EB900000000    jsr     creat                    * Call C create routine
344 000001FA DFFC00000006    adda.l  #6,a7                    * Pop parameters
345 00000200 3E00            move.w  d0,d7                    * Remember file number
346 00000202 6B66            bmi     badcreat                 * Can't create file
347        *
348        *   Now write the file, 4K at a time
349        *
350 00000204 2679000100AA    move.l  lastb,a3                 * a3 -> Last byte in the file
351 0000020A 49F900000055    lea     buffer,a4                * a4 -> beginning of buffer
352 00000210 4BEC1000   wloop:  lea   4096(a4),a5            * a5 -> buffer + 4K
353 00000214 B7CD            cmpa.l  a5,a3                    * Past end?
354 00000216 6402            bhis    do_wrt                   * No, just do 4K
355 00000218 2A4B            move.l  a3,a5                    * less than 4K remains
356 0000021A 260D       do_wrt: move.l  a5,d3                 * d3 = starting address
357 0000021C 968C            sub.l   a4,d3                    * Compute byte count
358 0000021E 3F03            move.w  d3,-(a7)                 * Push byte count
359 00000220 2F0C            move.l  a4,-(a7)                 * Push buffer address
360 00000222 3F07            move.w  d7,-(a7)                 * Push file number
361 00000224 4EB900000000    jsr     write                    * call write routine
362 0000022A DFFC00000008    adda.l  #8,a7                    * Pop parameters
363 00000230 B640            cmp.w   d0,d3                    * Did it all get written?
364 00000232 6646            bne     writerr                  * No, give error message
365 00000234 284D            move.l  a5,a4                    * Place to start next write
366 00000236 B9CB            cmp.l   a3,a4                    * Equal to end of buffer?
367 00000238 66D6            bne     wloop                    * No, Keep writing
368        *
369        *   Close output file
370        *
371 0000023A 3F07            move.w  d7,-(a7)                 * Push file number
372 0000023C 4EB900000000    jsr     close                    * Go close the file
373 00000242 548F            add.l   #2,a7                    * Pop parameter
374 00000244 4CDF7FFF        movem.l (a7)+,d0-d7/a0-a6        * Pop registers
375 00000248 4E75            rts                              * And return
376 0000024A                 .page
```

Listing 6.8 – The wrtfile routine

The Data Area

Listing 6.9 shows the remainder of the program—error routines, error messages, and data areas. The program handles error conditions by printing a message to the terminal screen and exiting. This type of error is sometimes called a *fatal error*, in that the program cannot recover and continue processing.

Notice that the majority of data is in the bss segment. This is not accidental. The buffer area is quite large, and placing it in the bss segment means that it is not stored on the disk. This reduces both disk storage requirements and the time it takes to load the program.

The PFIND Program

Listing 6.10 shows the main program for the PFIND command. This program calls the readfile routine to load the data file into memory. (For this program, we removed the code that created an empty data file.) The print routine then prints out all entries in the table that match the name specified in the single argument on the program's command line.

Reusing the readfile routine illustrates one of the great truths in programming: There ain't nothing new under the sun. Most programming efforts involve modifying existing code rather than writing new code. Writing modular code ensures that pieces from one program can readily be used in another program.

The Print Routine

The only new code in the PFIND program is the print routine. This is shown in Listing 6.11. The code at lines 147 through 159 forms a loop that checks each entry in the buffer using a local subroutine called match. The return parameter of match is the Z condition-code bit. The Z-bit is set when the record pointed to by A3 matches the string pointed to by A5. Using condition-code bits in this way saves a few instructions and is a useful technique for improving the performance of routines that are called frequently.

The match routine at lines 169 through 186 attempts to match the string (whose address is in A5) with the first and last name fields pointed to by A3. This routine checks only the command argument for termination so that a match occurs when the argument name is a prefix of the record name. For example, "White" will match "White," but it will also match "Whitehead." This is a useful feature if you can't remember the exact spelling of a name.

```
377
378                        *********************************************************
379                        *
380                        *       Error handling routines.  These routines print the appropriate error
381                        *       message and exit.
382                        *
383                        *********************************************************
384  0000024A 41F900000000 usage:    .globl  _printf          * C library printf routine
                                     lea     usagem,a0        * Usage message
385  00000250 602E                  bra     eprint           * Print it
386  00000252 41F900000033 badno:   lea     badnom,a0        * Bad phone # message
387  00000258 6026                  bra     eprint           * Print it
388
389  0000025A 41F90000004F badopen: lea     openmsg,a0       * Can't open file
390  00000260 601E                  bra     eprint           * Print it
391
392  00000262 41F900000068 boverfl: lea     bovfmsg,a0       * Buffer overflow
393  00000268 6016                  bra     eprint           * Print it
394
395  0000026A 41F900000079 badcreat: lea    creatm,a0        * Can't create file
396  00000270 600E                  bra     eprint           * print it
397
398  00000272 41F900000094 readerr: lea     readmsg,a0       * Read error
399  00000278 6006                  bra     eprint
400
401  0000027A 41F9000000AF writerr: lea     wrtmsg,a0        * Write error
402
403  00000280 2F08         eprint:  move.l  a0,-(a7)         * Push string address
404  00000282 4EB900000000          jsr     _printf          * Print it
405  00000288 DFFC00000004          adda.l  #4,a7            * Pop parameter
406  0000028E 4EB900000000          jsr     _exit            * Exit
407  00000000                       .data
408                        *
409                        *       Error Messages
410                        *
411  00000000 55736167653A2070 usagem: .dc.b  Usage: padd first middle last (aaa)eee-nnnn Xxxxx',10,0
```

Listing 6.9 – *The data area for the PADD program*

```
411 00000008 6164642006669273                badnom: .dc.b   'Incorrect telephone number',10,0
411 00000010 74206D6964646C65
411 00000018 206C617374202861
411 00000020 6161296565652D6E
411 00000028 6E6E6E6E205878787
411 00000030 780A00
412 00000033 496E636F72726563                openmsg:.dc.b   'Cannot open "PHONE.DAT"',10,0
412 0000003B 7420746C657068
412 00000043 6F6E65206E756D62
412 0000004B 65720A00
413 0000004F 43616E6E6F74206F                bovfmsg:.dc.b   'Buffer overflow',10,0
413 00000057 70656E20222504F84F
413 0000005F 4E452E444154220A
413 00000067 00
414 00000068 427566666572206F                creatm: .dc.b   'Cannot create "PHONE.DAT"',10,0
414 00000070 766572666C6F770A
414 00000078 00
415 00000079 43616E6E6F742063                readmsg:.dc.b   'Read error on "PHONE.DAT"',10,0
415 00000081 7265617465202250
415 00000089 484F4E452E444154
415 00000091 220A00
416 00000094 5265616420657272                wrtmsg: .dc.b   'Write error on "PHONE.DAT"',10,0
416 0000009C 6F72206F6E202250
416 000000A4 484F4E452E444154
416 000000AC 220A00
417 000000AF 5772697465206572                        .even
417 000000B7 726F72206F6E2022
417 000000BF 50484F4E452E4441                        .text
417 000000C7 54220A00
418 000000CC
418 000000CC
419 00000294
```

Listing 6.9 – *The data area for the PADD program (continued)*

```
420  00000294                        .page
421                         *******************************************************
422                         *
423                         *       Initialized data area
424                         *
425                         *******************************************************
426  000000CC              telfil:  .dc.b    'phone.dat',0          *    Data base file
427  000000CC 70686F6E652E6461
427  000000D4 7400
428                                 .even                          *    Force to word boundary
429                         *******************************************************
430                         *
431                         *       Uninitialized data area
432                         *
433                         *******************************************************
434  00000000                       .bss
435                                 .even
436  00000000              irec:    .ds.b    length                *    Input record space
437  00000055              buffer:  .ds.b    bufsize+length        *    File buffer area
438                        endbuff: .equ     *                     *    End of the buffer
439                                 .even                          *    Force word alignment
440  000100AA              lastb:   .ds.l    1                     *    Contains data end address
441  000100AE                       .end
```

Listing 6.9 – *The data area for the PADD program (continued)*

```
55   ****************************************************************
56   *
57   *                    P F I N D   P r o g r a m
58   *                    =============================
59   *
60   *      This program list phone numbers for a specified name.
61   *
62   *      Command:
63   *
64   *      A>pfind name
65   *
66   *      The program works as follows:
67   *
68   *      1).    Read the entire file into a temporary buffer
69   *      2).    Print each record that matches the specified name
70   *      3).    Exit.
71   *
72   *      Note that this technique requires that the entire file fit into memory
73   *      at once.  Using a 64K buffer gives about 800 phone number entries.
74   *
75   *
76   *      Main entry point.  This program is designed for use with the CP/M-68K
77   *      C runtime library, and hence can use argc/argv.
78   *
79   ****************************************************************
80   bufsize:.equ   $10000             *       64K buffer
81          .globl  _exit              *       Exit routine
82   *
83                                     *       Entry point
84   00000000  0C6F00020004  _main:    cmp.w   #2,4(a7)    *       Argc = 22
85   00000006  660000EE                bne     usage       *       No, print error message
86   0000000A  6110                    jsr     readfile    *       Read file into memory
87   0000000C  2A6F0006                move.l  6(a7),a5    *       a5 -> argv
88   00000010  2A6D0004                move.l  4(a5),a5    *       Second argument is match string
89   00000014  6174                    jsr     print       *       Call print routine
90   00000016  4EB900000000            jsr     _exit       *       Call exit routine
91   0000001C                          .page
```

Listing 6.10 – The main routine for the PFIND program

```
139
140    ****************************************************************
141    *        Print routine. This routine prints successive entries in the buffer
142    *        until all entries have been printed.
143    *
144    ****************************************************************
145 0000008A 48E7FFFE       print:  movem.l d0-d7/a0-a6,-(a7)    * Save registers
146 0000008E 47F900000000           lea    buffer,a3             * a3 -> buffer
147 00000094 613C           ploop:  bsr    match                 * Check a match
148 00000096 6626                   bne    pnext                 * NE => No match, don't print it
149 00000098 486B004E               pea    ext(a3)               *
150 0000009C 486B003F               pea    telno(a3)             * Push
151 000000A0 486B0000               pea    l_name(a3)            * printf
152 000000A4 486B002A               pea    m_name(a3)            *    arguments
153 000000A8 486B0015               pea    f_name(a3)            *    (reverse
154 000000AC 48790000 0000          pea    format                *     order)
155 000000B2 4EB900000000           jsr    printf                * Do the print
156 000000B8 DFFC00000018           adda.l #24,a7                * Pop arguments
157 000000BE D7FC00000055   pnext:  adda.l #length,a3            * a3 -> Next record
158 000000C4 B7F900011056           cmpa.l lastb,a3              * Done?
159 000000CA 65C8                   blo    ploop                 * No, continue to print
160 000000CC 4CDF7FFF               movem.l (a7)+,d0-d7/a0-a6    * Restore registers
161 000000D0 4E75                   rts                          * Return
162 00000000                        .data
163 00000000 252D3130732025 2D      format: .dc.b  '%-10s %-10s %-10s %-14s %-6s',10,0
163 00000008 31307320252D3130
163 00000010 7320252D31347320
163 00000018 252D36730A00
164                                 .even
165 000000D2                        .text
```

Listing 6.11 – The print routine of the PFIND program

```
166
167
168                              *
                                 *         Test for a match
                                 *
169  000000D2  49EB0000   match:    lea    l_name(a3),a4      *    a4 -> Comparison string
170  000000D6  2F0D                 move.l a5,-(a7)           *    Save argv string
171  000000D8  B90D       lmatch:   cmp.b  (a5)+,(a4)+        *    Do the compare
172  000000DA  6608                 bne    tryfirst           *    No match, try first name
173  000000DC  4A15                 tst.b  (a5)               *    Next byte null
174  000000DE  66F8                 bne    lmatch             *    Continue
175  000000E0  2A5F                 move.l (a7)+,a5           *    POP return register
176  000000E2  4E75                 rts                       *    Return (Note Z bit set)
177
178  000000E4  2A57       tryfirst: move.l (a7),a5           *    Reload argv string
179  000000E6  49EB0015             lea    f_name(a3),a4      *    Load first name pointer
180  000000EA  BB0C       fmatch:   cmp.b  (a4)+,(a5)+        *    Compare a byte
181  000000EC  6604                 bne    nomatch            *    No good, quit
182  000000EE  4A15                 tst.b  (a5)               *    Comparison done?
183  000000F0  66F8                 bne    fmatch             *    No, continue
184
185  000000F2  2A5F       nomatch:  move.l (a7)+,a5           *    Restore pointer
186  000000F4  4E75                 rts                       *    And quit
187  000000F6                       .page
```

Listing 6.11 – The print routine of the PFIND program (continued)

```
188                    *********************************************************
189                    *                                                       *
190                    *   Error handling routines.  These routines print the appropriate error
191                    *   message and exit.                                   *
192                    *                                                       *
193                    *********************************************************
194                             .globl  _printf          * C library printf routine
195 000000F6 41F90000001E  usage:   lea     usagem,a0        * Usage message
196 000000FC 6018                   bra     eprint           * Print it
197
198 000000FE 41F900000031  badopen: lea     openmsg,a0       * Can't open file
199 00000104 6010                   bra     eprint           * Print it
200
201 00000106 41F90000004A  boverfl: lea     bovfmsg,a0       * Buffer overflow
202 0000010C 6008                   bra     eprint           * Print it
203
204 0000010E 41F90000005B  readerr: lea     readmsg,a0       * Read error
205 00000114 4E71                   bra     eprint
206
207 00000116 2F08          eprint:  move.l  a0,-(a7)         * Push string address
208 00000118 4EB900000000           jsr     _printf          * Print it
209 0000011E DFFC00000004           adda.l  #4,a7            * Pop parameter
210 00000124 4EB900000000           jsr     _exit            * Exit
211 0000001E                        .data
212                        *
213                        *        Error Messages
214                        *
215 0000001E 5573616765733A2070  usagem:  .dc.b   'Usage: pfind name',10,0
215 00000026 66696E64206E616D
215 0000002E 650A00
```

Listing 6.12 – *The data area of the PFIND program*

```
216 00000049 00
217 0000004A 427566666572206F        bovfmsg:.dc.b   'Buffer overflow',10,0
217 00000052 766572666C6F770A
217 0000005A 00
218 0000005B 5265616420657272        readmsg:.dc.b   'Read error on "PHONE.DAT"',10,0
218 00000063 6F7220F6E202250
218 0000006B 484F4E452E444154
218 00000073 220A00
219                                           .even
220 0000012A                                  .text
221 0000012A                                  .page
222                        ***********************************************************
223                        *
224                        *       Initialized data area
225                        *
226                        ***********************************************************
227 00000076                                  .data
228 00000076 70686F6E652E6461        telfil: .dc.b   'phone.dat',0           * Data base file
228 0000007E 7400
229                                           .even                          * Force to word boundary
230                        ***********************************************************
231                        *
232                        *       Uninitialized data area
233                        *
234                        ***********************************************************
235 00000000                                  .bss
236                                           .even                          * Force word alignment
237 00000000                        buffer: .ds.b   bufsize+length           * File buffer area
238 00010056                        endbuff:.equ    *                        * End of the buffer
239 00010056                                 .even                           * Force word alignment
239 00010056
240 00010056                        lastb:  .ds.l   1                        * Contains data end address
241 0001005A                                .end
```

Listing 6.12 – The data area of the PFIND program (continued)

Data Area

Listing 6.12 shows the data area and error routines for the PFIND program. This data area is largely a subset of the PADD program.

The PLIST Program

The PLIST program is a trivial modification to the PFIND program, and is left as an exercise for the reader.

SUMMARY

In this chapter, we have touched briefly on a number of important topics. Among them are:

- The concept of records and the various types of records: fixed-length, variable-length and hybrid records.
- How records are arranged in memory: arrays and linked lists.
- Data structures: stacks, queues, and trees.
- Simple methods of sorting data: insertion sorts and interchange sorts.
- Sequential, binary and hash techniques of searching a table.
- The concept of recursive programming.
- Sample application of a phone directory.

In the next two chapters, we will progress from writing applications to writing low-level operating system software. This type of software makes extensive use of the stack and queue data structures.

EXERCISES

1. Derive the PLIST program from the PFIND program.
2. The Fibonacci series of numbers, denoted as F(n), is recursively defined as follows:
   a. F(0) = 0, and F(1) = 1.
   b. For all other numbers, F(n) = F(n − 1) + F(n − 2).

(For example, F(2) = F(1) + F(0) = 1; F(3) = F(2) + F(1) = 2, and so forth.) Write a recursive function called fib that returns in D0.W the Fibonacci number that corresponds to the number originally contained in D0.W.

3. Write a program called PNLIST that is similar to the PLIST program, but which prints the data sorted by phone number. (Hint: Use a bubble sort technique to sort the data before calling the print routine.)

4. Write a program called PDEL that deletes an entry from the telephone directory.

Exception Processing

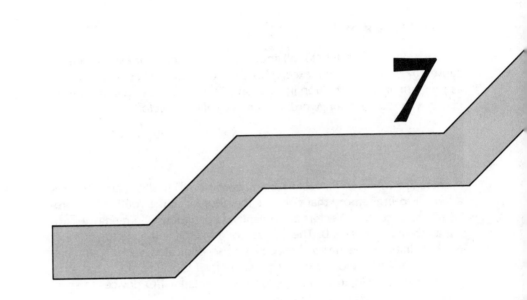

INTRODUCTION

This chapter will introduce you to the concept of a machine "exception," and to programming techniques used in processing exceptions. We will develop two sample programs that handle exceptions and discuss the types of exceptions possible on the 68000 chip.

WHAT IS AN EXCEPTION?

An exception is the machine's ability to interrupt what it is doing, do something else, and if necessary, return to the interrupted task. Exceptions caused by external events are called *interrupts*. Exceptions are also used by the 68000 for certain types of programming errors, such as division by zero.

A common use of the exception mechanism is to overlap I/O processing with computation. Since I/O devices are typically much slower than the CPU, sophisticated programs can perform both I/O and computations simultaneously. This technique reduces the time required to perform a task.

The exception mechanism is used as follows: the program starts an I/O operation and begins doing computations. When the I/O is complete, an exception occurs, causing the computational work to be suspended. If there is more I/O to be done, the program starts another I/O operation. Computation can then resume until another exception occurs. This type of I/O is commonly called *interrupt-driven I/O*.

General Exception Processing

Exceptions on the 68000 fall into one of two categories: exceptions caused by I/O devices and exceptions caused by internal operations, such as program errors or the *trap* instructions. Each possible exception is associated with a unique longword in memory called a *vector*.

Vectors

There are 256 possible vectors, numbered from 0 to 255. Each vector is a longword in memory that contains the address of the routine that processes the exception. Vectors are organized contiguously in memory, starting at absolute address 0. The address of a vector is the vector number times 4. Internally generated exceptions use dedicated vector numbers. There are seven dedicated vector numbers for I/O, called the *auto-vector interrupt vectors*. In addition, a mechanism exists for I/O devices to specify vectors to be used for I/O interrupts.

Table 7.1 lists the vector numbers that are preassigned by the 68000.

Locations 0 and 4 are used for the initial stack and Program counter when the processor is first powered up or when the RESET signal is applied. (Most microcomputer systems have a button for this purpose.)

A BUSERR (Bus Error) indicates a program reference to a memory location that does not exist. (This is colloquially known as "missing the bus.") References to a word or longword at an odd address cause an addressing-error exception. An illegal instruction (e.g., an op code of 4AFC) causes an exception through vector number 4. Two exceptions are op codes Axxx and Fxxx, which trap through the Line 1010 and Line 1111 vectors (10 and 11 respectively).

Division by zero causes an exception through vector 5. The CHK and TRAPV exceptions are caused by the CHK and TRAPV instructions (see Chapter 3). These instructions trap through vectors 6 and 7. A privilege violation exception results when a priviliged instruction is attempted while the processor is in user mode.

Many debugger programs use exception vector 9 (TRACE) for executing single instructions in a program to be debugged. The normal procedure for single-stepping is to (1) push the PC of the instruction to be debugged on the stack, (2) push the SR with the TRACE bit set (bit 15), and (3) execute an RTE instruction.

The processor will execute one instruction with the TRACE bit set, and then trap through the trace vector. Any instruction that affects all bits of the status register may set the trace bit.

Whenever a memory violation (BUSERR) occurs during an external interrupt, the spurious exception (vector 24) is taken. This is normally an error condition, but may possibly be used in an obscure manner by a hardware designer.

Vector	Address	Function
0	0	RESET initial SSP (supervisor stack pointer)
1	4	RESET initial PC (program counter)
2	8	BUSERR (nonexistent memory)
3	C	Address (boundary) error
4	10	Illegal instruction
5	14	Zero divide
6	18	CHK instruction
7	1C	TRAPV instruction
8	20	Privilege violation
9	24	TRACE
10	8	Line 1010 emulator
11	2C	Line 1111 emulator
12–14	30–38	Unassigned (reserved)
15	3C	Uninitialized interrupt vector
16–23	40–5C	Unassigned (reserved)
24	60	Spurious interrupt
25–31	64–7C	Level 0–7 autovector interrupts
32–47	80–BF	TRAP 0–15 instruction vectors
48–63	C0–FC	Unassigned (reserved)
64–255	100–3FF	User interrupt vectors

Table 7.1 – *Preassigned vectors*

WHAT HAPPENS DURING AN EXCEPTION?

When the 68000 recognizes an exception condition, several things occur:

1. The current values of the PC (which normally points to the next instruction to be executed) and status register are pushed onto the supervisor-mode stack.

2. The T bit in the status register is turned off and the S bit is turned on. This prevents a TRACE exception, and forces the 68000 into supervisor state. For external exceptions, the Interrupt Mask in the status register is also updated.

3. For a BUSERR or addressing error exception, extra information is pushed onto the stack.

4. The PC is loaded from the appropriate vector, and execution begins at this address.

The routine whose address is contained in the vector is called an *exception handler*. This routine normally saves the registers on the stack, performs some action, restores the registers, and executes an RTE instruction. Thus, the 68000 provides the ability to interrupt a program and later resume executing the program with no noticeable effect, other than increased processing time. This ability is normally used with interrupt-driven I/O.

RESET

A special pin on the 68000 chip called RESET causes a special exception to take place. A signal asserted on the RESET pin causes the processor to load the Supervisor stack pointer from location 0 and the Program counter from location 4. This provides a mechanism for starting the 68000 in a known state. RESET is normally used for the *bootstrap* button on 68000 microcomputers. This exception provides a mechanism for starting the 68000 when power is applied, as well as the ability to recover from catastrophic software failures.

BUSERR and Addressing Error Exceptions

Vectors 2 and 3 are used for errors detected in references to memory. The BUSERR exception (vector 2) indicates that the program has referenced memory that does not exist.

An addressing-error exception means that the program has referenced a memory word or longword at an odd address. If a program references a memory word or longword at an odd address that is also nonexistent (i.e., both bus and addressing error conditions), the processor will detect the addressing error first, and only the addressing error exception will take place.

These two exceptions differ from all other exceptions in that the processor puts extra information on the stack. On entry to the exception handler, the stack appears as shown in Figure 7.1.

The first word on the stack contains information about the type of memory access that caused the fault. Bits 5 through 15 of this word are undefined. If the access error occurred during a memory read, the R/W bit is 1. If the access error occurred during a memory write, the R/W bit is 0.

The I/N bit is 0 if the processor was processing an instruction, and 1 if the error was detected by an external device. (Most of these errors are the result of instruction processing.) The *Access code* contained in the lower

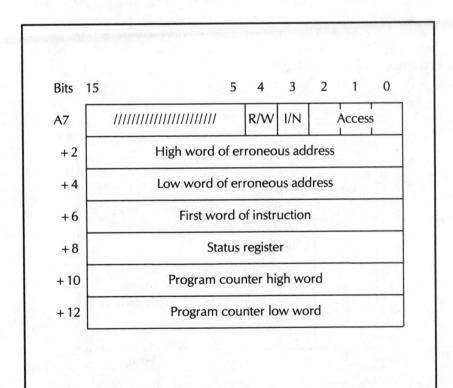

Figure 7.1 – *Stack after bus or addressing error*

three bits describes the type of memory access being performed. Table 7.2 shows the type of memory access indicated by each access code.

Thus, these bits tell you two things: whether the processor was referencing data or program instructions and whether the processor was in supervisor mode or user mode. Data references include all accesses to memory that use all addressing modes except the two PC-relative modes. Program references include the PC-relative addressing modes as well as fetching instruction words from memory.

The next two words on the stack give the address where the fault occurred. The processor saves a copy of the op code of the instruction that caused the fault in the next word on the stack. As with all other exceptions, the status register and Program counter are present. The value stored as the Program counter is advanced from the beginning of the instruction by two to ten bytes.

In the event that the error occurred when the instruction was being fetched, the stored Program counter will be in the vicinity of the previous instruction. Normally, this error is caused by taking a wild branch. In this case, the PC and op code word on the stack will indicate the branch instruction, rather than the erroneous address where transfer was attempted. The erroneous address words on the stack will contain the erroneous address (see Figure 7.1).

Code	Type of Access
000	(unassigned)
001	User mode data reference
010	User mode program reference
011	(unassigned)
100	(unassigned)
101	Supervisor mode data reference
110	Supervisor mode program reference
111	Interrupt acknowledge

Table 7.2 – Memory access codes

If the processor encounters a second BUSERR or addressing error during the processing of one of these errors, a situation called a *double bus fault* occurs. This can occur if the Supervisor stack pointer is corrupt and the processor is unable to save any information on the stack. The processor halts and can only be restarted using the RESET input on the chip.

Illegal Instruction Exceptions

Whenever the 68000 fetches an op code that cannot be interpreted as a legal 68000 instruction, an exception through vectors 4, 10, or 11 occurs. Vectors 10 and 11 are used for op codes that have 1010 or 1111 in the high order four bits. Vector 4 is used for all other illegal instructions. These include:

- Illegal op codes other than Axxx or Fxxx.
- Illegal addressing modes, such as PC-relative operands specified as an instruction destination.
- Illegal addressing mode or instruction combinations, such as byte operations on address registers.

A beneficial use of illegal instructions is software simulation of extended 68000 instructions. Op codes Axxx and Fxxx are normally used for this purpose. To simulate an extended instruction, first define an illegal op code pattern for this instruction and then write an exception handler for the appropriate illegal instruction vector that simulates the action of the instruction. A program can then make use of the instruction without knowing that the instruction is simulated. There is, of course, a significant cost in terms of processing speed.

This technique is often used for optional hardware extensions to a processor's instruction set, such as floating point. With simulation, you can write a program that uses floating-point operations and run that program on any machine, whether it has the floating-point hardware or not. The only difference is that the program will run much faster on a machine with the optional hardware.

TRAP Exceptions

The notion of an operating-system call instruction is similar to software simulation of illegal instructions. The program first issues an operating-system call instruction and then the operating system performs some function and returns an indication of its success or failure to the program.

The program can treat these operating-system calls as if they were single instructions. The operating system can provide a set of functions, sometimes called the *extended instruction set,* which is the same on machines that have substantially different hardware. This is the appeal of standard operating systems, which allow the same applications software to run unchanged on many different machines.

The 68000 has sixteen operating-system call instructions, TRAP 0 through TRAP 15. Illegal instructions could be used to extend this set almost infinitely. The TRAP instructions use vectors 32 through 47. The advantage of a large number of such instructions is that the operating system can dedicate a TRAP instruction to a frequently used operating system service and reduce the number of instructions required to perform this service. Less frequently called services may be invoked by requiring the application to load a function code into a register before performing the TRAP instructions.

The TRAP instruction allows a convenient transition between user mode and supervisor mode. Applications are normally run in user mode while the operating system normally runs in supervisor mode. To enter the operating system, the TRAP instruction automatically places the processor into supervisor mode.

When the RTE instruction is used to return to the user program, the user program's status register is loaded from the stack, causing the processor to go back to user mode. This mechanism also makes it possible for both supervisor mode and user mode programs to call the operating system, or even for the operating system to call itself.

Another advantage of the TRAP instruction is that the user program need not know the location of the operating system. Many systems require that the application program jump to some fixed address to call the operating system. The TRAP instruction allows the location of the operating system to change without affecting the application program.

Exceptions Used for Debuggers

The DDT-68K debugger explained in Chapter 3 provides two mechanisms for controlling program execution: breakpoints and single-instruction execution. These mechanisms make use of two 68000 exceptions: the illegal instruction and trace exceptions.

To set a breakpoint in a program being debugged, the most common technique is to save the instruction at the breakpoint location and place an illegal instruction at that location. The debugger then allows the program to execute until an illegal-instruction exception occurs. This technique will fail if a breakpoint is set in the middle of a multiword instruction or if the program uses the instruction as data. Also, continuing from a breakpoint requires that the instruction at the breakpoint be single-stepped before program execution resumes.

Single-stepping an instruction involves setting the Trace bit in the status register. The most common method is to stack the Program counter and status register, set the Trace bit in the stacked status register, and execute an RTE instruction. A trace exception will occur immediately following the execution of the target instruction. Some side effects of this technique are:

- Since an exception clears the trace bit, an exception caused by the instruction being traced causes the debugger to lose control, unless the debugger receives control when exceptions occur.

- TRAP instructions that call an operating-system function appear as a single instruction.

- Tracing an RTE instruction causes the debugger to lose control because the RTE instruction reloads the status register. Tracing an instruction which reloads SR has the same effect. These instructions include MOVE to SR, ANDI to SR, and EORI to SR.

- Tracing a MOVE from SR instruction can cause the program to malfunction because the trace bit will be set in the copy of the status register that the program receives. If the program compares this copy without masking the trace bit, it could execute incorrectly.

The real problems with this technique appear when the debugger is used on supervisor-mode programs (which are relatively rare). You can still debug a supervisor-mode program with this type of debugger if you exercise care in tracing the instructions which reload SR.

Other Error Exceptions

The TRAPV, CHK, and Zero divide exceptions are also mechanisms that detect malfunction. These exceptions are used to assist the application in detecting problems with overflow, array subscript range, and division by zero.

The application program may need to regain control after one of these exceptions in order to print out a message that identifies the error and its cause. High-level language programs may have a way of identifying the routine and its line number in the source program. Operating systems usually have some mechanism that allows the application program to regain control following an error exception.

Privilege Violation Exception

A user-mode program that attempts to execute a privileged instruction causes a privilege-violation exception through vector 8. This is normally an error condition. With some computer systems, however, you can use the privilege-violation exception to execute multiple supervisor-mode programs. The multiple supervisor-mode programs run in user state and a supervisor-mode monitor simulates the action of all the privileged-mode instructions. This technique is sometimes known as the *virtual machine* technique.

Virtual machines are used to run multiple operating systems on a single computer. A hardware device called a *Memory Management Unit,* or *MMU,* simulates different memory spaces for each operating system. This allows each system to have its own vector area as well as other dedicated memory locations. Since the operating systems are run in user mode, they do not interfere with each other.

The 68000 chip is capable of running a virtual machine system with a single exception—the MOVE from SR instruction is not privileged. If software that needs to run in supervisor state uses the MOVE from SR instruction and looks at the S bit, it may malfunction. On the 68010 chip, MOVE from SR is privileged.

An Exception-Processing Program

Listing 7.1 shows a sample program that handles exceptions. The program runs under CP/M-68K and handles the type of exceptions that are common program errors. When an exception occurs, the program prints out a message that identifies the type of exception, the contents of all registers, and the extra information on a BUSERR or addressing error exception.

Lines 11 through 19 are the program-initialization routine. Routine v_init is designed to be called by the applications program in order to set up the exception vectors. The technique used most frequently is to use the CP/M-68K service that allows applications to intercept exceptions. However, the purpose of Listing 7.1 is to illustrate how to deal directly with the 68000 hardware. Thus, the initialization routine stores the address of the exception handlers into the vector locations directly.

Lines 23 through 37 are the entry points for the exception handler. This table of BSR instructions (branch to subroutine) allows us, in a minimal

```
 1        *****************************************************************
 2        *
 3        *     Exception vector setup routine
 4        *
 5        *****************************************************************
 6        buserr: .equ   $08              * Buserr address
 7        endvec: .equ   $40              * First vector not initialized
 8                .globl binhex           * Hex conversion routine
 9                .globl prtstr           * String print routine
10                .globl v_init           * Vector initialization point
11 00000000 48E700C0      v_init: movem.l a0-a1,-(a7)  * Save work registers
12 00000004 41F900000008          lea     buserr,a0    * a0 -> vector
13 0000000A 43F900000022          lea     bsrtab,a1    * a1 -> routine
14 00000010 20C9          v_loop: move.l  a1,(a0)+     * Initialize a vector
15 00000012 5489                  addq.l  #2,a1        * Bump a1 by length of bsr.s
16 00000014 B1FC00000040          cmpa.l  #endvec,a0   * Past limit?
17 0000001A 65F4                  blo     v_loop       * No, continue to initialize
18 0000001C 4CDF0300              movem.l (a7)+,a0-a1  * Restore registers
19 00000020 4E75                  rts                  * And return
20
21        *
22        *     Exception entry points
23        *
23 00000022 611A          bsrtab: bsr.s   except       * 08  Buserr entry
24 00000024 6118                  bsr.s   except       * 0C  Addressing error entry
25 00000026 6116                  bsr.s   except       * 10  Illegal Instruction
26 00000028 6114                  bsr.s   except       * 14  Zero Divide
27 0000002A 6112                  bsr.s   except       * 18  CHK instruction
28 0000002C 6110                  bsr.s   except       * 1C  TRAPV instruction
29 0000002E 610E                  bsr.s   except       * 20  Privilege violation
30 00000030 610C                  bsr.s   except       * 24  Trace
31 00000032 610A                  bsr.s   except       * 28  Line 1010
32 00000034 6108                  bsr.s   except       * 2C  Line 1111
33 00000036 6106                  bsr.s   except       * 30  Reserved
34 00000038 6104                  bsr.s   except       * 34  Reserved
35 0000003A 6102                  bsr.s   except       * 38  Reserved
36 0000003C 4E71                  bsr.s   except       * 3C  Uninitialized vector
```

Listing 7.1 – Exception-processing program

```
37                               *
38                               *        Common exception processing entry point
39                               *
40  0000003E  23DF00000000  except: move.l  (a7)+,index       * Save word pushed by 'bsr'
41  00000044  48F9FFFF00000004      movem.l d0-d7/a0-a7,regs  * Save all registers at trap time
42  0000004C  2E3900000000          move.l  index,d7          * d7 = bsr return address
43  00000052  9EBC00000024          sub.l   #bsrtab+2,d7      * d7 = index
44  00000058  E38F                  lsl.l   #1,d7             *        into string table
45  0000005A  41F900000182          lea     strtab,a0         * a0 -> string table
46  00000060  20707000              move.l  0(a0,d7),a0       * a0 -> string to print
47  00000064  4EB900000000          jsr     prtstr            * Go print exception type
48  0000006A  41F90000023B          lea     estr,a0           * a0 -> "Exception"
49  00000070  4EB900000000          jsr     prtstr            * Print
50  00000076  41F900000247          lea     dstr,a0           * a0 -> "D "
51  0000007C  4EB900000000          jsr     prtstr            * print
52  00000082  43F900000004          lea     regs,a1           * a1 -> D registers
53  00000088  6100009C              jsr     pregs             * Print D registers
54  0000008C  41F90000024A          lea     astr,a0           * a0 -> "A "
55  00000092  4EB900000000          jsr     prtstr            * Print
56  00000098  43F900000024          lea     regs+32,a1        * a1 -> A registers
57  0000009E  61000086              jsr     pregs             * Print A registers
58                               *
59                               *  If exception was a BUSERR or addressing error, print the extra stack
60                               *  stuff
61                               *
62
63  000000A2  BEBC00000008          cmp.l   #8,d7             * Is d7 < 8?
64  000000A8  6E42                  bgt     prtpc             * No, print PC, SR
65  000000AA  41F90000024D          lea     func,a0           * a0 -> "Function="
66  000000B0  4EB900000000          jsr     prtstr            * Print
67  000000B6  301F                  move.w  (a7)+,d0          * Fetch exception function word
68  000000B8  610000BC              jsr     pword             * Print it
69  000000BC  41F900000257          lea     addr,a0           * a0 -> "Access Address"
70  000000C2  4EB900000000          jsr     prtstr            * Print this
71  000000C8  201F                  move.l  (a7)+,d0          * Fetch access address
72  000000CA  6100007C              jsr     plong             * Print it
```

Listing 7.1 – Exception-processing program (continued)

```
73  000000CE 41F900000268    lea    ir,a0          * a0 -> "Instruction register"
74  000000D4 4EB900000000    jsr    prtstr         * Print
75  000000DA 301F            move.w (a7)+,d0        * d0 = Instruction word
76  000000DC 6100009B        jsr    pword          * Print
77  000000E0 41F90000028E    lea    newline,a0     * a0 -> Newline sequence
78  000000E6 4EB900000000    jsr    prtstr         * print it
79
80                  *
81                  * Print PC, status register, and USP
82  000000EC 41F90000027F    prtpc: lea    srstr,a0   * a0-> "SR="
83  000000F2 4EB900000000    jsr    prtstr         * Print
84  000000F8 301F            move.w (a7)+,d0        * d0 = old SR
85  000000FA 6100007A        jsr    pword          * Print it
86  000000FE 41F900000283    lea    pcstr,a0       * a0-> "PC="
87  00000104 4EB900000000    jsr    prtstr         * Print it
88  0000010A 201F            move.l (a7)+,d0        * d0 = PC at fault
89  0000010C 613A            jsr    plong          * Print it
90  0000010E 41F900000288    lea    uspstr,a0      * a0-> "USP="
91  00000114 4EB900000000    jsr    prtstr         * Print
92  0000011A 4E68            move.l usp,a0          * Fetch User stack pointer
93  0000011C 2008            move.l a0,d0           * Put in d0
94  0000011E 6128            jsr    plong          * Print
95  00000120 303C0000        move.w #0,d0           * Exit       to CP/M
96  00000124 4E42            trap   #2
97  00000126                 .page
98                  ************************************************************
99                  *
100                 * miscellaneous print routines
101                 *
102                 ************************************************************
103 00000126 48E7C0C0    pregs: movem.l a0-a1/d0-d1,-(a7)   * Save work registers
104 0000012A 323C0007        move.w #7,d1           * Loop count
105 0000012E 2019        rloop: move.l (a1)+,d0        * Fetch next long
106 00000130 6116            jsr    plong          * print
```

Listing 7.1 – Exception-processing program (continued)

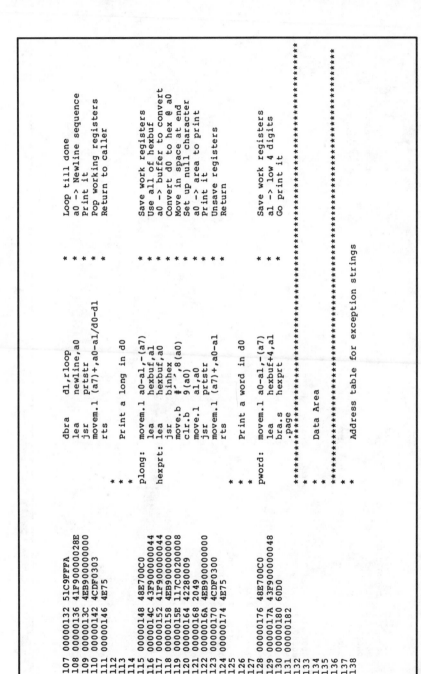

```
107  00000132  51C9FFFA              dbra    d1,rloop          *  Loop till done
108  00000136  41F90000028E          lea     newline,a0        *  a0 -> Newline sequence
109  0000013C  4EB900000000          jsr     prtstr            *  Print it
110  00000142  4CDF0303              movem.l (a7)+,a0-a1/d0-d1  *  Pop working registers
111  00000146  4E75                  rts                       *  Return to caller
112
113                                  *  Print a long in d0
114                                  *
115  00000148  48E700C0      plong:  movem.l a0-a1,-(a7)        *  Save work registers
116  0000014C  43F900000044          lea     hexbuf,a1         *  Use all of hexbuf
117  00000152  41F900000044          lea     hexbuf,a0         *  a0 -> buffer to convert
118  00000158  4EB900000000          jsr     binhex            *  Convert d0 to hex @ a0
119  0000015E  117C002000008         move.b  #' ',8(a0)        *  Move in space at end
120  00000164  42280009              clr.b   9(a0)             *  Set up null character
121  00000168  2049                  move.l  a1,a0             *  a0 -> area to print
122  0000016A  4EB900000000          jsr     prtstr            *  Print it
123  00000170  4CDF0300              movem.l (a7)+,a0-a1        *  Unsave registers
124  00000174  4E75                  rts                       *  Return
125
126                                  *  Print a word in d0
127                                  *
128  00000176  48E700C0      pword:  movem.l a0-a1,-(a7)        *  Save work registers
129  0000017A  43F900000048          lea     hexbuf+4,a1       *  a1 -> low 4 digits
130  00000180  60D0                  bra.s   hexprt            *  Go print it
131  00000182                        .page
132                                  ****************************************************
133                                  *
134                                  *  Data Area
135                                  *
136                                  ****************************************************
137                                  *
138                                  *  Address table for exception strings
```

Listing 7.1 – *Exception-processing program (continued)*

```
139                                      *
140 00000182 000001BA000001C1            strtab: .dc.l   busstr,addstr,illstr,zerstr,chkstr,trvstr,prvstr,trcstr,lnastr
140 0000018A 000001CF000001E3
140 00000192 000001EF000001F3
140 0000019A 000001F900000203
140 000001A2 00000209
141 000001A6 000002130000021D                    .dc.l   lnfstr,rsvstr,rsvstr,rsvstr,unistr
141 000001AE 0000021D0000021D
141 000001B6 00000226
142                                      *
143                                      *       Exception Strings
144                                      *
145 000001BA 425553455252                busstr: .dc.b   'BUSERR',0
146 000001C1 4164647265737320            addstr: .dc.b   'Address Error',0
146 000001C9 4572726F7200
147 000001CF 496C6C6567616C20            illstr: .dc.b   'Illegal Instruction',0
147 000001D7 496E737472756374
147 000001DF 696F6E00
148 000001E3 5A65726F20446976            zerstr: .dc.b   'Zero Divide',0
148 000001EB 69646500
149 000001EF 43484B00                    chkstr: .dc.b   'CHK',0
150 000001F3 545241505600                trvstr: .dc.b   'TRAPV',0
151 000001F9 50726976696C6567            prvstr: .dc.b   'Privilege',0
151 00000201 6500
152 00000203 547261636500                trcstr: .dc.b   'Trace',0
153 00000209 4C696E6520313031            lnastr: .dc.b   'Line 1010',0
153 00000211 3000
154 00000213 4C696E6520313131            lnfstr: .dc.b   'Line 1111',0
154 0000021B 3100
155 0000021D 5265736572766564            rsvstr: .dc.b   'Reserved',0
155 00000225 00
156 00000226 556E696E69746961            unistr: .dc.b   'Uninitialized Vector',0
```

Listing 7.1 – *Exception-processing program (continued)*

```
156  0000022E  6C697A6564642005665
156  00000236  63746F7200
157  0000023B  2045786365707469    estr:    .dc.b   ' Exception',10,0
157  00000243  6F6E0A00
158  00000247  4420                dstr:    .dc.b   'D ',0
159  0000024A  4120                astr:    .dc.b   'A ',0
160  0000024D  46756E6374696F6E    func:    .dc.b   'Function=',0
160  00000255  3D00
161  00000257  2041636365737320    addr:    .dc.b   ' Access Address=',0
161  0000025F  4164647265737333D
161  00000267  00
162  00000268  20496E7374727563    ir:      .dc.b   ' Instruction register=',0
162  00000270  74696F6E207265567
162  00000278  6973746572723D00
163  0000027F  53523D00            srstr:   .dc.b   'SR=',0
164  00000283  2050433D            pcstr:   .dc.b   ' PC=',0
165  00000288  205553503D00        uspstr:  .dc.b   ' USP=',0
166  0000028E  0A00                newline:.dc.b    10,0
167                                         .even
168                                *
169                                *        Unitialized data section
170                                *
171  00000000                      index:   .ds.l   1        * Return address temporary
172  00000000                               .bss
173  00000004                      regs:    .ds.l   16       * Room for registers
174  00000044                      hexbuf:  .ds.b   10       * Hex buffer
175  0000004E                               .end
```

Listing 7.1 – Exception-processing program (continued)

amount of space, to both handle all exceptions with a single routine and determine which exception occurred.

By taking the return address pushed by the BSR instruction, and subtracting the beginning of the table (in lines 41 through 44), we get the offset of the BSR instruction in the table. Multiplying this number by 2 gives us a zero-relative index into a table of long pointers. (That is, the value for BUSERR would be 0, for addressing error, 4, for illegal instruction, 8, and so on.)

Lines 45 through 48 compute the address of the string that corresponds to the exception. These lines of code also print this string, using the prtstr routine from Chapter 4. Lines 51 through 58 print the content of the registers using a subroutine called pregs, which we will look at later.

Lines 64 through 79 determine if the exception is a BUSERR or an addressing error. If the exception is either of these, the extra information is popped from the stack and printed. Hex numbers are printed with the routines called pword (which prints a 16-bit number) and plong (which prints a 32-bit number). If the exception was not a BUSERR or an addressing error, the branch at line 65 causes this code to be skipped.

Lines 83 through 95 print the status register, program counter, and user stack pointer. (The system stack pointer was previously printed as register A7.) Lines 96 through 97 return control to CP/M-68K.

It is not necessary to restore the interrupt vectors since CP/M-68K does this when each program exits. With another system, it might be necessary to save the old contents in the routine v_init, and then restore them before returning to the operating system.

Lines 104 through 112 form a routine called pregs, which on entry prints eight longwords pointed to by register A1. The routine called plong produces the actual output. Following the eight longwords, a line-feed character is printed, causing the terminal to advance to the beginning of the next line.

Lines 116 through 131 contain the routines plong and pword, which print 32-bit and 16-bit hex numbers. The pword routine prints the last four characters of the number, which is always converted to ASCII as a 32-bit quantity. The routine called binhex from Chapter 4 (see Listing 4.1) performs the conversion.

Interrupts

Exceptions that come from external sources are often called *interrupts.* The 68000 provides two techniques for external devices to interrupt the CPU: vectored interrupts and autovectored interrupts.

There are three pins on the 68000 chip that an external device may use to cause an interrupt. These pins are called IPL0, IPL1, and IPL2. IPL stands for *interrupt priority level*. These three inputs to the 68000 form a 3-bit code used to request interrupts. The special code 000 means no interrupt. Combinations 1 through 7 request an interrupt with priority 1–7. The 68000 chip recognizes an interrupt if the *interrupt mask* (contained in status register bits 8–10) is less than the priority presented on the IPL0–2 pins. Thus, an interrupt mask of 0 allows all interrupts and an interrupt mask of 7 allows no interrupts (except level 7).

When an interrupt occurs, the interrupt mask in the status register is set to the priority level of the interrupt. This prevents the interrupt, or any interrupt with the same or lower priority, from occurring until it is activated under software control.

Interrupt level 7 is a special case. Level-7 interrupts cannot be masked off. This interrupt level is normally reserved for extremely high-priority devices or for a "panic button" that can be used to recover from a runaway program. A level-7 interrupt is sometimes called a *Nonmaskable Interrupt* or NMI.

An interrupt requested at a lower level than the current processor priority remains pending until the processor priority is lowered. The maximum amount of time that an interrupt may remain pending is called *interrupt latency*. This time is determined by the maximum number of instructions a program can execute with interrupts masked off. Several applications, including instrumentation, industrial automation, and communications, require rapid interrupt response. In programming interrupt-driven software, there are usually restrictions on the amount of time interrupts can be disabled.

When the 68000 recognizes an interrupt, an additional control pin may be used to request an *autovectored interrupt*. Autovectored interrupts use vectors 25 through 31 for interrupt levels 1–7. If an autovectored interrupt is not requested, the 68000 reads a vector number from the device requesting the interrupt. Deciding which type of interrupt to use is the prerogative of the engineer who designs the 68000 computer system. Autovectored interrupts have the advantage of requiring less hardware, but are slower and may require more sophisticated software. Vectored interrupts provide better interrupt response time at the cost of extra hardware.

The association of a device with a particular vector and an interrupt priority-level is dependent on the physical connection between the 68000 and the hardware device. This relationship differs for each type (and possibly model) of computer. Interrupt programming usually requires different coding for each machine on which the program runs. (It is possible to write a fixed program that processes software exceptions, such as

BUSERR, addressing error, and so on, because these are a characteristic of the 68000 chip and do not change from machine to machine.)

INTERRUPT-DRIVEN SERIAL OUTPUT

Many devices communicate with a computer one bit at a time. To communicate a byte of information, the eight bits are sent one after another. The computer usually communicates through a device called a "serial port" that controls the conversion of data to and from serialized binary format. The amount of time required to send a single byte of information is quite large compared with the speed at which the computer executes instructions. For this reason, serial ports often interrupt the computer once per character transferred.

Sage IV Serial Output

The 68000 addresses external devices as if they were memory locations. This technique is called *Memory Mapped I/O,* and has the advantage that normal memory-reference instructions can be used to perform I/O. Listing 7.2 shows a program that uses I/O interrupts to print the string "Hello, world" on the (serial) terminal of a Sage IV microcomputer.

The terminal output port on the Sage IV responds to two addresses: FFC071 and FFC073. The first port is used to output data to the terminal. A byte placed in this location is transmitted to the terminal. The second port gives commands to the interface. A value of 25 hex causes the port to interrupt after each character has been transmitted. A value of 24 hex disables these interrupts.

The Sage IV microcomputer has a number of different devices connected to the autovector 1 interrupt. Upon receipt of an interrupt, it is necessary to poll an interrupt-controller device to determine which device actually requested the interrupt. The interrupt controller is located at location FFC041. A value of 0C written to this location requests a poll.

To find out which device interrupted, read location FFC041. Then, to prevent the interrupt from occurring again, write a value of 20 hex back to this location. The value read contains a device identifier in the low-order three bits. On the Sage IV, a value of 2 indicates the terminal.

Lines 28 and 29 of Listing 7.2 issue the CP/M-68K request to put the program in supervisor state. This is necessary to allow the program to use privileged instructions. Lines 31 and 32 save the old contents of the level-1 autovector location and set this location to the address of the interrupt-service routine. Lines 33 through 37 set up the transfer,

```
                                    ****************************************************
                                    *
                                    *               6 8 0 0 0   P r o c e s s o r   D e f i n i t i o n s
                                    *               ================================================
                                    *
                                    *               These are definitions for the 68000 and the SAGE IV.
                                    *
                                    ****************************************************

 1                                            .text
 2
 3
 4
 5
 6
 7
 8
 9  00000000
10                  enable:  .equ    $2000           *       Enable interrupts value for SR
11                  disable: .equ    $2700           *       Disable interrupts SR value
12                  al_vec:  .equ    $64             *       Autovector 1 location
13
14          *               Hardware Locations
15          *
16                  poll:    .equ    $ffc041         *       Interrupt poll port
17                  termout: .equ    $ffc071         *       Terminal output port
18                  termcmd: .equ    $ffc073         *       Terminal Command port
19          *
20          *               Miscellaneous hardware stuff
21          *
22                  rdvec:   .equ    $0c             *       Command to read vector
23                  clrint:  .equ    $20             *       Command to end interrupt
24          *
25          *               The following code sets up the interrupt driven output
26          *
27          init:
28  00000000  703E          move.l   #62,d0                  *       Set     supervisor
29  00000002  4E42          trap     #2                      *               supervisor
30  00000004  46FC2700      move.w   #disable,sr             *       Disallow interrupts
31  00000008  23F90000006400000008  move.l   al_vec,alsave   *       Save old vector contents
32  00000012  23FC0000004C00000064  move.l   #termint,al_vec *       Set I/O vector
33  0000001C  23FC0000000D00000000  move.l   #lmsg-1,bcount  *       Setup count
34  00000026  23FC0000000100000004  move.l   #msg+1,buff     *       Setup buffer address
35  00000030  13FC002500FFC073      move.b   #$25,termcmd    *       Enable terminal interrupts
```

Listing 7.2 – Interrupt-driven serial output

```
36  00000038  13F900000000FFC071        move.b   msg,termout          *    Output 1st character
37  00000042  46FC2000                  move.w   #enable,sr           *    Re-enable
38  00000046  60FE                      bra      x                    *    And loop forever
39
40  00000048  4280             exit:    clr.l    d0                   *    exit     to CP/M
41  0000004A  4E42                      trap     #2                   *
42  0000004C                            .page
43
44                   *******************************************************************
45                   *           T e r m i n a l   O u t p u t   I n t e r r u p t   H a n d l e r
46                   *           ======================================================
47                   *
48                   *    This code is entered by an interrupt through the 68000 Level 1
49                   *    autovector. The interrupt is first validated to make sure that it
50                   *    was, in fact, a terminal interrupt. If so, the next character is
51                   *    output. When all output is exhausted, the interrupt return is set
52                   *    to point to routine "exit", which returns control to CP/M.
53                   *
54                   *******************************************************************
55
56  0000004C  48E7FFFE         termint: movem.l  d0-d7/a0-a6,-(a7)    ***  Save registers
57  00000050  13FC000C00FFC041          move.b   #rdvec,poll          ***  Issue "read vector" command
58  00000058  10390 0FFC041             move.b   poll,d0              ***  Fetch vector
59  0000005E  13FC002000FFC041          move.b   #clrint,poll         ***  Indicate end of interrupt
60  00000066  4A00                      tst.b    d0                   ***  Was there really an interrupt?
61  00000068  6A4C                      bpl      noint                ***  Oops! no interrupt at all
62  0000006A  02400007                  andi.w   #7,d0                ***  Strip all but low 3 bits
63  0000006E  B03C0002                  cmp.b    #2,d0                ***  Was it a terminal interrupt?
64  00000072  6642                      bne      noint                ***  No, quit now
65  00000074  4AB900000000              tst.l    bcount               ***  Are we done?
66  0000007A  6E22                      bgt      nextchar             ***  No, continue to output
67  0000007C  23F9000000080000 0064     move.l   alsave,al_vec        ***  restore vector
```

Listing 7.2 – *Interrupt-driven serial output (continued)*

```
68  00000086  13FC002400FFC073          move.b   #$24,termcmd              ***   Get rid of terminal intrpts
69  0000008E  4CDF7FFF                  movem.l  (a7)+,d0-d7/a0-a6         ***   restore registers
70  00000092  4257                      clr.w    (a7)                      *     User mode SR
71  00000094  2F7C00000480002           move.l   #exit,2(a7)               *     Replace PC
72  0000009C  4E73                      rte                                *     Quit
73
74                                *     Here to output the next character
75                                *
76                                nextchar:
77  0000009E  20790000000004            move.l   buff,a0                   ***   a0 -> character to output
78  000000A4  13D800FFC071              move.b   (a0)+,termout             ***   output the character
79  000000AA  23C800000004              move.l   a0,buff                   ***   Save next address
80  000000B0  53B900000000              subq.l   #1,bcount                 ***   decrement count
81  000000B6  4CDF7FFF                  movem.l  (a7)+,d0-d7/a0-a6         ***   Restore registers
82  000000BA  4E73                      rte                                *     Exit to interrupted routine
83
84                                *     Data area
85                                *
86  00000000                            .data
87  00000000  48656C6C6F2C2057   msg:   .dc.b    "Hello, World",13,10
87  00000008  6F726C640D0A
88  00000008                     lmsg:  .equ     *-msg
89                                      .even
                                        .bss
90  00000000                     bcount: .ds.l   1                         *     Byte count to output
91  00000004                     buff:  .ds.l    1                         *     Buffer address to output
92  00000008                     alsave: .ds.l   1                         *     Vector save area
93  0000000C
94                                      .end
```

Listing 7.2 – Interrupt-driven serial output (continued)

including (1) enabling the terminal-output interrupt, (2) transferring the first character, and (3) enabling interrupts to allow the transfer to take place. The program loops at line 38 until the transfer is complete.

Level-1 autovector interrupts are handled starting at line 56. Lines 57 through 64 verify that an interrupt was a terminal-output interrupt. Lines 65 and 66 test for the presence of another character to output. If no characters remain, lines 67 through 72 (1) restore the vector, (2) disable terminal interrupts, and (3) alter the return address to point to the exit routine at lines 40 and 41. When the RTE instruction at line 72 is executed, control is returned to CP/M-68K.

If more characters remain to be output, the code at lines 77 through 82 output the next character, decrement the count, and return to the interrupted code.

This example glosses over a lot of the details of programming serial-output devices, but the purpose of the example is to illustrate 68000 interrupt coding. The programming for a serial device is largely dependent on the device, particularly how the device is addressed from the 68000 and how the device interrupts the 68000. This is different for each type of computer. How to program a particular device on a particular computer is usually documented by the computer manufacturer.

SUMMARY

In this chapter we have presented the exception conditions on the 68000, both internal and external, and how to write programs that use this feature. We have also explored some of the uses for exceptions that are not immediately obvious. The examples of coding contained in this chapter illustrate techniques for dealing with both program-error exceptions and I/O exceptions.

In the next chapter, we will combine exception processing with operating system concepts to produce a very small multitasking operating system. This will provide you with a better understanding of how I/O exceptions are generally used in larger systems.

EXERCISES

1. The 68000 lacks a block move instruction, i.e., a single instruction that transfers a block of memory from one place to another. Suppose we define such an instruction as in Figure 7.2, where An Src and An Dest are source and destination address register

specifications. Dn Cnt is a data register specification that gives byte count of the number of bytes to be transferred. Write an exception handler that simulates the action of such an instruction.

Bit	15	14	13	12	11	10	9	8	7	6	5	4	3	2	1	0
	1	1	1	1	An Src			An Dest			Dn Cnt			0	0	0

Figure 7.2 – *Instruction for transferring a block of memory from one place to another*

2. Write a privileged program that prints a trace of another program. The program to be traced should begin with *jsr trace*, where "trace" is your tracing routine. The output of the trace should include the PC, status register, and contents of all the CPU registers. You may assume that the program to be traced is a user mode program and you need not worry about RTE and MOVE SR instructions.

Case Study: A Sample Operating System

8

INTRODUCTION

In this chapter, we will look at writing operating systems for the 68000. We will first cover important concepts common to most operating systems and will then look at a simple operating system. This sample system is by no means complete—it lacks capabilities found in even the most rudimentary commercial systems. However, it is small enough so that you can understand the entire system in relatively short order. The sample system contains many of the design concepts found in large operating systems.

OPERATING SYSTEM CONCEPTS

An operating system is often likened to a traffic cop for a computer. The operating system controls the computing resources and allocates them to competing programs. The operating system also implements standard procedures for functions such as I/O, so that the underlying hardware may change, and still allow programs written for the operating system to continue to run. The relationship between an applications program, the operating system, and the hardware is shown in Figure 8.1.

Since an application program goes through the operating system to access the computer hardware, the hardware can change without affecting the application. It is important to preserve the applications programs because the cost of producing software is so high.

Multitasking

An important concept on the 68000 and other 16-bit microprocessors is the ability of the operating system to run more than one application program at a time. This is called *multitasking*. To perform multitasking, the operating system keeps a copy of each of the machine resources that are shared by the programs, such as the machine registers. Each program is

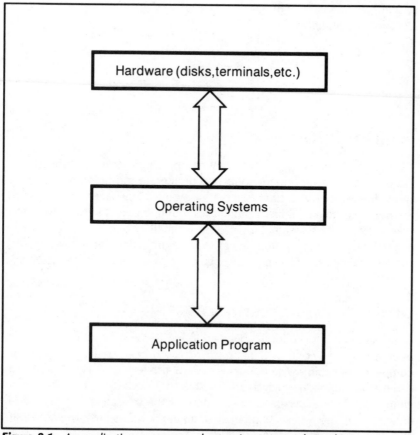

Figure 8.1 – An application program and operating system relationship

called a *task*. When it is time to switch from one program to another, the operating system saves the current copy of the resources and loads the next copy. This process is known as *context switching*.

A minimal context switch involves saving the current register set and the operating system's indicator of the current task. The registers for the new task are loaded and the operating system's global variables are set to indicate the new task. More complex context switching preserves the contents of various memory locations and I/O device registers for each task.

The real benefit of multitasking is the ability to keep more of a machine's resources busy at the same time. For instance, printing a document or a program listing is usually limited by the speed of the printer. The computer's disk drives and CPU are largely idle during this process. By overlapping printing with another computing task, such as running the assembler or linker, you can keep the CPU, disk, and printer busy. Adding another task, such as editing a file, keeps the computer operator busy as well. You don't have to wait for one task to finish before starting another.

Resource Management

The major problem posed by multitasking is that of *resource management*. Obviously, if you have one program using the printer, you shouldn't allow a second program to use the printer as well. To do so would result in the output of the first program mixed in with the output of the second. There are a number of things which the operating system must manage in a multitasking environment:

1. Memory. The operating system must control which tasks get which portions of memory, so that two tasks do not try to use the same memory area.

2. Nonshareable devices. A printer is an example of a device that is not shareable. Other examples are tape drives and terminals. Some devices that are normally shareable may have nonshareable uses. For instance, formatting a disk normally requires exclusive control of the disk drive. Thus, the operating system must provide some means for a task to gain and relinquish exclusive control of a device.

3. The CPU. Since there are now many tasks desiring to use the CPU, the operating system must have a policy for distributing CPU time.

4. A mechanism for tasks to cooperate and communicate with another. Many applications require the use of cooperating tasks.

Scheduling

The process of deciding which task may use the CPU's resources is called *scheduling*. The portion of the operating system that contains the code that makes this decision is called the *scheduler* or the *dispatcher*. There are a number of techniques used for allocating CPU time:

1. Priority-driven. In a priority-driven scheme, there is a priority associated with each task in the system. A priority-driven scheduler allocates the CPU to the highest priority task that is ready to run. The task keeps the CPU until it either terminates or requests some activity which prevents it from running, such as I/O. At this point, the dispatcher assigns the CPU to the highest priority task that is ready to run.

2. Preemptive priority-driven. The preemptive priority-driven technique forces a lower priority task to give up the CPU whenever a high-priority task becomes ready to use it. This prevents a high-priority task from being shut out by a low-priority task that uses a lot of CPU time.

3. Pure *time-slicing,* or *round robin.* This technique requires an external piece of hardware called a *clock* or a *tick* that interrupts the CPU at frequent intervals (normally 10 to 100 times a second). The time-slicing technique gives the CPU for some small fixed quantity of time to each task in turn.

4. Preemptive priority-driven with time-slicing. This technique modifies the preemptive priority-driven method so that tasks with equal priority are time-sliced.

Which Technique Is Best?

The preemptive priority-driven technique is preferred for systems that are strictly real-time in nature. This includes multitasking systems used for industrial control, instrumentation, and communications. The ability to guarantee a maximum response time is required for these applications. Preemptive priority-driven scheduling is the only way to achieve this goal.

Typical multiuser time-sharing systems try to guarantee each user an equal share of the computer. These systems tend to use some form of time-slicing technique. Simpler systems tend to use pure time-slicing, while more complicated systems require the preemptive priority-driven with time-slicing technique. These systems typically have both real-time requirements and time-sharing requirements. Fortunately, typical real-time tasks use very little of the CPU. However, a real-time task requires almost immediate response when it needs the CPU. It is possible to "steal" a little time from the time-sharing users to meet real-time requirements.

A further modification of the preemptive/time-sharing technique provides pure preemptive priority-driven scheduling above a certain priority level. This enhances real-time response without noticeably affecting the other tasks.

Who Gets Priority?

Assigning the priority for each task is sometimes a difficult task. Some systems dynamically vary the priority of a task as task behavior changes. In general, tasks that do a lot of I/O, especially I/O to slow devices, should be preferred over tasks that use large amounts of CPU time. This tends to keep the I/O devices, as well as the CPU active. Many large operating systems reevaluate task priority periodically and give more priority to tasks that have performed a large number of I/O operations since the last priority evaluations. Tasks that used most of the CPU time they had available are given less priority. Simple absence of I/O is not sufficient. A low-priority task may not have had a chance to do much since the last priority evaluation.

A task that performs a great deal of I/O is often called *I/O bound*. A task that requires a lot of CPU time is called *Compute bound* or *CPU bound*.

Reentrant Coding

A section of code is said to be *reentrant* if more than one task can be executing the same code simultaneously. Code is normally reentrant if it does not use global variables. Most multitasking systems have a data area for each task in the system. Using only these specific data areas and the stack allows most of the operating system to be reentrant.

The most commonly used technique is to have a global location in memory that contains the address of the task's data area for the task that is currently executing. Reentrant code in the operating system commonly loads this address into an address register and uses the "address register indirect with displacement" addressing mode to access fields in the specified task data area.

Mutual Exclusion

Obviously, all of the coding in an operating system cannot be reentrant. There must be global variables and be code that modifies these global variables. A section of code that modifies these shared variables is often called a *critical region*. The operating system must have some mechanism for making sure that only one task at a time can gain access to critical-region code. The same problem exists for variables that must be shared between task code and an interrupt routine.

Disabling Interrupts

Protecting critical-region code is often called *mutual exclusion*. The simplest form of mutual exclusion is simply to turn off interrupts while code in the critical region is executing. This works because an interrupt is required for a task swap to occur. This technique also protects variables that are shared between a task and interrupt code. The disadvantage to this form of mutual exclusion is that each instruction executed with interrupts that are turned off adds to the maximum response time for a real-time process. In order to protect critical-region code that is longer than a few instructions, other techniques are required.

A problem unique to microcomputers is that it may not be possible to disable interrupts completely. All microprocessor chips have at least one interrupt that may not be masked out. If the hardware designer connects this interrupt to something that interrupts frequently, it can pose a very difficult software-design problem. For example, one major computer manufacturer of Z-80 equipment used this interrupt for the clock! The computer receives an interrupt from this device thirty times a second. Designing an operating system to accommodate this design flaw required a lot of effort.

Practically all of the other techniques that have been developed to protect critical-region code employ some sort of queueing mechanism. These techniques include:

- Disabling dispatching
- Semaphores
- Monitor procedures
- Message switching

Disabling the Dispatcher

The simplest way to protect critical-region code that does not require an interrupt routine is to have a flag variable that the dispatcher interprets as prohibiting task swaps. This flag is set before entering a critical region and reset after leaving the critical region.

The disadvantage of this technique is that all critical-region code shares the same protection flag. This means that a high-priority task must wait for a low-priority task to exit a critical region, even though the high-priority task does not require access to the same critical-region code. This makes the maximum response time to a real-time event equal to the time required to execute the longest section of critical-region code in the operating system.

Semaphores

A better technique than disabling the dispatcher is the use of *semaphores*. A semaphore is a data structure consisting of a count and a pointer. The count is usually initialized to the value 1. There are two operations associated with a semaphore: wait and signal. These operations are defined as follows:

- A wait operation decrements the counter. If the result is not less than zero, the task is allowed to proceed. If the result is negative, the task is added to a list of tasks whose list head is the pointer variable of the semaphore.

- A signal operation increments the value of the counter. Then the first task in the list is allowed to run.

The semaphore data structure keeps track of the number of tasks waiting for a resource. The semaphore count is initialized to the number of these resources present in the system. For a situation requiring mutual exclusion, the count is set to one. Before entering a critical region, a process performs a wait on a semaphore associated with the critical region. Upon exiting the critical region, the process performs a signal operation on the semaphore. Each task in a semaphore operation waits only for other tasks that need access to the same protected resource. The real-time response using this method is a tremendous improvement over disabling the dispatcher.

Monitor Procedures

Monitor procedures are an extension of the semaphore technique. A monitor procedure is a subroutine that is protected by a semaphore or other mutual exclusion mechanism. Only one task at a time may execute a monitor procedure.

When programming a system with monitor procedures, the usual technique is to place all critical-region code that uses a set of shared variables inside a single monitor procedure. This technique is especially useful when the monitor construction is integrated into a programming language. An integration of this concept into the Pascal programming language is described in *The Architecture of Concurrent Programs* (New Jersey: Prentice-Hall, 1977).

Message Switching

Another technique for synchronizing processes is *message switching.* An operating system built on this architecture provides three functions for a task to communicate with another task. These functions are:

1. SEND data from one task to another.

2. RECEIVE data from another task.

3. REPLY to a message previously RECEIVED.

This technique uses the scheduling mechanism of the operating system itself to provide mutual exclusion.

A task that is similar in nature to a monitor procedure is set up to handle functions that would normally require critical-region code. This task, called a *server task,* receives messages from other tasks, performs the desired functions, and replies to each message as it completes each function. Messages not yet received are queued up in a "mailbox" associated with the task. This queue corresponds to the waiting queue for a semaphore.

Fork Queues

Providing synchronization between task-level code and interrupt code is a major concern in designing operating systems. One of the most clever schemes employed in many commercial systems is providing a way for an interrupt routine to schedule a high-priority task to execute as soon as an interrupt is finished. This normally involves setting up both some special code in the dispatcher and a queue of these "tasks," which are waiting to run.

This queue is usually known as the *fork queue.* The dispatcher checks the fork queue before it checks the normal list of tasks. Thus, a task in the fork queue has a higher priority than normal tasks. By allowing tasks in the fork queue to use some subset of the system calls that are normally available to ordinary tasks, you can use any of the previous techniques to synchronize task-level code with interrupt routines as well.

Deadlocks

When incorrectly applied, mutual exclusion can produce an unpleasant result. The area in which this problem is most often encountered is resource management. Suppose the system has two printers P1 and P2, and two tasks T1 and T2, that require both printers. If task T1 acquires printer P1 and asks for P2 and task T2 acquires P2 and asks for P1 at the same time, neither task will be able to finish. Since each task requires both printers and each task has one and is waiting for the other, they will both wait forever.

This situation is called a *deadlock* or a *deadly embrace*. There are many techniques to prevent this situation. One of the simplest is to require that all tasks acquire resources in the same order. In the example above, if both tasks acquired printer P1 and then printer P2, one of the tasks would wait until the other had finished, and no deadlock would occur.

Sample Operating System

The rest of this chapter is devoted to the sample operating system. This system, called LBOS (for "Little-Bitty Operating System"), is a message-switched system that allows user tasks to perform the following functions through the operating system:

- Delay for a period of time.
- Print a line on the terminal.
- Send a message to another task.
- Receive a message from another task.
- Reply to a message previously received.
- Enter dispatcher.

These functions are called *SVCs* (Supervisor Calls). The delay and print SVCs are implemented as tasks accessed through message-switching. LBOS uses a preemptive priority-driven scheduler without time-slicing. Tasks have fixed priorities. The system runs on the same SAGE IV microcomputer used in Chapter 7.

System Services

The system SVCs are accessed by executing a TRAP #0 instruction. Parameters are passed in registers. The application loads a code into register D0 that indicates the SVC desired. These codes are listed in Table 8.1.

In the event that a request could not be satisfied, register D0.L contains an error code following return from the TRAP #0 instruction. These codes are all less than zero, to allow a simple TST.L D0 / BLT sequence to test for errors.

Newtask SVC

The Newtask SVC provides a convenient means for a task to suspend itself. This SVC is used internally by the operating system to suspend a task that requests a service requiring that the task wait until the service is complete. The server tasks that provide the terminal output and delay capability also use this SVC to "put themselves to sleep" until an interrupt occurs.

Printline SVC

The Printline SVC writes a series of bytes on the SAGE IV terminal. The name Printline is actually a misnomer; the SVC just puts out a stream of bytes. This stream could contain many separate lines. The application requesting terminal output loads the address of the first byte to be output in register A0 and the number of bytes to be output in register D1.L. The task is suspended until the printing is complete.

Code	SVC
0	New task (enter dispatcher)
1	Print line on terminal
2	Delay
3	Send message
4	Receive message
5	Reply to message

Table 8.1 – LBOS SVC codes

Delay SVC

The Delay SVC allows a task to delay for an amount of time expressed in units of 1/100 second. The application puts the number of 1/100-second units desired into register D1.L. The task is suspended until the delay is complete.

Send Message SVC

The Send Message SVC sends a message to another task. The task that needs to send a message puts a byte count into register D1.L and an address into register A0. The task number to which the message is to be sent is contained in register D2.W. The task number is determined by a table inside the send code. The sending task is suspended until the task to which the message was sent has received the message and issues a REPLY SVC for that message.

Receive Message SVC

The Receive Message SVC suspends the issuing task until a message is available. Upon return from the TRAP #0 instruction, register D0.L contains the address of a data structure called a Message Control Block (MCB). This data structure contains all the parameters relevant to the message.

Reply to Message SVC

The Reply to Message SVC causes the task that originally sent the message to be marked dispatchable. The task issuing the Reply to Message SVC places the address of the Message Control Block (MCB) in register A0. The same address is returned by the Receive Message SVC in register D0.L.

Listing 8.1 contains the definitions for the SAGE IV hardware used, error codes returned, and equates for the SVC numbers. (The terminal hardware for this machine was explained in Chapter 7.) The clock is a single-interrupt count-down device. To use the clock, load a count into the clock-count register and get an interrupt some time later. To get another interrupt, you must reload the clock. LBOS uses the clock to interrupt at 1/100-second intervals.

Data Structures

LBOS uses two major data structures: a structure that represents each task, called a Task Control Block (TCB), and a structure for messages, called a Message Control Block (MCB). Both of these structures are elements on different linked lists. Listing 8.2 gives the definitions of both of these data areas.

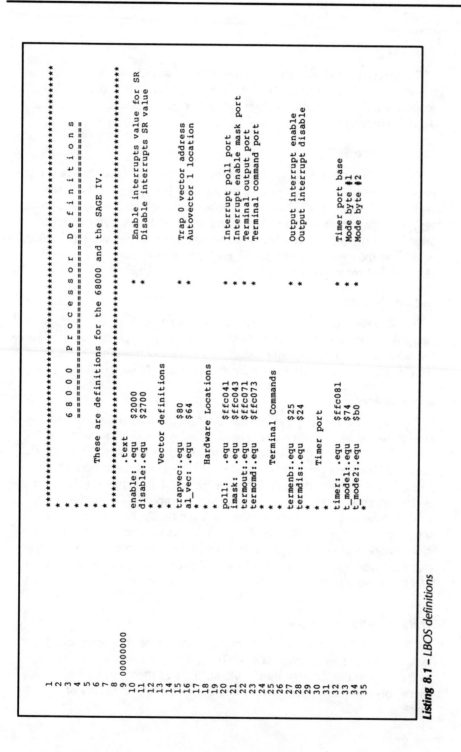

```
 1     *****************************************************
 2     *
 3     *        6 8 0 0 0   P r o c e s s o r   D e f i n i t i o n s
 4     *        ===============================================
 5     *
 6     *        These are definitions for the 68000 and the SAGE IV.
 7     *
 8     *****************************************************
 9 00000000     .text
10     enable: .equ  $2000           * Enable interrupts value for SR
11     disable:.equ  $2700           * Disable interrupts SR value
12     *
13     *              Vector definitions
14     *
15     trapvec:.equ  $80             * Trap 0 vector address
16     a1_vec: .equ  $64             * Autovector 1 location
17     *
18     *              Hardware Locations
19     *
20     poll:   .equ  $ffc041         * Interrupt poll port
21     imask:  .equ  $ffc043         * Interrupt enable mask port
22     termout:.equ  $ffc071         * Terminal output port
23     termcmd:.equ  $ffc073         * Terminal command port
24     *
25     *              Terminal Commands
26     *
27     termenb:.equ  $25             * Output interrupt enable
28     termdis:.equ  $24             * Output interrupt disable
29     *
30     *              Timer port
31     *
32     timer:  .equ  $ffc081         * Timer port base
33     t_mode1:.equ  $74             * Mode byte #1
34     t_mode2:.equ  $b0             * Mode byte #2
35     *
```

Listing 8.1 – LBOS definitions

```
36
37     *           Miscellaneous hardware stuff
38     *
39     rdvec:  .equ    $0C             *       Command to read vector
40 00000000
       clrint: .equ    $20             *       Command to end interrupt
41             .page
42     *******************************************************
43     *
44     *               L B O S   E r r o r   C o d e s
45     *               ===================================
46     *
47     *       The following error codes can be returned in D0.L if an error occurs
48     *       during the processing of an SVC.
49     *
       *******************************************************
50     e_badsvc: .equ  -1              *       Illegal SVC code in D0
51     e_nomcb:  .equ  -2              *       No MCB available for request
52     e_badtask:.equ  -3              *       Illegal task number
53     e_badmcb: .equ  -4              *       Illegal MCB address on reply
54
55     *******************************************************
56     *
57     *               S V C   C o d e   E q u a t e s
58     *               ===================================
59     *
60     *       These symbols are used by O/S tasks for referencing the SVC codes.
61     *
62     *******************************************************
63
64     SVCNEW: .equ    0               *       New task SVC
65     SVCPRT: .equ    1               *       Print on terminal SVC
66     SVCDLY: .equ    2               *       Delay SVC
67     SVCSND: .equ    3               *       Send SVC
68     SVCRCV: .equ    4               *       Receive SVC
69     SVCRPLY:.equ    5               *       Reply SVC
70 00000000
               .page
```

Listing 8.1 – *LBOS definitions (continued)*

```
71   *****************************************************************
72   *
73   *                    T C B  (Task Control Block) Layout
74   *                    ===================================
75   *
76   *        Each task in the LBOS system is represented by a data structure called
77   *        a "Task Control Block".  This area is used by the operating system to
78   *        store task-specific data.
79   *
80   *        Offset                      Contents                          Name
81   *        ======                      ========                          ====
82   *
83   *                  +---------------------------------------------+
84   *            0     ! Pointer to next TCB or Zero if no next TCB  !    t_link
85   *                  +---------------------------------------------+
86   *            4     ! Pointer to messages waiting to be RECEIVEd  !    t_msg
87   *                  +---------------------------------------------+
88   *            8     ! Pointer to messages awaiting REPLY          !    t_rply
89   *                  +---------------------------------------------+
90   *           12     ! Contents of task's USP when task is waiting !    t_usp
91   *                  +---------------------------------------------+
92   *           16     ! Contents of task's SSP when task is waiting !    t_ssp
93   *                  +---------------------------------------------+
94   *           20     ! Task flags word                             !    t_flag
95   *                  +---------------------------------------------+
96   *           24     ! Stack area for system                       !
97   *                  +---------------------------------------------+
98   *
99   *        The task's registers, PC, and status register are stored on the system
100  *        stack area within the TCB when the task is not running.
101  *
102  *****************************************************************
103  *
```

Listing 8.2 – LBOS data structures

```
104    *
105    *       Assembler definitions:
106    *
107    stacksize: .equ $100              *  Size of system stack
108    *
109    *       TCB offsets
110    t_link:  .equ  0                  *  Link word for task list thread
111    t_msg:   .equ  t_link+4           *  Link to waiting messages
112    t_rply:  .equ  t_msg+4            *  Link to messages received
113    t_usp:   .equ  t_rply+4           *  User Stack Pointer area
114    t_ssp:   .equ  t_usp+4            *  System Stack Pointer area
115    t_flag:  .equ  t_ssp+4            *  Flag word
116    t_stack: .equ  t_flag+4           *  Stack area
117    tcbsize: .equ  t_flag+4+stacksize *  Size of TCB in bytes
118                   t_stack
119    *
120    *       Flag word bits:
121    IWAIT:   .equ  0                  *  Waiting on interrupt
122    MWAIT:   .equ  1                  *  Waiting on message completion
123    RWAIT:   .equ  2                  *  Waiting on message receipt
124    00000000       .page
125    ***********************************************************
126    *
127    *           M e s s a g e   C o n t r o l   B l o c k
128    *           =======================================
129    *
130    *       LBOS performs system services by routing a message from the requesting
131    *       task to a task which performs the appropriate function.  Each message
132    *       is represented by a fixed length data area called a "Message Control
133    *       Block".  This area has the following layout:
```

Listing 8.2 – LBOS data structures (continued)

```
134   *
135   *
136   *              Offset    Contents                              Name
137   *              ======    ========                              ====
138   *
139   *                      +--------------------------------------+
140   *                0     ! Link to next MCB or zero if no next MCB !  m_link
141   *                      +--------------------------------------+
142   *                4     ! Buffer address (if required)         !  m_buff
143   *                      +--------------------------------------+
144   *                8     ! 32-bit count (byte count or delay time) !  m_count
145   *                      +--------------------------------------+
146   *                12    ! Requesting TCB address               !  m_rtcb
147   *                      +--------------------------------------+
148   *                16    ! Returned Status                      !  m_stat
149   *                      +--------------------------------------+
150   *
151   *       A message is sent using the SEND SVC and received using the RECEIVE
152   *       SVC. The issuing task is suspended until the serving task issues
153   *       a REPLY SVC.
154   *
155   *********************************************************************************
156   *
157   *              Assembler Definitions:
158   *
159   m_link: .equ    0            *       Link word
160   m_buff: .equ    m_link+4     *       Buffer address for I/O
161   m_count:.equ    m_buff+4     *       32-bit count
162   m_rtcb: .equ    m_count+4    *       Requesting TCB address
163   m_stat: .equ    m_rtcb+4     *       Status word
      mcbsize:.equ    m_stat+4     *       Size of MCB
              .page
164   00000000
```

Listing 8.2 – LBOS data structures (continued)

Task Control Block

Task control blocks (TCB) are kept in a singly-linked linear list. The first longword of the TCB is used for linkage. There are some portions of the LBOS code that depend on this fact. There are two list heads on the task control block that deal with messages. LBOS keeps a list of messages not yet received, as well as a list of messages that have been received, but for which no reply has been issued.

The TCB contains a stack to be used by the system when the task makes an SVC request or for an interrupt that occurs when the task is running. The contents of all the registers except the two stack pointers are saved on the stack when the task is not running. There are two separate longwords in the task control block that are used to save the two stack pointers.

The one remaining word in the TCB, the flag word, keeps track of whether or not the task may run. A task may be marked "not dispatchable" for three reasons:

1. The task is waiting for an interrupt. This flag is used by the server tasks to prevent dispatching while the tasks are waiting for some external event.

2. The task is waiting for a reply to a message.

3. The task is waiting to receive a message.

Message Control Block

Messages in the system are represented by a data structure known as a Message Control Block (MCB). The Message Control Block contains a link word that the operating system uses to link MCBs on the two lists of messages on the task control block. The contents of registers A0 and D1.L are stored in the MCB at the time the Send Message SVC was issued. Interpretation of these quantities is left up to the receiving task.

In order to provide the operating system with a way to associate the MCB with the task that originally sent the message, the address of the sending tasks task control block is maintained in the message control block. A longword is provided in the message control block for the receiving task. Anything stored in this word by the receiver will be placed in register D0.L when the sending task resumes execution. This allows an SVC to be implemented as a task rather than as a part of the operating system proper.

Initialization Code

LBOS is designed to be loaded under CP/M-68K, and to take over control of the machine. There is no way back to CP/M-68K from LBOS. To return to CP/M, the machine must be rebooted. Listing 8.3 contains the code that takes over from CP/M-68K and sets up LBOS.

Lines 180 and 181 issue the Set Supervisor request to CP/M so that LBOS can use privileged instructions. Lines 183 to 185 set up the SAGE IV hardware: loading the interrupt vectors and disabling the clock interrupt. Notice that instructions executed with interrupts off are tagged with three asterisks (* * *) in the comment field.

Lines 186 to 202 initialize the task control block fields for the four tasks in LBOS. A table in the initialized data area gives the TCB address and the initial PC and status register contents for each task in the system. The tasks are entered in this initialization table in order of priority. LBOS supports tasks that run in both supervisor and user modes.

Lines 206 to 213 link together an area of memory to become a linked list of message control blocks. When a Send Message SVC is issued, a free MCB is obtained from this area in memory. When the corresponding Reply SVC is issued, the MCB is placed back into this list.

The last two lines of initialization code start LBOS by entering the dispatcher. The longword at the label "current" always contains the address of the TCB of the currently executing task. When "current" is zero, no task is executing.

TRAP #0 Exception Handler

Listing 8.4 contains the code that is executed when a task executes a TRAP #0 instruction, indicating a request for an LBOS function. The application loads the code corresponding to the desired service into register D0.L. The code at lines 241 to 247 computes the address of the LBOS routine that performs the indicated function and jumps to this routine. Notice the use of a single unsigned branch to perform the range check on function numbers.

Lines 251 to 253 execute if the application requests an illegal function. The application's registers are restored, and −1 is loaded into register D0.L. The RTE instruction at line 253 returns control to the application.

The data at lines 258 to 264 forms a table of SVC routine addresses. The addresses are ordered by SVC number, so that the function number shifted left twice (times four) is the index into the table. Notice the use of an equate to define a symbol for the first illegal SVC number.

```
125   ******************************************************************
126   *
127   *                  M e s s a g e   C o n t r o l   B l o c k
128   *                  =========================================
129   *
130   *      LBOS performs system services by routing a message from the requesting
131   *      task to a task which performs the appropriate function. Each message
132   *      is represented by a fixed length data area called a "Message Control
133   *      Block". This area has the following layout:
134   *
135   *      Offset                   Contents                        Name
136   *      ======                   ========                        ====
137   *
138   *             +------------------------------------+
139   *        0    ! Link to next MCB or zero if no next MCB !      m_link
140   *             +------------------------------------+
141   *        4    ! Buffer address (if required)       !          m_buff
142   *             +------------------------------------+
143   *        8    ! 32-bit count (byte count or delay time) !      m_count
144   *             +------------------------------------+
145   *       12    ! Requesting TCB address             !          m_rtcb
146   *             +------------------------------------+
147   *       16    ! Returned Status                    !          m_stat
148   *             +------------------------------------+
149   *
150   *      A message is sent using the SEND SVC and received using the RECEIVE
151   *      SVC. The issuing task is suspended until the serving task issues
152   *      a REPLY SVC.
153   *
154   ******************************************************************
155   *
156   *      Assembler Definitions:
157   *
158   m_link: .equ   0            *       Link word
159   m_buff: .equ   m_link+4     *       Buffer address for I/O
160   m_count:.equ   m_buff+4     *       32-bit count
```

Listing 8.3 – LBOS initialization code

```
                                       m_rtcb: .equ    m_count+4              *       Requesting TCB address
                                       m_stat: .equ    m_rtcb+4               *       Status word
                                       mcbsize:.equ    m_stat+4               *       Size of MCB
    00000000                                   .page
                                       ******************************************************************************
                                       *
                                       *               L B O S   I n i t i a l i z a t i o n   C o d e
                                       *               ===============================================
                                       *
                                       *       Routine "init" performs initialization prior to LBOS receiving
                                       *       control.  Actions performed are:
                                       *
                                       *       1).     Initialize vector area to appropriate interrupt routines
                                       *       2).     Initialize TCB area
                                       *       3).     Initialize MCB free list
                                       *       4).     Jump to dispatcher
                                       *
                                       ******************************************************************************
                                       init:
    00000000 303C003E                          move.w  #62,d0                 *       Set
    00000004 4E42                              trap    #2                     *               Supervisor
    00000006 46FC2700                          move.w  #disable,sr            *       Disallow interrupts
    0000000A 23FC0000008E00000080              move.l  #trap0,trapvec         ***     Set trap vector
    00000014 23FC0000010600000064              move.l  #pollint,a1_vec        ***     Set I/O vector
    0000001E 08F9000000FFC043                  bset    #0,poll+2              ***     Disable timer interrupt
    00000026 41F900000018                      lea     initdata,a0            ***     a0 -> TCB init area
    0000002C 47F900000004                      lea     tcblist,a3             ***     a2 -> "previous TCB"
    00000032 2258                      inittcb: move.l (a0)+,a1               ***     a1 -> tcb area (uninit'ed)
    00000034 B3FC00000000                      cmpa.l  #0,a1                  ***     Done yet?
    0000003A 671E                              beq     tcbdone                ***     EQ => done with tcb area
    0000003C 42A9000C                          clr.l   t_usp(a1)              ***     Clear task's USP
    00000040 45E90118                          lea.l   t_stack(a1),a2         ***     a2 -> End of stack area
```

Listing 8.3 – *LBOS initialization code (continued)*

```
193  00000044  2518                            move.l   (a0)+,-(a2)             ***   Push task's "PC"
194  00000046  4A58                            tst.w    (a0)+                   ***   Skip high word of SR
195  00000048  3518                            move.w   (a0)+,-(a2)             ***   Push task's SR
196  0000004A  48E2FFFE                        movem.l  d0-d7/a0-a6,-(a2)       ***   save "registers"
197  0000004E  234A0010                        move.l   a2,t_ssp(a1)            ***   Set kernel stack
198  00000052  27490000                        move.l   a1,t_link(a3)           ***   Set previous tcb link word
199  00000056  2649                            move.l   a1,a3                   ***   Save previous tcb address
200  00000058  60D8                            bra      inittcb                 ***   Loop till done
201
202  0000005A  42AB0000            tcbdone:    clr.l    t_link(a3)              ***   Null out last link word
203
204                               *     Init Message control block area
205                               *
206  0000005E  203C00000004                    move.l   #nmcbs-1,d0             ***   d0 = number of mcbs to init
207  00000064  41F90000046C                    lea      mcbarea,a0              ***   a0 -> area
208  0000006A  23C80000468                     move.l   a0,mcblist              ***   Init list head
209  00000070  2248               mcbloop:     move.l   a0,a1                   ***   Save current address
210  00000072  41E80014                        lea      mcbsize(a0),a0          ***   a0 -> Next mcb
211  00000076  23480014                        move.l   a0,m_link(a1)           ***   Set link word
212  0000007A  51C8FFF4                        dbra     d0,mcbloop              ***   repeat till done
213  0000007E  42A90000                        clr.l    m_link(a1)              ***   set last link word to 0
214
215                               *     Prepare to enter dispatcher
216                               *
217  00000082  42B900000000                    clr.l    current                 ***   No current task
218  00000088  4EF90000000CE                   jmp      dispatch                ***   Go to dispatcher
```

Listing 8.3 - *LBOS initialization code (continued)*

```
*****************************************************************************
*
*               L B O S   Calling Conventions
*               =============================
*
*       LBOS supports 6 SVC's (SuperVisor Calls).  An SVC is requested by
*       loading the appropriate function code into D0.L and executing a
*       TRAP #0 instruction.  The following functions are available:
*
*       Function               D0        A0              D1            D2
*       ========               ==        ==              ==            ==
*       Newtask                0        N/A             N/A           N/A
*       Printline on terminal  1        Buffer Address  Byte Count    N/A
*       Delay                  2        N/A             Delay Count   N/A
*       Send Message           3        Buffer Address  Count         Task #
*       Receive Message        4        N/A             N/A           N/A
*       Reply to Message       5        MCB Address     N/A           N/A
*
*       The entry point for SVC routines is "trap0:".
*
*****************************************************************************
trap0:
                  movem.l d0-d7/a0-a6,-(a7)        * Save all registers
241 0000008E 48E7FFFE
242 00000092 B0BC00000006 cmp.l  #maxsvc,d0         * Is D0 in range?
243 00000098 640E         bhis   badsvc             * If HIS, no, return error
244 0000009A E588         lsl.l  #2,d0              * multiply d0 by 4
245 0000009C 4DF900000000 lea.l  svctab,a6          * a6 -> beginning of table
246 000000A2 2C760800     move.l 0(a6,d0.l),a6      * a6 -> svc routine
247 000000A6 4ED6         jmp    (a6)               * enter svc routine
248
*
```

***Listing 8.4** – Exception handler for the LBOS TRAP 0 instruction*

```
                                   *
                                   *      If function number out of range, return -1.
                                   *
251  000000A8  4CDF7FFF  badsvc:  movem.l  (sp)+,d0-d7/a0-a6      *      Restore registers
252  000000AC  70FF               move.l   #e_badsvc,d0          *      load return code
253  000000AE  4E73               rte                            *      Return to task code
                                   *
                                   *      Table of SVC routine addresses, in function code order
                                   *
257  00000000                     .data
258  00000000  000000B0  svctab:  .dc.l    newtask               *  0   Enter dispatcher
259  00000004  00000250           .dc.l    prtline               *  1   Terminal Output
260  00000008  00000256           .dc.l    delay                 *  2   Real-time delay
261  0000000C  0000013C           .dc.l    send                  *  3   Send a message
262  00000010  000001C2           .dc.l    recv                  *  4   Receive a message
263  00000014  000001F8           .dc.l    reply                 *  5   Reply to message
264                       maxsvc:  .equ    (*-svctab)/4          *      Max SVC number + 1
265  000000B0                     .text
266  000000B0                     .page
```

Listing 8.4 – *Exception handler for the LBOS TRAP 0 instruction (continued)*

Newtask SVC and Dispatcher

Listing 8.5 shows the Newtask SVC and the LBOS dispatcher. The New-task SVC provides a convenient method for a task to call the dispatcher. Lines 285 to 291 save the state of the user task. All exception-handling routines within LBOS are required to save all registers on the stack except A7. Notice that the contents of register D0 are in the first longword on the stack.

The dispatcher is located at lines 297 to 315. The dispatcher requires that the task registers (including both stack pointers) be saved, as is done in the Newtask SVC code. The dispatcher should, therefore, only be entered if there is no "current task." The dispatch algorithm is quite simple: scan down the list of TCBs until you find one that is not blocked. (Blocked tasks have at least one bit set in the TCB flag word.) Upon find-ing a dispatchable task, load location "current" with the TCB address (line 304), load up the task's registers (lines 305 to 308), and begin executing the task code (line 309).

The code at lines 313 to 314 executes if no task is dispatchable. The STOP instruction reduces the processor priority to zero and waits for an interrupt. The dispatch code is executed again to see if any tasks have been made dispatchable by the interrupt.

Data Area

Listing 8.6 contains the LBOS data area. Lines 329 to 335 contain initial data for four TCBs: a task to handle the clock (timer), a task to handle ter-minal output, and two applications tasks. The tasks are linked in priority order from the "tcblist" memory location. The storage for each of the TCBs is reserved in lines 342 to 345.

A linked list of free Message Control blocks is created by the initializa-tion code using the memory reserved by lines 349 to 351. Location "mcblist" contains the address of the first free MCB.

Interrupt Polling Routine

Both the clock and terminal-output interrupt are tied to the 68000 level 1 autovector interrupt. This is a modification of the routine used in Chap-ter 7 for the interrupt-driven serial output program.

On each interrupt, the registers are saved on the stack of the current task. If there is no current task, the last task to execute provides the stack

```
         *****************************************************************
         *                                                               *
         *              N e w t a s k   S V C   R o u t i n e            *
         *              ===================================              *
         *                                                               *
         *   SVC "newtask" is used to suspend the execution of the present task and
         *   schedule execution of the next task. This routine is called by other
         *   SVC routines when the current task becomes non-dispatchable.
         *                                                               *
         *   Entry Conditions:                                           *
         *                                                               *
         *         Registers and PC/SR stored on the stack in standard order.
         *                                                               *
         *   Exit Conditions:                                            *
         *                                                               *
         *         Task Context saved.  Exit to dispatcher               *
         *                                                               *
         *****************************************************************
         newtask: move.l  current,a0         *   a0 -> current TCB
                  cmpa.l  #0,a0              *   check to make sure there is one
                  beq     dispatch           *   EQ => No current task
                  move.l  usp,al             *   Fetch user stack pointer
                  move.l  al,t_usp(a0)       *   Save in TCB
                  move.l  a7,t_ssp(a0)       *   Save supervisor stack pointer
                  clr.l   current            *   Indicate no active task
                  *                                                      *
                  *   Here we try to dispatch the highest priority task.  If none, wait
                  *   until there is one
```

```
267
268
269
270
271
272
273
274
275
276
277
278
279
280
281
282
283
284
285  000000B0 2079000000000
286  000000B6 B1FC00000000
287  000000BC 6710
288  000000BE 4E69
289  000000C0 2149000C
290  000000C4 214F0010
291  000000C8 42B900000000
292
293
294
```

Listing 8.5 – The New task SVC and dispatcher

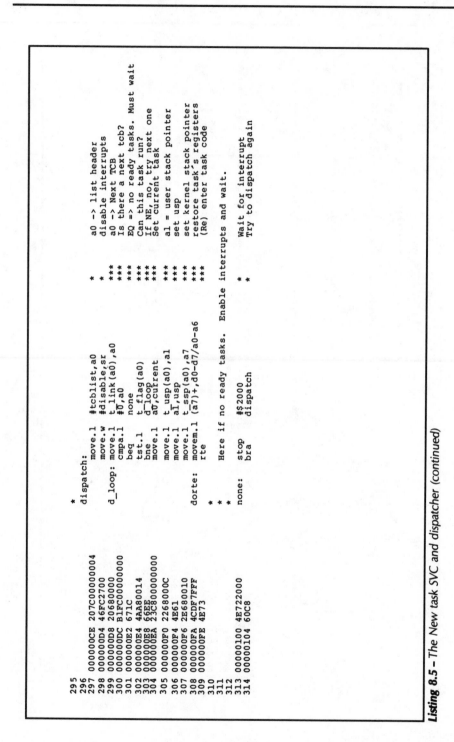

```
295             *
296             dispatch:
297  000000CE 207C00000004          move.l   #tcblist,a0       *    a0 -> list header
298  000000D4 46FC2700              move.w   #disable,sr       *    disable interrupts
299  000000D8 20680000      d_loop: move.l   t_link(a0),a0     ***  a0 -> Next TCB
300  000000DC B1FC00000000          cmpa.l   #0,a0             ***  Is there a next tcb?
301  000000E2 671C                  beq      none              ***  EQ => no ready tasks. Must wait
302  000000E4 4AA80014              tst.l    t_flag(a0)        ***  Can this task run?
303  000000E8 66EE                  bne      d_loop            ***  If NE, no, try next one
304  000000EA 23C800000000          move.l   a0,current        ***  Set current task
305  000000F0 2268000C              move.l   t_usp(a0),a1      ***  a1 = user stack pointer
306  000000F4 4E61                  move.l   a1,usp            ***  set usp
307  000000F6 2E680010              move.l   t_ssp(a0),a7      ***  set kernel stack pointer
308  000000FA 4CDF7FFF      dorte:  movem.l  (a7)+,d0-d7/a0-a6 ***  restore task's registers
309  000000FE 4E73                  rte                        ***  (Re) enter task code
310             *
311             *        Here if no ready tasks. Enable interrupts and wait.
312             *
313  00000100 4E722000      none:   stop     #$2000            *    Wait for interrupt
314  00000104 60C8                  bra      dispatch          *    Try to dispatch again
```

Listing 8.5 – The New task SVC and dispatcher (continued)

```
315 00000106              .page
316              ***************************************************************
317              *
318              *                   L B O S   D a t a   A r e a
319              *                   =============================
320              *
321              *      This area contains the data used by the operating system.
322              *
323              ***************************************************************
324 00000018              .data                          * Initialized data
325              *
326              *      Data for initialization routine
327              *
328              initdata: .globl applepa,app2epa         * Applications entry points
329 00000018 0000000800000025C
330 00000020 00002000       .dc.l timetask,timeepa,$2000 * Timer task tcb initialization
331 00000024 00000120000000310
331 0000002C 00002000       .dc.l termtask,termepa,$2000 * Terminal task tcb init.
332 00000030 0000023800000000
332 00000038 00000000       .dc.l appltask,applepa,0     * Application task #1
333 0000003C 0000035000000000
333 00000044 00000000       .dc.l app2task,app2epa,0     * Application task #2
334 00000048 00000000       .dc.l 0                      * End of list marker
335              *
336 00000000              .bss                           * Uninitialized data
337 00000000 current: .ds.l 1                            * -> Current task's TCB
338 00000004 tcblist: .ds.l 1                            * -> All TCB's in priority order
339              *
340              *      TCB storage area
341              *
342 00000008 timetask: .ds.b tcbsize                     * Timer task TCB area
343 00000120 termtask: .ds.b tcbsize                     * Terminal task TCB area
344 00000238 appltask: .ds.b tcbsize                     * Application task #1
345 00000350 app2task: .ds.b tcbsize                     * Application task #2
346              *
347              *      MCB storage area
348              *
349 00000468 mcblist: .ds.l 1                            * -> Free list of MCB's
350 0000046C nmcbs:   .equ  5                            * Number of free mcb's
351 00000106 mcbarea: .ds.b mcbsize*nmcbs                * Area for MCB's
352 00000106              .text
353 00000106              .page
```

Listing 8.6 – LBOS data area

space. If a decision is made to switch context as a result of the interrupt, only the two stack pointers need be saved.

The code shown in Listing 8.7 handles Level 1 interrupts. The interrupt-controller device is polled and the interrupt is cleared in lines 365 to 367. Lines 368 to 376 determine which device interrupted and jump to the appropriate interrupt-service code. LBOS uses only two of the devices on the interrupt controller, as indicated by the table at lines 378 to 386. All other interrupts are ignored by transferring to the label "noint," which returns to the interrupted task.

Send Message SVC

Listing 8.8 contains the code that performs the Send Message SVC. This code is entered from the TRAP #0 exception handler. Lines 401 to 406 allocate an MCB for the message. Notice that this is critical-region code. If the task were to get suspended between lines 402 and 406, another task could also issue a Send Message SVC, and the two tasks would try to use the same MCB. (The shared variable which must be protected is "mcblist".)

Lines 407 to 413 prepare the fields in the message control block. Line 414 marks the current task for suspension until the target task issues a Reply. Lines 415 to 418 compute the address of the receiving task task conrol block from the index passed by the sender in register D2. The task index is determined by the list of TCB addresses at line 436.

Lines 419 to 426 place the MCB in the receiving task's mailbox. To preserve the order in which the messages were sent, the message list ("m_link" in the TCB) is kept in strict FIFO order. This segment of code is also a critical region, protecting the task's entire list of MCBs.

Line 427 clears the bit in the receiving task's TCB that corresponds to "waiting to Receive a Message." If the receiving task is waiting for a message, it will now "wake up" and complete the Receive Message SVC. Line 428 branches to the Newtask SVC to cause another task to run. Notice that the current task is blocked, so a task swap is guaranteed.

The Send Message SVC can return two errors. The first, "e_badtask," occurs when the requesting task passes an invalid task index in register D2. The second, "e_nomcbs," occurs when no MCB is available to send the message.

Receive Message SVC

Listing 8.9 contains the code for the Receive Message SVC. Because it must protect the integrity of the receiving task's message lists, this entire

```
354                         ************************************************************
355                         *
356                         *       I n t e r r u p t   P o l l i n g   R o u t i n e
357                         *       ==================================================
358                         *
359                         *       Routine "pollint" determines the source of a level 1 autovector
360                         *       interrupt.  The standard stack arrangement is set up here.
361                         *
362                         ************************************************************
363                         pollint:
364  00000106  48E7FFFE              movem.l  d0-d7/a0-a6,-(a7)       * Save registers
365  0000010A  13FC000C00FFC041      move.b   #rdvec,poll             * Issue "read vector" command
366  00000112  103900FFC041          move.b   poll,d0                 * Fetch vector
367  00000118  13FC002000FFC041      move.b   #cirint,poll            * Indicate end of interrupt
368  00000120  4A00                  tst.b    d0                      * Interrupt pending?
369  00000122  6A12                  bpl      noint                   * Oops! no interrupt at all
370  00000124  02400007              andi.w   #7,d0                   * Clear all but vector bits
371  00000128  E548                  lsl.w    #2,d0                   * Multiply by 4
372  0000012A  41F90000004C          lea      vectable,a0             * a0 -> vector addresses
373  00000130  20700000              move.l   0(a0,d0.w),a0           * a0 -> Routine
374  00000134  4ED0                  jmp      (a0)                    * enter interrupt routine
375  00000136  4CDF7FFF      noint:  movem.l  (a7)+,d0-d7/a0-a6       * Restore registers
376  0000013A  4E73                  rte                             * Exit to interrupted routine
377  0000004C                        .data
378                         vectable:
379  0000004C  00000292              .dc.l    timeint                 * 0  Timer
380  00000050  00000136              .dc.l    noint                   * 1  Remote input
381  00000054  0000035A              .dc.l    termint                 * 2  Terminal output interrupt
382  00000058  00000136              .dc.l    noint                   * 3  Remote output
383  0000005C  00000136              .dc.l    noint                   * 4  Remote ring indicator
384  00000060  00000136              .dc.l    noint                   * 5  Centronics
385  00000064  00000136              .dc.l    noint                   * 6  Real-time clock
386  00000068  00000136              .dc.l    noint                   * 7  Software controlled
387  0000013C                        .text
388  0000013C                        .page
```

Listing 8.7 – LBOS interrupt-polling routine

```
389        **************************************************
390        *                                                *
391        *          S e n d   M e s s a g e   S V C        *
392        *          ===================================    *
393        *                                                *
394        *   Routine "send" is entered via TRAP or a JUMP from another SVC handler.
395        *   This routine allocates a message control block, and marks the task as
396        *   non-dispatchable.  It clears the RWAIT (Receive Wait) bit in the target
397        *   task.                                         *
398        *                                                *
399        **************************************************
400
401  0000013C  46FC2700      send:  move.w  #disable,sr         ***  Disable to allocate MCB
402  00000140  2C7900000468         move.l  mcblist,a6         ***  a6 -> first message block
403  00000146  BDFC00000000         cmpa.l  #0,a6              ***  Are there any?
404  0000014C  676A                 beq     nomcbs             ***  No, return an error
405  0000014E  23D600000468         move.l  (a6),mcblist       ***  Remove block from list
406  00000154  46FC2000             move.w  #enable,sr         ***  Allow interrupts
407  00000158  42AE0000             clr.l   m_link(a6)         *    Clear link word
408  0000015C  2D480004             move.l  a0,m_buff(a6)      *    Put buffer address into MCB
409  00000160  2D410008             move.l  d1,m_count(a6)     *    Put count into MCB
410  00000164  227900000000         move.l  current,a1         *    a1 -> Current task
411  0000016A  2D49000C             move.l  a1,m_rtcb(a6)      *    Save task's tcb address
412  0000016E  B4BC00000004         cmp.l   #maxtask,d2        *    Is d2 in range?
413  00000174  6438                 bhis    badtask            *    No, don't go any further
414  00000176  08E900010017         bset.b  #MWAIT,t_flag+3(a1) *   Make task wait for reply
415  0000017C  E582                 asl.l   #2,d2              *    multiply task index by 4
416  0000017E  45F90000006C         lea     tasktab,a2         *    a2 -> tasktable
417  00000184  D5C2                 adda.l  d2,a2              *    a2 -> address of TCB address
418  00000186  2452                 move.l  (a2),a2            *    a2 -> Target TCB
419  00000188  47EA0004             lea     t_msg(a2),a3       *    a3 -> message list
420  0000018C  46FC2700             move.w  #disable,sr        ***  Disable for queue search
```

Listing 8.8 – The Send Message SVC

```
421  00000190  4AAB0000      getmcb: tst.l   m_link(a3)        *** Zero link?
422  00000194  6706                  beq     mcbend            *** Yes, add in at end
423  00000196  266B0000              move.l  m_link(a3),a3     *** Advance to next list position
424  0000019A  60F4                  bra     getmcb            *** Continue until find null link
425  0000019C  274E0000      mcbend: move.l  a6,m_link(a3)     *** Link MCB in at end
426  000001A0  46FC2000              move.w  #enable,sr        *** Re-allow interrupts
427  000001A4  08AA00020017          bclr.b  #RWAIT,t_flag+3(a2)  * Indicate task dispatchable
428  000001AA  6000FF04              bra     newtask           * Go to new task.
429
430                          *       Here on error
431                          *
432  000001AE  2EBCFFFFFFFD  badtask: move.l  #e_badtask,(a7)  * Modify D0 on stack
433  000001B4  6000FF44              bra     dorte             * Go back to task code
434  000001B8  2EBCFFFFFFFE  nomcbs: move.l  #e_nomcb,(a7)     *** Modify D0 on stack
435  000001BE  6000FF3A              bra     dorte             *** Go back to task code
436  0000006C                       .data
437  0000006C  00000008000000120 tasktab:.dc.l timetask,termtask,appltask,app2task
437  00000074  000002380000000350

438                          maxtask: .equ  (*-tasktab)/4
439                          i_time:  .equ  0                  * Timer Task index
440                          i_term:  .equ  1                  * Terminal Task index
441  000001C2                       .text
```

Listing 8.8 – The Send Message SVC (continued)

routine is critical-region code. Lines 456 to 457 test for the presence of messages in the task's mailbox. If there are no messages, lines 464 to 467 cause the task to be suspended until another task sends a message to the current task. Lines 458 to 461 move the MCB from the "waiting for receive" list (t_msg) to the "waiting for reply" list (t_rply). Line 462 puts the address of the MCB into the receiving task's register D0.

Reply to Message SVC

Listing 8.10 contains the code for the Reply to Message SVC. Lines 480 to 488 attempt to find the MCB specified by the requesting task in register A0. If the specified MCB is not in the "waiting for reply" list, lines 498 and 499 return an error to the task that invoked the SVC. Line 489 removes the MCB from the "t_rply" list.

Lines 490 to 492 put the return code (which is placed by the receiving task in the MCB at the label "m_stat") in the sender's register D0.L. Line 493 makes the sending task dispatchable again. Lines 494 and 495 return the MCB to the free pool of MCBs. Line 497 exits to the dispatcher, since the sending task might have a higher priority than the receiving task.

Printline and Delay SVCs

Listing 8.11 gives the code for the Printline and Delay SVCs. This code is trivial due to the fact that these SVCs are handled by separate tasks. Since the registers used by the Printline and Delay SVCs correspond to the registers for the Send Message SVC, all that is necessary is to load the proper task index into register D2 and branch to the send code.

Timer Task Code

Listing 8.12 shows the code for processing the Delay SVC. Lines 534 to 535 perform a Receive SVC. Lines 536 to 544 load two global variables that communicate with the interrupt routine, mark the timer task nondispatchable, and call the dispatcher using the Newtask SVC. When the task becomes dispatchable again (after the delay), the task issues a Reply SVC. Only one delay can be active at a time.

The interrupt routine (lines 552 to 564) decrements the global counter ("tcount") until it reaches zero. When the count reaches zero, lines 560 to 564 cause the timer task to resume execution. The flag "tstatus" is used to prevent unnecessary timer interrupts when no delays are taking place.

```
442     *************************************************************
443     *
444     *           R e c e i v e   M e s s a g e   S V C
445     *           ===================================
446     *
447     *       Routine "recv" is used by a task desiring to receive a message from
448     *       another task.  Incoming messages are queued up in FIFO order by
449     *       "send".  The message is removed from the "t_msg" list and placed
450     *       in the "t_rply" list.
451     *
452     *************************************************************
453                     recv:    move.l  current,a0              *       a0 -> Current task's TCB
454  000001C2 207900000000        move.w  #disable,sr          ***     Disable interrupts
455  000001C8 46FC2700            tst.l   t_msg(a0)            ***     Any messages waiting?
456  000001CC 4AA80004            beq     nomsgs               ***     No, have to wait for one
457  000001D0 671A                move.l  t_msg(a0),a1         ***     a1 -> First message
458  000001D2 22680004            move.l  m_link(a1),t_msg(a0) ***     Remove from t_msg list
459  000001D6 216900000004        move.l  t_rply(a0),m_link(a1) ***    Put on   Reply list
460  000001DC 236800080000        move.l  a1,t_rply(a0)        ***     Replace DO contents
461  000001E2 21490008            bra     dorte                ***     Go back to task.
462  000001E6 2E89        nomsgs: bset.b  #RWAIT,t_flag+3(a0)  ***     Mark waiting for message
463  000001E8 6000FF10            move.l  #SVCNEW,a0           ***     Issue New task       SVC
464  000001EC 08E800020017        trap    #0                   ***
465  000001F2 7000                bra     recv                 ***     try receive again
466  000001F4 4E40                .page
467  000001F6 60CA
468  000001F8
```

Listing 8.9 – Receive Message SVC

```
                          **********************************************
                          *                                            *
                          *          R e p l y   T o   M e s s a g e   S V C
                          *          =======================================
                          *                                            *
                          *    Routine "reply" causes the task which originally sent a message to
                          *    resume execution, with D0 set equal to the returned status code
                          *    from the task which received and processed the message.
                          *                                            *
                          **********************************************

                          reply:
469
470
471
472
473
474
475
476
477
478
479
480 00001F8 247900000000        move.l  current,a2            * a2 -> current task TCB
481 00001FE 43EA0008            lea     t_rply(a2),a1         * a1 -> list header
482 0000202 46FC2700            move.w  #disable,sr           *** No interrupts in search
483 0000206 4AA90000   fndmcb:  tst.l   m_link(a1)            *** End of list?
484 000020A 673A                beq     badmcb                *** Yes, return error
485 000020C B1E90000            cmp.l   m_link(a1),a0         *** Does link point to right one?
486 0000210 6706                beq     found                 *** Yes, take out of list
487 0000212 22690000            move.l  m_link(a1),a1         *** Advance the list
488 0000216 60EE                bra     fndmcb                *** And try again
489 0000218 236800000000 found: move.l  m_link(a0),m_link(a1) *** take out of list
490 000021E 2668000C            move.l  m_rtcb(a0),a3         *** a3 -> Sender's TCB
491 0000222 286B0010            move.l  t_ssp(a3),a4          *** a4 -> Sender's D0
492 0000226 28A90010            move.l  m_stat(a1),(a4)       *** Put in status code
493 000022A 08AB00010017        bclr.b  #MWAIT,t_flag+3(a3)   *** Mark dispatchable
494 0000230 21790000468000000   move.l  mcblist,m_link(a0)    *** Put MCB
495 0000238 23C800000468        move.l  a0,mcblist            *** back in free list
496 000023E 46FC2000            move.w  #enable,sr            * Enable interrupts
497 0000242 6000FE6C            bra     newtask               *** And re-dispatch
498 0000246 2EBCFFFFFFFC badmcb: move.l #e_badmcb,(a7)        *** Set error code
499 000024C 6000FEAC            bra     dorte                 *** return to offender
500 0000250                     .page
```

Listing 8.10 – The Reply to Message SVC

```
501   *****************************************************************
502   *
503   *                  T e r m i n a l   O u t p u t   S V C
504   *                  =====================================
505   *
506   *       Routine "prtline" causes a buffer full of output to be sent to the
507   *       terminal. The task is suspended until the buffer is output.
508   *
509   *****************************************************************
510   prtline:
511   00000250  7401          move.l  #i_term,d2      *       Set appropriate index
512   00000252  6000FEE8      bra     send            *       And do send message
513
514   *****************************************************************
515   *
516   *                         D e l a y   S V C
517   *                         =================
518   *
519   *       Routine "delay" causes the issuing task to be delayed by the number of
520   *       clock ticks contained in register dl.
521   *
522   *****************************************************************
523   delay:
524   00000256  7400          move.l  #i_time,d2      *       Load task index
525   00000258  6000FEE2      bra     send            *       And do a send SVC
526   0000025C                .page
```

Listing 8.11 – *The Printline and Delay SVCs*

The subroutine called trset (lines 568 to 576) causes a timer interrupt after 1/100 second. The timer is a two-stage counter, which counts at a basic clock rate of 64,000 times per second. Lines 571 to 574 load the four bytes of the count register with appropriate constants to make the count register 640. The clock will then interrupt 1/100 second later. This subroutine must be called each time an interrupt is desired.

Terminal Output Task

Listing 8.13 contains the code for the task that handles the LBOS Printline SVC. Lines 590 and 591 execute a Receive Message SVC to get information on the output desired. Lines 592 to 603 set up the terminal output, mark the task as not dispatchable, and exit to the dispatcher via the New task SVC. This code actually puts out the first character, so the interrupt routine is always started by the completion of the character output. When the interrupt routine finishes outputting the buffer, the terminal task resumes execution. Lines 604 to 606 issue a Reply to Message SVC to wake up the task that originally requested the terminal output.

The terminal-output interrupt handler begins at line 612. If no more characters remain to be output, the task disables the serial port, and wakes up the terminal task (lines 612 to 617). If the count of characters is greater than 0, there is another character to be output. Lines 619 to 623 output the next character and decrement the character count.

Application Tasks

Listings 8.14 and 8.15 show two "applications" programs. The first application issues a Delay SVC for 2.5 seconds, and then prints a message on the terminal. The second application executes a CPU-intensive loop and outputs a similar message on the terminal. Since the first task has a higher priority than the second, both the clock and the CPU tend to remain busy.

SUMMARY

In this chapter, we have covered most of the basic concepts involved in writing multitasking operating systems. These topics are:

- Multitasking.
- Resource management.

```
527  ***************************************************************
528  *
529  *                    T i m e r   T a s k
530  *                    =====================
531  *
532  ***************************************************************
533
534  0000025C 7004              timeepa: move.l  #SVCRCV,d0              * Receive a message
535  0000025E 4E40                       trap    #0                     * From user task requesting delay
536  00000260 2040                       move.l  d0,a0                  * a0 -> MCB for request
537  00000262 23E80008000004D0           move.l  m_count(a0),tcount     * Copy count for interrupt rtn.
538  0000026A 227900000000               move.l  current,a1            * a1 -> our TCB
539  00000270 46FC2700                   move.w  #disable,sr            *** Disable interrupts
540  00000274 08F90000000004D4           bset.b  #0,tstatus             *** Turn on interrupt flag
541  0000027C 08B9000000000017           bset    #IWAIT,t_flag+3(a1)    *** Make ourselves non-dispatchable
542  00000282 614A                       bsr     trset                  *** Load timer registers
543  00000284 7000                       move.l  #SVCNEW,d0             *** Switch to next          task
544  00000286 4E40                       trap    #0
545  00000288 46FC2000                   move.w  #enable,sr             * Re-enable interrupts
546  0000028C 7005                       move.l  #SVCRPLY,d0            * Reply to MCB
547  0000028E 4E40                       trap    #0                     * Issue Reply SVC
548  00000290 60CA                       bra     timeepa                * Go around again
549
550  *
551  *       The following code is entered via timer interrupts
552  *
553  00000292 0839000000000004D4 timeint: btst.b #0,tstatus             *** Is timing desired?
554  0000029A 6604                       bne     tproc                  *** NE => yes, decrement count
555  0000029C 6000FE98                   bra     noint                  *** No, just exit
556  000002A0 53B90000004D0     tproc:   subq.l  #1,tcount              *** Decrement counter
557  000002A6 6706                       beq     twake                  *** EQ => delay finished
558  000002A8 6124                       bsr     trset                  *** Reload count registers
559  000002AA 6000FE8A                   bra     noint                  *** Otherwise, delay some more
```

Listing 8.12 – Code for the timer task

```
560 000002AE 08B90000000004D4  twake:  bclr.b  #0,tstatus            ***  Clear timer active flag
561 000002B6 41F900000008              lea     timetask,a0           ***  a0 -> our TCB
562 000002BC 08A800000017              bclr.b  #IWAIT,t_flag+3(a0)   ***  Make task part dispatchable
563 000002C2 08F9000000FFC043          bset    #0,imask              ***  disable timer interrupt
564 000002CA 6000FDE4                  bra     newtask               ***  enter dispatcher
565
566                             *
567                             *       Timer reset routine
                                *
568 000002CE 08F9000000FFC043  trset:  bset    #0,imask              ***  Disable timer interrupt
569 000002D6 13FC007400FFC087          move.b  #t_mode1,timer+6      ***  Set up    Timer
570 000002DE 13FC00B000FFC087          move.b  #t_mode2,timer+6      ***            Timer
571 000002E6 13FC004000FFC085          move.b  #$40,timer+4          ***  Load low count byte
572 000002EE 13FC000100FFC085          move.b  #$1,timer+4           ***  Load high count byte
573 000002F6 13FC000200FFC083          move.b  #2,timer+2            ***  Load next count stage
574 000002FE 13FC000000FFC083          move.b  #0,timer+2            ***  Load high byte
575 00000306 08B9000000FFC043          bclr    #0,imask              ***  Enable clock interrupts
576 0000030E 4E75                      rts
577 000004D0                           .bss
578 000004D0                   tcount: .ds.l   1                     *    Number of ticks remaining
579 000004D4                   tstatus:.ds.l   1                     *    Status word
580 00000310                           .text
```

Listing 8.12 – Code for the timer task (continued)

```
*************************************************************
*                                                          *
*           T e r m i n a l   O u t p u t   T a s k        *
*           ======================================         *
*                                                          *
*          This code performs terminal output for other tasks.
*                                                          *
*************************************************************
termepa:
581
582
583
584
585
586
587
588
589
590  00000310  7004               move.l   #SVCRCV,d0           * Receive output   request
591  00000312  4E40               trap     #0                   *
592  00000314  2040               move.l   d0,a0                * a0 -> MCB
593  00000316  23E8000800000004D8 move.l   m_count(a0),bcount   * Make local copy of
594  0000031E  24680004           move.l   m_buff(a0),a2        *            req. data
595  00000322  53B9000000004D8    subq.l   #I,bcount            * Decrement count
596  00000328  2279000000000      move.l   current,a1           * a1 -> our TCB
597  0000032E  46FC2700           move.w   #disable,sr          *** disable interrupts for startup
598  00000332  08E900000017       bset.b   #IWAIT,t_flag+3(a1)  *** mark us not dispatchable
599  00000338  13FC002500FFC073   move.b   #termenb,termcmd     *** Enable terminal interrupt
600  00000340  13DA00FFC071       move.b   (a2)+,termout        *** Output first character
601  00000346  23CA000004DC       move.l   a2,buff              *** Remember buffer address
602  0000034C  7000               move.l   #SVCNEW,d0           *** Execute next task
603  0000034E  4E40               trap     #0                   *
604  00000350  46FC2000           move.w   #enable,sr           * Re-enable interrupts
605  00000354  7005               move.l   #SVCRPLY,d0          * Reply to MCB
606  00000356  4E40               trap     #0                   * Issue reply SVC
607  00000358  60B6               bra      termepa              * Do next buffer
608                                                             *
609                                                             *  The following code is entered when each character is output.
610                                                             *
```

Listing 8.13 – Task code for terminal output

```
611
612  0000035A 4AB900004D8          termint:   tst.l    bcount            ***  Are we done?
613  00000360 6E18                            bgt      nextchar          ***  No, continue to output
614  00000362 13FC002400FFC073               move.b   #termdis,termcmd  ***  Disable terminal interrupt
615  0000036A 41F900000120                   lea      termtask,a0       ***  a0 -> our TCB
616  00000370 08A800000017                   bclr.b   #IWAIT,t_flag+3(a0) *** Clear wait bit
617  00000376 6000FD38                        bra      newtask           ***  Go find a new task
618
619  0000037A 207900004DC          nextchar:  move.l   buff,a0           ***  a0 -> character to output
620  00000380 13D800FFC071                    move.b   (a0)+,termout     ***  output the character
621  00000386 23C800004DC                    move.l   a0,buff           ***  Save next address
622  0000038C 53B900004D8                     subq.l   #1,bcount         ***  decrement count
623  00000392 6000FDA2                        bra      noint             ***  Resume interrupted task
624
625                             *              Data area
626                             *
627  000004D8            bcount:  .bss
628  000004D8            buff:    .ds.l    1                             *  Byte count to output
629  000004DC                     .ds.l    1                             *  Buffer address to output
630  000004E0                     .end
```

Listing 8.13 – Task code for terminal output (continued)

```
 1     *********************************************************************
 2     *
 3     *            L B O S   A p p l i c a t i o n   T a s k   # 1
 4     *            ================================================
 5     *
 6     *    This task simulates an "I/O bound" task: It issues a delay, followed
 7     *    by output to the terminal, and back to the delay, etc. The result
 8     *    is a task which consumes a lot of the terminal and delay resources,
 9     *    but very little of the CPU resource.
10     *
11     *********************************************************************
12             .globl   applepa
13     SVCTRM: .equ     1                      * Output SVC Code
14     SVCDEL: .equ     2                      * Delay  SVC Code
15     dlytim: .equ     250                    * Number of timer ticks to delay
16
17 00000000 7002         applepa: move.l  #SVCDEL,d0    * Set up delay SVC
18 00000002 223C000000FA          move.l  #dlytim,d1    * Delay time
19 00000008 4E40                  trap    #0            * Issue delay SVC
20 0000000A 7001                  move.l  #SVCTRM,d0    * Setup output SVC
21 0000000C 223C00000018          move.l  #msglen,d1    * Byte count to d1
22 00000012 41F90000001C          lea     msg,a0        * Buffer address to a0
23 00000018 4E40                  trap    #0            * Issue terminal output svc
24 0000001A 60E4                  bra     applepa       * Loop forever
25 0000001C 417070312D2D2D20 msg: .dc.b    'Appl -- Delay Complete',13,10
26                        msglen: .equ     *-msg        * Message byte count
27 00000034                       .end
```

Listing 8.14 – An I/O-bound task

```
 1  *****************************************************************
 2  *
 3  *        L B O S   A p p l i c a t i o n   T a s k   # 2
 4  *        ===============================================
 5  *
 6  *  This task simulates an "CPU bound" task:  It performs 655360 (640K)
 7  *  iterations of a loop and prints a message.  This process is repeated
 8  *  indefinitely.  The result is a process which consumes a tremendous
 9  *  amount of CPU resource and very little I/O resource.
10  *
11  *****************************************************************
12
13                          SVCTRM:  .globl app2epa
14                          app2epa: .equ  1               * Output SVC Code
15  00000000  303CFFFF              move.w #-1,d0           * DBRA maximum value
16  00000004  343C000A      o_loop: move.w #10,d2          * Outer loop beginning
17  00000008  4E71          loop:   nop                    * Loop
18  0000000A  51CAFFFC              dbra   d2,loop          * Inner loop
19  0000000E  51C8FFF4              dbra   d0,o_loop        * Loop till done
20  00000012  7001                  move.l #SVCTRM,d0       * Setup output SVC
21  00000014  223C00000018          move.l #msglen,d1       * Byte count to d1
22  0000001A  41F900000024          lea    msg,a0           * Buffer adress to a0
23  00000020  4E40                  trap   #0               * Issue terminal output SVC
24  00000022  60DC                  bra    app2epa          * Loop forever
25  00000024  41707032202D2D20 msg: .dc.b  'App2 -- Loop Complete',13,10
26  0000003C              msglen:  .equ   *-msg            * Message byte count
27                                  .end
```

Listing 8.15 – A CPU-bound task

- The various types of CPU scheduling: (1) priority-driven, (2) preemptive priority-driven, (3) pure time-slicing, and (4) preemptive priority-driven with time-slicing.

- Reentrant coding.

- The various forms of mutual exclusion techniques: (1) disabling interrupts, (2) disabling dispatching, (3) semaphores, (4) monitor procedures, (5) message switching, and (6) fork queues.

- A sample multitasking system.

EXERCISES

1. In a situation in which no task is dispatchable, why is an interrupt necessary for a task to become dispatchable?

2. What areas in LBOS have a potentially high interrupt latency? Can any of these be improved? How?

Answers to Exercises

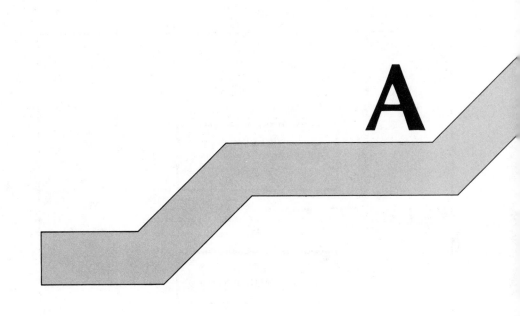

A

CHAPTER 1

This appendix gives the answers to the exercise questions found at the end of each chapter.

1. There are many correct solutions to this question. Here is one:

    1. Select the highest place value from the table that will divide into the number to be converted. Let the converted number be the initial remainder.
    2. Calculate the new quotient and remainder when the current remainder is divided by the present table entry.
    3. If place value table entries remain, repeat step 2 with the next table entry and the remainder just calculated.
    4. Read the answer as the successive quotients.

2. The flowchart for the above would look like Figure A.1.

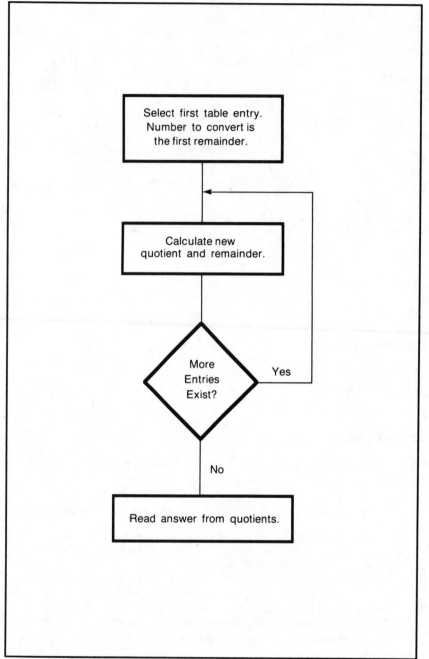

Figure A.1 – Flowchart for exercise 2

3. The machine language program would look like Table A.1.

Location	Contents	Instruction
100	1105	Load A from location 105
101	5104	Subtract location 104
102	3106	Store into location 106
104	0300	<Data>
105	0400	<Data>
106	0000	<Data>

Table A.1 *– Machine language program at location 100*

You must load the contents of location 105 first because the difference to be computed is (Location 105 − location 104). The subtraction instruction works by subtracting memory from the register. Therefore, you must have the contents of location 105 in the register to perform the subtraction operaton.

4. Moving to location 200 yields the results in Table A.2.

Location	Contents	Instruction
200	1205	Load A from location 205
201	5204	Subtract location 204
202	3206	Store into location 206
204	0300	<Data>
205	0400	<Data>
206	0000	<Data>

Table A.2 *– Machine language program at location 200*

5. The assembly language version is:

```
        LOAD        A,Y
        SUB         A,X
        STORE       A,Z
        STOP
X:      DC          300
Y:      DC          400
Z:      DC          0
```

6. To add the first five integers, a modified version of the previous program will work:

```
        LOAD        A,A
        ADD         A,B
        ADD         A,C
        ADD         A,D
        ADD         A,E
        STORE       A,F
        STOP
A:      DC          1
B:      DC          2
C:      DC          3
D:      DC          4
E:      DC          5
F:      DC          0
```

7. Conversion to hex and binary is shown in Table A.3.

Decimal	Hex	Binary
273	111	0001 0001 0001
421	1A5	0001 1010 0101
1024	400	0100 0000 0000
100	64	0000 0110 0100

Table A.3 – Conversion to hex and binary

8. Conversion to binary and decimal is shown in Table A.4.

Hex	Binary	Decimal
ABE	0000 1010 1011 1110	2750
100	0000 0001 0000 0000	256
64	0000 0000 0110 0100	100
1024	0001 0000 0010 0100	4132
505	0000 0101 0000 0101	1285

Table A.4 – Conversion to binary and decimal

9. Complements are shown in Table A.5.

Number	One's Complement	Two's Complement
0ABE	F541	F542
0100	FEFF	FF00
0064	FF9B	FF9C
1024	EFDB	EFDC
0505	FAFA	FAFB

Table A.5 – Complements

10. Binary operations are shown in Table A.6.

Number	Pair	AND	OR	XOR	ADD	C
A5A5	5A5A	0000	FFFF	FFFF	FFFF	0
FFFF	0001	0001	FFFF	FFFE	0000	1
1234	4321	0220	5335	5115	5555	0

Table A.6 – Binary operations

11. Shift and Rotate Tables:

Logical Shifts

Times	Left	Right
0	1111 1111 (FF hex)	1111 1111 (FF hex)
1	1111 1110 (FE hex)	0111 1111 (7F hex)
2	1111 1100 (FC hex)	0011 1111 (3F hex)
3	1111 1000 (F8 hex)	0001 1111 (1F hex)
4	1111 0000 (F0 hex)	0000 1111 (0F hex)
5	1110 0000 (E0 hex)	0000 0111 (07 hex)
6	1100 0000 (C0 hex)	0000 0011 (03 hex)
7	1000 0000 (80 hex)	0000 0001 (01 hex)
8	0000 0000 (00 hex)	0000 0000 (00 hex)

Times	Left	Right
0	0101 0101 (55 hex)	0101 0101 (55 hex)
1	1010 1010 (AA hex)	0010 1010 (2A hex)
2	0101 0100 (54 hex)	0001 0101 (15 hex)
3	1010 1000 (A8 hex)	0000 1010 (0A hex)
4	0101 0000 (50 hex)	0000 0101 (05 hex)
5	1010 0000 (A0 hex)	0000 0010 (02 hex)
6	0100 0000 (40 hex)	0000 0001 (01 hex)
7	1000 0000 (80 hex)	0000 0000 (00 hex)
8	0000 0000 (00 hex)	0000 0000 (00 hex)

Arithmetic Shifts

Times	Left	Right
0	1111 1111 (FF hex)	1111 1111 (FF hex)
1	1111 1110 (FE hex)	1111 1111 (FF hex)
2	1111 1100 (FC hex)	1111 1111 (FF hex)
3	1111 1000 (F8 hex)	1111 1111 (FF hex)
4	1111 0000 (F0 hex)	1111 1111 (FF hex)
5	1110 0000 (E0 hex)	1111 1111 (FF hex)
6	1100 0000 (C0 hex)	1111 1111 (FF hex)
7	1000 0000 (80 hex)	1111 1111 (FF hex)
8	0000 0000 (00 hex)	1111 1111 (FF hex)

Times	Left	Right
0	0101 0101 (55 hex)	0101 0101 (55 hex)
1	1010 1010 (AA hex)	0010 1010 (2A hex)
2	0101 0100 (54 hex)	0001 0101 (15 hex)
3	1010 1000 (A8 hex)	0000 1010 (0A hex)
4	0101 0000 (50 hex)	0000 0101 (05 hex)
5	1010 0000 (A0 hex)	0000 0010 (02 hex)
6	0100 0000 (40 hex)	0000 0001 (01 hex)
7	1000 0000 (80 hex)	0000 0000 (00 hex)
8	0000 0000 (00 hex)	0000 0000 (00 hex)

Rotates

Times	C Left	Right C
0	0 1111 1111 (FF hex)	1111 1111 0 (FF hex)
1	1 1111 1110 (FE hex)	0111 1111 1 (7F hex)
2	1 1111 1101 (FD hex)	1011 1111 1 (BF hex)
3	1 1111 1011 (FB hex)	1101 1111 1 (DF hex)
4	1 1111 0111 (F7 hex)	1110 1111 1 (EF hex)
5	1 1110 1111 (EF hex)	1111 0111 1 (F7 hex)
6	1 1101 1111 (DF hex)	1111 1011 1 (FB hex)
7	1 1011 1111 (BF hex)	1111 1101 1 (FD hex)
8	1 0111 1111 (7F hex)	1111 1110 1 (FE hex)
9	0 1111 1111 (FF hex)	1111 1111 0 (FF hex)

Times	C Left	Right C
0	0 0101 0101 (55 hex)	0101 0101 0 (55 hex)
1	0 1010 1010 (AA hex)	0010 1010 1 (2A hex)
2	1 0101 0100 (54 hex)	1001 0101 0 (95 hex)
3	0 1010 1001 (A9 hex)	0100 1010 1 (4A hex)
4	1 0101 0010 (52 hex)	1010 0101 0 (A5 hex)
5	0 1010 0101 (A5 hex)	0101 0010 1 (52 hex)
6	1 0100 1010 (4A hex)	1010 1001 0 (A9 hex)
7	0 1001 0101 (95 hex)	0101 0100 1 (54 hex)
8	1 0010 1010 (2A hex)	1010 1010 0 (AA hex)
9	0 0101 0101 (55 hex)	0101 0101 0 (55 hex)

CHAPTER 2

1. The instructions would result in:

    MOVE.B D0,A0

    This instruction is illegal because address registers can only be accessed as words or longs. Give yourself extra points if you knew that an Illegal Instruction exception would occur.

    MOVE.W D0,A0

    This instruction causes the contents of register A0 to become FFFF8000. Remember that word moves to an address register cause sign extension.

    MOVE.B D0,(A0)+

    The byte at location 1000 becomes 0. Register A0 becomes 1001.

    MOVE.B D0, – (A7)

    The byte at memory location 10000 becomes 0. The contents of register A7 becomes FFFE. Remember that A7 is the hardware stack pointer, and is incremented or decremented by 2 in byte operations.

2. The instructions as modified are:

Instruction	Hex	Changes
ADD.L D1,D0	D081	D0=01234566
ADD.L A1,D0	D089	D0=01234566
ADD.L (A1),D0	D091	D0=01234566
ADD.L (A1)+,D0	D099	D0=01234566
ADD.L –(A1),D0	D0A1	D0=01234566
ADD.L 4(A1),D0	D0A9 0004	D0=01234566
ADD.L 4(A1,A2.L),D0	D0B1 A804	D0=01234566
ADD.L $1000,D0	D0B8 1000	D0=01234566
ADD.L $10000,D0	D0B9 0001 0000	D0=01234566
ADD.L $100(PC),D0	D0BA 0100	D0=01234566
ADD.L $10(PC,A1.L)	D0BB 9810	D0=01234566
ADD.L #$10002000,D0	D0BC 1000 2000	D0=11234566

3. The pre-decrement and post-increment modes may be used to implement a stack as follows:

PUSH operation is MOVE.s xxx,(An)+

POP operation is MOVE.s −(An),xxx

The difference between this technique and a stack that grows toward lower addresses is that the address register no longer contains the address of the top item of the stack. Instead, the register points to the next stack location to be used. By changing the addressing modes to pre-increment and post-decrement (+(An) and (An)−), the stacking would be equivalent to the present technique.

CHAPTER 3

1-2. There aren't any answers back here. Either you can use your system or you can't. If you can't, you should first learn how. The basic mechanical steps are essential, and you will learn to program faster if you can do the mechanics well.

3. The ADDX and SUBX instructions perform arithmetic on multiple memory locations. You must start with the least significant digit in doing arithmetic. Comparisons, however, must be done starting with the most significant digit.

4. The RTE instruction reloads the status register (SR). This changes the Trace bit in the status register. Normally, the Trace bit is cleared by an RTE instruction. This prevents the instruction from being traced, and causes the debugger to lose control. Other instructions that can clear the Trace bit will have the same effect: MOVE to SR, ANDI to SR, and EORI to SR.

CHAPTER 4

1. The long division routine.

```
***************************************************
* 32-bit division routine.
* Enter with:
*    D0 = dividend
*    D1 = divisor
* Exit with:
*    D0 = quotient
*    D1 = remainder
***************************************************
        .globl  ldiv
ldiv:   movem.l d2-d3,-(sp)   * Temporary registers.
        clr.l   d2           * Quotient
        clr.l   d3           * Sign flag
        tst.l   d0           * Dividend < 0?
        bge     x1           * If gt, no
        addq.l  #1,d3        * Increment flag
        neg.l   d0           * Make positive
x1:     tst.l   d1           * Divisor < 0?
        bge     loop         * If ge, no
        addq.l  #1,d3        * Increment flag
        neg.l   d1           * Make positive
loop:   cmp.l   d0,d1        * Dividend : divisor
        bgt     done         * If gt, don't subtract
        sub.l   d1,d0        * Subtract divisor
        addq.l  #1,d2        * Increment quotient
        bra     loop         * Loop again
done:   btst    _#0,d3       * Like signs?
        beq     x2           * Yes, skip negate
        neg.l   d2           * Make negative
        neg.l   d0           *
x2:     move.l  d0,d1        * This is remainder
        move.l  d2,d0        * This is quotient
        movem.l (sp)+,d2-d3  * Restore registers
        rts                  * Return
```

Handling negative numbers is not required for the next question. The real disadvantage to doing division in this manner is the excessive amount of time required to divide a very large number by a very small one. It can take several minutes for a single division operation.

2. This is the modified binary to decimal ASCII-conversion routine.

```
***************************************************
* Binary to decimal ASCII conversion routine.
*
* Enter with:
*    D0.L = number to convert
*    A0  -> Output area (10 bytes)
***************************************************
        .globl  bindec
        .globl  ldiv
bindec: movem.l d0-d2/a0,-(sp)  * Save registers
        move.b  #' ',d1         * Assume positive
        tst.l   d0              * Negative?
        bpl     notneg          * No, use ' '
        move.b  #'-',d1         * Negative, use '-'
```

```
              neg.l     d0                        * Convert to positive
      notneg: move.b    dl,(a0)+                   * Move in sign
              adda.l    #9,a0                     * A0 -> end of area
              move.w    #8,d2                     * Count register
      loop:   move.l    #10,dl                    * Set divisor
              jsr       ldiv                      * Divide by 10
              move.b    dl,-(a0)                  * Remainder to area
              add.b     #'0',(a0)                 * Adjust to ASCII
              dbra      d2,loop                   * Loop until done
              movem.l   (sp)+,d0-d2/a0            * Restore registers
              rts
```

3. The finished conversion program looks like this:

```
      ********************************************************
      *
      * This program converts decimal numbers to hex.
      * Numbers are input from the keyboard and output to
      * the screen.
      *
      ********************************************************
              .globl    prtstr                   * Line-print routine
              .globl    binhex                   * Output converter
              .globl    bindec                   * Output converter
              .globl    decbin                   * Input converter
              .globl    getlin                   * Keyboard input
      loop:   lea       prompt,a0                * A0 -> output area
              jsr       prtstr                   * Print prompt
              lea       inbuf,a0                 * A0 -> input  area
              jsr       getlin                   * Get keyboard input
              tst.b     (a0)                     * Null line?
              bne       gotnum                   * No, continue to process
              rts                                * Yes, exit to CP/M
      gotnum: jsr       decbin                   * Convert to binary
              lea       hexbuf,a0                * A0 -> conversion area
              jsr       binhex                   * Convert to hex
              lea       decbuf,a0                * Reconvert to decimal
              jsr       bindec                   *
              jsr       prtstr                   * Print answer
              bra       loop                     * Repeat until ^C
              .data
      prompt: .dc.b     'Enter decimal number: ',0
      decbuf: .dc.b     'XXXXXXXXX decimal is '
      hexbuf: .dc.b     'XXXXXXX hex',10,0
              .bss
      inbuf:  .ds.b     80                       * Input buffer
              .end
```

Notice that the only change required was to expand the size of the decimal output conversion area.

4. The hex conversion routine looks like this:

```
*************************************************
*
* This subroutine converts hex ASCII to
* longword binary.
*
* Enter with:
*        A0 -> Hex string
* Exit with:
*        D0 =  Converted number
*
*   Conversion terminates on first nonhexadecimal
*   character. No overflow detection.
*
*************************************************
          .globl  hexbin
hexbin: movem.l  d1-d2/a0,-(sp) * Save starting registers
          clr.l    d0           * Zero out accumulator
loop:    clr.l    d1            * Zero out D1
          cmpi.b   #'9',(a0)    * Upper bound
          bhi      notdec       * Not a decimal digit
          cmpi.b   #'0',(a0)    * Lower bound
          blo      nothex       * Not a hex digit
          move.b   #'0',d1      * Correction factor
          bra      gotdig       * Accumulate
notdec: cmpi.b   #'A',(a0)     * Check letters
          blo      nothex       * Not a hex digit
          cmpi.b   #'F',(a0)    * Upper case hex?
          bhi      notuc        * No, try lower
          move.b   #'A'-10,d1   * Correction factor
          bra      gotdig       * Got digit
notuc:  cmpi.b   #'a',(a0)     * Lower case?
          blo      nothex       * No
          cmpi.b   #'f',(a0)    * Test upper bound
          bhi      nothex       * Not hex
          move.b   #'a'-10,d1   * Correction factor
gotdig: clr.l    d2            * Zero high byte
          move.b   (a0)+,d2     * Get next digit
          sub.l    d1,d2        * Convert to binary
          lsl.l    #4,d0        * Multiply by 16
          add.l    d2,d0        * Add in digit
          bra      loop         * Try another digit
nothex: movem.l  (sp)+,a0/d1-d2 * Unsave registers
          rts                   * Return to caller
```

A slightly tricky piece of code to yield the proper binary nibble uses register D1 as the factor to be subtracted from the ASCII byte.

5. The program for converting hex to decimal can be derived from the earlier solution to converting the longword decimal to hex.

```
****************************************************
*
* This program converts hex numbers to decimal.
* Numbers are input from the keyboard and output to
* the screen.
*
****************************************************
        .globl  prtstr          * Line-print routine
        .globl  binhex          * Output converter
        .globl  bindec          * Output converter
        .globl  hexbin          * Input converter
        .globl  getlin          * Keyboard input
loop:   lea     prompt,a0       * A0 -> output area
        jsr     prtstr          * Print prompt
        lea     inbuf,a0        * A0 -> input  area
        jsr     getlin          * Get keyboard input
        tst.b   (a0)            * Null line?
        bne     gotnum          * No, continue to process
        rts                     * Yes, exit to CP/M
gotnum: jsr     hexbin          * Convert to binary
        lea     hexbuf,a0       * A0 -> conversion area
        jsr     binhex          * Convert to hex
        lea     decbuf,a0       * Reconvert to decimal
        jsr     bindec          *
        lea     hexbuf,a0       * A0 -> Answer
        jsr     prtstr          * Print answer
        bra     loop            * Repeat until ^C
        .data
prompt: .dc.b   'Enter hex number: ',0
hexbuf: .dc.b   'XXXXXXXX hex is '
decbuf: .dc.b   'XXXXXXXXX decimal',10,0
        .bss
inbuf:  .ds.b   80              * Input buffer
        .end
```

CHAPTER 5

1. The summation program is:

```
**********************************************
* Sum of first five integers using printf
**********************************************
        .globl  _main
        .globl  _printf
_main:  move.w  #1,d0       * First integer
        move.w  #4,d1       * Counter
        clr.l   d2          * Accumulator
loop:   add.w   d0,d2       * Add next integer
        add.w   #1,d0       * increment
        dbra    d1,loop     * Loop until done
        move.w  d2,-(sp)    * Push answer
        pea     format      * Push format string
        jsr     _printf     * Call printf
        add.l   #6,sp       * Pop arguments
        rts                 * Exit
        .data
format: .dc.b   "The sum is %d",10,0
```

2. The program to generate the powers of two is:

```
*************************************************
* Table of powers of two using fprintf
*************************************************
        .globl   _fopen
        .globl   _printf
        .globl   _fprintf
        .globl   _fclose
        .globl   _main
_main:  move.w   4(sp),d0        * argc
        move.l   6(sp),a5        * -> argv
        cmp.w    #2,d0           * One argument?
        bne      argerr          * No, quit now
        pea      wstr            * -> "w"
        move.l   4(a5),-(sp)     * -> filename
        jsr      _fopen          * Try to open file
        add.l    #8,sp           * Pop arguments
        move.l   d0,d3           * Save stream pointer
        beq      openerr         * Couldn't open
        move.l   #1,d4           * First power of two
        clr.w    d5              * Power counter
loop:   move.l   d4,-(sp)        * Push
        move.l   d4,-(sp)        * Twice
        move.w   d5,-(sp)        * Push power number
        pea      format          * -> Format string
        move.l   d3,-(sp)        * Push Stream pointer
        jsr      _fprintf        * Do the print
        add.l    #18,sp          * Pop arguments
        add.w    #1,d5           * Bump counter
        cmp.l    #$100000,d4     * Compare against limit
        beq      done            * EQ => just printed last
        lsl.l    #1,d4           * Shift right one place
        bra      loop            * Do another one
done:   move.l   d3,-(sp)        * Prepare to close
        jsr      _fclose         * Do the close
        add.l    #4,sp           * Pop arguments
        rts                      * Exit
argerr: pea      err1            * Push error message
        bra      errcom          * Merge
openerr:pea      err2            * Push error message
errcom: jsr      _printf         * Call printf
        add.l    #4,sp           * Pop arguments
        rts                      * Exit
        .data
format: .dc.b    "2**%2d = %91d (decimal) %81x (hex)",10,0
wstr:   .dc.b    "w",0
err1:   .dc.b    "Invalid argument count",10,0
err2:   .dc.b    "Unable to open output",10,0
```

3. The copy function is:

```
*************************************************
* Memory copy function for C. Calling sequence:
*
* mcpy(src,dst,length);
*
* Where "src" is the source address
```

```
*          "dst" is the destination address.
*          "length" is the number of bytes to copy.
*
* No return parameter.
**************************************************
           .globl   _mcpy
_mcpy:     move.l   4(sp),a0      * Source address
           move.l   8(sp),a1      * Destination address
           move.w   12(sp),d0     * Length
           sub.w    #1,d0         * Decrement for dbra
loop:      move.b   (a0)+,(a1)+   * Copy a byte
           dbra     d0,loop       * Loop until done
           rts                    * Return
```

CHAPTER 6

1. The PLIST program can be derived from the PFIND program as follows:

   1. Change line 84 to compare "argc" to 1 instead of 2.

   2. Delete lines 87–88 and 148.
      You can also delete lines 147 and 169–186, and put the "ploop:" label on line 149. Notice that the program will still work with the useless code in place.

2. The Fibonacci program is:

```
**************************************************
*          Recursive Fibonacci routine
*
*          Enter with number in D0.W
*          Exit  with answer in D0.W
**************************************************
           .globl   fib
fib:       cmp.w    #1,d0         * Easy?
           bgt      dofib         * No, do recursion
           rts                    * Done
dofib:     move.w   d0,-(a7)      * Save present value
           sub.w    #1,d0         * Decrement
           jsr      fib           * Take F(n-1)
           move.w   d0,-(a7)      * Save result
           move.w   2(a7),d0      * Restore n
           sub.w    #2,d0         * Decrement
           jsr      fib           * Take F(n-2)
           add.w    (a7)+,d0      * Compute sum
           add.l    #2,a7         * Pop saved word
           rts                    * Quit
```

3. The sort routine is as follows:

```
*************************************************************************
*
*       Sort routine. This routine performs an in-place sort on the buffer,
*       using a bubble-sort technique.
*
*************************************************************************
sort:   movem.l  d0-d7/a0-a6,-(a7)      *      Save the registers
        move.l   lastb,a2               *      A2 -> buffer end
sloop:  lea      buffer,a0              *      A0 -> buffer beginning
        clr.w    d0                     *      Clear exchange flag
sloopl: lea      length(a0),a1          *      A1 -> Next record
        cmpa.l   a1,a2                  *      Past end?
        blos     send                   *      Yes, see if another pass needed
        bsr      scmp                   *      Compare (a0) : (a1)
        bne      snext                  *      NE => don't swap
        bsr      xchang                 *      Swap (a0) and (a1)
        move.w   #1,d0                  *      Set flag
snext:  lea      length(a0),a0          *      Advance A0 to next entry
        bra      sloopl                 *      And compare the next two
send:   tst.w    d0                     *      Did last pass exchange?
        bne      sloop                  *      Yes, make another pass
        movem.l  (a7)+,d0-d7/a0-a6      *      Unstack registers
        rts                            *      Return
*
*       Comparison routine. Compares (A0) to (A1). Returns NE condition code
*       if no exchange necessary.
*
scmp:   move.w   #numlen+extlen,d1      *      D1 = DBRA-adjusted count
        lea      telno(a0),a4           *      A4 -> 1st telephone #
        lea      telno(a1),a5           *      A5 -> 2nd telephone #
cloop:  cmp.b    (a4)+,(a5)+            *      Compare a digit
        bgt      noswt                  *      Switch only if lt
        dbne     d1,cloop               *      If eq, continue loop
        clr.w    d1                     *      Set Z bit
noswt:  rts                            *      Return
*
*       Exchange routine. Exchanges (A0) with (A1)
*
xchang: move.w   #length-1,d1           *      D1 = DBRA-adjusted count
        move.l   a0,a4                  *      A4 -> record 1
        move.l   a1,a5                  *      A5 -> record 2
xloop:  move.b   (a4),d2               *      Pick up a byte
        move.b   (a5),(a4)+            *      Swap
        move.b   d2,(a5)+             *                byte
        dbra     d1,xloop              *      Count down
        rts                            *      Return
```

4. The PDEL program is derived from the PADD program as follows:

1. Alter the code in the main routine to call subroutine "delete" instead of "insert."

2. Alter the code in subroutine "setfield" to accept three names as arguments. Remove the code for the telephone number and extension.

3. Replace the "insert" subroutine with the following code:

```
****************************************************************************
*
*       Delete routine. This routine removes the record at "irec" from the
*       buffer. The buffer is moved up to remove the deleted entry.
*
****************************************************************************
delete: movem.l d0-d7/a0-a6,-(a7)      *       Save registers
        lea     buffer,a1              *       A1 -> Buffer
        move.l  lastb,a3               *       A3 -> End of buffer
find:   lea     irec,a0                *       A0 -> Comparison string
        cmpa.l  a3,a1                  *       Past the end
        bhis    found                  *       Yes, insert at end
        jsr     ncmp                   *       Compare the two
        tst.w   d0                     *       Record : buffer
        beq     found                  *       Found record to delete
        bmi     norec                  *       MI => Can't find it
        adda.l  length,a1              *       A1 -> Next record in buffer
        bra     find                   *       Loop until done
*
*       Now move the buffer up to delete the entry
*
found:  move.l  a3,a4                  *       Copy end of buffer
        sub.l   length,a4             *       A4 -> New end of buffer
        move.l  a4,lastb               *       Record this
        lea     length(a1),a2          *       A2 -> next record
moveit: move.b  (a2)+,(a1)+            *       Transfer a byte
        cmpa.l  a3,a2                  *       Just moved last?
        blo     moveit                 *       No, continue to move
        movem.l (a7)+,d0-d7/a0-a6      *       Pop registers
        rts                            *       And return
```

CHAPTER 7

1. This is the block-move handler program.

```
****************************************************************************
*       This exception handler simulates the block move instruction.
****************************************************************************
        .globl  LineF            *       Make globl
LineF:  movem.l d0-d7/a0-a6,regs *       Save the registers
        move.l  2(a7),a0         *       A0 = PC
        add.l   #2,2(a7)         *       Advance PC to next
        move.w  (a0),d0          *       D0 = instruction
        move.w  d0,d1            *       Copy to D1
        andi.w  #7,d1            *       Low-order 3 bits=0?
        bne     dorte            *       No, quit
        lsr     #3,d0            *       Get rid of low 3 bits
        lea     regs,a0          *       A0 -> registers
        bsr     get3             *       Get 3 bits in D1
        move.l  0(a0,d1.w),d7    *       D7 = Data register contents
        bsr     get3             *       Get 3 more bits in D1
        move.l  32(a0,d1.w),a4   *       A4 = An dst contents
        bsr     get3             *       Get next field
        move.l  32(a0,d1.w),a5   *       A5 = An src contents
```

```
loop:   move.b  (a5)+,(a4)+     *    Move a byte
        subq.l  #1,d7           *    Down
        bne     loop            *              count
dorte:  movem.l regs,d0-d7/a0-a6 *   Restore registers
        rte
*
*       Get 3 bits out of D0.W
*
get3:   move.l  d0,d1           *    Copy
        lsr.l   #3,d0           *    Get rid of bits
        andi.w  #7,d1           *    Isolate bits
        lsl.w   #2,d1           *    Make long index
        rts                     *    Return
        .bss
regs:   .ds.l   15              *    Register storage area
```

2. This is the trace program.

```
**********************************************************************
* The program-trace routine
**********************************************************************
tracev: .equ    $24             *    Trace vector
        .globl  binhex          *    Hex conversion routine
        .globl  prtstr          *    String-print routine
        .globl  trace           *    Entry point
trace:  movem.l d0-d7/a0-a6,regs *   Save registers
        move.l  (a7)+,retpc     *    Save return address
        move.l  #xtrace,tracev  *    Load vector
        move.w  #62,d0          *    Set
        trap    #2              *              super
        movem.l regs,d0-d7/a0-a6 *   Restore registers
        move.l  retpc,-(sp)     *    Push return PC
        move.w  #$8000,-(sp)    *    And status register
        rte                     *    Begin trace
*
*       Trace Trap Entry
*
xtrace: movem.l d0-d7/a0-a7,regs *   Save all registers at trap time
        lea     dstr,a0         *    A0 -> "D "
        jsr     prtstr          *    Print
        lea     regs,a1         *    A1 -> D registers
        jsr     pregs           *    Print D registers
        lea     astr,a0         *    A0 -> "A "
        jsr     prtstr          *    Print
        lea     regs+32,a1      *    A1 -> A registers
        jsr     pregs           *    Print A registers
*
*       Print PC, status register, and USP
*
        lea     srstr,a0        *    A0-> "SR="
        jsr     prtstr          *    Print
        move.w  (a7),d0         *    D0 = old SR
        jsr     pword           *    Print it
        lea     pcstr,a0        *    A0-> "PC="
        jsr     prtstr          *    Print it
        move.l  2(a7),d0        *    D0 = PC at fault
        jsr     plong           *    Print it
        lea     uspstr,a0       *    A0-> "USP="
        jsr     prtstr          *    Print
        move.l  usp,a0          *    Fetch user stack pointer
        move.l  a0,d0           *    Put in D0
        jsr     plong           *    Print
        lea     newline,a0      *    Print new line
        jsr     prtstr          *    Print it
```

```
          lea    newline,a0              *    Print another new line
          jsr    prtstr                  *    Print blank line
          movem.l regs,d0-d7/a0-a7       *    Restore registers
          rte                            *    Do next instruction

***************************************************************************
*         miscellaneous print routines

***************************************************************************
pregs:    movem.l a0-a1/d0-d1,-(a7)      *    Save work registers
          move.w  #7,d1                  *    Loop count
rloop:    move.l  (a1)+,d0               *    Fetch next long
          jsr     plong                  *    Print
          dbra    d1,rloop               *    Loop until done
          lea     newline,a0             *    A0 -> Newline sequence
          jsr     prtstr                 *    Print it
          movem.l (a7)+,a0-a1/d0-d1      *    Pop working registers
          rts                            *    Return to caller
*
*         Print a long in D0
*
plong:    movem.l a0-a1,-(a7)            *    Save work registers
          lea     hexbuf,a1             *    Use all of hexbuf
hexprt:   lea     hexbuf,a0             *    A0 -> buffer to convert
          jsr     binhex                *    Convert D0 to hex    A0
          move.b  #' ',8(a0)            *    Move in space at end
          clr.b   9(a0)                 *    Set up null character
          move.l  a1,a0                 *    A0 -> area to print
          jsr     prtstr               *    Print it
          movem.l (a7)+,a0-a1           *    Unsave registers
          rts                           *    Return
*
*         Print a word in d0
*
pword:    movem.l a0-a1,-(a7)           *    Save work registers
          lea     hexbuf+4,a1          *    A1 -> low four digits
          bra.s   hexprt              *    Go print it
          .page
***************************************************************************
*
*         Data Area
*
***************************************************************************
dstr:     .dc.b   'D ',0
astr:     .dc.b   'A ',0
srstr:    .dc.b   'SR=',0
pcstr:    .dc.b   ' PC=',0
uspstr:   .dc.b   ' USP=',0
newline:  .dc.b   10,0
          .even
*
*         Uninitialized data section
*
          .bss
regs:     .ds.l   16                    *    Room for registers
hexbuf:   .ds.b   10                    *    Hex buffer
retpc:    .ds.b   4                     *    Return PC
          .end
```

CHAPTER 8

1. An interrupt is required because only an external event can make a task dispatchable in this case. If no tasks are dispatchable, then "app1" must be waiting on the timer and "app2" must be waiting for a terminal I/O operation to complete.

2. There are two primary areas: the dispatcher and the Send Message SVC. The dispatcher cannot really be improved. The Send SVC can be improved by using a tail pointer on the message control block list on the task's task control block. This would eliminate the loop to find the end of the message control block list.

ASCII Character Set

Dec	Hex	Character	Dec	Hex	Character	Dec	Hex	Character
042	2A	*	043	2B	+	044	2C	,
045	2D	-	046	2E	.	047	2F	/
048	30	0	049	31	1	050	32	2
051	33	3	052	34	4	053	35	5
054	36	6	055	37	7	056	38	8
057	39	9	058	3A	:	059	3B	;
060	3C	<	061	3D	=	062	3E	>
063	3F	?	064	40	@	065	41	A
066	42	B	067	43	C	068	44	D
069	45	E	070	46	F	071	47	G
072	48	H	073	49	I	074	4A	J
075	4B	K	076	4C	L	077	4D	M
078	4E	N	079	4F	O	080	50	P
081	51	Q	082	52	R	083	53	S
084	54	T	085	55	U	086	56	V
087	57	W	088	58	X	089	59	Y
090	5A	Z	091	5B	[	092	5C	\
093	5D	]	094	5E	^	095	5F	_
096	60		097	61	a	098	62	b
099	63	c	100	64	d	101	65	e
102	66	f	103	67	g	104	68	h
105	69	i	106	6A	j	107	6B	k
108	6C	l	109	6D	m	110	6E	n
111	6F	o	112	70	p	113	71	q
114	72	r	115	73	s	116	74	t
117	75	u	118	76	v	119	77	w
120	78	x	121	79	y	122	7A	z
123	7B	{	124	7C	|	125	7D	}
126	7E	~	127	7F	DEL(ete)			

The following table gives the ASCII (American Standard Code for Information Interchange) character set.

Dec	Hex	Character	Dec	Hex	Character	Dec	Hex	Character
000	00	CTL-@ NULL	001	01	CTL-A SOH	002	02	CTL-B STX
003	03	CTL-C ETX	004	04	CTL-D EOT	005	05	CTL-E ENQ
006	06	CTL-F ACK	007	07	CTL-G BELL	008	08	CTL-H BS
009	09	CTL-I HT	010	0A	CTL-J LF	011	0B	CTL-K VT
012	0C	CTL-L FF	013	0D	CTL-M CR	014	0E	CTL-N SO
015	0F	CTL-O SI	016	10	CTL-P DLE	017	11	CTL-Q DC1
018	12	CTL-R DC2	019	13	CTL-S DC3	020	14	CTL-T DC4
021	15	CTL-U NAK	022	16	CTL-V SYN	023	17	CTL-W ETB
024	18	CTL-X CAN	025	19	CTL-Y EM	026	1A	CTL-Z SUB
027	1B	CTL-[ESC	028	1C	FS	029	1D	GS
030	1E	RS	031	1F	US	032	20	SPACE
033	21	!	034	22	"	035	23	#
036	24	$	037	25	%	038	26	&
039	27	'	040	28	(	041	29	)

ASCII Character Set

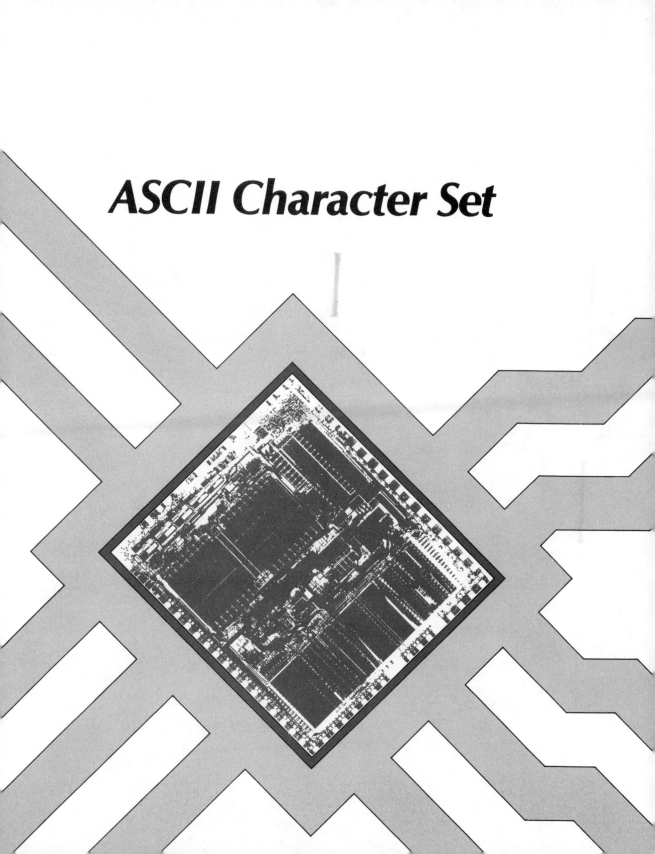

The characters marked "CTL-x" can be generated on most terminals by holding down the CONTROL key and typing the indicated character. For example, the hex character value 07 is generated by typing CONTROL-G. Control characters are used to perform some device-control function. Some of the common control characters and their functions are:

- Control-G is used to sound the terminal buzzer, beeper, or bell.

- Control-H (Backspace) causes the terminal cursor to move back one character space. Some older terminals do not support this character.

- Control-I (Tab) causes the next character to be printed at the next tab stop to the right. Tab stops are typically placed every eight characters.

- Control-J (Line feed) causes the device to move down one line.

- Control-L (Form feed) causes the device to move to the top of the next page.

- Control-M (Carriage return) causes the cursor to move to the beginning of the present line.

- Control-Q (XON) causes suspended output to resume.

- Control-S (XOFF) causes output to be suspended until the receipt of a Control-Q.

Programming Style

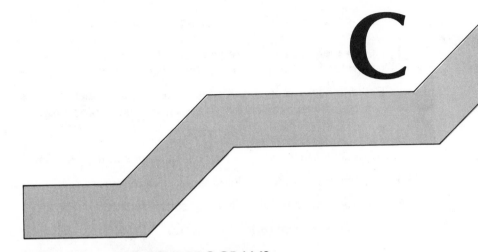

WHAT IS A "GOOD" PROGRAM?

Now that we've written several programs, let's stop and consider the program creation process. A few guidelines were developed during the history of programming that will help you write better programs.

Before we discuss these guidelines, however, we must first define what is meant by a "good" program. What makes one program better than another? Is it possible to tell by looking at a program whether it is a "good" program or a "bad" program?

This is an area in which programming is similar to other kinds of creative endeavor. A great deal of program "goodness" is in the eye of the beholder. One programmer might value the use of "meaningful labels," another the smallest possible code size, and so on. The old adage about one man's trash being another man's treasure is also true in the software world.

The one objective measure of how good a program is whether it works for the problem you are trying to solve. A program may be well-designed, well-coded, extensible, modular, but if it fails in only one case, these programming virtues are of no value if *your case* is the one on which the program fails. The value of a program is how well the program solves the problem it is designed to address.

The guidelines outlined in this appendix are generally accepted in the computer software industry as rules that produce good software. Every program is different, however, and you should adapt the guidelines to suit your environment and programming style.

PROGRAMMING GUIDELINES

Here then, are some guidelines for writing good programs:

1. Design the program before you code it. Planned programs can be written faster and with fewer bugs than unplanned programs.

2. Design modular programs. Modular programs are easier to debug and extend than nonmodular (i.e., "spaghetti code") programs.

3. Design the top-level modules first.

4. Follow consistent coding conventions throughout the program.

5. Integrate program testing into the development process.

6. Document the code liberally using comment lines.

7. Have someone else review your work.

Let's look at each of these areas in greater detail.

Top-Down Program Design

Like any other construction project, a program works better if built from a plan. The time invested in planning a program will more than pay for itself in time saved during the coding and debugging phases of the program.

Program planning consists of three activities:

1. Write a description of how the program will work. For very large programs, it is a good idea to write user documentation (or external specifications) before coding begins. The external specification should describe how to operate the program and any data input and output by the program.

2. Design the data structures before writing any code. Data structures often dictate the design of the code that uses them.

3. Partition the program into modules, and design the inter-module calling sequences. Write a description (called *pseudocode*) of the activities performed by each module.

4. Decide how you are going to test the program to verify that it works.

Modular Programming

As we saw in Chapter 6, modular programs lend themselves to borrowing code from an existing program to write a new program. Partitioning a large program into modules makes it easier to write, debug, and modify. Here are some guidelines to follow in partitioning a program into modules:

- Structure the program in a hierarchical fashion. Put detail work as far down the hierarchy as you can. Ideally, the top level should do nothing but call the lower levels.

- Use the principle of "hiding information." Wherever possible, isolate all uses of each data structure to a single module. This makes it possible to overhaul the data structure without major surgery on the entire program.

- Avoid "pathological connections." A pathological connection is one module relying on the structure of another module. Altering the second module can cause bugs to appear in the first.

- Strive for singularity of function for each module. Don't try to put unrelated functions into a module to save time or space.

Figure C.1 shows a module chart for the PADD program.

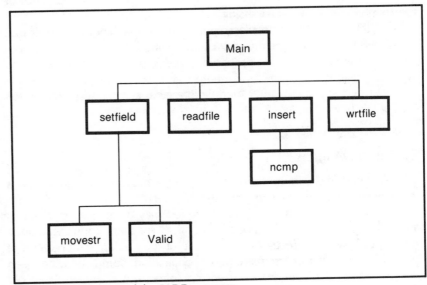

Figure C.1 – *Diagram of the PADD program*

The PADD program consists of four basic functions:

1. Format the fields on the command line.

2. Read the file into memory.

3. Insert the record.

4. Write the file from memory to disk.

Each of these functions are fairly independent. Except for the shared global variables, none of these routines know anything of the workings of the other modules.

Top-Down Implementation and Testing

Top-down design means that you begin design at the top levels and progress to the lower levels. You should also follow this philosophy for implementation and testing. Yourdon, in *Managing the Structured Techniques* (New York: Yourdon Press, 1979), describes a system for implementing software that codes and tests the complete system in a top-down fashion. This technique requires that you build the top module and dummy out its subordinate modules. The dummy routines are often called *stubroutines*. These are routines which either just return, return a constant value, or return after some trivial processing.

Once this scaffolding is in place, put it on the machine, and try it out. Then, one by one, replace the stubroutines with the real implementation. Test the system as you go. Be prepared to redesign the top modules as the subordinate modules are implemented. You will avoid a lot of effort wasted in redesigning the inter-module interfaces at the last minute by following this technique.

Coding Techniques

The primary evaluation criteria of whether a program is a good one is whether or not it performs its intended function.

The manner in which a program is coded may determine its eventual success or failure. Programs coded using the "spaghetti code" technique may, in fact, work perfectly. However, one of the fundamental realities of programming is that programs require modification. Somewhere between 70 to 80 percent of the money spent on software is spent on fixing old programs, not on building new ones. So, unless your programs are easy to modify, odds are that you are spending more time, energy, and money than necessary in modifying them. Also, programs that are not easy to modify tend to be abandoned or rewritten rather than maintained, entailing more needless expense.

Most coding techniques for writing maintainable code are simply common sense. The programming environment has been improved significantly over the past several years, yet still you see software being written for fourth generation computers using second generation techniques.

Readability is Key

Efficiency used to be *the* key consideration, especially in older microcomputer systems. The days when microseconds were precious and bytes were worth their weight in gold are gone forever. Although it is not possible to completely ignore efficiency considerations, it is no longer the primary consideration.

Brooks, in *The Mythical Man-Month* (Reading, Mass.: Addison-Wesley, 1979), suggests that a program has two audiences—the machine and the humans that will maintain the program. Computer hardware has progressed to the point where we can give the human audience higher priority for most programs.

In writing programs, you should focus on how well the program can be understood by another programmer. Here are some guidelines in this area:

1. Don't use instructions as data, or worse, modify instructions as the program executes. This practice creates programs that are extremely difficult to understand.

2. Try to make every program module fit on a single page (exclusive of documentation). If a module won't fit on a page, make part of it a subroutine and put that on a separate page. An example of this technique is the "ncmp" subroutine in Listing 6.7.

3. Strive to make branch targets lower on the page than the branch instruction. This follows the normal reading pattern for most people. (This is obviously impossible for branches that form the end of a loop.)

4. When using conditional branches, try to make branch failure the "normal" case, particularly where the branch destination is relatively far away. This means that most of the time, the branch will

not be taken and the first-time reader can ignore the branch and still understand the program.

5. Create modules that have a single entry and a single exit point. Try to place the entry at the top of the page and the exit at the bottom.

6. Avoid branches or jumps that span page boundaries. This is not always possible, as in the case with the LBOS interrupt routines (see Listing 8.7), which must jump to the dispatcher on occasion. Another exception is a disaster bail-out, where you branch to an error routine with no intention of returning.

7. Always use symbolic names for record fields, absolute addresses, and constants that are likely to change.

8. Try to use labels and names for data items that suggest their functions.

Avoiding Bugs

One of the best ways to avoid bugs in your programs is to structure your coding so that it's hard to put the bugs into your program in the first place. This is called *defensive programming*. Some examples of defensive programming techniques are:

1. Range check parameters coming into a routine or structure the code so that nothing harmful is done when one of these parameters is out of range. The best solution is to print an error message that identifies both the parameter in error and the location in the program.

2. Limit return values from a function to one register. Always make it the same register. Don't expect this register to come back unchanged from a subroutine call.

3. Save and restore all the registers (except possibly the return parameter register) at the beginning and end of each module. This eliminates the process of figuring out which registers to save and restore. It also prevents the "Who clobbered register D3?" crisis.

4. Avoid mixing stack pushes and pops with conditional branches. If you push something on the stack, try not to have a conditional

branch before the item is popped off the stack. One of the hardest errors to find is the condition where you execute an RTS or RTE instruction with the stack pointer pointing to the wrong data. This causes some random address to be loaded into the PC, resulting in a "wild branch." Using the LINK and UNLK instructions at the beginning and end of each subroutine can alleviate this problem.

5. When using an address register to access fields in a record, always use the "address register indirect with displacement" addressing mode. *Don't* use pre-decrement or post-increment addressing to step through the fields in a record. This effectively prohibits adding, deleting, or rearranging record fields.

6. Avoid other "clever" uses of the pre-decrement / post-increment addressing modes. For instance, the CMP.L (A0)+,(A1) instruction can be used to add 4 to both A0 and A1. However, if either of these registers contains a nonexistent or odd address, an exception will result.

7. Don't use immediate fields as variables.

```
          MOVE.L    #18,D0
XYZ:      .EQU      * – 4        * Used to reference data
                      .
                      .
                      .
          MOVE.L    D2,XYZ
```

Many computer systems have memory protection devices called *memory management units,* which prohibit writing to memory that contains instructions.

Program Documentation

"Document unto others as you would have them document unto you."
Program documentation is the most neglected aspect of the programming process. It is often said in professional programming circles that nothing is later than software—except documentation. The value of good program documentation is only realized after the program has been in use for a while and the time comes to fix it. This problem has been

around for a long time. The quotation above was written in 1971 (Kreitzberg et al., *The Elements of FORTRAN Style* [New York: Harcourt, Brace, Jovanovich, 1971). Yet today, one of the biggest problems in software development is inadequately documented code.

There are essentially two types of documentation for a piece of software: user documentation, which describes how to operate the program, and implementor's documentation, which describes how the program is constructed internally. User documentation is usually packaged in a separate manual. Most users are totally unconcerned with *how* a program does what it does. He or she is strictly concerned with *what* a program does, and what magic incantations he or she must recite to get the program to do what he wants.

The implementor's documentation should normally be kept in the program, for two reasons. First, it is impossible to lose the program's internal documentation without also losing the source code. Second, when the program is changed, it is *much* more likely that the documentation will be updated as well. There are few things less useful than program documentation that no longer matches the program.

In documenting a program, try to anticipate the questions that another programmer might have in modifying your code. Here are some suggestions for documenting assembly-language code:

1. Put a description of what the program is and what it does at the very beginning. An overview of the operating procedures is often helpful.

2. Instructions for rebuilding the program should be included near the beginning. Ideally, you should have an automated procedure for doing this, such as a UNIX "Makefile," or a CP/M "SUBMIT" file, which performs all the steps necessary to reconstruct the program from its source code.

3. Include descriptions for each of the major data structures, preferably with block diagrams, before the code begins. See Listing 6.1 for an example.

4. For each subroutine, include a narrative section that describes the overall function of the subroutine and the input and output parameters. Any unusual coding techniques or external dependencies should be mentioned in this section.

5. Include a description of each section of code that performs a different function at the beginning of that section of code. Also explain code that is tricky or hard to understand in any way.

6. Use blank lines, white space, and page breaks liberally to make the program listing more readable.

7. Wherever you can, include a comment at the end of each line. This is especially valuable when a section of code is hard to understand.

Code Reviews

Arrange to have someone else review your code. You should take advantage of every opportunity to do this. Weinberg, in *The Psychology of Computer Programming* (New York: Van Nostrand Reinhold Company, 1971), first suggested this technique, citing the example of a thirteen-line program in which twenty errors were found by other people reviewing the code. Many software organizations formalize this process, called a *code walkthrough*. There are several benefits to be reaped from doing this:

1. The other person can spot bugs that you can't. Often in programming, you will find yourself so close to a program that you overlook an error many times. Someone not as familiar with the problem as you are may spot the problem immediately.

2. You may learn something. Unless the other person's technical background is very similar to yours, she or he may see a better way of doing something in your program.

3. The other person may learn something. The best way to learn programming is by example. Something in your program may help the reviewer solve one of his or her programming problems.

4. You will learn which areas of your program are difficult to understand.

5. In the process of explaining your program, you may uncover bugs yourself.

CONCLUSION

"If carpenters built houses the same way programmers write programs, then the first woodpecker would destroy civilization" (Weinberg, op. cit.).

Writing good programs is hard work. Fixing bad programs is even harder. The effort spent in writing maintainable programs will more than be repaid when the time comes to add that next feature or remove "the last bug." Many successful books have been written on software engineering. The ones mentioned in this appendix are widely regarded as classics, and are strongly recommended. Another important source is your own experience. You will find that your ability to write software increases dramatically with your level of experience. There is absolutely no substitute for getting on the machine and doing it yourself.

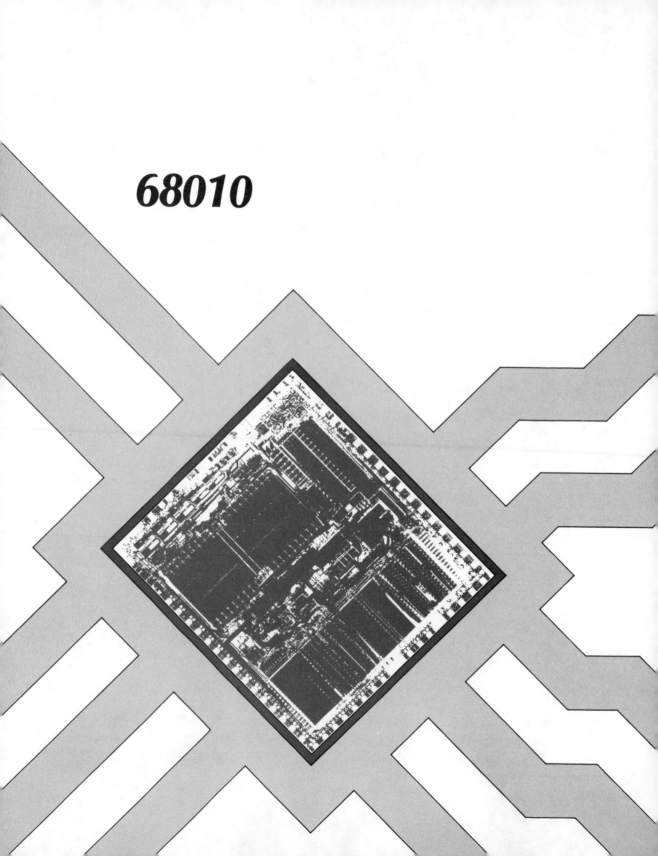

68010

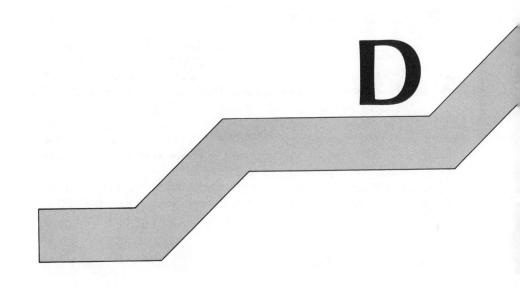

D

INTRODUCTION

The 68010 processor chip is the second generation of 68000 processors. This appendix outlines the differences between the 68010 and its older brothers, the 68008 and 68000. These differences lie in four major areas:

1. Extra registers in the 68010.

2. Extra instructions in the 68010.

3. Differences in the 68010 exception mechanism.

4. The addition of a Loop Mode for repeated instructions.

The 68010 is also appreciably faster than the 68000, as the basic processor clock is faster (12.5 Mhz as opposed to 8 Mhz). Some of the instructions also require fewer clock cycles to execute.

EXTRA REGISTERS IN THE 68010

The 68010 has three more registers than the 68000 or 68008—the vector base register (VBR), source function code (SFC) register, and destination function code (DFC) register. These registers are accessed through a special instruction, the move to/from control register (MOVEC) instruction.

Vector Base Register (VBR)

The vector base register (VBR) specifies a base for the vector area of memory. On the 68000, this area is constrained to memory addresses 0 to 3FF. The 68010 adds the contents of the vector base register to any vector address. The register is 32 bits long, and should always be loaded with an even address. If we place the quantity 1000 hex in the VBR and execute a TRAP #0 instruction, the vector will be loaded from address 1080 hex rather than 80 hex as on the 68000. If the VBR is loaded with a number that places a vector on an odd boundary or in non-existent memory, the 68010 will halt upon attempting to access the vector.

The vector base register is initialized to zero during the RESET exception, which is required for the processor to begin execution. If the VBR is not modified, the 68010 will use the same vector area as the 68000.

SFC and DFC Registers

One of the additional instructions on the 68010 is the Move Address Space (MOVES) instruction. This instruction allows the programmer to specify the function code that appears on the 68010 FC0 to FC2 pins, while moving data between memory and a register. This is a useful feature when the function-code pins are decoded by external hardware. For instance, a hardware designer might elect to put data memory in different physical memory than program memory. Without the MOVES instruction, there would be no way to load a program into memory on such a system.

The source function code and destination function code registers are 3-bit registers that contain the function code to appear on the FC0 to FC2 pins when the MOVES instruction specifies memory as a source and a destination, respectively.

The bits are numbered from the right, so pin FC0 is loaded from the low-order bit of the SFC or DFC registers.

ADDITIONAL INSTRUCTIONS IN THE 68010

The 68010 has four extra instructions:

1. The Move from Condition Code Register (MOVE CCR) instruction. Allows nonprivileged access to the Condition Codes.

2. The Move Control Register (MOVEC) instruction. Allows loading and storing the contents of one of the three extra registers described above.

3. The Move Address Space (MOVES) instruction. Allows a supervisor mode program to access memory with an arbitrary function code on the 68000 function code pins (FC0 to FC2).

4. The Return and Deallocate (RTD) parameters. Allows a subroutine to remove arguments from the stack while returning to a procedure that has invoked the subroutine.

In addition, the MOVE from Status Register (MOVE from SR) instruction has privileged status, so that any access to the System byte of the Status Register is now privileged.

MOVE From CCR Instruction

The Move From CCR instruction allows a user or supervisor mode program to copy the condition code register to an effective address operand. The operation is constrained to word size, with the low-order byte of the destination receiving the User byte of the Status Register, and the high-order byte of the destination receiving all zeros.

Addressing Modes:

Dn	An	(An)	(An) +	– (An)	x(An)	x(An,xr.s)
Yes	No	Yes	Yes	Yes	Yes	Yes
x.w	**x.l**	**x(PC)**	**x(PC,xr.s)**	**#x**	**SR**	**CCR**
Yes	Yes	No	No	No	No	No

Data Size: Word

Condition Codes Affected: None

Assembler Syntax: MOVE   CCR, <ea>

Machine Code Format:

Bit	15	14	13	12	11	10	9	8	7	6	5	4	3	2	1	0
	0	1	0	0	0	0	1	0	1	1	Effective		Address			

← Mode → | ← Reg. →

MOVE Control Register Instruction

The Move Control Register (MOVEC) instruction allows a supervisor mode program to copy the contents of any of the 68010 control registers to or from an address or data register. All transfers are 32 bits, regardless of the length of the control register. When copying DFC or SFC to a register, bits 4 to 31 are zeroed in the destination.

Data Size: Long

Condition Codes Affected: None

Assembler Syntax: MOVEC   Rc,Rn
                  MOVEC   Rn,Rc

Rc is the control register, either VBR, DFC, USP, or SFC. Rn specifes an address or data register.

Machine Code Format:

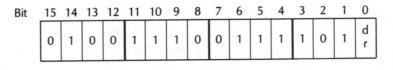

Bit	15	14	13	12	11	10	9	8	7	6	5	4	3	2	1	0
	0	1	0	0	1	1	1	0	0	1	1	1	1	0	1	d r

A	Register	Control Register

Dr is the direction: 0 for control register as the source, 1 for control register as the destination. "Register" is the number of the general register. A is 1 if this register is an address register, 0 if a data register. The Control Register field specifies the control register to be used, as shown below.

Control Register Field	Register	
0000 0000 0000 (000 hex)	Source Function Code	(SFC)
0000 0000 0001 (001 hex)	Destination Function Code	(DFC)
1000 0000 0000 (800 hex)	User Stack Pointer	(USP)
1000 0000 0001 (801 hex)	Vector Base Register	(VBR)

MOVE to/from Address Space

The Move to/from Address Space (MOVES) instruction allows a supervisor mode program to move a byte, word, or longword to or from memory with an arbitrary function code on the 68010 function code pins (FC0–FC2). When memory is used as a source, the function code is obtained from the Source Function Code (SFC) register. When memory is used as a destination, the function code is obtained from the Destination Function Code (DFC) register.

The transfer must occur between memory and an address or data register. When moving to an address register, the source is sign-extended to 32 bits. All 32 bits of the address register are affected by the transfer.

Addressing Modes Allowed (memory operand):

Dn	An	(An)	(An) +	– (An)	x(An)	x(An,xr.s)
No	No	Yes	Yes	Yes	Yes	Yes
x.w	**x.l**	**x(PC)**	**x(PC,xr.s)**	**#x**	**SR**	**CCR**
Yes	Yes	No	No	No	No	No

Data Size: (Byte, Word, Long)

Condition Codes Affected: None

Assembler Syntax: MOVES   Rn,<ea>

MOVES   <ea>,Rn

Rn specifies an address or data register.

Machine Code Format:

Bit	15	14	13	12	11	10	9	8	7	6	5	4	3	2	1	0
	0	0	0	0	1	1	1	0	Size		Effective			Address		

← Mode → | ← Reg. →

A	Register	d r	0	0	0	0	0	0	0	0	0	0	0

Size specifies the data size: 00 for bytes, 01 for words, and 10 for longs. Register specifies the general register to be used for the transfer. A is a 1 if this register is an address register, 0 if a data register. dr specifies the direction of the transfer: 0 for <ea> to register, and 1 for register to <ea>.

RTD Instruction

The ReTurn and Deallocate parameters (RTD) instruction allows a subroutine to return to its caller and simultaneously pop a parameter list from the stack. The instruction first pops the longword at the top of the stack into the PC, as with the RTS instruction. Next, a 16-bit displacement is sign-extended and added to the stack pointer. The final value of the stack pointer is the old stack pointer plus the displacement plus four.

Data Size: Unsized

Condition Codes Affected: None

Assembler Syntax: RTD #<displacement>

Machine Code Format:

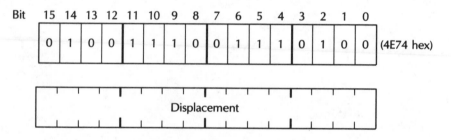

Bit	15	14	13	12	11	10	9	8	7	6	5	4	3	2	1	0	
	0	1	0	0	1	1	1	0	0	1	1	1	0	1	0	0	(4E74 hex)

| Displacement |

The Displacement field specifies the displacement to be added to the stack pointer. Due to the sign extension process, the displacement must be less than 32K (32768 decimal) to deallocate space from the stack.

DIFFERENCES IN THE 68010 EXCEPTION MECHANISM

The 68010 is quite different from the 68000 and 68008 in the area of exception-processing. It is, however, possible to write exception processing code that functions on any 68000 processor. The 68010 exception mechanism differs from the 68000 and 68008 in the following areas:

- The 68010 programmer can move the address of the vector area to any even location in memory, using the vector base register (VBR).

- The format of information pushed on the stack by an exception is different on the 68010. The 68010 pushes an extra word for all exceptions, and pushes more information on the stack for the BUSERR and addressing error exceptions.

- When an invalid stack format is encountered by an RTE instruction, an extra vector is reserved for use by the 68010.

Vector Base Register

To change the vector area on the 68010, set up a new vector area somewhere in addressable memory, and load the address into the vector base register. Listing D.1 shows a sample sequence for performing this function.

This code copies the contents of the old vector area (at absolute location 0) into a new vector area (at "newvec"). It is safe to load the address of the new vector area into VBR only after the copy is made.

```
            lea     newvec,a0     * A0 -> New vector area
            move.l  a0,a1         * Copy
            suba.l  a2,a2         * A2 -> Old vector area
            move.l  #255,d0       * D0 = Vector count
    mloop:  move.l  (a2)+,(a0)+   * Copy
            dbra    d0,mloop      *         vectors
            movec   a1,vbr        * Load VBR
```

Listing D.1 – *Changing the vector area on the 68000*

Stack Format Differences

The 68010 has a different format for the information pushed on the stack by an exception. There are two different formats: one pushed by a BUSERR or addressing error (called *long format*), and one pushed by all other types of exceptions (called *short format*). Both of these formats are different from those on the 68000 and 68008.

Short Format

The short format for exceptions on the 68010 stack frame is shown in Figure D.1.

The fourth word on the stack is the difference between this format and the 68000 short-format exception stack frame. The zeroes in the upper nibble of this word indicate that it is a short-format exception. A long-format exception is indicated by a value of 1000 in these four bits.

The RTE instruction looks at these four bits to determine how many words to remove from the stack. If you attempt an RTE instruction with a format code that is neither 0000 nor 1000, a format exception takes place. This exception uses vector 14 (offset 3C hex).

Long Format

The long-stack frame format is pushed by a BUSERR or addressing error exception. Figure D.2 shows how the long-stack frame format appears.

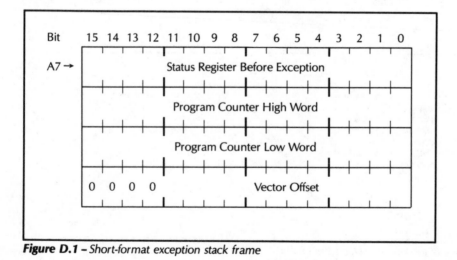

Figure D.1 – *Short-format exception stack frame*

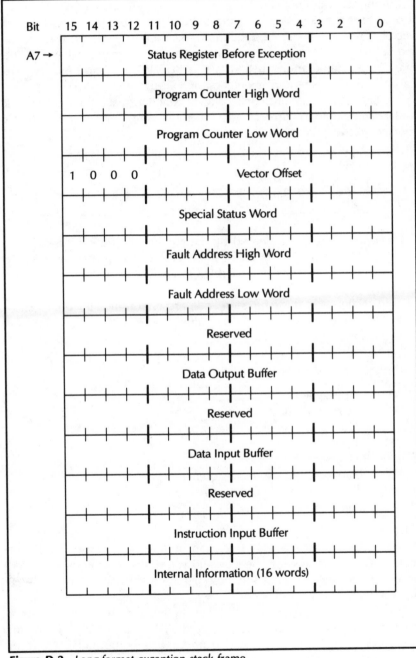

Figure D.2 – *Long-format exception stack frame*

This format is also not compatible with the corresponding 68000 format. It does have the advantage that the status register, program counter, and vector offset have the same position on the stack relative to register A7 as the 68010 short format. The purpose of the long format is to enable the 68010 to continue an instruction after a BUSERR exception occurs. This capability permits the implementation of a virtual-memory machine.

The Special Status Word contains additional information about the fault and it can be used to correct the fault with software. Here is the format of the Special Status Word:

Bit	15	14	13	12	11	10	9	8	7	6	5	4	3	2	1	0
	RR	*	*	IF	DF	RM	HB	BY	RW	*	*	*	*	*	*	*	*	*	*	Function

The RR (ReRun) bit is cleared by the exception. If this bit is not set, when an RTE instruction executes, the processor will rerun the memory access that failed. Setting this bit prior to an RTE instruction causes the processor to skip the failing access.

The Function field is the function code present on the 68010 pins FC0–FC2 during the fault. The possible values and their interpretation are shown below.

Code	Type of access
000	Unassigned
001	User mode data reference
010	User mode program reference
011	Unassigned
100	Unassigned
101	Supervisor mode data reference
110	Supervisor mode program reference
111	Interrupt acknowledge

The access codes are only important when the memory hardware makes use of them. If this is the case and you desire to simulate the failed access in software, you must use these bits in combination with a MOVES instruction.

The RW (Read / Write) bit indicates whether the failed access was a memory read (RW = 1) or a memory write (RW = 0). Simulating a memory write requires copying the data from the data output buffer word on the stack to the address indicated by the fault address words on the stack.

The IF (Instruction Fetch) bit indicates that the processor was trying to read data from memory into the instruction input buffer. If you are simulating the failed access in software, you must write the data from the fault address into the instruction input buffer word on the stack.

The DF (Data Fetch) bit indicates that the processor was trying to read data from memory into the data input buffer. Simulating the failed access requires writing the data from the fault address to the data input buffer word on the stack. The DF bits and IF bits may both be set. If this is the case, the data from the faulted address must be written to both the instruction input buffer and the data input buffer.

The RM bit indicates that the interrupted memory access occurred during a read-modify-write cycle, as from a Test And Set (TAS) instruction. Allowing the processor to rerun the cycle (by leaving the RR bit clear) will cause both the read and write memory cycles to be repeated. Simulating a TAS read-modify-write cycle with software requires that you:

1. Write the original contents of the memory location to the data input buffer word on the stack.

2. Set the most significant bit of the memory location at the faulted address.

3. Set the condition codes in the status-register image on the stack according to the state of the byte before it was written.

The BY and HB bits are used in byte transfers. The BY bit has a value of 1 if the failed access was to a byte. If this is the case, the HB bit specifies whether the high byte (HB = 1) or the low byte (HB = 0) was being transferred.

Virtual Memory

A virtual memory system is one in which only a part of the program is in physical memory. This part of the program is called the program's *working set*. When the program makes a reference to an address that is not in memory, the memory management unit causes a BUSERR exception. The operating system loads the memory page containing the fault address and continues the failed instruction. The 68010 allows you to rerun the failing access or to simulate the access in software.

It is possible to have more than one access failure on a single instruction. For example, the instruction MOVE.B $10000,$40000 could cause three separate faults—one when the instruction is fetched from memory, and separate faults on both the source and destination operands.

LOOP MODE

A final change in the 68010 is the hardware *loop mode* capability. The 68010 has a special optimization for the DBcc instruction. If a program executes a two-instruction loop consisting of a one-word instruction and a DBcc instruction with a displacement of − 4, the 68010 completes the loop without refetching the instructions. This doubles the speed of a copy operation from memory to memory.

Listing D.2 shows a sequence of code optimized on the 68010.

```
        lea     src,a0      * A0 -> Source
        lea     dst,a1      * A1 -> Destination
        move.w  #length,d0  * D0 =  Byte count
loop:   move.b  (a0)+,(a1)+ * Loop
        dbra    d0,loop     *         mode
```

Listing D.2 – *Optimized code on the 68010*

The move.b and dbra instructions are optimized by the 68010 loop mode. Once the instructions have been fetched, the 68010 accesses only data until the loop is completed. On the 68000, by comparison, six bytes of instructions are fetched to move one byte of data.

Glossary

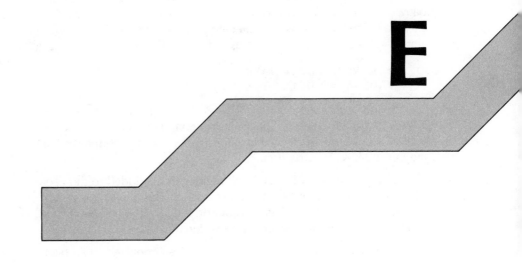

E

68000. A 16-bit microprocessor chip that forms the basis of this book.

68008. A version of the 68000 that has an 8-bit data bus. This chip is usually employed in low-cost computer systems.

68010. A version of the 68000 that has improved performance, virtual memory capability, and additional instructions. The 68010 is described in Appendix D.

68010 destination function code register (DFC). A 3-bit register used with the 68010 MOVES (Move Address Space) instruction. This register contains the memory access code (FC0–2), which is used when memory is the destination operand in the MOVES instruction.

68010 format exception. An exception through vector 14 (offset 38 hex) that indicates that an RTE instruction was attempted with an improper format code in the top four bits of the fourth word on the stack. Valid format code words are 0xxx hex and 8xxx hex. Any other combination of these four bits causes the 68010 format exception.

68010 loop mode. The ability of the 68010 to execute a one-word instruction followed by a DBcc instruction without refetching the operands. For example, the following code would execute in loop mode until the DBRA condition failed (i.e., when D0 becomes − 1):

```
LOOP.     MOVE.B    (A0) + ,(A1) +
          DBRA      D0,LOOP
```

68010 source function code register (SFC). A 3-bit register used with the 68010 MOVES (Move Address Space) instruction. This register contains the memory access code (FC0–2) that is used when memory is the source operand in the MOVES instruction.

68010 vector base register (VBR). A 32-bit register that is added to the vector address generated during exception processing. This allows the vector area to start at any even address in memory on the 68010. The 68000 vector address always starts at absolute address zero.

8-bit peripheral devices. I/O devices designed to be connected to an 8-bit data bus, rather than the 16-bit data bus on the 68000. The 68000 MOVEP instruction is designed to work with these devices.

Absolute long. A 68000 addressing mode in which the 32-bit longword following the instruction contains the address of the data to be used by the instruction.

Absolute short. A 68000 addressing mode in which the 16-bit word following the instruction contains the address of the data to be used by the instruction. This form of addressing is limited to the first 32K (32,768) bytes of memory.

Accumulator variable. A variable used as a total. The variable usually starts with an initial value of zero and is then augmented on each pass of a loop.

Addressing error exception. An exception through vector 3 (offset 0C hex) that occurs when a program references a memory word or longword using an odd address.

Addressing mode. Also known as an "Effective Address." On the 68000, this addressing mode is one of several techniques for obtaining data for an instruction. Data may be in a register, in memory, or in the status register. The 68000 has fourteen addressing modes (refer to Chapter 2 for a comprehensive description of the addressing modes).

Address register. One of eight 32-bit registers used to contain memory addresses. These registers may be accessed as either 16- or 32-bit quantities.

Address register direct. A 68000 addressing mode in which an address register contains the data for the instruction.

Address register indirect. A 68000 addressing mode in which an address register contains the memory address of the data for the instruction.

Address register indirect with displacement. A 68000 addressing mode in which an address register plus the word following the instruction is the memory address of the data for the instruction.

Address register indirect with index. A 68000 addressing mode in which an address register plus an 8-bit displacement plus an index register is the memory address of the data for the instruction.

Address register indirect with post-increment. A 68000 addressing mode in which an address register contains the memory address of the data for the instruction. The address register is incremented by the data size (1, 2, or 4) after execution of the instruction.

Address register indirect with pre-decrement. A 68000 addressing mode in which an address register is decremented by the data size (1, 2, or 4). The address register then contains the memory address of the data for the instruction.

Algorithm. A step-by-step procedure for performing some action. Algorithms often form the basis for programs.

ALU. Arithmetic and Logical Unit. Performs arithmetic and logical operations on the data passing through it. The ALU is a major component of the Central Processing Unit (CPU).

AND. A logical operation that takes two binary numbers and produces a third binary number. This binary number has a 1 in every bit position where both of the operands have a 1, and 0 in all other bit positions.

Arithmetic and logical unit (ALU). The central part of the CPU. The ALU performs all the basic data operations, i.e., addition, subtraction, and so on.

Arithmetic shift left. An operation on a single binary number in which each bit is transferred to the left one or more positions. Bits shifted out of the high-order bit position are transferred into a Carry bit. Zero bits are added on the right.

Arithmetic shift right. An operation on a single binary number in which each bit is transferred to the right one or more positions. Bits shifted out of the low-order position are transferred into a Carry bit. The high-order bit is preserved.

Array. A method of allocating memory to a group of data items (records) by placing them in contiguous locations.

ASCII. American Standard Code For Information Interchange. ASCII is a system by which each character (letters, digits, punctuation, and so on) is assigned a unique 7-bit binary code. These codes are given in Appendix B.

Assembler. A program that transforms assembly language into machine code.

Assembler directive. An assembly language statement that does not directly generate a machine operation, but which directs the assembler to perform some action. An example is the ".page" directive, which instructs the assembler to advance the listing to the top of the next page.

Assembly language. A programming language that allows a programmer to specify individual machine instructions in symbolic form, but which does not require assigning addresses for each instruction or data item. A program called an assembler performs this task. The assembler also converts the instruction mnemonics into their corresponding binary codes.

Autovector interrupt. An interrupt that uses the automatic vector assignment mechanism for the 68000. Automatic vectoring assigns all interrupts of a given priority level to a single vector. This feature can be used on systems that do not have many interrupting devices in order to save hardware costs.

Backspace. An ASCII character that causes a terminal or printer to move left one space.

BASIC. Beginner's All-Purpose Symbolic Instruction Code. BASIC is a programming language designed for the novice programmer. It is easy to learn and use. BASIC does not work well on large programs.

BCD. Binary Coded Decimal. BCD numbers store one decimal digit in every four bits. BCD is widely used in hardware devices and commercial applications.

Binary. A number system in which each digit (called a bit) can have one of two values, zero or one. The binary number scheme is used by most digital computers.

Binary search. A high-speed algorithm for finding an item in an ordered table. The binary search consists of taking two pointers, which initially point to the beginning and end of the table, and examining the item halfway between the two pointers. The appropriate pointer is moved to the halfway point and the process is repeated until the desired data item is found.

Binary tree. A tree structure in which each node may have at most two children. See also Child node.

Bit. Binary digIT. A bit is a single digit of a binary number, and may have one of two values, zero or one.

Boolean operations. Logical operations on binary numbers that are "bitwise" in nature. The most common Boolean operations are AND, OR, and Exclusive OR.

Bootstrap. The process by which a computer starts up. The 68000 RESET operation is used to start most bootstrap operations. The term comes from pulling oneself up by one's bootstraps. In the early days of computing, a bootstrap operation often required reading in part of a program that could read in some more of the program which could read in more of the program, and so on.

Branch condition. A combination of the condition codes that is interrogated by a conditional branch instruction. If the branch condition is met (i.e., the condition codes are set appropriately), the branch operation takes place. Otherwise, the next instruction is executed.

Branch instruction. An instruction that alters the normal flow of instructions. A branch instruction can be conditional (branching only when certain conditions are met) or unconditional (branching whenever the instruction is encountered).

Breakpoint. A location at which a debugger stops a program so that intermediate results may be examined.

Bubble sort. A sorting technique that examines consecutive data elements, swapping if necessary.

Buffer. An area of memory, usually used to hold data for I/O operations.

Buffered I/O. An I/O technique used by the C run-time library for performing I/O a few bytes at a time. The library routines buffer the transfer in a *stream buffer* to minimize the I/O overhead.

Bug. Any instruction (or set of instructions) in a program that causes an error or unexpected result.

BUSERR exception. A 68000 exception through vector 2 (location 8), which results from an attempt to access nonexistent memory.

Byte. An 8-bit binary number. Most computers are constructed to work on one or more bytes at a time.

C. A high-level language suitable for use as a systems language.

Cards. An antique storage device that placed 80 or 96 characters on a piece of paper. The characters were encoded as a combination of punched holes that generated binary codes.

Carriage return. An ASCII character (decimal value 13) that causes a terminal or printer to go to the beginning (i.e., left-hand side) of the current line.

Carry bit. A bit used as an extension bit to the ALU. For example, during an ADD operation, the carry bit receives the binary carry value that results from the addition of the two high-order bits.

CCR. See Condition code register.

Central Processing Unit. See CPU.

Child node. In a binary tree structure, a node that is below another node, which is called the node's "parent."

Circular buffer. A queue structure that is implemented as an array. A circular buffer contains a linear array of elements and insertion and deletion pointers. When a pointer advances beyond the end of an array, it is "wrapped around" to the beginning of the buffer.

Circular linked lists. A linked list in which the last element points either to the list head or to the first element in the list.

COBOL. COmmon Business Oriented Language. COBOL is one of the first high-level programming languages, and is especially suited for business software. Over 70 percent of existing software is in COBOL.

Comment line. In a program listing, a line inserted next to a line or lines of coding which aids the human reader of the program to understand the purpose or function of the coding.

Compute-bound task. See CPU-bound task

Computerese. The often obscure terminology that has developed in response to computer technology.

Conditional branch. An instruction that either branches to another location in the program or continues to the next instruction, depending on the setting of the condition codes in the status register.

Condition code register (CCR). The low-order byte of the 68000 status register. The CCR contains the eXtend (X), Negative (N), oVerflow (V), Zero (Z), and Carry (C) status bits. This register is also called the User byte of the Status register.

Context switching. The process of saving volatile machine resources (such as registers and dedicated memory locations) for one task and resetting them for another task. This is also called a task swap.

Conversion routines. Code that converts data from one representation to another. These routines are often used to convert binary data to ASCII format and vice versa.

CP/M-68K. A rather simple operating system for the 68000. CP/M-68K developed from CP/M-80 for 8080 and Z-80 machines.

CP/M SUBMIT file. A file of CP/M commands that can be executed without operator intervention.

CPU. Central Processing Unit. The CPU is a combination of the Control Unit (CU) and the Arithmetic-Logical Unit (ALU) and is the heart of every computer. The CPU controls a computer's memory and I/O devices. The 68000 chip is an example of a CPU.

CPU-bound task. A program or routine that performs substantially more computation than I/O.

Critical region. In a multitasking system, a critical region is an area of code that cannot be executed by more than one task at once. Critical-region code is the opposite of reentrant code.

CRT. Cathode Ray Tube. A computer's terminal is often referred to as a CRT, even though the term refers strictly to the televison tube containing the display screen.

C Run-time library. A collection of subroutines used by C programs for I/O and other common functions.

Data register. One of eight 32-bit registers in the 68000 used for temporary data storage. Many 68000 operations require a data register as one of the operands.

Data register direct. A 68000 addressing mode in which the data for the instruction is contained in a data register.

Data structures. Logical data structures that are superimposed on top of data stored as linked lists or arrays. Common examples of such data structures are stacks, queues, and trees.

DDT-68K. The debugger that comes with CP/M-68K. It is used in this book to illustrate the 68000 instruction set.

Deadlock. A situation that can arise in a multitasking environment in which a number of tasks are waiting on resources held by other tasks. Since the tasks which hold the resources are also waiting, all the tasks wait forever.

Deadly embrace. See Deadlock.

Debugger. A program that allows interactive control of the execution of another program. Examples are DDT-68K under CP/M-68K and SDB under UNIX.

Decimal. A number scheme in which each digit has one of ten values, 0 to 9.

Defensive programming. A programming style that attempts to minimize the probability of bugs in a program.

Dequeues. A "double-ended queue." Data items in a dequeue can be inserted or removed at either end.

Device-independent I/O. An operating system technique that attempts to remove device considerations from I/O programming. The usual technique to achieve this is to treat all devices as if they were files. UNIX I/O is device-independent.

Direct file access. Also called random access. File I/O in which the records are not processed in sequential order.

Disabling dispatching. A technique for providing mutual exclusion in an operating system by disallowing context swaps while executing critical-region code.

Disabling interrupts. A technique for providing mutual exclusion in an operating system by masking off interrupts while executing critical-region code.

Disassembly. The process of going from binary machine code to assembly language.

Disk. A device that can be accessed in a random fashion and on which data can be modified on a block-by-block fashion. Blocks (also called "sectors") are typically 128–2048 bytes in length. Disks are usually round platters of magnetic media.

Dispatcher. Operating system code that decides which program should run next.

Documentation. Written information that describes some aspect of a computer system. Documentation is usually written for one of two audiences—the users of the computer, who require functional descriptions of how the software and hardware operates, or computer programmers and technicians, who require detailed technical descriptions of the computer system.

Double-bus fault. A situation in which the 68000 references illegal memory during the processing of an exception. The processor halts as a result. A double-bus fault can be caused by a corrupted system stack pointer (SSP) or an incorrect vector base register (only on the 68010).

Doubly-linked list. A linked list in which each item points to both the previous item and the next item.

Effective address operand. An operand of an instruction which may use one of the fourteen 68000 addressing modes.

Efficiency. Software efficiency is measured in terms of size and speed. A size-efficient program packs a lot of functionality into a small area of memory. A speed-efficient program performs its function rapidly. The two types of efficiency are often mutually exclusive.

End of file. A condition that occurs during a read operation when there is no more data to be read. The operating system normally returns an error to the program in this case.

Error condition. A condition that is not the normal case. A program may or may not recover from an error. Errors that a program cannot recover from are often called "fatal" errors.

Exception. The capability of the 68000 to interrupt the processing of the current program and do something else. Exceptions can be caused by program errors or external events.

Exception handler. Code that processes an exception condition.

Exclusive OR. An operation on two binary numbers that produces a third binary number. The result has a 1 in every position where one of the two operands has a 1. The result has a 0 in every position where both operands have a zero or both operands have a 1.

Executable file. A file that contains a machine-language program that can be loaded into memory and executed by the operating system.

Extend bit. The X bit in the condition code register. The extend bit is used to provide a carry for multiprecision operations on the 68000.

External symbols. Labels used in an assembly-language program that are defined in another program that assembled separately. The linker program resolves the references between programs.

File. A collection of bytes, normally stored on a disk device, that has a name and is handled as a unit by the computer system.

File close. A file operation provided by the operating system which terminates a program's access to a file.

File create. A file operation provided by the operating system which allows a program to create a new file.

File descriptor. A 16-bit quantity returned by the unbuffered C run-time routines that identifies an open file.

File open. A file operation provided by the operating system which allows a program to access an existing file.

File read. A file operation provided by the operating system which transfers data from a file into memory.

File system. That part of the operating system that performs file operations.

File write. A file operation provided by the operating system that transfers data from memory to a file.

First In First Out (FIFO). A scheduling discipline for organizing data on a stack. The first data item to arrive is the first to get service. FIFO scheduling is used by the QUEUE data structure.

Fixed length records (FLR). A technique of organizing information such that each piece of information takes up the same amount of memory.

Flowchart. A technique for representing an algorithm in a visual form.

Fork queues. A scheduling technique used by operating systems, that allows interrupt code to use the operating system resources normally available only to tasks in the operating system.

Form feed. An ASCII character (decimal value 12) that causes a printer to advance to the top of the next page.

FORTRAN. FORmula TRANslation. FORTRAN was the first high-level language and is still widely used in scientific work.

Frame pointer. An address register used to address data allocated on the stack via the LINK instruction.

Hardware stack pointer. Register A7, which is used by the 68000 instruction set to point to the top of a stack.

Hash code. The result of a hash function. Hash codes are used to determine an item's position in a table used by the hashing technique.

Hash collision. The situation which arises when using hashing in which two different elements have the same hash code.

Hash function. The algorithm for determining a hash code for a given data item. A good hash function is one that results in few hash collisions for ordinary data.

Hashing. A technique for searching tables in which a desired data item is placed in a table according to a hash code. Hash codes for the data items are determined by a hash function.

Hexadecimal. A number system in which each digit can have one of sixteen values, 0–9 or A–F (values zero–15). Hexadecimal numbers can be easily converted to or from binary.

Hex debugger. A debugger with which the user must specify addresses in hex. See also Symbolic debugger.

High-level language. A programming language that communicates with the computer at a higher level than machine instructions. Examples include BASIC, C, COBOL, FORTRAN, and Pascal.

Hybrid records. A technique of organizing information such that each piece of information occupies a fixed length and a variable-length area of memory.

Illegal instruction exception. An exception through vector 4 (address 10 hex) which results from the 68000 trying to execute a memory word that did not contain a valid 68000 machine instruction.

Immediate mode. A 68000 addressing mode in which the data for the instruction immediately follows the instruction.

Implementor's documentation. Documentation that describes in technical terms how a program does what it does. This documentation is typically used by a programmer to modifying a program.

Index register. An address or data register used by the address register indirect with index addressing mode or program counter relative with index addressing mode. The index register is added to the address register or the program counter and the displacement to obtain the memory address of the data.

Information hiding. A technique of decomposing a program into modules such that the organization of major data structures is hidden from all modules except one.

Insertion sort. A sorting technique in which the data items are placed in an ordered list one at a time.

Instruction. An operation which the computer can perform in hardware.

Interchange sort. A group of sorting techniques that rearranges the data in place. A bubble sort is an example of an interchange sort.

Interrupt. An exception caused by an external device.

Interrupt-driven I/O. The process of starting an I/O operation and waiting for the device to interrupt upon completion of the I/O operation. Computations may be overlapped with the I/O using the interrupt-driven technique.

Interrupt latency. The maximum time between an external device requesting an interrupt and the beginning of the interrupt service code. This interval is determined by the largest number of instructions executed with interrupts masked off.

Interrupt mask. Bits 8–10 of the status register. The 68000 will not recognize an interrupt that is less than or equal to the value in the interrupt mask. (Level 7 interrupts may not be masked off in this fashion.)

I/O. Input / Output. The process by which a computer exchanges information with the outside world.

I/O-bound task. A program whose execution speed is limited by I/O rather than computations.

I/O devices. One of several devices, such as a terminal or printer, that can be connected to a computer for purposes of giving information to or receiving information from the computer.

K. An abbreviation for "Kilo" (1,000), which has been adapted to mean 1,024 in computer terminology.

Kb. See Kilobyte.

Kilobyte. 1,024 bytes. Kilobyte is often abbreviated Kb.

Label. In assembly language, a label is a symbolic tag associated with an instruction or a data area. Instructions may refer to the label, and the assembler will assign the correct address in memory.

Last In First Out (LIFO). A storage discipline in which the last item added to a data structure is the first one removed. Stacks are an example of LIFO data structures.

Leaf node. A leaf node of a tree structure is one with no descendant nodes. See also Binary tree.

Level 7 interrupt. A level 7 interrupt is an external interrupt that may not be masked off.

Linear linked lists. A linked list in which the last element contains a value that indicates there are no more elements in the list.

Line 1010 exception. An exception executed through vector 10 (address 28 hex) which results whenever the 68000 encounters an instruction word with values between A000–AFFF hex.

Line 1111 exception. An exception executed through vector 11 (address 2C hex) which results whenever the 68000 encounters an instruction word with values between F000–FFFF hex.

Line feed. An ASCII character (decimal value 10) which causes a terminal to advance to the next line.

Linked list. A storage discipline in which each item in a set of records contains the address of the next item in logical order.

Linked list tail pointer. A variant on the linked list technique in which the address of the last element in the list is maintained in a separate pointer.

Linker. A program that combines multiple assembly object files into a single executable file. The linker resolves the use of external symbols among the different program segments.

List head. A memory location that contains the address of the first item in a linked list.

Listing file. A file produced by the assembler that shows the source program and the machine code produced by the assembler.

Load file. See Executable file.

Load module. See Executable file.

Logical left shift. An operation on a single binary number in which each bit is moved to the left one or more positions. Zeroes are added on the right. The last bit shifted out of the high-order bit position is preserved in the Carry bit.

Logical right shift. An operation on a single binary number in which each bit is moved to the right one or more positions. Zeroes are added on the left. The last bit shifted out of the low-order bit position is preserved in the Carry bit.

Longword. A 32-bit quantity (4 bytes).

Loop. A series of instructions that are executed repetitively.

Looping primitive. An instruction designed to facilitate programming loops. The 68000 looping primitive is the DBcc instruction.

M. An abbreviation for "Mega"(1,000,000), which has been adapted to mean 1,048,576 (1042 × 1024) in computer terminology.

Machine language. The binary code which is executed by the computer.

Mailbox. In a message-switched operating system, a mailbox is a storage area for messages that a task has not yet received.

Mb. See Megabyte.

Megabyte. 1,048,576 bytes (abbreviated Mb).

Memory. A device capable of storing and retrieving information. Computer memories usually store and retrieve 8, 16, or 32 bits at a time.

Memory access codes (FC0–FC2). Three output signals on the 68000 that indicate to external devices what kind of memory access is being performed.

Memory address. A mechanism for specifying which memory location is to be affected in a memory operation.

Memory bus. The physical connection between the CPU and memory.

Memory data. Contents of a memory location.

Memory management unit. An external device which translates the addresses output by the CPU (called "logical addresses") to real memory addresses. The MMU is used to provide memory protection, i.e., to prevent a program from destroying another program or the operating system.

Memory mapped hardware. External devices connected to the 68000 that appear to be memory locations.

Memory read. A memory operation that retrieves the contents of a memory location.

Memory write. A memory operation that sets the contents of a memory location.

Message switching. A technique for achieving mutual exclusion in an operating system. Critical regions in the system are contained in tasks, which process messages one at a time. See also Critical region.

Mnemonic. A symbol recognized by the assembler to represent a particular machine language instruction.

Modem. MOdulator DEModulator. A device for connecting two computers over a telephone line.

Modularity. The degree to which a program is constructed of discrete building blocks.

Monitor procedures. A technique for achieving mutual exclusion in an operating system. A monitor procedure is a section of code which can be executed by only one task at a time.

Multitasking. The ability to run multiple programs simultaneously.

Mutual exclusion. Allowing only one task at a time to execute a given piece of code.

Negative bit. A bit in the condition code register that is set when the high-order bit of the result of an operation is set, which in turn indicates a result less than zero.

Nibble. A group of four bits; one half of a byte.

Nonmaskable interrupt (NMI). An interrupt that cannot be disabled by software.

Nonshareable devices. I/O devices, such as printers, that cannot be used by more than one program at a time.

No operation instruction. An instruction which does nothing (except take time).

Object code portability. The ability to take an executable file from one system and run it on another system.

Object file. The binary code file created by the assembler.

One's complement. An operation on a single binary number that inverts the state of all bits in the number. All zero bits become one and all one bits become zero.

Op code. A binary pattern that instructs the computer to perform some action.

Operand. Data on which an instruction operates.

Operating system. A program that controls the execution of other programs and coordinates the functions of a computer system.

Overflow bit. A bit in the 68000 status register that is set when the result of an operation is too large to represent.

Parent node. In a binary tree, a parent node is a node that has descendant nodes.

Pascal. A high-level language widely used to teach budding computer scientists.

Pathological connection. A case where one area of a program makes some assumption about the inner workings of another area. Changing the second area often introduces bugs in the first.

PL/I. Programming Language I. A high-level language that contains all of the features in FORTRAN and COBOL. PL/I is commonly used on mainframe computers.

Pop. An operation that removes the top item of a stack.

Portability. The ability to move a program from machine to machine.

Preemptive priority-driven scheduling. A scheduling technique in which a high-priority task can usurp the CPU from a lower-priority task that is currently using the CPU.

Preemptive scheduling with time-slicing. A modified preemptive scheduling technique which provides time-slicing among tasks that have equal priority. See also Time-slicing.

Printer. A device that outputs data on "hardcopy" (paper).

Priority-driven scheduling. A technique in which a task receives CPU time on a priority basis.

Priority order queue. A queue arranged in some order other than time of arrival.

Privileged instruction. An instruction that potentially compromises the integrity of a computer system. These instructions, such as RESET, can only be executed when the 68000 is in Supervisor mode.

Privilege violation exception. An exception that occurs through vector 8 (address 20 hex) when a user mode program attempts to execute a privileged instruction.

Program. A group of instructions and data that performs a particular function.

Program counter. A 32-bit register that contains the address of the next instruction to be executed.

Program counter with displacement. A 68000 addressing mode in which the program counter is added to the word following the instruction to obtain the memory address of the data for the instruction.

Program counter with index. A 68000 addressing mode in which the program counter is added to an index register and an 8-bit displacement to obtain the memory address of the data for the instruction.

Programming language. A method of communicating with a computer in order to perform some task. Computers may be programmed in machine, assembly, or high-level languages.

Push. An operation that adds an element to the top of a stack.

Queue. A data structure in which items are added and removed on a First in First Out (FIFO) basis.

Read-modify-write operation. An operation that guarantees that a memory flag has been read and modified with no other device allowed to access the flag.

Record. An aggregate of data that have an underlying relationship to each other.

Recursion. The process of defining a structure or algorithm in terms of itself.

Reentrant code. Code that can be executed by more than one task at a time.

Register. A temporary memory location within the CPU that is used for temporary data storage.

Resource management. The regulation, usually by an operating system, of the various aspects of a computer system by other programs. This includes CPU scheduling, I/O device management, and memory allocation.

Ring buffer. See Circular buffer.

ROM. Read only memory.

Root. The topmost element of a tree.

Rotate left. An operation on a single binary number in which each bit is moved to the left a number of positions. Bits shifted out the high-order end of the number are shifted back in the low-order end, possibly through an external Carry bit.

Rotate right. An operation on a single binary number in which each bit is moved to the right a number of positions. Bits shifted out the low-order end of the number are shifted back in the high-order end, possibly through an external Carry bit.

Round robin scheduling. See time-slicing.

Scheduling. The process of allocating CPU time to a number of competing tasks.

Screen. The output (visual) side of a computer's CRT Terminal.

Searching. The process of finding a specific data item in a group of data items.

Semaphore. A data structure used to control shared access to a critical hardware or software resource such as a printer or block of memory.

Sequential search. The process of finding an item in a table by starting at the front of the table and looking at each item until the data item is located.

Sibling nodes. In a tree data structure, nodes that are children of the same parent node.

Sign bit. The high-order bit of a binary number. This bit is set when the number is less than zero in two's complement arithmetic.

Sign extension. The process of expanding the bits in a binary quantity by replicating the top bit of the source in all of the extra bits in the destination.

Sorting. The act of taking unordered data and arranging them to meet some ordering criteria.

Source code. Text which the user enters into an assembler in order to produce an object file. See also Object file.

Source code portability. The ability to move a program in source form from one system to another.

Source file. A text file containing program source code.

Spaghetti code. A derogatory term for a poorly organized program.

Stack. A data structure in which the last item added is the first item removed. Also a Last In First Out (LIFO) data structure.

Stack frame. A specific data area allocated on the stack using the LINK instruction.

Stack overflow. Trying to push an item on a stack that has no more available space.

Stack pointer. A register or memory location that gives the location of the top item on a stack.

Stack underflow. Trying to remove an item from an empty stack.

Status register. The 16-bit CPU register in the 68000 containing the trace, supervisor, interrupt mask, and condition code bits.

Status register addressing. A 68000 addressing mode in which the status register is the destination of an instruction.

Status register system byte. The upper byte of the status register. This byte contains the trace, supervisor, and interrupt mask bits.

Status register user byte. The lower byte of the status register, which contains the condition codes.

Stream I/O. See Buffered I/O.

String. A set of ASCII characters arranged in contiguous memory locations.

Structures. Data structures.

Subroutine. A group of instructions that may be used at several different points in a program through subroutine call and return instructions.

Subroutine call. An instruction that places the address of the next instruction on the stack and then branches to an address specified in the instruction.

Subroutine return. An instruction that pops an address off the stack and branches to it.

Subtree. Any node of a tree and all its descendants.

Supervisor bit. Bit 13 in the status register, which governs the execution of privileged instructions.

Supervisor mode. The condition when bit 13 of the status register is set, indicating that the 68000 will execute privileged instructions.

Supervisor stack pointer (SSP). The stack pointer used when the 68000 is in supervisor mode.

Symbolic debugger. A debugger that allows you to specify memory addresses using the symbols in the program.

System bit. Bit 13 of the status register, which governs execution of privileged instructions.

Tape. A device that records data on a long strip of magnetic material. Tape devices usually require that the data be processed sequentially.

Task. A program that executes independently.

Terminal. A device that allows a computer user to display and input ASCII data.

Text editor. A program that allows you to create and modify (i.e., edit) ASCII files.

Time-slicing. A CPU scheduling technique that gives the CPU to each task for a brief period, on a rotating basis. Task swaps occur 10 to 100 times a second to give the illusion of simultaneous execution.

Top-down implementation. Implementing the top level of a program first, testing it, then implementing the lower levels, one at a time, testing as you go.

Top-down program design. A discipline of program design that involves designing the top levels of a program first, followed by the lower levels.

Trace bit. Bit 15 of the status register. When this bit is set, a trace exception will occur at the end of the next instruction.

Trace exception. An exception that occurs through vector 9 (address 24 hex) as a result of executing an instruction with the trace bit on.

TRAP exception. An exception that occurs through vectors 32–47 (addresses 80–BC hex) when a TRAP 0–15 instruction is executed.

Trees. A data structure in which each item may point to more than one next item.

Two's complement. A system of binary arithmetic that represents negative numbers as the two's complement of the corresponding positive number.

UCSD p-System. An operating system based on the Pascal programming language that is available for the 68000.

Unbuffered I/O. A method of doing I/O through the C run-time library that does not require intermediate buffering.

Unconditional branch. A branch instruction that is not dependent on the condition codes. An unconditional branch is always executed.

UNIX. An operating system written in the C language that runs on the 68000.

Unsigned arithmetic. Considering a binary number to be always positive. This changes the range of a 16-bit number, for instance, from $-32768 \rightarrow 32767$ to $0 \rightarrow 65535$.

User documentation. Program documentation that describes how to use a program.

User mode. The condition that results when the Supervisor bit in the status register is not set.

User mode stack pointer (USP). The stack pointer used by the 68000 when the processor is in user mode.

Variable length records (VLR). A technique of organizing information such that each piece of information is not constrained to occupy the same size memory area. This requires a method for determining the length of each record.

Vector. A memory location associated with an exception that gives the address of the code which handles the exception.

Vectored interrupts. A 68000 interrupt technique in which the interrupting device specifies which vector is to be used in processing the interrupt.

Virtual memory. A technique by which a program may execute with only a portion of its code in memory. This reduces the amount of physical memory required to run a given program. The 68010 can support a virtual memory system, but the 68008 and 68000 cannot.

Wild branch. An error condition in which a branch is made to an erroneous address. This condition can also result from an erroneous RTS or RTE instruction.

Word. A 16-bit binary number.

Zero bit. A bit in the status register that is set when the result of an operation is zero.

Reading List

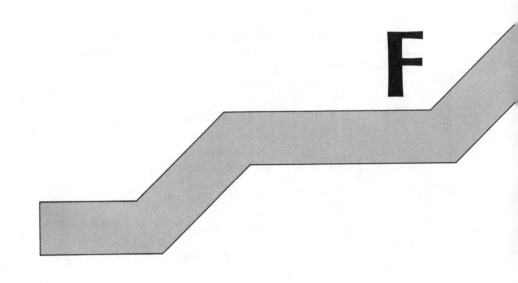

68000 BOOKS

Motorola, Inc. MC68000 16/32-Bit Microprocessor Programmer's Reference Manual (New Jersey: Prentice-Hall, 1984).

Kane et al., *68000 Assembly Language Programming* (New York: Osborne/McGraw-Hill, 1981).

PROGRAMMING IN GENERAL

F.P. Brooks, *The Mythical Man-Month* (Reading, Mass.: Addison-Wesley, 1979).

E.W. Dijkstra, *A Discipline of Programming* (New Jersey: Prentice-Hall, 1976).

G.M. Weinberg, *The Psychology of Computer Programming* (New York: Van Nostrand Reinhold, 1971).

E.N. Yourdon, *Techniques of Program Structure and Design* (New Jersey: Prentice-Hall, 1975).

E.N. Yourdon, *Managing the Structured Techniques* (New York: Yourdon Press, 1979).

ADVANCED CONCEPTS

J.J. Donovan, *Systems Programming* (New York: McGraw-Hill, 1972).

C.W. Gear, *Computer Organization and Programming* (New York: McGraw-Hill, 1969).

D.E. Knuth, *Fundamental Algorithms* (Reading, Mass.: Addison-Wesley, 1973).

D.E. Knuth, *Sorting and Searching* (Reading, Mass.: Addison-Wesley, 1973).

OPERATING SYSTEMS

P. Brinch Hansen, *The Architecture of Concurrent Programs* (New Jersey: Prentice-Hall, 1973).

P. Brinch Hansen, *Operating System Principles* (New Jersey: Prentice-Hall, 1973).

S. Madnick and J.J. Donovan, *Operating Systems* (New York: McGraw-Hill, 1973).

J. Welsh and M. McKeag, *Structured System Programming* (New Jersey: Prentice-Hall, 1980).

68000 Quick Reference

EFFECTIVE ADDRESS SUMMARY

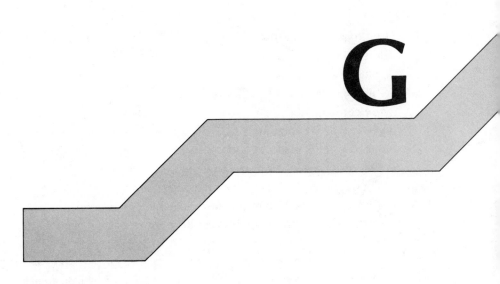

Addressing Mode Name	Syntax	Mode	Register
Data Register Direct	Dn	000	Data Register
Address Register Direct	An	001	Address Register
Address Register Indirect	(An)	010	Address Register
Address Register Indirect Postincrement	(An)+	011	Address Register
Address Register Indirect Predecrement	–(An)	100	Address Register
Address Register Indirect with Displacement	w(An)	101	Address Register
Address Register Indirect with Index	b(An,Rx)	110	Address Register
Absolute Short	w	111	000
Absolute Long	l	111	001
Program Counter with Displacement	w(PC)	111	010
Program Counter with Index	b(PC,Rx)	111	011
Immediate	#x	111	100
Status Register	SR	111	100
Condition Code Register	CCR	111	100

Legend:

Dn Data Register   (n is 0-7)

An Address Register (n is 0-7)

b   08-bit constant

w   16-bit constant

l   32-bit constant

x   8-, 16-, or 32-bit constant

Rx Index Register Specification, one of:

　　　Dn.W　　Low 16 bits of Data Register

　　　Dn.L　　All 32 bits of Data Register

　　　An.W　　Low 16 bits of Address Register

　　　An.L　　All 32 bits of Address Register

Bit

Index

Extension Word:

Bit	15	14	13	12	11	10	9	8	7	6	5	4	3	2	1	0
	A	Register			Sz	0	0	0	8-bit Displacement							

"A" is the type of index register: 1 for an address register, 0 for a data register. "Sz" is 1 for a long index, 0 for word.

Operation Code Summary

Bits 12 through 15	Operation
0000	Bit Manipulation/MOVEP/Immediate
0001	Move Byte
0010	Move Long
0011	Move Word
0100	Miscellaneous
0101	ADDQ/SUBQ/Scc/DBcc
0110	Bcc / BSR
0111	MOVEQ
1000	OR / DIV / SBCD
1001	SUB / SUBX
1010	(unassigned)
1011	CMP / EOR
1100	AND / MUL / ABCD / EXG
1101	ADD / ADDX
1110	ASL/ASR/ROL/ROR/ROXL/ROXR
1111	(unassigned)

Symbol	Meaning
*	Set according to result of operation
—	Not affected
0	Cleared
1	Set
U	Outcome (state after operation) undefined
I	Set by immediate data

NUMERICAL INSTRUCTION SUMMARY

Instruction	Machine Code Format	Condition Codes

ORI

15–12	11	10	9	8	7	6	5	4	3	2	1	0
0000	0	0	0	0	Size		Effective		Address			

X N Z V C
- * * 0 0

BTST
(Dynamic)

15–12	11	10	9	8	7	6	5	4	3	2	1	0
0000	D Reg.			1	0	0	Effective		Address			

X N Z V C
- - * - -

BCHG
(Dynamic)

15–12	11	10	9	8	7	6	5	4	3	2	1	0
0000	D Reg.			1	0	1	Effective		Address			

X N Z V C
- - * - -

BCLR
(Dynamic)

15–12	11	10	9	8	7	6	5	4	3	2	1	0
0000	D Reg.			1	1	0	Effective		Address			

X N Z V C
- - * - -

BSET
(Dynamic)

15–12	11	10	9	8	7	6	5	4	3	2	1	0
0000	D Reg.			1	1	1	Effective		Address			

X N Z V C
- - * - -

MOVEP

15–12	11	10	9	8	7	6	5	4	3	2	1	0
0000	D Reg.			1	Dr	Sz	0	0	1	Address Register		

X N Z V C
- - - - -

Instruction	Machine Code Format	Condition Codes

ANDI

15–12	11	10	9	8	7	6	5	4	3	2	1	0
0000	0	0	1	0	Size		Effective		Address			

X N Z V C
- * * 0 0

SUBI

15–12	11	10	9	8	7	6	5	4	3	2	1	0
0000	0	1	0	0	Size		Effective		Address			

X N Z V C
* * * * *

ADDI

15–12	11	10	9	8	7	6	5	4	3	2	1	0
0000	0	1	1	0	Size		Effective		Address			

X N Z V C
* * * * *

BTST
(Static)

15–12	11	10	9	8	7	6	5	4	3	2	1	0
0000	1	0	0	0	0	0	Effective		Address			

X N Z V C
- - * - -

BCHG
(Static)

15–12	11	10	9	8	7	6	5	4	3	2	1	0
0000	1	0	0	0	0	1	Effective		Address			

X N Z V C
- - * - -

BCLR
(Static)

15–12	11	10	9	8	7	6	5	4	3	2	1	0
0000	1	0	0	0	1	0	Effective		Address			

X N Z V C
- - * - -

BSET
(Static)

15–12	11	10	9	8	7	6	5	4	3	2	1	0
0000	1	0	0	0	1	1	Effective		Address			

X N Z V C
- - * - -

Instruction	Machine Code Format	Condition Codes

EORI

15–12	11	10	9	8	7	6	5	4	3	2	1	0
0000	1	0	1	0	Size		Effective		Address			

```
X N Z V C
- * * 0 0
```

CMPI

15–12	11	10	9	8	7	6	5	4	3	2	1	0
0000	1	1	0	0	Size		Effective		Address			

```
X N Z V C
* * * * *
```

MOVES
(68010)

15–12	11	10	9	8	7	6	5	4	3	2	1	0
0000	1	1	1	0	Size		Effective		Address			

```
X N Z V C
- - - - -
```

MOVE.B

15–12	11	10	9	8	7	6	5	4	3	2	1	0
0001	Register			Mode			Mode			Register		

← Destination → | ← Source →

```
X N Z V C
- * * - -
```

MOVEA.L

15–12	11	10	9	8	7	6	5	4	3	2	1	0
0010	Register			0	0	1	Mode			Register		

← Destination → | ← Source →

```
X N Z V C
- - - - -
```

MOVE.L

15–12	11	10	9	8	7	6	5	4	3	2	1	0
0010	Register			Mode			Mode			Register		

← Destination → | ← Source →

```
X N Z V C
- * * 0 0
```

| *Instruction* | *Machine Code Format* | *Condition Codes* |

MOVEA.W

15-12	11 10 9	8	7	6	5 4 3	2 1 0
0011	Register	0	0	1	Mode	Register

← Destination → | ← Source →

X N Z V C
- - - - -

MOVE.W

15-12	11 10 9	8 7 6	5 4 3	2 1 0
0011	Register	Mode	Mode	Register

← Destination → | ← Source →

X N Z V C
- * * 0 0

NEGX

15-12	11	10	9	8	7 6	5 4 3 2 1 0
0100	0	0	0	0	Size	Effective Address

X N Z V C
* * * * *

MOVE From SR

15-12	11	10	9	8	7	6	5 4 3 2 1 0
0100	0	0	0	0	1	1	Effective Address

X N Z V C
- - - - -

CHK

15-12	11 10 9	8	7	6	5 4 3 2 1 0
0100	D Reg.	1	1	0	Effective Address

X N Z V C
- * U U U

LEA

15-12	11 10 9	8	7	6	5 4 3 2 1 0
0100	A Reg.	1	1	1	Effective Address

X N Z V C
- - - - -

Instruction	Machine Code Format	Condition Codes

CLR

15–12	11	10	9	8	7	6	5	4	3	2	1	0
0100	0	0	1	0	Size		Effective		Address			

X	N	Z	V	C
-	0	1	0	0

MOVE From CCR *(68010)*

15–12	11	10	9	8	7	6	5	4	3	2	1	0
0100	0	0	1	0	1	1	Effective		Address			

X	N	Z	V	C
-	-	-	-	-

NEG

15–12	11	10	9	8	7	6	5	4	3	2	1	0
0100	0	1	0	0	Size		Effective		Address			

X	N	Z	V	C
*	*	*	*	*

MOVE to CCR

15–12	11	10	9	8	7	6	5	4	3	2	1	0
0100	0	1	0	0	1	1	Effective		Address			

X	N	Z	V	C
I	I	I	I	I

NOT

15–12	11	10	9	8	7	6	5	4	3	2	1	0
0100	0	1	1	0	Size		Effective		Address			

X	N	Z	V	C
-	*	*	0	0

MOVE to SR

15–12	11	10	9	8	7	6	5	4	3	2	1	0
0100	0	1	1	0	1	1	Effective		Address			

X	N	Z	V	C
I	I	I	I	I

Instruction	Machine Code Format	Condition Codes

NBCD

15–12	11	10	9	8	7	6	5	4	3	2	1	0
0100	1	0	0	0	0	0	Effective		Address			

X N Z V C
* U * U *

SWAP

15–12	11	10	9	8	7	6	5	4	3	2	1	0
0100	1	0	0	0	0	1	0	0	0	D Reg.		

X N Z V C
- * * 0 0

PEA

15–12	11	10	9	8	7	6	5	4	3	2	1	0
0100	1	0	0	0	0	1	Effective		Address			

X N Z V C
- - - - -

EXT.W

15–12	11	10	9	8	7	6	5	4	3	2	1	0
0100	1	0	0	0	1	0	0	0	0	D Reg.		

X N Z V C
- * * 0 0

MOVEM
(Regs to EA)

15–12	11	10	9	8	7	6	5	4	3	2	1	0
0100	1	0	0	0	1	Sz	Effective		Address			

X N Z V C
- - - - -

EXT.L

15–12	11	10	9	8	7	6	5	4	3	2	1	0
0100	1	0	0	0	1	1	0	0	0	D Reg.		

X N Z V C
- * * 0 0

TST

15–12	11	10	9	8	7	6	5	4	3	2	1	0
0100	1	0	1	0	Size		Effective		Address			

X N Z V C
- * * 0 0

Instruction	Machine Code Format	Condition Codes

TAS

15–12	11	10	9	8	7	6	5	4	3	2	1	0
0100	1	0	1	0	1	1	Effective		Address			

X N Z V C
- * * 0 0

ILLEGAL

15–12	11	10	9	8	7	6	5	4	3	2	1	0
0100	1	0	1	0	1	1	1	1	1	1	0	0

X N Z V C
- - - - -

MOVEM
(EA to Regs)

15–12	11	10	9	8	7	6	5	4	3	2	1	0
0100	1	1	0	0	1	Sz	Effective		Address			

X N Z V C
- - - - -

TRAP

15–12	11	10	9	8	7	6	5	4	3	2	1	0
0100	1	1	1	0	0	1	0	0	Vector			

X N Z V C
- - - - -

LINK

15–12	11	10	9	8	7	6	5	4	3	2	1	0
0100	1	1	1	0	0	1	0	1	0	A Reg.		

X N Z V C
- - - - -

UNLK

15–12	11	10	9	8	7	6	5	4	3	2	1	0
0100	1	1	1	0	0	1	0	1	1	A Reg.		

X N Z V C
- - - - -

**MOVE
to USP**

15–12	11	10	9	8	7	6	5	4	3	2	1	0
0100	1	1	1	0	0	1	1	0	0	A Reg.		

X N Z V C
- - - - -

Instruction	Machine Code Format													Condition Codes
	15–12	11	10	9	8	7	6	5	4	3	2	1	0	X N Z V C

MOVE from USP

15–12	11	10	9	8	7	6	5	4	3	2	1	0
0100	1	1	1	0	0	1	1	0	1	A Reg.		

X N Z V C
‑ ‑ ‑ ‑ ‑

RESET

15–12	11	10	9	8	7	6	5	4	3	2	1	0
0100	1	1	1	0	0	1	1	1	0	0	0	0

X N Z V C
‑ ‑ ‑ ‑ ‑

NOP

15–12	11	10	9	8	7	6	5	4	3	2	1	0
0100	1	1	1	0	0	1	1	1	0	0	0	1

X N Z V C
‑ ‑ ‑ ‑ ‑

STOP

15–12	11	10	9	8	7	6	5	4	3	2	1	0
0100	1	1	1	0	0	1	1	1	0	0	1	0

X N Z V C
I I I I I

RTE

15–12	11	10	9	8	7	6	5	4	3	2	1	0
0100	1	1	1	0	0	1	1	1	0	0	1	1

X N Z V C
I I I I I

RTD
(68010)

15–12	11	10	9	8	7	6	5	4	3	2	1	0
0100	1	1	1	0	0	1	1	1	0	1	0	0

X N Z V C
‑ ‑ ‑ ‑ ‑

RTS

15–12	11	10	9	8	7	6	5	4	3	2	1	0
0100	1	1	1	0	0	1	1	1	0	1	0	1

X N Z V C
‑ ‑ ‑ ‑ ‑

Instruction	Machine Code Format	Condition Codes

TRAPV

15–12	11	10	9	8	7	6	5	4	3	2	1	0
0100	1	1	1	0	0	1	1	1	0	1	1	0

X N Z V C
- - - - -

RTR

15–12	11	10	9	8	7	6	5	4	3	2	1	0
0100	1	1	1	0	0	1	1	1	0	1	1	1

X N Z V C
I I I I I

MOVEC
(68010)

15–12	11	10	9	8	7	6	5	4	3	2	1	0
0100	1	1	1	0	0	1	1	1	1	0	1	Rd

X N Z V C
- - - - -

JSR

15–12	11	10	9	8	7	6	5	4	3	2	1	0
0100	1	1	1	0	1	0	Effective		Address			

X N Z V C
- - - - -

JMP

15–12	11	10	9	8	7	6	5	4	3	2	1	0
0100	1	1	1	0	1	1	Effective		Address			

X N Z V C
- - - - -

ADDQ

15–12	11	10	9	8	7	6	5	4	3	2	1	0
0101	IData			0	Size		Effective		Address			

X N Z V C
* * * * *

Scc

15–12	11	10	9	8	7	6	5	4	3	2	1	0
0101	Condition				1	1	Effective		Address			

X N Z V C
- - - - -

Instruction	Machine Code Format	Condition Codes

DBcc

15–12	11 10 9 8	7	6	5	4	3	2 1 0
0101	Condition	1	1	0	0	1	D Reg.

X N Z V C
- - - - -

SUBQ

15–12	11 10 9	8	7 6	5 4 3	2 1 0
0101	Data	1	Size	Effective	Address

X N Z V C
* * * * *

Bcc

15–12	11 10 9 8	7 6 5 4 3 2 1 0
0110	Condition	8-bit Displacement

X N Z V C
- - - - -

BSR

15–12	11	10	9	8	7 6 5 4 3 2 1 0
0110	0	0	0	1	8-bit Displacement

X N Z V C
- - - - -

MOVEQ

15–12	11 10 9	8	7 6 5 4 3 2 1 0
0111	D Reg.	0	8-bit Data Value

X N Z V C
- * * 0 0

OR

15–12	11 10 9	8	7 6	5 4 3	2 1 0
1000	D Reg.	Dr	Size	Effective	Address

X N Z V C
- * * 0 0

DIVU

15–12	11 10 9	8	7	6	5 4 3	2 1 0
1000	D Reg.	0	1	1	Effective	Address

X N Z V C
- * * * 0

Instruction	Machine Code Format	Condition Codes

SBCD

15–12	11 10 9	8	7	6	5	4	3	2 1 0
1000	Dest Reg	1	0	0	0	0	DA	Src Reg

X N Z V C
* U * U *

DIVS

15–12	11 10 9	8	7	6	5	4 3 2 1 0
1000	D Reg.	1	1	1	Effective Address

X N Z V C
- * * * 0

SUB

15–12	11 10 9	8	7 6	5 4 3 2 1 0
1001	D Reg.	Dr	Size	Effective Address

X N Z V C
* * * * *

SUBA

15–12	11 10 9	8	7	6	5 4 3 2 1 0
1001	A Reg.	Sz	1	1	Effective Address

X N Z V C
- - - - -

SUBX

15–12	11 10 9	8	7 6	5	4	3	2 1 0
1001	Dest Reg	1	Size	0	0	DA	Src Reg

X N Z V C
* * * * *

CMP

15–12	11 10 9	8	7 6	5 4 3 2 1 0
1011	D Reg.	0	Size	Effective Address

X N Z V C
- * * * *

CMPA

15–12	11 10 9	8	7	6	5 4 3 2 1 0
1011	A Reg.	Sz	1	1	Effective Address

X N Z V C
- * * * *

Instruction	Machine Code Format	Condition Codes

EOR

15–12	11 10 9	8	7 6	5 4 3	2 1 0
1011	D Reg.	1	Size	Effective	Address

X N Z V C
\- * * 0 0

CMPM

15–12	11 10 9	8	7 6	5	4	3	2 1 0
1011	Dest Reg	1	Size	0	0	1	Src Reg

X N Z V C
\- * * * *

AND

15–12	11 10 9	8	7 6	5 4 3	2 1 0
1100	D Reg.	Dr	Size	Effective	Address

X N Z V C
\- * * 0 0

MULU

15–12	11 10 9	8	7	6	5 4 3	2 1 0
1100	D Reg.	0	1	1	Effective	Address

X N Z V C
\- * * 0 0

ABCD

15–12	11 10 9	8	7	6	5	4	3	2 1 0
1100	Dest Reg	1	0	0	0	0	DA	Src Reg

X N Z V C
* U * U *

EXG
(2 D regs)

15–12	11 10 9	8	7	6	5	4	3	2 1 0
1100	D Reg.	1	0	1	0	0	0	D Reg.

X N Z V C
\- - - - -

EXG
(2 A regs)

15–12	11 10 9	8	7	6	5	4	3	2 1 0
1100	A Reg.	1	0	1	0	0	1	A Reg.

X N Z V C
\- - - - -

Instruction	Machine Code Format	Condition Codes

EXG
(A and D reg)

15–12	11	10	9	8	7	6	5	4	3	2	1	0
1100		D Reg.		1	1	0	0	0	1		A Reg.	

X N Z V C
- - - - -

MULS

15–12	11	10	9	8	7	6	5	4	3	2	1	0
1100		D Reg.		1	1	1		Effective		Address		

X N Z V C
- * * 0 0

ADD

15–12	11	10	9	8	7	6	5	4	3	2	1	0
1101		D Reg.		Dr	Size			Effective		Address		

X N Z V C
* * * * *

ADDA

15–12	11	10	9	8	7	6	5	4	3	2	1	0
1101		A Reg.		Sz	1	1		Effective		Address		

X N Z V C
- - - - -

ADDX

15–12	11	10	9	8	7	6	5	4	3	2	1	0
1101		Dest Reg		1	Size		0	0	RM	Src Reg		

X N Z V C
* * * * *

ASR
(Memory form)

15–12	11	10	9	8	7	6	5	4	3	2	1	0
1110	0	0	0	0	1	1		Effective		Address		

X N Z V C
* * * * *

ASL
(Memory form)

15–12	11	10	9	8	7	6	5	4	3	2	1	0
1110	0	0	0	1	1	1		Effective		Address		

X N Z V C
* * * * *

Instruction	Machine Code Format	Condition Codes

LSR
(Memory form)

15–12	11	10	9	8	7	6	5	4	3	2	1	0
1110	0	0	1	0	1	1	Effective Address					

X N Z V C
* * * 0 *

LSL
(Memory form)

15–12	11	10	9	8	7	6	5	4	3	2	1	0
1110	0	0	1	1	1	1	Effective Address					

X N Z V C
* * * 0 *

ROXR
(Memory form)

15–12	11	10	9	8	7	6	5	4	3	2	1	0
1110	0	1	0	0	1	1	Effective Address					

X N Z V C
* * * 0 *

ROXL
(Memory form)

15–12	11	10	9	8	7	6	5	4	3	2	1	0
1110	0	1	0	1	1	1	Effective Address					

X N Z V C
* * * 0 *

ROR
(Memory form)

15–12	11	10	9	8	7	6	5	4	3	2	1	0
1110	0	1	1	0	1	1	Effective Address					

X N Z V C
- * * 0 *

ROL
(Memory form)

15–12	11	10	9	8	7	6	5	4	3	2	1	0
1110	0	1	1	1	1	1	Effective Address					

X N Z V C
- * * 0 *

Instruction	*Machine Code Format*	*Condition Codes*

ASR
(Register form)

15–12	11 10 9	8	7 6	5	4	3	2 1 0
1110	Cnt/Reg	0	Size	IR	0	0	D Reg.

X N Z V C
* * * * *

ASL
(Register form)

15–12	11 10 9	8	7 6	5	4	3	2 1 0
1110	Cnt/Reg	1	Size	IR	0	0	D Reg.

X N Z V C
* * * * *

LSR
(Register form)

15–12	11 10 9	8	7 6	5	4	3	2 1 0
1110	Cnt/Reg	0	Size	IR	0	1	D Reg.

X N Z V C
* * * 0 *

LSL
(Register form)

15–12	11 10 9	8	7 6	5	4	3	2 1 0
1110	Cnt/Reg	1	Size	IR	0	1	D Reg.

X N Z V C
* * * 0 *

ROXR
(Register form)

15–12	11 10 9	8	7 6	5	4	3	2 1 0
1110	Cnt/Reg	0	Size	IR	1	0	D Reg.

X N Z V C
* * * 0 *

ROXL
(Register form)

15–12	11 10 9	8	7 6	5	4	3	2 1 0
1110	Cnt/Reg	1	Size	IR	1	0	D Reg.

X N Z V C
* * * 0 *

Instruction	Machine Code Format	Condition Codes

ROR
(Register form)

15–12	11 10 9	8	7 6	5	4 3	2 1 0
1110	Cnt/Reg	0	Size	IR	1 1	D Reg.

X N Z V C
- * * 0 *

ROL
(Register form)

15–12	11 10 9	8	7 6	5	4 3	2 1 0
1110	Cnt/Reg	1	Size	IR	1 1	D Reg.

X N Z V C
- * * 0 *

Legend:

Size   Specifies instruction data size:

    00 Byte
    01 Word
    10 Long

Dr   Specifies instruction direction:

    0 EA or Memory to Dn
    1 Dn to EA or Memory

Sz   Specifies instruction data size:

    0 Word
    1 Long

Rd   Specifies instruction direction:

    0 Control register to General Register
    1 General register to Control Register

IData   3 bits of immediate data:

    000   Specifies the value "8".
    001–111 Specify values 1–7.

Condition Specifies a branch condition:

Condition	Instruction	Condition	Instruction
0000	BRA	1000	BVC
0001	(NONE)	1001	BVS
0010	BHI	1010	BPL
0011	BLS	1011	BMI
0100	BCC	1100	BGE
0101	BCS	1101	BLT
0110	BNE	1110	BGT
0111	BEQ	1111	BLE

DA Specifies the type of registers used:

0 Data Registers
1 Address Registers

Cnt Reg Specifies a count or a register value:

If the IR field is 0, then 3-bit IData format
If the IR field is 1, then Data Register Number

ALPHABETICAL INSTRUCTION SUMMARY

Instruction	Machine Code Format	Condition Codes

ABCD

15–12	11 10 9	8	7	6	5	4	3	2 1 0
1100	Dest Reg	1	0	0	0	0	DA	Src Reg

X N Z V C
* U * U *

ADD

15–12	11 10 9	8	7 6	5 4 3	2 1 0
1101	D Reg.	Dr	Size	Effective	Address

X N Z V C
* * * * *

Instruction	Machine Code Format	Condition Codes

ADDA

15–12	11 10 9	8	7	6	5 4 3	2 1 0
1101	A Reg.	Sz	1	1	Effective	Address

X N Z V C
- - - - -

ADDI

15–12	11	10	9	8	7 6	5 4 3	2 1 0
0000	0	1	1	0	Size	Effective	Address

X N Z V C
* * * * *

ADDQ

15–12	11 10 9	8	7 6	5 4 3	2 1 0
0101	IData	0	Size	Effective	Address

X N Z V C
* * * * *

ADDX

15–12	11 10 9	8	7 6	5	4	3	2 1 0
1101	Dest Reg	1	Size	0	0	DA	Src Reg

X N Z V C
* * * * *

AND

15–12	11 10 9	8	7 6	5 4 3	2 1 0
1100	D Reg.	Dr	Size	Effective	Address

X N Z V C
- * * 0 0

ANDI

15–12	11	10	9	8	7 6	5 4 3	2 1 0
0000	0	0	1	0	Size	Effective	Address

X N Z V C
- * * 0 0

ASL
(Register form)

15–12	11 10 9	8	7 6	5	4	3	2 1 0
1110	Cnt/Reg	1	Size	IR	0	0	D Reg.

X N Z V C
* * * * *

Instruction	Machine Code Format	Condition Codes

ASL
(Memory form)

15–12	11	10	9	8	7	6	5 4 3 2 1 0
1110	0	0	0	1	1	1	Effective Address

X N Z V C
* * * * *

ASR
(Register form)

15–12	11 10 9	8	7 6	5	4	3	2 1 0
1110	Cnt/Reg	0	Size	IR	0	0	D Reg.

X N Z V C
* * * * *

ASR
(Memory form)

15–12	11	10	9	8	7	6	5 4 3 2 1 0
1110	0	0	0	0	1	1	Effective Address

X N Z V C
* * * * *

Bcc

15–12	11 10 9 8	7 6 5 4 3 2 1 0
0110	Condition	8-bit Displacement

X N Z V C
- - - - -

BCHG
(Dynamic form)

15–12	11 10 9	8	7	6	5 4 3 2 1 0
0000	D Reg.	1	0	1	Effective Address

X N Z V C
- - * - -

BCHG
(Static form)

15–12	11	10	9	8	7	6	5 4 3 2 1 0
0000	1	0	0	0	0	1	Effective Address

X N Z V C
- - * - -

BCLR
(Dynamic form)

15–12	11 10 9	8	7	6	5 4 3 2 1 0
0000	D Reg.	1	1	0	Effective Address

X N Z V C
- - * - -

Instruction	Machine Code Format	Condition Codes

BCLR
(Static form)

15–12	11	10	9	8	7	6	5	4	3	2	1	0
0000	1	0	0	0	1	0	Effective		Address			

X N Z V C
- - * - -

BSET
(Dynamic form)

15–12	11	10	9	8	7	6	5	4	3	2	1	0
0000	D Reg.			1	1	1	Effective		Address			

X N Z V C
- - * - -

BSET
(Static form)

15–12	11	10	9	8	7	6	5	4	3	2	1	0
0000	1	0	0	0	1	1	Effective		Address			

X N Z V C
- - * - -

BSR

15–12	11	10	9	8	7	6	5	4	3	2	1	0
0110	0	0	0	1	8-bit Displacement							

X N Z V C
- - - - -

BTST
(Dynamic form)

15–12	11	10	9	8	7	6	5	4	3	2	1	0
0000	D Reg.			1	0	0	Effective		Address			

X N Z V C
- - * - -

BTST
(Static form)

15–12	11	10	9	8	7	6	5	4	3	2	1	0
0000	1	0	0	0	0	0	Effective		Address			

X N Z V C
- - * - -

CHK

15–12	11	10	9	8	7	6	5	4	3	2	1	0
0100	D Reg.			1	1	0	Effective		Address			

X N Z V C
- * U U U

Instruction	Machine Code Format	Condition Codes

CLR

15-12	11	10	9	8	7 6	5 4 3	2 1 0
0100	0	0	1	0	Size	Effective	Address

X N Z V C
- 0 1 0 0

CMP

15-12	11 10 9	8	7 6	5 4 3	2 1 0
1011	D Reg.	0	Size	Effective	Address

X N Z V C
- * * * *

CMPA

15-12	11 10 9	8	7	6	5 4 3	2 1 0
1011	A Reg.	Sz	1	1	Effective	Address

X N Z V C
- * * * *

CMPI

15-12	11	10	9	8	7 6	5 4 3	2 1 0
0000	1	1	0	0	Size	Effective	Address

X N Z V C
- * * * *

CMPM

15-12	11 10 9	8	7 6	5	4	3	2 1 0
1011	Dest Reg	1	Size	0	0	1	Src Reg

X N Z V C
- * * * *

DBcc

15-12	11 10 9 8	7	6	5	4	3	2 1 0
0101	Condition	1	1	0	0	1	D Reg.

X N Z V C
- - - - -

DIVS

15-12	11 10 9	8	7	6	5 4 3	2 1 0
1000	D Reg.	1	1	1	Effective	Address

X N Z V C
- * * * 0

Instruction	Machine Code Format	Condition Codes

DIVU

15–12	11 10 9	8	7 6	5 4 3 2 1 0
1000	D Reg.	0	1 1	Effective Address

```
X N Z V C
- * * * 0
```

EOR

15–12	11 10 9	8	7 6	5 4 3 2 1 0
1011	D Reg.	1	Size	Effective Address

```
X N Z V C
- * * 0 0
```

EORI

15–12	11	10	9	8	7 6	5 4 3 2 1 0
0000	1	0	1	0	Size	Effective Address

```
X N Z V C
- * * 0 0
```

EXG
(2 D regs)

15–12	11 10 9	8	7	6	5	4	3	2 1 0
1100	D Reg.	1	0	1	0	0	0	D Reg.

```
X N Z V C
- - - - -
```

EXG
(2 A regs)

15–12	11 10 9	8	7	6	5	4	3	2 1 0
1100	A Reg.	1	0	1	0	0	1	A Reg.

```
X N Z V C
- - - - -
```

EXG
*(A and
D reg)*

15–12	11 10 9	8	7	6	5	4	3	2 1 0
1100	D Reg.	1	1	0	0	0	1	A Reg.

```
X N Z V C
- - - - -
```

EXT.L

15–12	11	10	9	8	7	6	5	4	3	2 1 0
0100	1	0	0	0	1	1	0	0	0	D Reg.

```
X N Z V C
- * * 0 0
```

Instruction	Machine Code Format	Condition Codes

EXT.W

15–12	11	10	9	8	7	6	5	4	3	2	1	0
0100	1	0	0	0	1	0	0	0	0	D Reg.		

X N Z V C
- * * 0 0

ILLEGAL

15–12	11	10	9	8	7	6	5	4	3	2	1	0
0100	1	0	1	0	1	1	1	1	1	1	0	0

X N Z V C
- - - - -

JMP

15–12	11	10	9	8	7	6	5	4	3	2	1	0
0100	1	1	1	0	1	1	Effective		Address			

X N Z V C
- - - - -

JSR

15–12	11	10	9	8	7	6	5	4	3	2	1	0
0100	1	1	1	0	1	0	Effective		Address			

X N Z V C
- - - - -

LEA

15–12	11	10	9	8	7	6	5	4	3	2	1	0
0100	A Reg.			1	1	1	Effective		Address			

X N Z V C
- - - - -

LINK

15–12	11	10	9	8	7	6	5	4	3	2	1	0
0100	1	1	1	0	0	1	0	1	0	A Reg.		

X N Z V C
- - - - -

LSL
(Register form)

15–12	11	10	9	8	7	6	5	4	3	2	1	0
1110	Cnt/Reg		1	Size		IR	0	1	D Reg.			

X N Z V C
* * * 0 *

Instruction	Machine Code Format	Condition Codes

LSL
(Memory
form)

15–12	11	10	9	8	7	6	5	4	3	2	1	0
1110	0	0	1	1	1	1	Effective		Address			

X N Z V C
* * * 0 *

LSR
(Register
form)

15–12	11	10	9	8	7	6	5	4	3	2	1	0
1110	Cnt/Reg			0	Size		IR	0	1	D Reg.		

X N Z V C
* * * 0 *

LSR
(Memory
form)

15–12	11	10	9	8	7	6	5	4	3	2	1	0
1110	0	0	1	0	1	1	Effective		Address			

X N Z V C
* * * 0 *

**MOVE
from CCR**
(68010)

15–12	11	10	9	8	7	6	5	4	3	2	1	0
0100	0	0	1	0	1	1	Effective		Address			

X N Z V C
- - - - -

**MOVE
from SR**

15–12	11	10	9	8	7	6	5	4	3	2	1	0
0100	0	0	0	0	1	1	Effective		Address			

X N Z V C
- - - - -

**MOVE
from USP**

15–12	11	10	9	8	7	6	5	4	3	2	1	0
0100	1	1	1	0	0	1	1	0	1	A Reg.		

X N Z V C
- - - - -

**MOVE
to CCR**

15–12	11	10	9	8	7	6	5	4	3	2	1	0
0100	0	1	0	0	1	1	Effective		Address			

X N Z V C
I I I I I

| Instruction | Machine Code Format | Condition Codes |

MOVE to SR

15–12	11	10	9	8	7	6	5	4	3	2	1	0
0100	0	1	1	0	1	1	Effective			Address		

X N Z V C
I I I I I

MOVE to USP

15–12	11	10	9	8	7	6	5	4	3	2	1	0
0100	1	1	1	0	0	1	1	0	0	A Reg.		

X N Z V C
- - - - -

MOVE.B

15–12	11 10 9	8 7 6	5 4 3	2 1 0
0001	Register	Mode	Mode	Register

← Destination → ← Source →

X N Z V C
- * * 0 0

MOVE.L

15–12	11 10 9	8 7 6	5 4 3	2 1 0
0010	Register	Mode	Mode	Register

← Destination → ← Source →

X N Z V C
- * * 0 0

MOVE.W

15–12	11 10 9	8 7 6	5 4 3	2 1 0
0011	Register	Mode	Mode	Register

← Destination → ← Source →

X N Z V C
- * * 0 0

MOVEA.L

15–12	11 10 9	8	7	6	5 4 3	2 1 0
0010	Register	0	0	1	Mode	Register

← Destination → ← Source →

X N Z V C
- - - - -

Instruction	Machine Code Format	Condition Codes

MOVEA.W

15–12	11	10	9	8	7	6	5	4	3	2	1	0
0011	Register			0	0	1	Mode			Register		

← Destination → ← Source →

X N Z V C
- - - - -

MOVEC
(68010)

15–12	11	10	9	8	7	6	5	4	3	2	1	0
0100	1	1	1	0	0	1	1	1	1	0	1	Rd

X N Z V C
- - - - -

MOVEM
(Regs to EA)

15–12	11	10	9	8	7	6	5	4	3	2	1	0
0100	1	0	0	0	1	Sz	Effective		Address			

X N Z V C
- - - - -

MOVEM
(EA to Regs)

15–12	11	10	9	8	7	6	5	4	3	2	1	0
0100	1	1	0	0	1	Sz	Effective		Address			

X N Z V C
- - - - -

MOVEP

15–12	11	10	9	8	7	6	5	4	3	2	1	0
0000	D Reg.			1	Dr	Sz	0	0	1	Address Register		

X N Z V C
- - - - -

MOVEQ

15–12	11	10	9	8	7	6	5	4	3	2	1	0
0111	D Reg.			0	8-bit Data Value							

X N Z V C
- * * 0 0

MOVES
(68010)

15–12	11	10	9	8	7	6	5	4	3	2	1	0
0000	1	1	1	0	Size		Effective		Address			

X N Z V C
- - - - -

Instruction	Machine Code Format	Condition Codes

MULS

15–12	11	10	9	8	7	6	5	4	3	2	1	0
1100	D Reg.			1	1	1	Effective			Address		

```
X N Z V C
- * * 0 0
```

MULU

15–12	11	10	9	8	7	6	5	4	3	2	1	0
1100	D Reg.			0	1	1	Effective			Address		

```
X N Z V C
- * * 0 0
```

NBCD

15–12	11	10	9	8	7	6	5	4	3	2	1	0
0100	1	0	0	0	0	0	Effective			Address		

```
X N Z V C
* U * U *
```

NEG

15–12	11	10	9	8	7	6	5	4	3	2	1	0
0100	0	1	0	0	Size		Effective			Address		

```
X N Z V C
* * * * *
```

NEGX

15–12	11	10	9	8	7	6	5	4	3	2	1	0
0100	0	0	0	0	Size		Effective			Address		

```
X N Z V C
* * * * *
```

NOP

15–12	11	10	9	8	7	6	5	4	3	2	1	0
0100	1	1	1	0	0	1	1	1	0	0	0	1

```
X N Z V C
- - - - -
```

NOT

15–12	11	10	9	8	7	6	5	4	3	2	1	0
0100	0	1	1	0	Size		Effective			Address		

```
X N Z V C
- * * 0 0
```

Instruction	Machine Code Format	Condition Codes

OR

15–12	11 10 9	8	7 6	5 4 3	2 1 0
1000	D Reg.	Dr	Size	Effective	Address

X N Z V C
- * * 0 0

ORI

15–12	11	10	9	8	7 6	5 4 3	2 1 0
0000	0	0	0	0	Size	Effective	Address

X N Z V C
- * * 0 0

PEA

15–12	11	10	9	8	7	6	5 4 3	2 1 0
0100	1	0	0	0	0	1	Effective	Address

X N Z V C
- - - - -

RESET

15–12	11	10	9	8	7	6	5	4	3	2	1	0
0100	1	1	1	0	0	1	1	1	0	0	0	0

X N Z V C
- - - - -

ROL
(Register form)

15–12	11 10 9	8	7 6	5	4	3	2 1 0
1110	Cnt/Reg	1	Size	IR	1	1	D Reg.

X N Z V C
- * * 0 *

ROL
(Memory form)

15–12	11	10	9	8	7	6	5 4 3	2 1 0
1110	0	1	1	1	1	1	Effective	Address

X N Z V C
- * * 0 *

ROR
(Register form)

15–12	11 10 9	8	7 6	5	4	3	2 1 0
1110	Cnt/Reg	0	Size	IR	1	1	D Reg.

X N Z V C
- * * 0 *

Instruction	Machine Code Format	Condition Codes

ROR
(Memory form)

15–12	11	10	9	8	7	6	5	4	3	2	1	0
1110	0	1	1	0	1	1	Effective		Address			

X	N	Z	V	C
-	*	*	0	*

ROXL
(Register form)

15–12	11	10	9	8	7	6	5	4	3	2	1	0
1110	Cnt/Reg			1	Size		IR	1	0	D Reg.		

X	N	Z	V	C
*	*	*	0	*

ROXL
(Memory form)

15–12	11	10	9	8	7	6	5	4	3	2	1	0
1110	0	1	0	1	1	1	Effective		Address			

X	N	Z	V	C
*	*	*	0	*

ROXR
(Register form)

15–12	11	10	9	8	7	6	5	4	3	2	1	0
1110	Cnt/Reg			0	Size		IR	1	0	D Reg.		

X	N	Z	V	C
*	*	*	0	*

ROXR
(Memory form)

15–12	11	10	9	8	7	6	5	4	3	2	1	0
1110	0	1	0	0	1	1	Effective		Address			

X	N	Z	V	C
*	*	*	0	*

RTD
(68010)

15–12	11	10	9	8	7	6	5	4	3	2	1	0
0100	1	1	1	0	0	1	1	1	0	1	0	0

X	N	Z	V	C
-	-	-	-	-

RTE

15–12	11	10	9	8	7	6	5	4	3	2	1	0
0100	1	1	1	0	0	1	1	1	0	0	1	1

X	N	Z	V	C
I	I	I	I	I

Instruction	Machine Code Format	Condition Codes

RTR

15–12	11	10	9	8	7	6	5	4	3	2	1	0
0100	1	1	1	0	0	1	1	1	0	1	1	1

X N Z V C
I I I I I

RTS

15–12	11	10	9	8	7	6	5	4	3	2	1	0
0100	1	1	1	0	0	1	1	1	0	1	0	1

X N Z V C
- - - - -

SBCD

15–12	11 10 9	8	7	6	5	4	3	2 1 0
1000	Dest Reg	1	0	0	0	0	DA	Src Reg

X N Z V C
* U * U *

Scc

15–12	11 10 9	8	7	6	5 4 3	2 1 0
0101	Condition		1	1	Effective	Address

X N Z V C
- - - - -

STOP

15–12	11	10	9	8	7	6	5	4	3	2	1	0
0100	1	1	1	0	0	1	1	1	0	0	1	0

X N Z V C
I I I I I

SUB

15–12	11 10 9	8	7 6	5 4 3	2 1 0
1001	D Reg.	Dr	Size	Effective	Address

X N Z V C
* * * * *

SUBA

15–12	11 10 9	8	7	6	5 4 3	2 1 0
1001	A Reg.	Sz	1	1	Effective	Address

X N Z V C
- - - - -

Instruction	Machine Code Format	Condition Codes

SUBI

15–12	11	10	9	8	7	6	5	4	3	2	1	0
0000	0	1	0	0	Size		Effective		Address			

X N Z V C
* * * * *

SUBQ

15–12	11	10	9	8	7	6	5	4	3	2	1	0
0101	Data			1	Size		Effective		Address			

X N Z V C
* * * * *

SUBX

15–12	11	10	9	8	7	6	5	4	3	2	1	0
1001	Dest Reg			1	Size		0	0	DA	Src Reg		

X N Z V C
* * * * *

SWAP

15–12	11	10	9	8	7	6	5	4	3	2	1	0
0100	1	0	0	0	0	1	0	0	0	D Reg.		

X N Z V C
- * * 0 0

TAS

15–12	11	10	9	8	7	6	5	4	3	2	1	0
0100	1	0	1	0	1	1	Effective		Address			

X N Z V C
- * * 0 0

TRAP

15–12	11	10	9	8	7	6	5	4	3	2	1	0
0100	1	1	1	0	0	1	0	0	Vector			

X N Z V C
- - - - -

TRAPV

15–12	11	10	9	8	7	6	5	4	3	2	1	0
0100	1	1	1	0	0	1	1	1	0	1	1	0

X N Z V C
- - - - -

| *Instruction* | | | | | | | *Machine Code Format* | | | | | | | | | | *Condition Codes* |

TST

15–12	11	10	9	8	7	6	5	4	3	2	1	0
0100	1	0	1	0	Size		Effective			Address		

X N Z V C
- * * 0 0

UNLK

15–12	11	10	9	8	7	6	5	4	3	2	1	0
0100	1	1	1	0	0	1	0	1	1	A Reg.		

X N Z V C
- - - - -

ALPHABETICAL INSTRUCTION SUMMARY

EXCEPTION VECTORS

Vector	Address	Use
0	0	RESET Initial SSP
1	4	RESET Initial PC
2	8	BUSERR (Non-existent Memory)
3	C	Address (Boundary) Error
4	10	Illegal Instruction
5	14	Zero Divide
6	18	CHK Instruction
7	1C	TRAPV Instruction
8	20	Privilege Violation
9	24	TRACE
10	28	Line 1010 Emulator
11	2C	Line 1111 Emulator
12–13	30–34	Unassigned (Reserved)
14	38	68010 Stack Format Error
15	3C	Uninitialized Interrupt Vector
16–23	40–5C	Unassigned (Reserved)
24	60	Spurious Interrupt
25–31	64–7C	Level 0–7 Autovector Interrupts
32–47	80–BF	TRAP 0–15 Instruction Vectors
48–63	C0–FC	Unassigned (Reserved)
64–255	100–3FF	User Interrupt Vectors

BUSERR / ADDRESSING ERROR STACK FRAME (68000/68008)

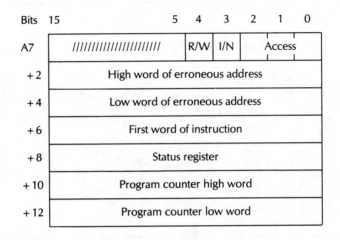

BUSERR / ADDRESSING ERROR STACK FRAME (68010)

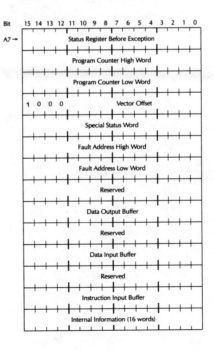

Bit	15	14	13	12	11	10	9	8	7	6	5	4	3	2	1	0
	RR	**	IF	DF	RM	HB	BY	RW	**	**	**	**	**	Function		

SPECIAL STATUS WORD FORMAT

RR	ReRun Bit Set by software for no hardware rerun
IF	Instruction fetch
DF	Data fetch
RM	Read-modify-write cycle
HB	Processor accessing high byte
BY	Byte access
RW	Read / Write bit
Function	Function codes FC0–FC2

Index

Selections from The SYBEX Library

THE MACINTOSH™ TOOLBOX
by Huxham, Burnard, and Takatsuka
300 pp., illustr., Ref. 0-249
This tutorial on the advanced features of the Macintosh toolbox is an ideal companion to The Macintosh BASIC Handbook.

THE MACINTOSH™ BASIC HANDBOOK
by Thomas Blackadar/Jonathan Kamin
800 pp., illustr., Ref. 0-257
This desk-side reference book for the Macintosh programmer covers the BASIC statements and toolbox commands, organized like a dictionary.

PROGRAMMING THE MACINTOSH™ IN ASSEMBLY LANGUAGE
by Steve Williams
400 pp., illustr., Ref. 0-263
Information, examples, and guidelines for programming the 68000 microprocessor are given, including details of its entire instruction set.

SYSTEMS PROGRAMMING IN C
by David Smith
275 pp., illustr., Ref. 0-266
This intermediate text is written for the person who wants to get beyond the basics of C and capture its great efficiencies in space and time.

THE PROGRAMMER'S GUIDE TO UNIX SYSTEM V
by Chuck Hickev/Tim Levin
300 pp., illustr., Re.f 0-268
This book is a guide to all steps involved in setting up a typical programming task in a UNIX systems environment.

REAL WORLD UNIX™
by John D. Halamka
209 pp., Ref. 0-093
This book is written for the beginning and intermediate UNIX user in a practical, straightforward manner, with specific instructions given for many business applications.

For a complete catalog of our publications:

SYBEX, Inc. 2344 Sixth Street, Berkeley, California 94710
Tel: (415) 848-8233   Telex: 336311